AN ILLUSTRATED HISTORY OF
ENGLISH RUGBY

AN ILLUSTRATED HISTORY OF
ENGLISH RUGBY

**FUN, FACTS AND STORIES FROM OVER 150 YEARS
OF MEN'S INTERNATIONAL RUGBY**

JAMES STAFFORD

Illustrated by Raluca Moldovan

*With additional art by
Carys Feehan, Josel Nicolas,
Ched De Gala and Anne Cakebread*

This edition first published in 2023 by

POLARIS PUBLISHING LTD
c/o Aberdein Considine
2nd Floor, Elder House
Multrees Walk
Edinburgh
EH1 3DX

Distributed by
Birlinn Limited

www.polarispublishing.com

ISBN: 9781913538767
eBook ISBN: 9781913538774

British Library Cataloguing-in-Publication Data
A catalogue record for this book is available on request from the British Library.

Designed and typeset by Polaris Publishing, Edinburgh
Printed in Great Britain by CPI Group (UK) Ltd, Croydon, CR0 4YY

To my father, who started this book with me but, sadly, was unable to finish it with me. I owe you so much. Rest well.

And to my two favourite English sides:
London Japanese RFC and Plymouth University Ladies RFC.

Ronald Poulton won 17 caps for England between 1909 and 1914.

CONTENTS

INTRODUCTION

A team of rugby players clad in white with a red rose on their chest first took to the field more than one and a half centuries ago. Their opponents for the first ever rugby international in 1871 were Scotland.

Lennard Stokes of Blackheath and Guy's Hospital was one of England's first rugby captains.

Rugby was such a young sport at the time that until Ireland arrived in 1874, Scotland and England were the only international sides in the world. It would be a decade until Wales (1881) joined the international fold, 32 years before New Zealand and South Africa appeared and a full 36 years before France took to the field. Today, rugby's governing body, World Rugby, oversees 120 national unions.

The world that first England side were born into was one of empire, invention, class struggle and, crucially for this book, sport. It wasn't just international rugby that was new; the sport of rugby itself was an infant. Sports like football and rugby had only recently codified their rules and they were rapidly becoming a crucial part of British life.

Queen Victoria sat upon the throne when England began to play international rugby.

The story we relate in this volume begins in the reign of Queen Victoria, at a time when cowboys still roamed the Wild West of America, and ends in an era of Twitter and TikTok. Most readers will be familiar with the exploits of players like Owen Farrell, Jonny Wilkinson or Martin Johnson and many will be aware of the adventures of Will Carling or Andy Ripley. But relatively few will know much about heroes like Ronnie Poulton or Herbert 'Octopus' Gamlin. We hope to show that each era of English international rugby is as fascinating as any other.

Some chapters feature tales of fortune and glory, others of famine and decline. Some sections relate great feats which led to English hands lifting prestigious trophies; other sections deal with incompetence, snobbery and failure. We've got stories of fateful rhino encounters and anecdotes about players flagging down planes to be able to reach a stadium in time for kick-off. So put your feet up and enjoy a trip into the spectacular (and at times surreal) history of the England rugby team.

1871–95: BEGINNINGS

	PLAYED	WON	DRAWN	LOST
HOME CHAMPIONSHIP	32	21	3	8
HOME UNION TESTS (NON- CHAMPIONSHIP)	21	12	6	3
TOURING TEAMS	1	1	0	0
TOTAL	54	34	9	11

Championships (3)

1883 (Triple Crown), 1884 (Triple Crown), 1892 (Triple Crown)

Shared Championships (2)

1886, 1890

'We need not pause long to discuss the much-abused shoving matches of the days when twenty-a-side were played. They have gone, never to return, regretted by none.'

HARRY VASSALL (ENGLAND FORWARD, FIVE CAPS BETWEEN 1881 AND 1883)

'The evolution of the Rugby Union game since the foundation of the Union has been a remarkable feature of national life. It has resulted in a schoolboy game, under wise guidance, becoming a great winter sport . . . frequently graced by Royalty. Under a strictly amateur code of laws there has developed a great sport in which players of all classes meet in equality and keen rivalry on the field . . . '

O.L. OWEN (RFU HISTORIAN)

HOW RUGBY BEGAN

The story of rugby's beginning is carved in stone. Quite literally. Visit Rugby School in the town of Rugby in England and you can see a plaque that pays tribute to William Webb Ellis, a former pupil of theirs, which reads:

THIS STONE
COMMEMORATES THE EXPLOIT OF
WILLIAM WEBB ELLIS
WHO WITH A FINE DISREGARD FOR THE RULES OF FOOTBALL
AS PLAYED IN HIS TIME
FIRST TOOK THE BALL IN HIS ARMS AND RAN WITH IT
THUS ORIGINATING THE DISTINCTIVE FEATURE OF
THE RUGBY GAME
A.D. 1823

This story is so established that William now lends his name to the coveted gold trophy that international teams compete for every four years at the World Cup. But how true is it? Well, probably not very true at all. But let's take a quick look at it anyway.

In the early 19th century, almost all public schools in England had their own games to play. 'Foot-ball', as it was commonly called, was not the football we know today. In fact, each school's rules varied according to tradition, individual players' tastes, and even were adapted depending on the trees, walls, cobblestones, fences or whatever else lay in or around the playing fields. Schools with more grass tended to allow more

Cheating Bill in action.

rough activities and permit things like 'hacking' and tripping. Rugby School recorded a game in 1817 that involved sides with 40 or more players each. Running ball in hand up the field was not in the rules at that time.

When William (supposedly) picked up the inflated pig's bladder that was used for a ball back then, he would most certainly have been violating the spirit of the game. It was said later that William was a man known to take 'unfair advantage at football'. However, within 20 years, Rugby School had legitimised handling the ball (in certain circumstances) in its version of football. In 1846, the Head of Rugby School appointed a committee of eight pupils to formalise the rules of football at the school. All 37 rules were then crammed into a book that was small enough to be carried by those taking part in matches, making it easy to resolve disputes.

So far, so simple, right? The problem is, this version of rugby's creation was most likely a well-crafted myth dreamed up well after the supposed event occurred. It was not until 1876, four years after William had passed away, that a letter was published outlining his alleged contribution to the game. Even the date of this supposed founding moment flipped between 1823, 1824 and 1825 (after William had left the school). In 1895, this story was 'investigated' by rugby union figures and a plaque installed to mark the event. Why was there such a desire to formalise this story? Well, some believe that it was an attempt by educated classes to lay a formal claim to the origin of the game and combat the increased influence of the working classes in organised sports such as rugby (we'll get to this a bit later).

RUGBY'S ANCIENT ORIGINS?

'Football'-type games can be found throughout history. Some say the Chinese game cuju is like modern football. Others say the Ancient Greeks and Romans may have helped shape modern sport. Medieval Britain had all sorts of 'football' games. The Welsh had *cnapan*, a brutal football form played in areas like Pembrokeshire and Carmarthenshire. Like lots of medieval football, whole towns or villages would compete against each other and games could last a whole day (or more in some versions).

In *cnapan*, the ball was boiled in animal fat to make it hard to catch and the aim of the game was to take the ball to the church in a rival village. This, of course, meant the playing arena could be many miles wide. Poor folk played on foot and rich folk could ride a horse. Slightly unfair, no?

SHAPING MUSCULAR CHRISTIANS

Versions of football became popular in public schools as it was believed they helped shape 'muscular Christians'. The Victorian era saw a rising belief in the idea that sport, particularly team sports, helped develop physical and moral health. In an age of empire and war, it was also seen as a good way to develop leaders and soldiers. An added benefit, especially in boarding schools, was it helped exhaust young men and limit their enthusiasm for mischief in class or at night.

Here are some of the laws that were laid down at Rugby School in 1845:

- All matches are drawn after five days, but after three if no goal [*a goal meant a converted try*] has been kicked.
- No hacking with the heel, or above the knee, is fair.
- No player may wear projecting nails or iron plates on the heels or soles of his shoes or boots.
- Nobody may wear a cap or jersey without leave from the head of the house.

THE FOUNDING OF THE RUGBY FOOTBALL UNION

Football was spread to wider society by ex-pupils of public schools who wished to continue playing after their schooldays had ended, either in university or in adult life. However, as each school had such different rules, each university or club side would have to decide to follow a particular set of rules. This was, of course, a major problem when a team came up against another side that favoured a different set of rules. For instance, ex-pupils of Eton were horrified at the preference from former Rugby School pupils for handling. And where some schools had immensely enjoyed hacking at each other's shins during games, others had been far less keen and were revolted by the injuries such tactics caused. It soon became obvious that formal rules were going to be needed for organised sport to work and grow.

On 26 October 1863, in London, the Football Association (FA) was formed by 11 London-based clubs. A great split had developed in football circles between those who favoured the version of the sport that was dribbling based, and those that preferred the handling-based code. The clubs that formed the FA were also against hacking. Many of those that refused to join the FA (such as Blackheath) felt that hacking was vital to the spirit of the game and that men developed character by overcoming and ignoring pain and injury. Indeed, some of the clubs that formed the FA went on to play rugby again later on.

For many years the 'rugby' faction were proud that they had no need of formal organisation. But continuing confusion about the rules of the sport when opposing clubs met inevitably led to a need to codify the game. In addition, even some of the rugby clubs were turning against hacking and became mindful of how injuries were a lot more difficult to deal with when you were an adult with a job or family to support, rather than a carefree schoolboy or student.

So, in the Pall Mall Restaurant in London on 26 January 1891, 32 men (drawn from two schools and 19 clubs) got together to standardise the rules (and hopefully limit the violence that plagued the game). The founding clubs of the Rugby Football Union (RFU) were:

- Addison
- Belsize Park
- Blackheath
- Civil Service
- Clapham Rovers
- Flamingoes F.C.
- Gipsies
- Guy's Hospital
- Harlequin F.C.
- King's College Hospital
- Lausanne
- The Law Club
- Marlborough Nomads
- Mohicans
- Queen's House
- Ravenscourt Park
- Richmond
- St Paul's
- Wellington College

- West Kent
- Wimbledon Hornets

According to legend, Wasps were absent from the meeting as the club's representative went to the wrong venue and missed it. Notably, Rugby School were not represented either. Rugby historian Jed Smith wrote that the schoolboys at Rugby School 'had always been unwilling to hand control of their game to school masters, so were even less likely to hand it over to a foreign body'.

A YOUNG MAN'S SPORT (ON AND OFF THE FIELD)

Today, rugby is a young person's game, usually run by older, greyer heads. But in 1871 the sport itself was so young there had not been time for the sport to develop a senior set of administrators. The average age of the founding members of the RFU was just 23. It meant, of course, that they also selected themselves when it came to picking the England team.

WHY DOES RUGBY HAVE LAWS, NOT RULES?

If ever you've referred to rules at a rugby game or on social media, chances are some mirthless pedant has corrected you by saying: 'Rugby has laws, not rules.' Why is this? Well, the three men charged with formulating the 1871 rule book were lawyers. It seems simply they just found it more appropriate to use a more legal term like 'laws', rather than 'rules'.

HIGHLIGHTS OF THE EARLY LAWS

After all the fuss about hacking, the original 1871 RFU laws removed it from the game anyway. It's interesting to note that a law was created which allowed for players to pass hand to hand to each other. However, this was seen as most cowardly and it would take the best part of two decades before it was accepted as smart play.

The aim of rugby at this stage in its evolution was to register as many goals as possible. A 'goal' is an old-fashioned way of saying a converted try, a drop goal or goal from mark (more on that later). One goal beat any number of unconverted tries. A last-minute 'goal' would be enough to deliver victory over a team that had scored 20 unconverted tries! In fact, that's where the term 'try' came from. Touching the ball down over the try line allowed you to have a 'try' at kicking at the posts to make a goal.

It's worth noting too, that games involved 20 players per side (although this wasn't stated in the law book at the time). There were 59 laws laid down in all, and here are some of the quirkier ones:

• Law 11: A *scrummage* takes place when the holder of the ball being in the field of play puts it down on the ground in front of him and all who have closed round on their respective sides endeavour to push their opponents back and by kicking the ball to drive it in the direction of the opposite goal line.

• Law 18: In the event of any player holding or running with the ball being tackled and the ball being fairly held he must at once cry *down* and there put it down.

- Law 38: The sides shall change goals as often as and whenever a goal is obtained unless it has been otherwise agreed by the captains before the commencement of the match.
- Law 57: No hacking or hacking over or tripping up shall be allowed under any circumstances.
- Law 58: No one wearing projecting nails, iron plates or gutta percha on any part of his boots or shoes shall be allowed to play in the match.
- Law 59: The captains of the respective sides shall be the sole arbiters of all disputes.

Traditionalists were outraged at the banning of hacking, saying it would make the game soft and even encourage Frenchmen to play.

THE FIRST INTERNATIONAL
A Scotch victory

Despite the FA being formed in 1863, rugby can officially lay claim to the first ever representative international football match. There had been 'soccer' matches in 1870 and 1871 between England and 'Scotland' before this date, but FIFA does not recognise them as it claimed the Scottish side was not truly representative of the nation.

Inspired by these 'international' contests, the RFU accepted an invitation to Raeburn Place, Edinburgh on 27 March 1871 to face Scotland. As the RFU laws had not yet been formally codified, the match was played under Scottish laws.

The game was played with 20 players per team, over

50-minute halves and on a pitch that was 110 metres by 50 metres (smaller than standard English pitches of the era). England's captain was Frederick Stokes of Blackheath. He was aged just 20 years and 258 days and still holds the record as the youngest England captain of all time. Fittingly, perhaps, the side contained 11 former Rugby School pupils.

A PICTORIAL REPRESENTATION of
THE PIONEERING MEN OF ALBION
1871

The first ever England team.

Four thousand spectators turned out on a fine day to see a 'war of attrition' between the packs. As each team had ten forwards and passing was not really a thing back then, the game's attritional nature was hardly surprising. There was no score in the first half. Both teams used three full-backs, standard for the day, and their roles were purely defensive. They were also expected to clear their lines by drop-kicking, not punting. Punting was looked down upon as a tactic and it would be many years before it became the preferred way of kicking up field.

After the break, the home pack began to dominate and Scotland's Angus Buchanan scored the first ever international try. It was converted and turned into a precious 'goal' by William Cross. England forward Reginald Birkett soon laid claim to the first ever English try, but it went unconverted. Before the match ended, William Cross added another Scottish try. As no points were awarded in those days, the result was a Scottish win by one goal and one try to one try.

Fittingly for a sport that to this day (even with video technology) sees so much controversy around tries, both Scotland's scores were the matter of some dispute. Scottish umpire, Dr Hely Hutchinson Almond, later explained his reason for allowing one Scottish try saying: 'When an umpire is in doubt, I think he is justified in deciding against the team which makes the most noise. They are probably in the wrong.'

It's interesting to note that newspapers in those days would use the term 'Scotch' rather than 'Scots'. Search through old papers and you'll see things like: 'Time being up, the Scotch were declared the winners'.

England wore white shirts with a red rose. The shirt of forward John Clayton still survives and can be seen at Twickenham's World Rugby Museum. Why did England choose a rose as their emblem? It is believed the coat of arms of Rugby School, which contains roses, inspired the design.

The first English XX: (backs) A.G. Guillemard (West Kent), R.R. Osborne (Manchester), A. Lyon (Liverpool), W. MacLaren (Manchester), J.E. Bentley (Gipsies), F. Tobin (Liverpool), J.F. Green (West Kent); (forwards) R.H. Birkett (Clapham Rovers), B.H. Burns (Blackheath), J.H. Clayton (Liverpool), C.A. Crompton (Blackheath), A. Davenport, J.M. Dugdale (Ravenscourt Park), A.S. Gibson (Manchester), A. St G. Hamersley (Marlborough Nomads), J.H. Luscombe (Gipsies), C.W. Sherrard (Blackheath), F. Stokes (Blackheath, captain), D.P. Turner (Richmond), H.J.C. Turner (Manchester).

Did you know? There was no referee on the pitch for this first international, as it was still up to captains to settle disputes (see Law 59 of 1871). There were, however, two umpires. These umpires, one from each side, patrolled the sidelines and only got involved if one of the captains lodged an appeal. It was not until 1875 that a referee took charge of an English Test match. In these early years of international rugby, the referees would be provided by the home union and often refereed while dressed in formal clothes.

FOOTBALL, RUGBY OR SOCCER?

In musty old newspapers and dusty books you'll often see rugby being called football. In the Victorian era, rugby, and what we now call football or soccer, were simply seen as different 'codes' of football. Whatever code was most popular in a certain area or region was called football. When newspapers wanted to avoid confusion, they might write 'association football' or 'rugby football' in their articles. For a long time, rugby tended to be called football as often as it was called rugby.

Even today, according to where you are in the world, 'football' can refer to soccer, rugby union, rugby league, American football, Gaelic football, Australian Rules football and Canadian football. The word 'soccer' comes from the word 'association'. Association football is the full name of the sport most people in the UK call football. There's a misconception that soccer is an American word. But soccer has been used for over 200 years and was a popular term in the UK in the 1980s – even among football fans. Even today, one of the most popular UK football shows is called *Soccer AM*.

REVENGE AT HOME
An 'Oval' victory

A few months after the loss in Scotland, the RFU invited Scotland to London for a rematch in 1872. The match was played at the Oval (the famous cricket ground), which was to remain the home venue for England until 1879. Frederick Stokes was again captain, but there were 14 new caps in the side (there were still 20 players in a team). Unlike 1871, the side was selected after a set of trial games.

England benefited from the wide home pitch (it was said the English halves kept running off the narrow field the year before) and after an early Scottish score, Stokes's men won comfortably by one goal, one drop goal and two tries to a solitary Scottish drop goal.

COBBLERS, CARTS AND HORSES OF WAR

In 1873, England and Scotland struggled to a scoreless draw in the sludge of a snowy and wet Glasgow field. But were England denied the spoils due to the actions of a local cobbler? Before the game, captain Frederick Stokes had arranged for his players' boots to be altered by adding leather bars to the soles to better cope with the slushy field. However, two of the backs (Harold Freeman and Cecil Boyle) never got their boots back and at least one of them (reports differ as to whether it was one or both players) had to play in 'dress boots'.

After the match there was a small scandal when one of the English players was 'found driving one of Her Majesty's mail carts in the middle of Glasgow'!

Cecil Boyle was a fascinating individual and as well as being capped once for England, he played first-class cricket, once even getting a hat-trick for Oxford. He fought in the Second Boer War and took 30 of his own horses to South Africa. He was killed in action in 1900.

AND THEN THERE WERE THREE

In 1875 Ireland joined the international arena, meeting England at the Oval on a wet pitch on a Monday afternoon in front of 3,000 spectators. The poor conditions probably saved the visitors from an even bigger hiding than the one goal, one drop goal and one try to nil result suggests. The Irish team selection consisted of ten players picked by the Northern Irish Union and ten from the Southern Irish Union (the modern

IRFU was not founded until 1879). Not only did the players barely know each other, two never even showed up, causing a late reshuffle and forcing backs and forwards to switch around once replacements had been found. The Irish pack, nonetheless, acquitted itself well, but their stamina ultimately failed them.

A SCANDAL IN EDINBURGH

Players getting in trouble after too much alcohol is by no means a curse of modern rugby. On Monday, 8 March 1875, Scotland and England once again met in a scoreless draw. It seems that there was more action after the match when 'boisterous' England players, drunkenly waiting to return home on the 10.40 p.m. train, ended up scuffling with the engine driver and one player even whacked a police officer.

The *Edinburgh Evening Post* reported: ' . . . one of the Englishmen gave an engine-driver a blow on the breast, which sent him reeling against a carriage. The engine-driver, generously enough, did not press any charge against his assailant, and the players were hustled into a carriage and the doors locked upon them. Just before the starting of the train, however, one of them got out and struck a railway policeman. The policeman attempted to detain him, but two of the others, coming to their comrade's assistance, gave the officers some rough treatment. While the party were struggling, the train moved off, leaving the three Englishmen in the custody of the railway officials who came to the policeman's assistance. They struggled violently to free themselves, kicking and using their sticks in a savage manner. The policeman received a severe kick while he was lying on the ground, which nearly broke the bridge of his nose.'

One of the troublemakers was Reginald Birkett, scorer of England's first ever try back in 1871. Birkett, who played as a 'forward' (there was no specialisation then) has perhaps one of the most fascinating biographies in the annals of rugby. A player with Clapham Rovers, he was one of the founding members of the RFU. Rovers played rugby and football, often playing both codes the same weekend as they had enough players for multiple sides. Birkett won four England caps, but also played in two FA Cup finals as a goalkeeper. In 1879 Rovers lost to Old Etonians F.C., but in 1880, with Birkett again in goal, they tasted victory over Oxford University. He also won an England international cap in football in 1879.

Reginald Birkett was a sporting man.

Sporting success ran in the family as his brother (Louis) and his son (John) also won caps for England. Birkett's life ended tragically in 1898. Aged just 49, suffering from delirium during a severe bout of illness, he leapt out of his bedroom window to his death as he was being helped into bed.

AND THEN THERE WERE FIFTEEN

The 1877 encounter with Ireland at the Oval was the first England international in which both sides played 15-a-side. Cambridge and Oxford universities can be credited with leading the move to smaller sides. England won by two goals and two tries to nil.

KICKING THE GAME FORWARD

The 1877 game also saw the debut of 30-year-old Albert Hornby of Preston Grasshoppers (who was also a Test cricketer). The threequarter was famous for punting, rather than drop-kicking the ball. As mentioned earlier, this technique had been frowned upon. But Hornby said it was natural to him as this was the way the ball was kicked at his school (Harrow), where drop kicks were forbidden.

THE CALCUTTA CUP IS BORN

Today, rugby fans associate England v Scotland games with the famous Calcutta Cup. But it was not until 1879, the ninth time these sides met, that the trophy was put on the line. The story behind its creation reflects the age of empire in which it was forged.

In 1872 a rugby club had been formed by soldiers and Brits working or living in India. By 1874, calling itself the Calcutta Club, it had joined the RFU. However, when many of the military personnel who made up the team started to move away, it was clear the club could not survive. In 1878 members decided to use the remaining club funds to do something that would be of 'lasting good . . . for the cause of Rugby Football'. Two hundred and seventy silver rupees were melted down by the skilled silversmiths of Calcutta and used to create one of the most elegant and unique trophies in all of sport. The Calcutta Club suggested the cup be used as a kind of FA Cup for rugby clubs to compete for. But this was seen as against the 'ethos' of rugby and far too 'professional'. Instead, it was decided to award the cup to the winners of the annual Scotland and England game.

Interestingly, the base of the trophy, which lists the winners, includes all games back to 1871, even though these are not classed as Calcutta Cup matches.

A GLORIOUS RUN OF SUCCESS

In 1880, England defeated Ireland by one goal and one try to one try in Lansdowne Road, Dublin. It was the start of an astonishing decade of success in which England lost just two of the 22 games they played in. The win in Dublin didn't come easy though. Several of the players were taken sick after a rough crossing of the Irish Sea. Ernie Woodward, an English student in Dublin, was called into the side when one player failed to recover in time for the match. The late selection gave a good account of himself, but never won another cap.

England strolled to victory against Wales in 1881.

TAMING BABY DRAGONS

Wales entered the international scene in 1881, meeting England at Blackheath. The Welsh Rugby Union had not yet been founded and the side was not truly representative of the growing strength of the game in Wales. England won by seven converted tries (goals), one drop goal and six tries to nil. Today that would be 82-0. England had agreed to play Wales to set a 'good example to the other nationalities'. Amusingly, England had one try disallowed because the scoring pass was so long and unusual it was deemed 'unsporting' by the RFU's own referee. Wales also lost two players to injury in the first half. Alas, in those days there were no replacements, so Wales played over half the game with just 13 men.

The scale of the defeat was so great it was said that Wales were 'lucky to get nil'. The following season Wales played against an English regional side instead of a full Test team. But by late 1882, Wales were on the fixture list for good.

THIS TRAIN IS BOUND FOR GLORY

Frank Wright (Manchester/Edinburgh Academy) won his only cap in the draw against Scotland at Raeburn Place in 1881. He owed his selection to the fact that Blackheath's Henry Herbert Taylor missed the train to Scotland for the match.

MY CAPTAIN! MY CAPTAIN!

Albert Neilson Hornby was the first man to captain England

in both cricket and rugby. As a rugby man he was a full-back or threequarter who played for Preston Grasshoppers and Manchester Football Club. He won nine caps in total in rugby. He is perhaps more famous as being leader of the England cricket team that lost to Australia in 1882 and which led to this famous 'obituary' to English cricket being published in a newspaper:

In Affectionate Remembrance of ENGLISH CRICKET, which died at the Oval on 29th AUGUST, 1882, Deeply lamented by a large circle of sorrowing friends and acquaintances R.I.P. N.B. – The body will be cremated and the ashes taken to Australia.

This is the origin of what we now know as the Ashes. In his final game as England captain, he became the first player to be stumped in both innings. He was 36 years old when he captained both the cricket and rugby sides. His sporting prowess also saw him play a game of football for Blackburn Rovers.

WHOSE SIDE ARE YOU ON?

Scotland's two try to nil win over England at Whalley Range, Manchester in 1882 was the first international to be controlled by a neutral referee, when Mr. H.L. Robinson of Ireland was the man in the middle. He wasn't the man with the whistle though. It wasn't until 1886 that referees were given whistles and umpires provided with 'sticks'. Until then, they had to shout loudly to get players' attention.

THE HOME NATIONS CHAMPIONSHIP

The tournament we now know as the Six Nations can, astonishingly, be traced back to the 1882–83 season.

England, Ireland, Scotland and Wales played a total of five matches among themselves between December 1882 and March 1883. Not all the teams played the same number of games. The Irish and Welsh had fallen out rather badly over the refereeing in their most recent encounter and refused to meet each other. As a result, England and Scotland played three games each and Wales and Ireland just two. As the results below show, England claimed the first ever Triple Crown.

1883 TRIPLE CROWN

MATCH ONE: Wales (nil) England (two goals, four tries) (St. Helen's, Swansea)

While easily defeated, Wales were praised for their development since the 1881 match.

MATCH TWO: England (one goal, three tries) Ireland (one try) (Whalley Range, Manchester)

Ireland had to play most of their game against England a man short as one player failed to recover from seasickness and left the field early.

MATCH THREE: Scotland (one try) England (two tries) (Raeburn Place, Edinburgh)

This was England's first win on Scottish soil.

The official idea of a championship didn't come into being until several years later. The first time a table of results was published was in 1896 when *The Times* newspaper ran one. It was common for many years for teams to play an uneven number of games. As we'll see soon, in the late 1880s, England and Scotland had such a big row over a knock-on that they refused to play each other for years. If you were to make a table for the 1883 Championship, it would look like this.

TEAM	PLAYED	WON	LOST
ENGLAND	3	3	0
SCOTLAND	3	2	1
IRELAND	2	0	2
WALES	2	0	2

It was all about the glory anyway.

Did England like their Triple Crown trophy? Well, no. There wasn't one. Neither was there one for winning the Championship. Rugby was passionately amateur in those days and many of the ever so highly principled people who ran the game saw trophies as a bit too unsporting or even, whisper it quietly, professional. The demands of modern marketing led to the first Championship trophy being created in 1993, 110 years later. The 'mythical' Triple Crown was finally made into a physical object in 2006.

A FALLING OUT OF OLD FRIENDS

In 1884, England again won the Triple Crown. But the fallout from a disputed score in the Scottish match was so severe it would change rugby forever and led to the formation of what is now known as World Rugby, the game's global governing body.

1884 TRIPLE CROWN

MATCH ONE: England (one goal, two tries) Wales (one goal) (Cardigan Fields, Leeds)

MATCH TWO: Ireland (nil) England (one goal) (Lansdowne Road)

MATCH THREE: England (one goal) Scotland (one try)

For the infamous match with Scotland, England were led by Edward Temple Gurdon (Richmond), considered one of the greatest forwards of the Victorian era. On a cold, but sunny day, 8,000 spectators saw Scotland edge ahead with a try in the first half. Crucially, they failed to convert.

After the break, what is arguably the most controversial decision in rugby history occurred. England forward Richard Kindersley (Oxford University/Exeter) scored a try near the posts after a scrum close to the Scottish line. However, the game was held up for ten minutes as both sides argued heatedly over the score. England rugby historian Barry Bowker, in his 1978 version of events wrote:

'There followed a delay of nearly ten minutes, the Scots claiming that they had earlier knocked the ball back and that there should have been a scrum down. The English claimed that a side should not profit from its own mistake (there was no such thing as advantage then), that knocking back was legal anyway and that, as England had not appealed (appeals were still essential), subsequent play was legal.'

The conversion eventually followed from Wilfred Bolton (Blackheath) and England held on to win. But that was far from the end of it. Furious Scottish players continued to argue their point after the game and the Scottish Rugby Union (SRU) even tried to have the result overturned – something that could technically happen until as late as 1969.

The RFU would not even entertain the idea of the very laws they had formulated in 1871 being challenged, especially with the game having been played in England. A flurry of furious letters were exchanged, including one from the RFU stating: *'I was told by the referee that no Englishman appealed. I am not admitting that knocking back is illegal, but simply pointing out that if it is, the act was done by a Scotchman who has to suffer for his mistake.'*

In the end, there was such bad blood that the 1885 Calcutta

Cup fixture was cancelled. Puts a disputed TMO try in today's rugby into context doesn't it?

MENDING, BREAKING AND MENDING BROKEN FENCES

After this dramatic dispute over the laws of the sport, something had to be done to clear up the messy matter of the game's laws. In 1886 Wales, Ireland and Scotland got together to form the IRFB (eventually to become the IRB, and today it is known as World Rugby) which would set the laws for the sport. This upset England, especially as the Welsh, Irish and Scots said each country should have the same number of representatives in the IRFB. England believed they should have more as they had more clubs and refused to join.

The Celtic unions said no members of the IRFB could play England until they joined the newly created organisation. England were exiled from international rugby and missed the 1888 and 1889 Home Nations Championships. Eventually, in 1890, the matter was resolved when, cheekily, England demanded to have six representatives on the IRFB. The Welsh, Irish and Scots, who only had two representatives each, reluctantly agreed. This meant England, who originally wanted no part of it, had exactly the same number of officials and voting rights on the IRFB as all the founding members put together.

With everyone on board and finally talking again, the IRFB became the lawmakers of the game and everyone could get back to arguing on the field again, rather than off it.

CHARLES, CHARLES, CHARLES

The England v Wales match in Yorkshire in January 1884 saw Charles Chapman win his first and only cap for England. Also winning his first cap that day for Wales was a Charles Taylor. Wales grabbed a try through Charlie Allen and added a conversion from Charles Lewis. In total, England had four players called Charles playing that day, and Wales had three with that name and one called Charlie. The four English Charles were the happier as their side won by one goal and two tries to one goal.

INNOVATIONS IN BACK PLAY

In 1884, Wales, thanks to innovations at Cardiff RFC,

introduced the modern rugby formation of eight forwards and seven backs. The addition of an extra threequarter transformed the game. It wasn't an instant success, and England were slow to follow. But England too were playing their part in changing the way the sport was played. In the early 1880s it had become acceptable to 'heel' the ball back in a scrum (rather than booting it forward towards the opponent's goal line as used to be the preferred tactic). This approach was encouraged by English players like Harry Vassall. At Oxford University, Vassall had played in the centre and been part of the development of 'Oxford passing'. In the 1880s people were amazed to see Oxford players practising passing, not kicking or dribbling, before a game. These players would throw the ball 'hand to hand, not high in the air, but about the level of the hands from the ground'.

In his five caps wearing the red rose of England, Vassall pushed England to heel the ball from the scrum and get his half-backs (who played on the right and left, rather than scrum-half and fly-half as we know now) to pass to their threequarters. This may not seem much to us now, but it was a significant innovation at the time.

THE STRANGEST CHAMPIONSHIP OF THEM ALL?

England are listed in some sources as the winners of the 1885 Championship, as even though they never met Scotland due to the 1884 dispute, they beat both Wales and Ireland. Official records, however, list the Championship as incomplete. Amusingly, Ireland and Wales were also on bad terms and refused to meet (the same happened the following season too). Making things even stranger, the Ireland v Scotland game in Belfast was abandoned after 25 minutes due to a storm. Scotland refused to have a rematch in Ireland and arrogantly declared they would claim a win unless the replay was in Scotland! The Irish agreed and Scotland won the home version of the fixture.

IRISH EYES ARE (FINALLY) SMILING

In 1887 Ireland defeated England by two goals to nil at Lansdowne Road. It was the Red Roses' first loss in 13 fixtures against the Irish. One Irish player, John Macaulay, was desperate to play in the game but had no annual leave left at work to take. Needing an excuse, he decided to get married on the morning of the game so he could get the necessary time off. After exchanging vows with his beloved, he ran off to help beat England in the afternoon!

THE UNIQUE TEAM OF 1888

England played no matches in 1888 as they had been sent into 'exile' by the other Home Unions. However, the RFU picked a team and, incredibly, awarded each player selected a cap. Two of these players, Percy Robertshaw (Bradford) and Harry Eagles (Salford), never actually got on the field in an England shirt. These caps, however, are not listed in official records today.

A PANTS BIT OF BEHAVIOUR BY THE HOME SIDE
1889 – England 7 New Zealand Native Team (Māoris) 0 (Rectory Field, Blackheath)

The New Zealand Native Team was the first major touring

side from the southern hemisphere to visit Europe. Made up primarily of Māori players, the touring party played a mind-blowing 107 matches on this tour, 74 of them in Britain! This tour was the first time that British rugby fans got to see a haka performed. The Test match with England caused a huge controversy which led to the visitors having to make two official apologies. When you read what happened, you'll probably feel the apology should have come from the home side.

England back Andrew Stoddart (Blackheath) had his shorts ripped while in possession of the ball. To protect his dignity, other players stood around Stoddart until his modesty could be restored. When this kind of thing happened, it usually meant play was over. However, forward Frank Evershed (Burton) decided to pick up the ball and score in the corner unopposed by the Native team who were simply showing sportsmanship to their opponents. The visitors remonstrated with the referee, the RFU's own Rowland Hill. As this was happening, Evershed then strolled over to the posts and touched down again. And the try was awarded! Rightly incensed, three of the Native team left the field in protest. Eventually, the tour manager persuaded them to return, but the RFU were enraged and the visiting team were forced to grovel in apology, the RFU threatening to prevent their clubs playing any more games against the tourists. The first apology, sent later by telegram by the tourists' manager, was not deemed enough, and a second one was demanded and received.

Interestingly, this was the first England game for which points were recorded, rather than just a tally of goals, tries and drop goals.

MAKING A POINT (OR MORE)

By the time the 1891 Championship arrived, a points system had been universally agreed on and implemented by the IRFB. A try was worth just one measly point.

At the start of the scoring era, as you can see in the table below, you could score three points from a goal from mark. Today, marks can only be called inside your own 22 when catching a ball. Back then, a mark could be called anywhere. Successfully called, a player (or even for a time another nominated player) could then take a drop goal or place kick at goal if they wished. It wasn't as easy as it sounds. You had to be completely static when catching the ball and calling for a mark. Then, when kicking, opposing players could try to charge it down by running up to the point of the mark (meaning the kicker had to retreat to take it). Amazingly, this method of scoring existed until 1977.

HISTORY OF SCORING VALUES IN RUGBY

	TRY	CONVERSION	DROP GOAL	PENALTY	GOAL FROM MARK
1890–91	1	2	3	2	3
1891–92	2	3	3	3	3
1892–93	2	3	4	3	4
1893–94 TO 1904–05	3	2	4	3	4
1905–06 TO 1947–48	3	2	4	3	3
1948–49 TO 1970–71	3	2	3	3	3
1971–72 TO 1976–77	4	2	3	3	3
1977–78 TO 1992	4	2	3	3	NO LONGER POSSIBLE
1992 TO PRESENT	5	2	3	3	NO LONGER POSSIBLE

BACK WITH A (SHARED) BANG

England celebrated their return to the Home Nations Championship by sharing the title with Scotland. In those days, points difference (or even league table points) did not exist; champions were decided by total wins. Although England defeated Scotland, they lost for the first time to Wales. With England and Scotland on two wins each, they shared the spoils.

THE DRAGON FINALLY BURNS THE RED ROSE
1890 – England 0 Wales 1 (Crown Flatt, Dewsbury)

In a blizzard of snow and sleet, and nine years on from the massacre of 1881, Wales gained their first ever win over England.

Wales were gaining a reputation for using smart thinking to compensate for their lack of size compared to other nations. Some felt they used a sneaky move to score in this game. The winning try came from half-back 'Buller' Stadden (during this period, backs would throw into the line-out). Stadden pretended he was going to throw long and both sets of forwards edged back to compete for the ball. Instead, he bounced the ball near his own feet, picked it up, beat a couple of defenders and went over for the try. Sixteen years later this move was outlawed from the game.

England were still using nine forwards and struggled with the style and verve of their opponents, who employed an extra back instead. Not helping matters, Fred Bonsor (Bradford), one of England's star backs, dropped out before the game.

This allowed his club teammate James Wright to win his first cap. Sadly for them both, neither ever got capped again. Many think it was because the RFU believed Bonsor had intentionally pulled out of the game as a favour to his buddy.

UNGRATEFUL WALES?

After Wales's win, RFU president, Arthur Budd, said: 'All Englishmen looked upon the progress of football in Wales with great satisfaction . . . England was the parent of football in Wales, but whether the precocity of the child showed sufficient gratitude to the parent was not a question he was inclined to answer.'

PLEASE, SIR, CAN I GET SOME EXPENSES?

In 1891, more than half the clubs in the RFU voted in favour of compensation payments for players who lost earnings due to having to take time off work to play or travel in relation to rugby. Despite the majority of clubs backing these 'broken-time' payments, the motion failed as a two-thirds majority was needed to pass. The fanatics in the RFU, who held steadfastly to the amateur spirit of rugby, were nervous and battened down the hatches. One RFU official, Rowland Hill (secretary) revealed he would rather rugby fell apart than become professional.

IT'S OVAL BETWEEN US

In 1892 the RFU made it compulsory for all rugby balls to be oval, not round!

WINNERS AGAIN . . . BUT NOT FOR LONG

England once more claimed the Triple Crown in 1892. However, dark times were on the horizon – perhaps the darkest in 150 years of the England international side. The Championship would not be won by England again until 1910. The core reason for this decline was 'the great split' which saw many of England's powerful northern clubs break away from the RFU to become professional. But before the English game was torn apart, there was one last dose of glory.

1892 TRIPLE CROWN

MATCH ONE: England 17 Wales 0 (Rectory Field, Blackheath)

With tries now worth two points, Wales took a hammering on the scoreboard as England grabbed four of them. The score might have been worse, if one of England's conversion attempts hadn't been prevented due to a bizarre law. After one try, two England players handled the ball before the conversion. Wales, knowing the laws well, appealed. At the time only the placer (place kicks had to involve a player holding the ball in place for the kicker back then) was allowed to bring the ball out. As another player had touched it, the conversion attempt was not allowed to proceed.

MATCH TWO: England 7 Ireland 0 (Whalley Range, Manchester)

The game was said to be so brutal that players were frequently given brandy to revive them after being knocked out.

MATCH THREE: Scotland 0 England 5 (Raeburn Place, Edinburgh)

By keeping a clean sheet, the 1892 England side became the only side to ever win a Triple Crown without conceding a point. In fact, no other side in the history of the tournament that is now the Six Nations has ever kept a clean sheet in every game. Thirteen of this England side hailed from northern clubs, including all six backs. These were the clubs represented in this game:

Blackheath, Bradford, Bramley (2), Brighouse Rangers, Hartlepool Rovers (2), Heckmondwike, Huddersfield, Leigh, Liversedge, Salford, Tadcaster, Wellington, Wigan.

THE MYSTERY SCORERS

Today, thanks to technology woven into players' shirts and an army of analysts, you can find out how far and fast players ran, how many tackles they made and a hundred other things besides. Back in 1892, it wasn't even clear who scored the points in a Test match. The scorers for the 1892 win over Scotland are a source of debate. Today it is thought that William Bromet (Tadcaster) scored the try and Richard Lockwood (Heckmondwike) kicked the extras. However, other reports had Sammy Woods (Wellington) scoring the try and Frederic Alderson (Hartlepool Rovers) kicking the conversion!

THE AGE-OLD ISSUE OF DUAL INTERNATIONALS

There's a misconception that 'flexible' approaches to nationality in international sport are a new phenomenon. But nothing could be further from the truth. In 1892, James Marsh (Swinton) turned out for England to win his first cap. However, it was not his first Test cap as he had actually played for Scotland in 1889. While there have been lots of dual internationals in the history of rugby, this is the only example of a player lining up for two Home Union sides.

It wasn't just rugby either where players turned out for different sides. Sammy Woods won 13 caps for England in rugby between 1890 and 1895. But he also represented both Australia and England in cricket!

Three other England rugby players have represented another side at Test level:

• Frank Mellish: six caps for England (1920–21) and six caps for South Africa (1921–24)

• Barry Holmes: four caps for England and two caps for Argentina (all caps in 1949)

• Jamie Salmon: seven caps for New Zealand (1980–81) and 12 for England (1985–87)

GO FOR THE POSTS . . . NO, REALLY!
1893 – Wales 12 England 11 (Cardiff Arms Park, Cardiff)

England lost thanks to the first ever penalty goal in international rugby after legendary Welsh full-back Billy Bancroft slotted Wales to glory (although after arguing with his captain he drop-kicked it rather than place-kicked it!). The option to kick a goal was a relatively fresh addition to the law book. The late score did, however, lead to some confusion among spectators and many Welsh fans left the ground thinking the final score was 14-14. Welsh scoring rules at club level were still different to international rules and a member of the WRU had to confirm to the press after that Wales had won!

ADVANTAGE BEGINS

The 1893–94 season came with several great changes in the law book. As well as the three-point try coming into being, it was the first season in which referees could whistle whenever they felt that laws were being transgressed. Until that point, they responded to appeals from the players. This year also saw the 'advantage' law written into the records. And today, around 130 years later, almost no fan, player or referee can agree on how it should work.

WELCOME TO 1886, FINALLY!
1894 – England 24 Wales 3 (Birkenhead Park)

England made a mockery of the form book by dismantling the Welsh team that had claimed the Triple Crown the year before. In this game England finally joined the 'modern age' and followed the Welsh innovation of playing with four threequarters and only having eight forwards. Cardiff and Wales had toyed with this format as early as 1886. England also had innovators of their own. Half-back Cyril Wells of Harlequins, at a time when half-backs usually both stood near the base of a scrum (often taking a left and right position), would stand deeper and leave his partner to man the scrum alone and then distribute the ball. However, it would be around a decade before Wells was allowed to do this for the far more conservative national side.

FOR THE LOVE OF THE GAME

Modern England internationals are well paid for their work and can often collect extra cash for advertising and media work. But from 1881 to 1995, rugby union was amateur.

In the Victorian era, many people believed sport should be played purely for the love of the game. In fact, the word amateur comes from the Latin and French word *amour*, which means love. To take money or reward for athletic skill was seen as 'ungentlemanly'.

Those running the game thought that once money was introduced it would lead to cheating, corruption and abuse of officials. These people didn't just prefer amateurism, they were FANATICAL about it. To them, the idea of being paid to play was morally disgusting. Arthur Budd, an early president of the RFU, once said: 'The history of all sports over which professionalism has gained sway is a catalogue of corruptibility and decay.'

A LEVEL FIELD FOR THE WORKING MEN

As rugby became popular with working men in the north of England and Wales, this commitment to amateurism became a problem. In these areas many players wanted to get what was called 'broken-time' payments. Until changes to working laws that gave workers a half day on a Saturday, working men usually worked six days a week and weren't allowed to play sport on a Sunday for religious reasons. They often had to take time off to play rugby.

As a result, many in rugby wanted small expenses or match fees to be allowed as a form of compensation for time missed at work. It's worth remembering that if a player picked up an injury and couldn't earn money, he could have trouble feeding his family or paying the bills. Not being paid also made it difficult for working-class players to travel to away games due to cost and time. But those in rugby's corridors of power refused to budge.

'GET THESE COMMONERS AWAY FROM ME!'

There were other reasons some wanted rugby to stay amateur. Gentlemen, who only played once a week, knew they would be no match for full-time professionals. They had seen it happen in football in the 1880s as working men 'took over' the sport they felt was spiritually theirs.

An even uglier reason for rugby staying amateur was that some 'gentlemen' simply didn't like working men playing what they saw as 'their game'. Some clubs ignored amateur rules and would leave money in players' clothes for them to secretly collect after a game. This became known as 'shamateurism' as it made a sham of amateurism.

The biggest 'threat' to amateurism in rugby came from the north of England and Wales. Everyone in the RFU knew lots of Welsh players were getting illicit cash, but the English mostly turned a blind eye. In the 1890s, the big four teams of Wales – Cardiff, Llanelli, Newport and Swansea – were huge attractions when they played across the border and nobody wanted to miss out on the money from ticket sales they brought in. Money, you see, wasn't always bad – particularly if it paid for food, drink and travel for committee members.

THE GREAT SPLIT

In 1895, after years of arguments about the issue of players getting money for playing, the matter exploded. In August of that year, 22 clubs in the north of England resigned from the Rugby Football Union and formed the Northern Union. Initially the Northern Union only allowed payments for time missed from work due to playing, but soon it permitted full professionalism. From this Northern Union the modern game of rugby league was created. As we will see in the next chapter, the impact of this decision on the England team was devastating. It was like ripping the heart and guts out of the national side and the following years were characterised by famine and decline on the international field.

The split of 1895 meant any rugby union player who played professional rugby with the Northern Union was, until 1995, not allowed to play, coach, referee or do anything related to rugby union ever again. Just talking to a rugby league official could see a player banned from union for life. Sometimes, players who turned professional weren't even allowed into a rugby union clubhouse for a beer with old teammates. Bizarrely, you could play any other sport professionally – such as cricket, football, boxing or tennis – and there was nothing stopping you playing union again. But play rugby league once and that was it, no more union.

Rugby union itself would fight off the spectre of professionalism for 100 years. Well, almost. Rugby union was to remain amateur for 99 years and 364 days after the decision to split!

1871–95: THE STAR PLAYERS

FREDERICK STOKES

Club: Blackheath
Position: Forward
Caps: 3 (1871–73)
Points: 0

As a former Rugby School pupil, it was perhaps fitting that

Frederick Stokes was the first ever England captain. At 20 years and 258 days old in that inaugural game of 1871, he still remains the youngest ever player to lead the side. A founding member of the RFU, he also became its president aged just 24, having retired from international rugby aged 22. He also remains the youngest person to have been RFU president. As a player he was described by a fellow player as 'one of the very best examples of a heavy forward, always on the ball and first-rate either in the thick of a scrum or in a loose rally'. He was also useful with the boot and could play half-back when needed too.

EDWARD TEMPLE GURDON

Club: Richmond
Other notable teams: South of England, Cambridge University
Position: Forward
Caps: 16 (1878–86)
Points: N/A (1 try)

A hard-working, tireless forward, Gurdon won what was then a monumental 16 caps (a record not broken until 1913). He captained Cambridge University for two seasons and went on to lead England nine times, never suffering a defeat. That impressive record included back-to-back Triple Crowns. The Reverend Frank Marshall, one of the key historians of the early rugby game, ranked him among the greatest forwards to have pulled on the white shirt as well as 'one of the most massive and muscular forwards' to have played for England.

His brother, Charles, was also a fiercely respected England forward of the era, winning 14 caps. After his playing days, Temple served as president of the RFU and was also elected to the IRFB.

LENNARD STOKES

Club: Blackheath
Position: Full-back, threequarter
Caps: 12 (1875–81)
Points: N/A (17 conversions, 2 drop goals)

His older brother, Frederick, may have set a couple of notable 'firsts' in his short England career, but Lennard set several records which required more than just being the first person to do something. A full-back or threequarter, many argue that Lennard was the first true star of English rugby. A superb athlete, he had all the traits to succeed. He was strong and quick, hard to tackle, sure of hand, a superb defender, owner of an accurate and powerful boot and, to top it all off, a scientific brain for the game. His 12 caps may not seem much, but it must be remembered that only from 1881 did England usually play three games a season. Between 1875 and 1880 England played only two, or even one, games a year.

He kicked six conversions against a hapless Wales in 1881, contributing to a career total of 17 international conversions. This would remain an English record for more than a century. His 12 appearances included five as captain and only once was he on the losing side at Test level. Arthur Guillemard, an early rugby historian, writing in the early 1890s, felt that Lennard had had no equal 'either in science or play . . . from the date of the foundation of the Union'.

SAMMY WOODS

Clubs: Cambridge University, Bridgwater, Blackheath
Position: Forward
Caps: 13 (1890–95)
Points: 6 (1 try, 1 conversion)

So varied was Sammy Woods's sporting life, it's hard to know what bit of it was most impressive. Was it the 13 caps for England? Or the five times he captained the side? Or was it the fact he played over 400 first-class cricket matches? Perhaps it was his three caps for the English cricket team? Or maybe his three Tests for the Australian cricket team (he was born in Australia)? Added to these glorious achievements, he played hockey and football at county level and won blues at Cambridge in both rugby and cricket.

On the rugby field, he was a tough-tackling forward, known for his mobility. It was said he played 'cricket like a rugger forward and [rugby] like a fast bowler . . . he was a demon both in the tight scrums and the loose mauls and when he went down the field he went with the fury of a charging rhino'. One player said that it might be better to be hit by a car than tackled by Woods.

RICHARD LOCKWOOD

Clubs: Heckmondwike, Dewsbury
Athletic and Football Club
Position: Threequarter
Caps: 14 (1887–94)
Points: 28 (5 tries, 8 conversions)

'Little Dick, the World's Wonder' was the first ever working-class captain of England. Just 166cm in height (5ft 4.5 in), the Crigglestone-born threequarter was once described by rugby historian Tony Collins as 'the greatest player that most fans of rugby . . . have never heard of'. Collins also said Lockwood was 'a rather tubby little man who . . . did not look a bit like a great footballer, but revealed the mark of "class" as soon as the game started'.

He made his senior rugby debut for Dewsbury aged just 16 and was known for his spectacular runs, often from deep within his half. He had peerless positional sense, excellent tactical decision-making skills and always seemed to pop up in the most useful of places. He was rumoured to have flirted with professionalism (possibly taking £1 a game for his club) and as a result had a short spell out of the national side. But he eventually was honoured with the captaincy against the Welsh in the impressive 24-3 win in 1894, in which he bagged a try and three conversions.

Sadly for England, he turned professional after the split of 1895. He went on to have a fantastic career in rugby league, captaining Wakefield Trinity for four seasons.

- 1871: Lewis Carroll publishes *Through the Looking-Glass*.

- 1872: The first ever FA Cup final takes place. Wanderers F.C. (a team made up of former pupils of English public schools) win 1-0 over Royal Engineers A.F.C.

- 1873: Elizabeth Garrett Anderson is the first woman to gain membership of the British Medical Association. Soon after, women are barred from joining and no other woman is admitted for 19 years.

- 1874: Red becomes the standard colour of post and pillar boxes.

- 1877: England and Australia play the first ever cricket Test match. Australia win by 45 runs.

- 1878: Alexander Graham Bell shows off his new-fangled telephone invention to Queen Victoria and electric street lighting appears in London for the first time.

- 1879: The Battle of Rourke's Drift takes place, one of the most famous encounters of the Anglo-Zulu War.

- 1880: The first cricket Test match to be played on English soil sees the home side defeat Australia.

- 1881: The Natural History Museum opens in London.

- 1882: Old Etonians F.C. win the FA Cup, beating Blackburn Rovers. It is the last time an amateur team wins the tournament.

- 1883: 183 children die in a crush at Victoria Hall (Sunderland) as they clamour for prizes being handed out from the theatre stage and are trapped by a bolted door.

- 1884: In football, England, Ireland, Scotland and Wales compete in the first British Home Championship.

- 1885: *King Solomon's Mines* by H. Rider Haggard is published.

- 1886: Atheist Charles Bradlaugh, after six years of campaigning and even time spent in prison, is finally allowed to affirm (rather than take) the traditional oath which allows an elected politician to formally take their seat in Parliament.

• 1887: Arthur Conan Doyle's first Sherlock Holmes novel is published.

• 1888: Jack the Ripper murders several women in the East End of London over a terrifying period of several months.

• 1889: Birmingham is granted city status.

• 1890: Joseph Merrick, the Elephant Man, dies.

• 1891: Rachel Beer becomes the first woman to edit a national newspaper (the *Observer*).

• 1892: Queen Victoria interferes with the appointment of the Cabinet, refusing to allow Henry Labouchere, a radical, to take his place.

• 1893: 135 people die in an underground explosion in West Yorkshire (Combs Pit, Thornhill).

• 1894: *The Jungle Book* by Rudyard Kipling is published for the first time in book form.

• 1895: The original FA Cup is stolen and never recovered.

1896–1914: DECLINE AND RESURRECTION

	PLAYED	WON	DRAWN	LOST
HOME CHAMPIONSHIP/ FIVE NATIONS	62	26	4	32
TOURING TEAMS	4	0	1	3
FRANCE (NON-CHAMPIONSHIP)	4	4	0	0
TOTAL	70	30	5	35

Championships (3)

1910, 1913 (Grand Slam), 1914 (Grand Slam)

Shared Championships (1)

1912

'. . . such a chapter of misfortune is unequalled in the English history of the game. A wave of mediocrity has swept over English Rugby football in these last few seasons . . . English forward play has degenerated, and its decline began when the English authorities began to soar after the Welsh style and to seek success by imitation of the subserviency of the forward to the backs.'

THE TIMES (13 MARCH 1899)

'Rugby is too good a game to be confined to a particular class.'

RONALD POULTON (ENGLAND THREEQUARTER, 17 CAPS BETWEEN 1909 AND 1914)

ENGLAND SAYS FAREWELL
TO THE VICTORIAN ERA

As the 19th century drew to a close, so too did the reign of Queen Victoria. In 1901, after 63 years upon the throne, Victoria died and Edward VII become monarch. Although Edward himself died in 1910, to be succeeded by George V, the years 1901 to 1914 are generally referred to as the Edwardian era.

Coming before the horrors of the First World War, the period is often overly romanticised in popular culture. American writer, Samuel Hynes, said it was a 'leisurely time when women wore picture hats and did not vote, when the rich were not ashamed to live conspicuously, and the sun really never set on the British flag'.

Ronald Poulton symbolised the glory and the tragedy of the era.

In reality, the period was one of momentous change, political conflict, class struggle, great wealth inequality and saw rapidly developing technology that transformed the way people lived and worked. In politics, the Conservatives (also known as the Unionists) and the Liberals were the two main parties. Despite the ferocity of their battles in the corridors of power, the Liberal Party were able to pass many important and humane laws relating to working hours and minimum wages – to the fury of the Conservatives. While this was happening, the Suffragette Movement (the campaign to give women the right to vote) was reaching a peak, with seemingly constant protests and riots led by women who, quite rightly, wanted to have a say in the way their country was governed.

Technology was drastically reshaping the world, most notably with the rapid development of motorised vehicles and improved long-distance communications through radiotelegraphy. By 1899, London had its first bus in action. In 1896, at Crystal Palace, the first known case of a pedestrian being killed by a motor car occurred when 44-year-old Bridget Driscoll was struck by a vehicle supposedly being driven at no more than 4.5 miles per hour. The coroner said afterwards he hoped 'such a thing would never happen again'.

The British Empire still flew its flag (sometimes nicknamed the Butcher's Apron) over huge chunks of the world. British politicians were not afraid to send the empire's forces into action to 'defend' national interests. The Second Boer War (1899–1902) in South Africa, involving the British Empire and two independent Boer states, was sparked by the discovery of gold and diamonds in the Boer states and a disagreement over who had the right to the benefit from this natural wealth. While Britain ultimately won the conflict, it triggered huge debate about the ethics of British foreign policy and the ability of Britain to maintain such a vast empire.

Newspapers, in the form of popular journalism, were booming. Many of the new publications hitting the newsstands focused less on international and political news than their predecessors and more on gossip, celebrities, sport and crime.

The Edwardian era also saw a huge shift in the way children were raised and treated by society. Thanks to changes in child labour and education laws in the late 19th century, there were fewer children in the workforce and by 1918 school was made compulsory up to the age of 14. A 'cult of childhood' developed in which children were no longer seen as 'small adults', and it was felt attention and care should be spent on ensuring their early years helped them develop and learn.

THE DIMMING OF THE NORTHERN STARS

The split of 1895 changed English rugby forever. The immediate impact could be seen in the poor run of results that followed in the decade or so after the Northern Union was formed. The RFU would eventually lose 136 Yorkshire clubs to the Northern Union, with just 14 staying loyal. Unsurprisingly, England's national side struggled to cope with so many of its key clubs and star players so suddenly ineligible to play the amateur game. Even now, in the 21st century, huge swathes of the north of England are more devoted to rugby league than union and thousands of talented athletes never even try to play the union game. And while both codes are now fully professional, allowing players to swap between the two as they wish, most players, naturally, stay with the sport they grew up with.

However, England did recover to again win Triple Crowns and Championships (and by 1910 claiming the newly available Grand Slam). But war soon brought all rugby to a halt. Many young men who proudly wore the red rose of their nation on the playing field were soon to make the ultimate sacrifice for their country on the battlefield.

Tough times were ahead for England.

NORMAL SERVICE CONTINUES?

1896 – England 25 Wales 0 (Rectory Field, Blackheath)

It briefly seemed that the great split would have little impact on England's international fortunes. The first game after the schism saw Wales (down to 14 men after just 15 minutes due to injury) comprehensively dismantled. But appearances were deceiving: ten of the Red Rose team for this clash were from the north as many clubs and players were, at this point, yet to 'defect'. The result turned out to be a rare glimpse of light in a dark period.

A DISMAL DECLINE

From 1896 to 1905, England played 39 internationals. They won a mere ten, suffering 25 defeats and enduring four draws. They were not to win the Championship again until 1910.

1896 – England 4 Ireland 10 (Meanwood Road, Leeds)

Nearly 18,000 fans saw a fiery Irish side ultimately subdue the supposedly superior home pack. Ireland began to fade in the second half and it seemed England had a chance to pull it back. But ten minutes from time, Oxford University threequarter Edward Baker blew a certain score. After successfully crossing the line with ball in hand, he attempted to get nearer the posts to make the conversion easier. Instead, he stepped out of the field of play. England's chance for a comeback was gone.

1897 – Wales 11 England 0 (Rodney Parade, Newport)

This was the first real beating England had ever taken from their

Welsh neighbours and a dramatic turnaround from the 25-0 win a year earlier. It wasn't just on the scoreboard either. Wales, who were usually the most lightweight of the Home Unions in terms of size, began selecting 'Rhondda-type forwards'. These were extremely tough men – often policemen or manual labourers – who could dish it out and stand toe-to-toe with anyone. These players helped give the silky Welsh backs enough ball to run free with and create havoc. This was to be the foundation of Wales's first golden era, which lasted from 1900 to 1911. England would win just once against Wales in the next dozen years and would not taste success on Welsh soil between 1895 and 1913. It was a far cry from the massacre of 1881 when the gap was so great the English decided not to even play the Welsh the following season.

1897 – England 12 Scotland 3 (Fallowfield, Manchester)

Another impact of the split within the rugby union game was England's 'retreat' to the south for home games, rather than spreading fixtures around the nation. This was to be the final international England played in the north until 1997. The Red Roses at least said farewell with a rare Calcutta Cup win – the first since 1893. The home side's pack played superbly to subdue the Scottish forwards and make room for the backs to finish off the match. England's full-back Fred Byrne (Moseley) used his boot to excellent effect to either pin back the Scots or to kick points (he bagged a conversion and drop goal).

However, there were no immediate English celebrations with the Calcutta Cup after the match as the Scottish had not brought it with them! Whether this was due to forgetfulness, or an arrogant belief that they would not lose, is not known.

1898 – England 14 Wales 7 (Rectory Field, Blackheath)

A crowd of 20,000 witnessed England snatch their last win over Wales for 12 years, with the brothers Percy and Frank Stout (both Gloucester) grabbing two of England's four tries. The next match England were to play, against the same opposition to boot, was to be one of the darkest moments of a black era.

1899 – Wales 26 England 3 (St Helen's, Swansea)

England travelled to west Wales with seven new caps. For a short time they had Wales on the back foot, but soon the Swansea tide turned. Thanks to four tries from winger Willie Llewellyn and a mesmerising display from the legendary James brothers of Swansea, Wales beat England with what *The Times* called 'a severity unknown in English international games'. At the time it was their largest ever defeat. England were criticised for trying to play like Wales, rather than focusing on old-fashioned forward play.

About the only positive for the visitors was the debut of Red Rose great Herbert 'Octopus' Gamlin (Devonport Albion) at full-back.

AN OUTRAGE AGAINST THE SPIRIT OF THE GAME

Wales's 1899 success didn't go down too well with some English writers. The *Yorkshire Post* newspaper grumbled that the Welsh team had got together to practise on the Thursday before the match. The writer, Old Ebor, moaned it was 'too business-like for amateur sport'.

THE FIRST WHITEWASH

After the Welsh loss, England fell 6-0 to Ireland in Dublin and 5-0 at home in Blackheath to Scotland. It was the first time England had been 'whitewashed' in the Home Championship and they had only scored a meagre three points all tournament (a try against Wales by George Carmichael 'Tot' Robinson of Percy Park). The 1899 season saw Ireland win the Triple Crown and title. It was to be their last outright title until 1936. The only points Ireland conceded were from a penalty. It was remarkable at the time as the penalty had been awarded for a player being tackled off the ball – the first occasion such an offence had been penalised at this level.

Meanwhile, *The Times* reacted furiously to the loss to Scotland at Blackheath, blasting the forwards in particular: 'While possessed of weight, the English forwards' game was being repeatedly spoilt by one or two of their men kicking too hard, which meant that the Scottish, with all their dexterity, were being helped by their opponents. And the fact that these delinquents in the scrummage were mostly from the north revives the opinion that by some means or other the blending of the two schools of southern and northern scrummagers has to answer for many of England's disasters.'

Sadly for England, whitewashes were no longer to be an unusual result. They were to plumb the white depths again in 1901, 1903, 1905 and 1907.

ONLY THE OCTOPUS HANGS ON
1900 – England 3 Wales 13 (Kingsholm, Gloucester)

In response to the humiliations of 1899, the English selectors welcomed in the 20th century by making 14 changes to the side that finished the previous season against Scotland. An astonishing 13 of these were new caps. Only Herbert 'Octopus' Gamlin at full-back retained his place. The other previously capped player was scrum-half and captain Richard Cattell (Moseley), who was a priest in the Church of England. The entire England pack, therefore, was uncapped.

This was the only England international ever played in Gloucester, and the disappointing crowd of 15,000 saw Wales win with ease. One of Wales's try scorers, Dick Hellings, played almost the whole game with a fractured arm as no replacements were permitted. Indeed, in 1901, it was decided that stoppages for injuries could only last for three minutes. People were concerned about how much time was being taken up by injuries!

The great Welsh team that defeated England at Gloucester in 1900.

A PROPHET LEADS THE RED ROSES

One of England's captains in this period was John 'The Prophet' Daniell. A powerful forward who played club rugby with Cambridge University, he was arguably an even more talented cricketer. Some contemporaries considered Daniell one of the great forwards of the era and it was agreed he was a hugely inspirational captain.

While he won seven caps for England between 1899 and 1904, he played cricket for Somerset for 15 seasons and was captain for all but two of them. He took a break from cricket in 1904 when he moved to India to work on the family tea estates! Daniell returned to England and played for Somerset until 1927. It was said he was so tough he had a disdain for cricketers wearing boxes to protect their private parts.

OUT WITH THE (NOT VERY) OLD
AND (BRIEFLY) IN WITH THE NEW

England selectors of the period were notoriously fickle. As the national side floundered, the selectors would fumble around for fresh faces. Alongside the 13 new caps to face Wales in 1900, history shows other reckless selection examples of the period. In 1909, England used 31 players in just four matches (bear in mind, there were no replacements or squad rotation back then).

The hacking up of teams, and constant switching around in selection, hindered England hugely as more settled opponents could take advantage of English unfamiliarity.

This was particularly damaging against Wales. At the time, the fixture with the Dragons would, unless weather caused a postponement, be the first fixture of the season. Blooding a load of new caps or trying out fresh combinations against the tournament's best team (and one of the greatest of any era) was not conducive to good team development. Welsh captain Gwyn Nicholls said: 'An English XV is more or less a scratch side. The men are drawn from a great variety of clubs playing various styles of game, and almost totally unfamiliar with each other.'

Rugby historian Huw Richards has noted that between 1900 and 1909, England awarded an astonishing 71 new caps against Wales. Richards also points out that between 1899 and 1951, England never once picked the same half-back combination to play the Welsh in consecutive fixtures.

It wasn't always the fault of RFU selectors when players had to be changed. In 1910, in the first international at Twickenham, centre Barney Solomon (Redruth) made a successful debut in a rare win against Wales. However, after the match he informed the selectors he no longer wished to be considered as the travel from Cornwall to London was simply too much.

WHERE HAVE YOU BEEN, MR ROBINSON?

For the 1902 encounter with Wales at Blackheath, English selectors called upon John Robinson in the forwards to win his second cap. Remarkably, his previous cap had been earned in 1893 against Scotland. The nine-year gap between caps was a record that would not be equalled until 1965. Robinson had been a Cambridge University player when first called up, but on his dramatic recall he was playing for Headingley. He was the first player capped from that club.

1902 – England 6 Scotland 3 (Inverleith, Edinburgh)
England scored a rare win over their oldest enemy – their first since 1897 and last until 1906. Star of the match was Herbert 'Octopus' Gamlin at full-back. His famously fierce tackling saved his side many a time, particularly in the final quarter. Welsh writer J.B.G. Thomas wrote: 'None passed where Gamlin guarded the way.'

WHEN HAVING AN EXTRA MAN BACKFIRES
1903 – Wales 21 England 5 (St Helen's)
After just 15 minutes of this match, Welsh winger and captain Tom Pearson departed injured after he ran into the rock that · was Herbert Gamlin. The injury reduced Wales to 14 men and they were forced to take Jehoida Hodges out of the pack and place him on the wing. Sadly for England, any hope this would help them to a rare win in Wales were instantly dashed as Hodges scored three tries before half-time! England at least managed a try, their only one in Wales between 1899 and 1911. Unsurprisingly, England's season ended in another whitewash.

WOODEN PLAYERS
With England in the doldrums, the English press, much like their counterparts today, were not slow in putting the boot in.

The *Daily Chronicle* wrote: 'There is no reason why English players should be less intelligent or less gifted but it is a fact that, relatively, English football is wooden.'

A DOUBLE TRAGEDY

England lost at Lansdowne Road in 1903 by 6-0. But the result was utterly insignificant when compared to what happened afterwards. Rugby historian John Griffiths records that three of the travelling party caught typhoid fever in Dublin. Of these two died: winger Reggie Forrest (Blackheath) and R.W. Whalley, a former RFU president. The third victim, scrum-half Bernard Oughtred, recovered.

CLUBS OF A DIFFERENT ERA

Modern rugby fans may be surprised to see the clubs that supplied the players to the national team in this period. Take the 1903 loss to Scotland: the England side was made up of players from Devonport Albion (2), Rockcliff, Liverpool O.B., Lennox, Blackheath (2), Streatham & Croydon, Birkenhead Park, Liverpool, Old Merchant Taylors' FC, Percy Park, Newton Abbot, Richmond and Oxford University.

'OUR SCRUM, YOUR PUT IN'
1904 – England 14 Wales 14 (Welford Road, Leicester)

Scottish referee Crawford Findlay penalised Welsh scrum-half Dicky Owen so much at scrum time that Owen refused to place the ball in the scrum after a while as he expected to be penalised each time. Instead, he gave it to his opponent Walter Butcher (Bristol) to place in the tunnel. Referee Findlay was known to dislike the working-class element in Welsh teams. The Scottish official once gave a speech in which he said he was 'surprised that Wales selected miners, steelworkers and policemen' and that they would be more suited to rugby league in the north of England.

England led by four points with very little time remaining, when a very rare event occurred which gave Wales a draw. The Dragons' Will Joseph called a mark, allowing the visitors a shot at goal (see page 33 for more details). Until 1921, a goal from mark could be taken by a different player to the one who had called it. Welsh full-back Bert Winfield stepped up and slotted a goal worth four points! The following year this would be reduced to a three-point score.

A RARE BRIGHT SPOT

1904 – England 19 Ireland 0 (Rectory Field, Blackheath)

This dominating win over Ireland was a rare highlight in a grim era. Led by John 'The Prophet' Daniell and a strong pack, the home side scored 16 second-half points to dismantle the overwhelmed visitors. Winger Elliott Vivyan (Devonport Albion) and forward Norman Moore (Bristol) bagged two tries apiece. Vivyan added a conversion too to give him ten points, which was then an English record in the Championship.

THE NORTH LOOMS LARGE

It is taken for granted now that rugby union is a far larger sport than rugby league in England. In 1904, however, the Northern Union actually overtook the RFU in terms of affiliated clubs.

THE ORIGINAL ALL BLACKS ARRIVE

1905 is one of the most celebrated years in the history of rugby. For this was the year when the first major international team from the southern hemisphere arrived to play in Europe: New Zealand.

The 1905 Home Championship had been another disaster for England with the men in white left whitewashed and clinging on to the dreaded wooden spoon. The season started with a 25-0 loss in Cardiff (until 1972, this was the biggest defeat England had suffered in the Championship), a 17-3 thrashing from Ireland in Cork and an 8-0 loss in Richmond to the Scots. It was a set of results that would hardly worry the approaching All Blacks.

1905 – Ireland 17 England 3 (Mardyke, Cork)

If it wasn't bad enough playing for England at this time, the travelling was a test of endurance too. After the long sea crossing to Ireland, the RFU had the players travel third-class on the train from Dublin to Cork, a far from ideal way of preparing for an international. There was further embarrassment for the RFU on the field too. The star of the match was Ireland's centre Basil Maclear who scored and converted his own try, set up two more and gave a commanding performance. Maclear was wearing the emerald green shirt (it was his debut too) because the RFU president, Rowland Hill, had previously declared Maclear 'not good enough' to play for England.

The scorned threequarter, who qualified for Ireland based on his residency in Cork, would wear white gloves while he played. Tragically, he was killed in the First World War – one of eight Irish internationals to lose their lives in the conflict.

THE COLONIES ARRIVE TO TEACH THE MOTHER COUNTRY A LESSON

Today New Zealand is known far and wide as the world's premier rugby nation. Since their first game in 1903, they have either been the leading team at Test level, or just one or two steps behind. Their greatness was established as early as 1905 when the 'Original All Blacks' travelled to Europe and North America for their now legendary tour. The team would change rugby forever and establish rugby union as the national game of New Zealand.

The All Blacks played 35 games on the tour and won 34 of them. Few of the games were close. The tourists conceded just 59 points, scored an incredible 976 and 23 of their opponents didn't even manage to score against them at all.

ARE WE NEARLY THERE YET?

The 1905 All Blacks left on 30 July by boat and, after two short stops, arrived in England on 8 September. They returned home (after two games in Canada) on 6 March 1906.

SHAPING A NATION

The 1905 tour helped shape the identity of modern New Zealand. In the early years of the 20th century many British people considered places like New Zealand and Australia as mere colonies of the British Empire, rather than unique, vibrant countries in their own right. Yet the All Blacks were so dominant over the teams of the 'Mother Country' – and the visiting players seemed so athletic, healthy and muscular compared to the Home Union ones – that many feared it showed a decline in the masculinity of men of all classes in Britain.

At the start of the tour plenty of folk in Britain and Ireland, full of smug superiority, thought the visitors would struggle. When Devon lost 55-4 in the opening game, some newspapers ran the score the other way around, unable to believe the reported score was correct.

GAME CHANGERS

Not only were the New Zealanders remarkably fit and strong, they also brought a new style of rugby with them that most European teams were unable to react to. In the scrum, the New Zealanders specialised with each player having a specific role. In contrast, British and Irish teams still had forwards pack down at scrums in the order they arrived. The All Blacks used a 2-3-2 formation in the scrum: two hookers, three in the middle row and two in the back. The other forward, the wing-forward or 'rover', placed the ball in the scrum and the scrum-half awaited it at the back, ready to whip it away quickly. This rover, usually superhuman tour captain Dave Gallaher, was accused of obstructing defenders and the role caused home teams all sorts of problems.

Another way they excelled was in line-out play, where they practised obsessively, and they had a different back formation – they played what they called two fifth-eighths. One reason the Kiwis were fitter was that they used to play 45 minutes a half back home but in the UK games were 35 minutes a half. Some even thought the 'silk' shirts the All Blacks wore made them hard to grab.

1905 – England 0 New Zealand 15 (Crystal Palace, London)

A crowd of 45,000 gathered to watch the first clash of black and white in international rugby (although some sources claim it was as many as 70,000). The tourists had already swatted away the challenge of 19 English club sides as well as Ireland, Munster, Scotland and the West of Scotland. Few had much hope for the Red Roses before the game and, it turned out, they were right not to. England, with eight new caps, played five threequarters in an attempt to bolster their defence. The New Zealand players, however, saw this as a sign of weakness and lack of confidence. The Kiwis, having already played against most of the England players in club and county games during the tour, felt the RFU selectors had not picked the best team possible. In preparation, England had taken the unusual step of getting together four days before the match for training. Ultimately, the tactics and training mattered little as the English pack simply couldn't live with the visitors. New

Zealand brushed off the home side with five unconverted tries, four of them from winger Duncan McGregor.

The *Daily Express* wrote: 'Ninety-nine people out of a hundred expected her to lose. It was the fact that England had never looked in the smallest degree like making a close fight of it that gave rise to a sense of dissatisfaction . . . The England team were never anything but losers.'

THE MIRROR MAN AND THE RANKS OF HUMANITY

The sheer size of the crowd at Crystal Palace for the game took up many column inches in the days that followed the game. *The Times* reported that 'Never in the history of rugby football has such a multitude assembled to watch a game. The vast attendance was a wonderful tribute to the fame of the New Zealand football team. People came to the Palace to see the New Zealanders play and not to see England win.'

The most remarkable description of the day was to be found in the *Daily Mail*: 'The slopes above the field of play were black with humanity . . . Every tree that commanded a view was laden with spectators and one daring spirit climbed the tall central pole of Maxim's captive flying machine. But the height of ingenuity was reached by an elderly enthusiast who made no attempt to raise himself above his fellows. Instead, he stood at the back of the crowd with a long pole on which were fixed two mirrors, the upper one tilted so as to reflect a view of the game upon the lower glass. There he stood, holding his pole aloft and gazing serenely into his looking glass, oblivious of the gibes of his neighbours.'

1905 ALL BLACKS TOUR RECORD

Played: 35
Won: 34
Lost: 1 (Wales)
Points for: 976
Points against: 59
Average tour score: NZ 28 Opponents 2
Players known to have worn hats while playing: George Gillett

NO LONGER A RIGHT (AND LEFT) WAY OF PLAYING

Such was the devastation the New Zealanders caused among the Home Unions, there was a realisation among the four national sides that they had to evolve the way they played the game. Wales and Ireland experimented with the seven forwards, eight backs split the All Blacks had used. Wales in particular had success with the model and used it as late as 1907. England, meanwhile, began to change the way their half-backs played. Traditionally they had played a left and right half-back, but in 1906 shifted to what we now recognise as a scrum-half and outside-half. The game was growing internationally too, with France (who had also faced New Zealand) added to England's fixture list for the first time.

1906 – Scotland 3 England 9 (Inverleith)

England shocked the rugby community with this surprise win away from home against Scotland. It was England's first win since 1904 and ended a 'very long spell of ill-fortune' and a seven-game losing streak. At scrum-half for this game was the legendary Adrian Stoop (Harlequins) – a player so influential in the history of English rugby (see 'Star Players' section) that the home stadium of rugby aristocrats Harlequins bears his name.

THE REMARKABLE STORY OF JIMMY PETERS

In the victory over Scotland in 1906, history was made as England's first black player was capped. Jimmy Peters was born in Salford in 1879 to an English mother and Jamaican father, both of whom worked in a travelling circus. As a young boy his father died a 'shocking death in a lion's cage'. His mother, unable to support Jimmy, allowed him to join another circus where he was trained as a bareback horse rider. When the young

Peters broke his arm aged 11, he was sent to an orphanage in Southwark.

Jimmy Peters led a most remarkable life.

Peters excelled at rugby, cricket and athletics, and trained as a carpenter. As an adult he joined Bristol FC, where a committee man resigned in anger at the selection of a non-white player. One Bristol newspaper complained he was keeping a white player out of the team and referred to him in a derogatory manner.

Eventually he moved to Plymouth Albion and won representative honours with Devon. Upon his England call-up, the *Yorkshire Post* wrote that his 'selection is by no means popular on racial grounds'. Peters was nicknamed 'Darkie' and after his assured debut for the national side, *The Sportsman* wrote that the 'dusky Plymouth man did many good things, especially in passing'.

As a working-class black man in Edwardian England, Peters

must have been an exceptional player to overcome the prejudices of the time and win a total of seven England caps. And while, looking back, it may be said the selectors showed a welcome 'progressive' streak in selecting Peters, it appears he was not considered to face the 1906 South Africans on racial grounds. Rugby journalist E.H.D. Sewell wrote that the Springboks 'preferred not to play against a coloured man' and, by not even selecting Peters for the two trial games before the international, it appears the RFU, shamefully, took note of that.

In 1910, Peters lost three fingers in a working accident. His club, Plymouth Albion, arranged a testimonial match to help raise funds for him. Sadly, this tainted his status as an amateur. He moved to rugby league and played until 1914. Despite his extraordinary life, his death in 1954 was almost unmarked in the national newspapers. It wasn't to be until 1988 that another black player, Chris Oti, lined up in an England team.

1906 – France 8 England 35 (Parc des Princes, Paris)

The first encounter in one of rugby's great fixtures ended in a simple win for England, in which they scored nine tries. France were babies on the international scene, having played their first Test on New Year's Day a few months before, against the touring All Blacks. One French player later described the experience of playing England as like facing 'a series of white avalanches'. The addition of France to the international calendar was a blessing for England as, with hardly any wins coming in this period against their traditional Home Union rivals, they could usually use France as a punching bag and secure at least one victory.

THE AFRICAN CHALLENGE

Following hot on the heels of the 1905 All Blacks, the Springboks arrived in 1906. With British rugby still reeling from the impact of the Kiwis, the Springboks came along and asked further questions of the game in the Mother Country. Just as the All Blacks did, the visitors helped to evolve the game, most notably with their use of the 3-4-1 scrum formation (which is how teams pack down today).

The men in green won 26 of their 29 games (they suffered two defeats and had one draw). The two losses came to Scotland and Cardiff (a shocking 17-0).

1906 – England 3 South Africa 3 (Crystal Palace)

The Times said the rain that fell in London on this day was bad for the 40,000 spectators but great for the 'fifteen Englishmen who took part' who, it was claimed, benefited from the dire conditions on the unsuitable Crystal Palace field. It was felt the wet weather curtailed the superb South African passing game and, furthermore, the home side were fortunate that South Africa had key players missing. In the first half, the backs mainly did nothing but watch the forwards battle in the mud.

After the match, the South African captain, Paul Roos, spoke of the success of the tour. He did, however, have one reservation. According to *The Times* he 'took exception to one thing in British football without wishing to give offence. This was that when a man dropped on the ball with forwards coming on him his life was in danger, and that in South Africa the foot was not used so dangerously.'

WHOOPS, YOU'VE BEEN CAPPED FOR ENGLAND

In the 1906 South African game, Arnold Alcock gained his first and only cap. A forward, he was a student at Guy's Hospital and a somewhat surprise selection for such a big game. It turned out his call-up was a complete error. The selectors had, in fact, meant to pick Lancelot Slocock (Liverpool)! Luckily for Lancelot, he got his cap in the very next game against France and went on to win eight in total.

1907 – Wales 22 England 0 (St Helen's)

This thrashing took Wales ahead in the series between the nations by 11 wins to 10. *The Times* wrote: 'Wales was the last of the four countries of the United Kingdom to be admitted as a competitor to the international championship . . . its early attempts at competing were disastrous and discouraging . . . At last the tide turned, and ever since it has set strongly in favour of Wales.'

The Dragons played just seven forwards and still held off the challenge of the English pack easily (one paper said they were a 'helpless rabble'). This was said to be the first game in which England were to use set positions for players when packing down in the scrum. It didn't help them much. In 1908 England would begin to use specialised half-backs too. The times were a-changing.

THE DESIRABILITY OF FRENCH TOURNAMENT RUGBY

With France now added to the fixture list, talk soon began about turning the Home Union Championship into the Five

Nations. *The Times* wrote rather poetically about this: 'French athletes have all the qualities of good Rugby Union football players, and they only need frequent practice in the company of those who play better than themselves to improve.'

By 1909, the *Daily Mail* was impressed enough by the improvement of French rugby to write that 'Frenchmen do not play "Comic" football' any more. France officially joined the Championship in 1910.

1909 – England 3 Australia 9 (Rectory Field, Blackheath)

The public had seemingly grown accustomed to visitors from faraway lands and the first tour of the Wallabies failed to generate the excitement of the appearances of the New Zealanders and South Africans. The visiting players reluctantly performed a war dance on this tour, encouraged to do so by their union who knew the All Blacks' haka had gone down well. Despite the relative indifference of the public, the Australians had a very good tour record with 25 wins, five losses and a draw. They were too good for an England side with ten new caps.

Australia wore a light blue shirt (the colours of New South Wales) with an embroidered waratah (a plant from Australia). The British press originally nicknamed them 'The Rabbits', but the visitors didn't like it and took on the mantle of 'The Wallabies' instead. This was the last England match played at Blackheath.

SCOTTISH AND IRISH PURITY

Ireland and Scotland refused to face the Australians as they didn't like the fact that the Australian players were permitted to claim three shillings a day in expenses! This was akin to the horror of professionalism. The Scottish Rugby Union, the always 'honourable' defenders of purity and amateurism, even considered cancelling their fixture with England in 1909 in protest. The match eventually went ahead and the uncorrupted Scots won 18-8.

1909 – Ireland 5 England 11 (Lansdowne Road)

This was England's first win in Ireland since 1895. Only one player, full-back Edward John Jackett (Leicester) had played in the Emerald Isle before. In fact, the selectors were so frequently chopping and changing at this time that the only other players in the side to have ever faced Ireland before at all were forwards Alf Kewney (Rockcliff) and captain Robert Dibble (Bridgwater Albion). England had used an incredible 31 players in their four 1909 Championship games (remember, there were only 15 players used per game back then!).

THE CABBAGE PATCH HELPS
ENGLAND BLOSSOM

In 1910 England found themselves a new home at Twickenham. Costing £5,573, the ground was sourced by the RFU's Billy Williams and affectionately became known as 'Billy Williams's Cabbage Patch' due to the fact that, well, it had once been a cabbage patch.

It was also later nicknamed, only half-jokingly, 'HQ' (as it was the 'headquarters of rugby'). The ground was immediately a source of good luck as England ended a terrible run of results against the Welsh and went on to claim their first title in 18 years. Here are the highlights from that season:

1910 – England 11 Wales 6 (Twickenham, London)

Due to the visitors being caught up in traffic, the opening international fixture at Twickenham began 15 minutes late. It was written that 'Perhaps never before had such a large crowd been seen on a Metropolitan rugby ground as that which gathered around the arena when the game commenced.'

But once the contest got under way, the new home of English rugby had the most extraordinary baptism. Wales kicked off to England's captain Adrian Stoop who threw convention to the wind and decided to run, not punt. England quickly made inroads into the Welsh half and with quick hands, fleet feet and soft passing, winger and debutant Frederick Chapman (Westoe) was over in the corner (Chapman also kicked a conversion and a penalty).

Twickenham had humble beginnings.

Wales never recovered and fell to their Auld Enemy for the first time in 12 years. To the delight of England fans in the coming years, Twickenham seemed to paralyse Wales, who would not win at the ground until 1933. Considering how one-sided the fixture had become since 1895, it was a remarkable change of fortunes.

This match also saw the debut of England legend Charles 'Cherry' Pillman (Blackheath). Pillman is considered by many to be one of the key figures in the development of the 'roving' flank forwards. Interestingly, England half-back Dai Gent was a fluent Welsh speaker, extremely useful in an era when the Welsh players often discussed tactics in their native language.

1910 – Scotland 5 England 14 (Inverleith)
England followed up the Welsh win at Twickenham with a less thrilling 0-0 draw against Ireland on their next appearance at their new home. The subsequent 11-3 win over France in Paris was par for the course, but what came next was a shock. Since 1897 England had managed just two wins over Scotland, who were enjoying one of their strongest periods in their history. Their 'rather unexpected' away win over the Scots gave England their first title since 1892. Played in front of 30,000 spectators (the largest match on Scottish soil to that point), the English were praised for making the most of limited attacking opportunities, with the Scottish forwards in the ascendancy until at least the halfway point before the visitors pulled clear.

Centre John Birkett (Harlequins) bagged two of England's four tries. Birkett was the son of Reginald Birkett, who played in the first ever international in 1871.

A NEUTRAL LINE

Rugby historian John Griffiths relates that on the same day the above match took place, the IRFB met and a proposal was made that when neutral touch judges were appointed, they should have the power to point out foul play to the referee. The wise decision was passed into law . . . 70 years later!

TAKING THE KNEE OUTLAWED

In 1911 a new law was brought in that made it illegal to pick the ball up in the scrum with your legs!

FATIGUED FRANCE

1911 – England 37 France 0

Weeks before France made their debut at HQ, they shocked the rugby world with a win over Scotland in Paris, the first international win they had ever enjoyed. Alas, France suffered several withdrawals before travelling and then three major injuries during their match with England. As there were no replacements then, it meant they finished with just 12 fully fit men. As a result, an 8-0 half-time deficit for the visitors became 37-0 by the end. *The Times* reported the visiting forwards had very 'little knowledge' of their duties! Winger Douglas Lambert (Harlequins) scored what was in that era an astonishing 22 points with five conversions, two tries and two penalties.

NUDE OR GLORY?

1911 – England 13 Scotland 8 (Twickenham)

England retained the Calcutta Cup for the first time since 1884 with this win. The fixture was described by one paper as being 'regarded by sportsmen as the most chivalrous, if not the most scientific, contest in the series of international matches'. Gentlemanly qualities were certainly the order of things on this day. During the dying minutes of the match, Scottish centre George Cunningham broke through the English defence and was in the clear, just 'ten yards' from the line. However, England full-back Samuel Williams (Newport) grabbed the Scot's shorts and they came off. Rather than score in half a birthday suit, Cunningham simply sat down on the field to protect his dignity. The chance to draw level was lost and Scotland suffered a narrow loss.

This game also marked the beginning of a 46-game streak in which England would score at least one try in every match (the run would end in 1927).

NO SUCH THING AS A FREE (SICK) LUNCH

To get a sense of how strictly amateur regulations were applied in this period, look no further than the story of how RFU treasurer William Cail dealt with expense claims. After a player had submitted his expenses for his trip to Ireland with the national side, Cail asked him how his journey had been. When the player revealed the sea crossing had made him unwell, Cail cancelled the player's claim for lunch expenses. He reasoned if the player was truly sick he would not have eaten anything.

THE TRAGIC DEATH OF A TEENAGE SENSATION

Richard Stafford (Bedford) made his debut for England aged just 18 years old and while still a schoolboy. Picked to face Wales at prop, he appeared in all four matches as England shared the title with Ireland. He was 190.5cm (6ft 3in) tall and seen as a prodigy. Stafford had made his club debut for Bedford aged just 15 and captained them at 17. Early in the 1912–13 season, when he was captain, he had to stop playing due to illness and injury. Within three weeks of being diagnosed as having spinal cancer, he was dead. He was just 19. It is the youngest age an England international has died.

1913 – England 3 South Africa 9 (Twickenham)

After the draw in 1906, South Africa were the first side to record a victory in the series between these teams. Despite the thrilling runs of Ronald Poulton (Harlequins) in the centre, one of which led to a try as 'dramatic' as had ever been seen, the humongous South Africa pack wore the home forwards down and took the tourists over the finish line.

BACK-TO-BACK GRAND SLAMS

England not only achieved their first Grand Slam in 1913, they put together back-to-back clean sweeps with another in 1914, as the national side finally emerged fully from the depression that had set in after the 1895 schism. Tragically, the horrors of the First World War were soon to bring sport to a halt and plunge the world into darkness. The captain of the 1913 Grand Slam, forward Norman Wodehouse (Royal Navy/United Services RFC), survived the First World War, but was to perish at sea in the Second World War after coming out of retirement to help the war effort.

1913 GRAND SLAM

MATCH ONE: Wales 0 England 12 (Cardiff Arms Park)

Norman Wodehouse led England to the first win in Cardiff since 1895, putting his men on the way to Grand Slam glory. Centre Ronald Poulton was so dominant that the fixture is sometimes referred to as 'Poulton's match'. Several key players began establishing themselves in the English side, two of whom were winning just their second cap: winger Cyril Lowe (Cambridge University) and fly-half William 'Dave' John Abbott Davies (Royal Navy/United Services RFC). Both of these players would go on to become icons in English rugby history. The latter was born in Pembrokeshire, Wales and was only once on the losing side in 22 matches for England. This caused a great deal of regret in Wales, summed up by a poem that was published in the match programme for this game:

'Hurrah for the Leek, the succulent Leek, That hall-marks our lads as true metal!

Hurrah for the Rose, the real English Rose — Except for the Pembrokeshire petal.'

Wales were so upset by the defeat, eight of the team never wore the red shirt again.

MATCH TWO: England 20 France 0 (Twickenham)

After this routine five-try victory, E.D.H. Sewell wrote of France that: 'Their game suffers from each forward having a fixed position in the scrum.'

MATCH THREE: Ireland 4 England 15 (Lansdowne Road)

Ireland's drop goal was the only score conceded by England during the Championship. Winger Vincent Coates (Bath) grabbed a brace of tries taking his tally to an impressive six tries in his first three Tests. Yet, he would only win five caps in total and not play after 1913.

MATCH FOUR: England 3 Scotland 0 (Twickenham)

Around 25,000 spectators roared England on to their first Grand Slam. The home crowd were disappointed by the wastefulness of the English backs (described as 'variable as the English summer'), but a try in the corner just before half-time from Oxford University wing-forward Leonard Graham Brown (known as Bruno Brown) was enough to secure a first ever Grand Slam.

1914 GRAND SLAM

MATCH ONE: England 10 Wales 9 (Twickenham)

Led by Ronnie Poulton, England held off a late Welsh onslaught for the narrowest of wins. Tries from Charles Pillman and Bruno Brown and two conversions from Hartlepool Rovers centre Fred Chapman were enough to get England on track to defend their title. Wales once again found Twickenham was not a lucky ground for them. Indeed, before their 1912 loss, one Welsh fan said: 'There is an indefinable something in the atmosphere and the surroundings at Twickenham which is not congenial to the Celtic temperament.'

MATCH TWO: England 17 Ireland 12 (Twickenham)

This match took place with the debate over Home Rule (independence) for Ireland looming large in political and public life in England. As a result, the game got a lot more press attention than was usual and many feared Irish nationalists would disrupt the contest. Ireland were tough to break down, but a superb individual score from Dave Davies, involving multiple dummies and swerves, knocked Ireland out of the running.

Welsh official Tom Schofield took no prisoners when it came to refereeing scrums. If a pack was not scrummaging straight on, he would promptly kick the player at the back of the scrum on the backside.

MATCH THREE: Scotland 15 England 16 (Inverleith)

England secured the Triple Crown in fine style in a thriller of a match. Captain Ronnie Poulton had one of his great performances in the white shirt and claimed a try. Cyril Lowe managed three tries, while his teammate at Cambridge University, George Will, grabbed two for Scotland (the pair had even had a bet the night before on whether they would manage to score). Charles Pillman broke his leg and, after 18 caps in which he had established himself as one of the key players of the era, he never played for England again.

Tragically, 11 of the players from this game would die in the First World War.

A change in captain? Or not?

Between the Scottish and French matches, captain Ronnie Poulton changed his legal name to Poulton-Palmer as a condition of benefiting from his uncle's will. Whatever his name, he had a storming campaign in 1914 and some felt he was the key player in each Triple Crown game. An extraordinary human being (see 'Star Players' section), he was to meet a cruel fate in the coming war.

Ronald Poulton ranks among the finest men to wear the red rose.

MATCH FOUR: France 13 England 39 (Stade Colombes, Paris)

With war about to unleash horror upon Europe, this was to be England's last game until 1920. England claimed the Grand Slam in style (captain Ronald Poulton helped himself to four tries) and set a bunch of records in the process:

- Cyril Lowe grabbed a hat-trick for the second consecutive game, the first time this had happened in successive Tests.
- This was England's ninth successive win, a national record.
- The six conversions from forward John Greenwood (Cambridge University) were an England record.
- The nine tries England scored were the most they had scored in a Championship game.

The Parisian crowd 'hooted' the England team, leading *The Times* to write: 'The match was unfortunately marred by two things – the rough play by one or two of the French team and the exceedingly bad behaviour of the large crowd of spectators. We have come to associate chivalry with the name of France, but if the behaviour of the columns of spectators is typical of French crowds they have learned very little by the lesson of playing Rugby football. However much their teams improve in skill, it will avail little in the eyes of their opponents until they see the necessity in their play of learning to recognize good play on both sides, and also how to take a beating.'

THE FALLEN OF THE FIRST WORLD WAR

'Every player who represented England in Rugby international matches last year has joined the colours.'
***The Times*, 30 November 1914**

For all the grimness of England's record from 1895 until 1910, and the joy the revival of 1911 to 1914 brought, it was all to pale into utter insignificance in 1914 when Britain went to war in one of the most grotesque, barbaric and pointless conflicts in human history. The rugby community rallied to the war effort and the willingness of fit, strong rugby men to sign up to fight was often used by the government as a shining example of patriotism. In total, 28 England internationals were to die as a result of the war.

Some of these men were so keen to fight for King, country and empire, they found ways to overcome barriers that should have prevented them going to the battlefield. Edgar Mobbs (Northampton), who won seven caps for England between 1909 and 1910, was considered too old to fight at 32. In response he brought 264 men to the recruitment office and was then allowed to join himself. He died at Passchendaele.

Jack King (Headingley), who had been described as a 'pocket Hercules' on account of his small stature (he was 165.1cm/5ft 5in tall), was not allowed to enlist due to his height. He simply refused to take no for an answer until the recruiters relented and let him in. He was killed on the Somme.

The only England international to receive the Victoria Cross (the highest order of merit that can be bestowed on an individual in the armed forces) was Lieutenant-Commander Arthur Leyland Harrison who won two caps as a forward in the 1914 Grand Slam. Harrison led an assault on a machine gun emplacement in the raid on Zeebrugge in 1918. At one point, his jaw was broken by a piece of shrapnel and he was knocked out. He recovered and personally led his raiding party onwards into the path of enemy machine gun fire. The report on the action said: 'though already severely wounded and undoubtedly in great pain, [Harrison] displayed indomitable resolution and courage of the highest order in pressing his attack, knowing as he did that any delay in silencing the guns might jeopardise the main object of the expedition.' Harrison was killed in this brave action and was awarded the Victoria Cross posthumously.

It is reported when the great Ronnie Poulton-Palmer was felled by a sniper's bullet in 1915, his last words were: 'I shall never play at Twickenham again.'

28 England internationals died in the First World War:

- Harry Alexander (7 caps, aged 36)
- Henry Berry (4 caps, aged 32)
- Henry Brougham (4 caps, aged 34 and died in 1923 of war wounds)
- Arthur Dingle (3 caps, aged 23)
- George Dobbs (2 caps, aged 32)
- Leonard Haigh (7 caps, aged 35)
- Reginald Hands (2 caps, aged 29)
- Arthur Harrison (2 caps, aged 32)
- Harold Hodges (2 caps, aged 32)

- Rupert Inglis (3 caps, aged 53)
- Percy Kendall (3 caps, aged 36)
- John King (12 caps, aged 32)
- Ronald Lagden (1 cap, aged 25)
- Douglas Lambert (7 caps, aged 32)
- Alfred Maynard (3 caps, aged 22)
- Edgar Mobbs (7 caps, aged 35)
- William Nanson (2 caps, aged 34)
- Francis Oakeley (4 caps, aged 23)
- Robert Pillman (1 cap, aged 23)
- Ronald Poulton-Palmer (17 caps, aged 25)
- John Raphael (9 caps, aged 35)
- Reginald Schwarz (3 caps, aged 43)
- Lancelot Slocock (8 caps, aged 29)
- Francis Tarr (4 caps, aged 27)
- Alexander Todd (2 caps, aged 41)
- James Watson (3 caps, aged 24)
- Arthur Wilson (1 cap, aged 30)
- Charles Wilson (1 cap, aged 43)

1896–1914: THE STAR PLAYERS

HERBERT 'OCTOPUS' GAMLIN

Clubs: Devonport Albion, Blackheath
Position: Full-back
Caps: 15 (1899–1904)
Points: 3 (1 penalty)

Herbert Gamlin had one of rugby's greatest nicknames. He was called 'Octopus' for his hard-hitting ability in the tackle, where he was effective at preventing attackers from getting passes away. He occasionally tackled two players at the same time. It was also said he did not tackle a man, he crushed him.

Gamlin was known for a powerful, if not precise, punt and a super ability to read and shut down attacking plays – a skill that frequently saved England from conceding scores in what was a grim era for the national side. Sadly, he only tasted victory four times in his Test career. His teammates spoke in reverential terms about his defence. As a schoolboy, Gamlin also played county cricket with Somerset.

ADRIAN STOOP

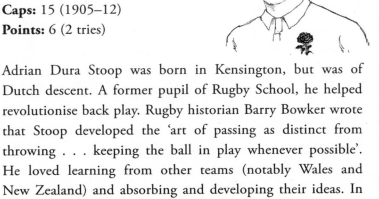

Clubs: Harlequins, Oxford University
Position: Fly-half
Caps: 15 (1905–12)
Points: 6 (2 tries)

Adrian Dura Stoop was born in Kensington, but was of Dutch descent. A former pupil of Rugby School, he helped revolutionise back play. Rugby historian Barry Bowker wrote that Stoop developed the 'art of passing as distinct from throwing . . . keeping the ball in play whenever possible'. He loved learning from other teams (notably Wales and New Zealand) and absorbing and developing their ideas. In particular he helped formalise the changing role of the half-backs. Previously, teams tended to play a 'left' and 'right' half-back. But Stoop saw the advantage to developing more specialised positions, thereby creating a distinct scrum-half and outside-half. His defence, however, was less refined. He was also known to blow hot and cold when it came to form. One contemporary said he was 'on one day positively brilliant and another not worth playing'.

His system thrived at his club Harlequins, who enjoyed great success with Stoop as captain. His last game for the Harlequins was 1938. He was 56! Today, his name is still known to most rugby folk through the name of the Quins' home ground: The Stoop.

CHARLES 'CHERRY' PILLMAN
Club: Blackheath
Position: Wing-forward (flanker)
Caps: 18 (1910–14)
(British Isles, 2 caps, 4 points,
2 conversions)
Points: 26 (8 tries, 1 conversion)

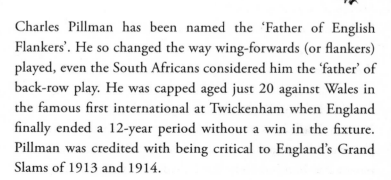

Charles Pillman has been named the 'Father of English Flankers'. He so changed the way wing-forwards (or flankers) played, even the South Africans considered him the 'father' of back-row play. He was capped aged just 20 against Wales in the famous first international at Twickenham when England finally ended a 12-year period without a win in the fixture. Pillman was credited with being critical to England's Grand Slams of 1913 and 1914.

Pillman always packed down on the side of the opposing fly-half at scrum time and would harass not just the fly-half, but all the backline as he would cover across the field. His ability to disrupt the attack of opponents was like nothing the game had seen before. On the 1910 British Isles tour, Pillman played one Test at fly-half where he was so outstanding a South African witness said he 'played a game apparently invented by himself'.

He broke his leg in the penultimate game before the First World War and his spot was taken by his younger brother Robert Pillman for the following match. Robert was killed in the First World War and Charles was not capped again after the conflict.

Pillman also served in the war and won the Military Cross in 1918. Tragically, two of his three sons died within weeks of each other during the Second World War. It is said he never recovered from the grief the deaths brought on.

RONALD POULTON-PALMER

Clubs: Oxford University, Harlequins, Liverpool
Position: Centre, wing
Caps: 17 (1909–14)
Points: 28 (8 tries, 1 drop goal)

Ronald 'Ronnie' Poulton (who later changed his surname to Poulton-Palmer), is one of the most fascinating individuals to have ever pulled on the white shirt of England. He was remarkable both on and off the field. On it, he was said to be the 'idol of English rugby'. Historian Barry Bowker wrote that Poulton ran 'with his head well back and the ball in both hands at arms' length; he had an instinct for seeing a gap and, thanks to a peculiar trick of crossing his feet without stumbling, the ability to swerve either way without losing speed. He was a Rugby genius and one of the best players to don an England jersey.'

Poulton made his debut aged 19 and captained the 1914 Grand Slam team. As England captain, he did not wish to hold the ball in team photos (as is standard for captains) as he did not wish to stand out.

His finest hour in an England shirt was the win over Wales in 1913, described as 'Poulton's match'. Such was his fame that before the match there were posters for the game in Wales that proclaimed 'Come and see R.B. Poulton'. Afterwards, one of the defeated Welsh team said: 'How can one stop him when his head goes one way, his arms another and his legs keep straight on?'

But his off-the-field life was similarly fascinating. Although he was born into wealth, he was, as rugby historian Huw Richards wrote, 'by rugby standards a radical'. He was not shy of criticising the RFU. He openly spoke out when the union banned ten West Country players and officials who had broken rules on amateurism. Poulton believed that such a decision risked making rugby a game for one class only. He even went as far as to publicly call for broken-time payments for players who could not afford to take time off work to play. This was a bold move, considering this was the issue that split English rugby in two in 1895. (The letter is published below this biography.)

At university he was an advocate of the Balliol Boys' Club, a society which helped the homeless and hungry and Poulton would often clash at Oxford with Eton elites who mocked the efforts of groups like the Balliol Boys' Club. He was known to give up his free time to volunteer for lads' clubs in Manchester and Reading and played rugby not just with the glamorous Harlequins of London, but also Liverpool.

In 1914 he became heir to a biscuit fortune (as part of the inheritance arrangement he had to change his name to Poulton-Palmer). He was angered by the idea of civilised nations going to war, but patriotically enlisted when war arrived. Poulton was killed by a sniper's bullet aged just 25. It is said his last words were regret that he would never again play at Twickenham.

In 2018, soil from Twickenham was taken to Poulton's grave in Belgium and soil from his grave taken back to Twickenham and buried pitchside.

Poulton's Letter to *The Sportsman*, December 1912

THE RUGBY UNION AND PROFESSIONALISM.

It is with much apprehension that I read this morning the finding of the General Committee of the Rugby Union concerning the charges brought against certain players in Devonshire clubs of having received money for 'broken time'.

If it is the desire of the Rugby Union Committee practically to limit the game to players who learn it at the Public Schools, and in the Services and Universities, such a finding is reasonable. But I cannot believe such is their desire.

Was not this, then, the opportunity to put the game on

an immovable basis among all classes of the community by making an alteration in the laws of the game relating to professionalism, so as to legislate for a carefully arranged payment for 'broken time' for men who are paid weekly or monthly for the hours they work?

And it is difficult to see how such an offence can be construed as professionalism. A man does not, or under careful regulation would not, receive any addition to this normal weekly wage, but would be paid merely for the hours of work missed through football. Such hours of work would, of course, not include 'overtime'.

He would then be exactly in the position of many business men who, in the enjoyment of a settled income, leave their work an hour or so earlier to catch the necessary train to the match. The most optimistic must feel that such an action as the R.U. Committee have taken will do much to prevent the expansion of the Rugby game, and so reduce the value to England of the most democratic of sports.

I only venture to write this to find out if there are any other present or past players of the game who think as I do.

Yours truly,

RONALD W. POULTON.

16 Portland Place, Reading

1896–1914 NOTABLE EVENTS IN ENGLISH HISTORY

• 1896: A pedestrian is killed by a car for the first time. It is hoped 'such a thing will never happen again'.

• 1897: George Smith, a London taxi driver, becomes the first person to be convicted of drink-driving.

• 1898: The first stepless escalator in the UK is installed in Harrods, London.

• 1899: The Second Boer War begins in South Africa (the United Kingdom versus the Boers of the Transvaal and Orange Free State).

• 1900: The US win the first Davis Cup in tennis.

• 1901: Queen Victoria dies after 63 years on the throne.

• 1902: 25 people die and over 500 are injured when a stand at Glasgow's Ibrox Stadium collapses during a Scotland v England football match.

• 1903: The *Daily Mirror* newspaper is launched – it is originally pitched as a newspaper by women, for women.

• 1904: The speed limit for motor cars is set at 20 miles per hour.

• 1907: New Zealand is granted dominion status by the British government (meaning it was recognised as self-governing).

• 1908: The Olympics are held in London.

• 1909: The 1908 Children Act becomes law and abolishes hanging for children under 16.

• 1910: Dr Crippen becomes the first criminal to be captured thanks to wireless telegraphy. He murdered his wife in London and is caught entering Canada.

• 1912: Both boats sink in the annual Boat Race between the universities of Oxford and Cambridge.

• 1914: The First World War begins.

1919–39: BETWEEN THE WARS

	PLAYED	WON	DRAWN	LOST
HOME CHAMPIONSHIP/ FIVE NATIONS	72	44	7	21
TOURING TEAMS	4	2	0	2
TOTAL	76	46	7	23

Championships (7)

1921 (Grand Slam), 1923 (Grand Slam), 1924 (Grand Slam), 1928 (Grand Slam), 1930, 1934 (Triple Crown), 1937 (Triple Crown)

Shared Championships (3)

1920, 1932, 1939

'I had a very easy war, with only a bullet wound through the left arm.'

JOHN GREENWOOD (ENGLAND FORWARD, 13 CAPS BETWEEN 1912 AND 1920)

'Handling the ball is only a minor part of your job, so don't give much thought to it.'

DAI GENT (ENGLAND FLY-HALF, FIVE CAPS BETWEEN 1905 AND 1910)

AFTER 'THE WAR TO END ALL WARS' (AND BEFORE THE NEXT ONE)

England's revival on the playing field was cut short by the First World War. After the game had been torn apart by the split of 1895, England had been forced to endure over a decade of misery and failure. The 1913 and 1914 Grand Slams ended that period of defeat, but war was to cruelly cut down the lives of many of those rugby heroes as well as countless others who may have gone on to represent England had they not lost life or limb on the battlefield.

While the personnel had changed (England's first game after the war saw 11 debutants line up), England's return as a serious international force continued with a run of success in the early 1920s and further glory before war again brought sport to a halt in 1939.

The impact of the First World War on life in England was to vary massively between different sections of society. The decade is often referred to as the 'Roaring Twenties'. For some, war had brought peace, profits and prosperity. Those who had supplied or manufactured vital goods during the war (or even weapons) reaped the financial rewards. Many young aristocrats or members of the upper classes who had avoided service in the war enjoyed a carefree, even reckless, approach to life (some say war had shown them life was too short to waste) in a decade of jazz, literature, cocktails and nightclubs. For others, however, especially the working classes, there was little to enjoy about the 1920s.

By the middle of the decade, the short boom that followed the war was well and truly over and more than two million people were out of work in the UK. Unemployment was a cruel fate for the men who had fought through the horrors of the Western Front, only to find themselves living in misery and perhaps even poverty upon their return. Unemployment was to be a major issue until the Second World War. The Wall Street Crash of 1929, in which the US stock market collapsed, further threw the economy into a death spiral and began the period known as the Great Depression. In the highly industrialised areas such as the north of England, unemployment reached as high as 70 per cent.

There was major social progress amid the economic gloom. Women over 30 had been given the vote in 1918 and, with women playing such a crucial part in the war effort (often working in tough manual and physical labour and doing all sorts of jobs previously performed by men), the call for equal voting rights intensified. By 1928 all women over 21 were eligible to vote, just like their fellow male citizens.

THE FOUL-MOUTHED ENGLISHMAN
KILLED BY A RHINOCEROS

Denys Douglas Dobson, a forward, won six caps for England between 1902 and 1903. He also toured with the 1904 British Isles team to Australia. Playing for the latter team, he was dismissed in one game for use of foul language. Sending offs were almost unheard of at that time. His punishment was an eight-month ban, despite the fact there was no consensus among players and referee on what terms where supposedly used by Dobson.

Dobson has the unfortunate claim to fame of suffering perhaps the most bizarre death of any England international. He was killed in 1916 in Nyasaland (now Malawi) by a rhinoceros. It is claimed that one associate of Dobson responded to news of his untimely death by saying the departed had 'always had a weak hand-off'.

THE CAPPING OF THE UNCAPPED PLAYER
1920 – Wales 19 England 5 (St Helen's)

England's first match after the First World War was a convincing defeat. Eleven new caps had been selected in the line-up due to a combination of Father Time's work (six years had passed since the last game in Paris) and the ravages of war.

There was an interesting footnote to this match though. England winger Wilfrid Lowry (Birkenhead Park) lined up with his teammates before the game for the team photo. But when the sides ran out a short while later, he was nowhere to be seen. Between the photo and the kick-off, the English selectors had decided Harold Day (Leicester) would be better suited to the wet west Wales conditions. Slightly more oddly, they said Lowry had given an 'indifferent exhibition' the previous week when playing for his club. Which begs the question as to why he was selected. Even more bizarrely, Lowry had already been presented with his cap! His replacement Day actually scored all of England's points with a try and conversion. Thankfully, Lowry was picked for the next game against France and won a proper cap.

There was another odd omission from the side. The legendary Dave Davies was not selected in a decision England captain John 'Jenny' Greenwood (Cambridge University) said confirmed that the English selectors 'were not very bright'.

England shared the 1920 Championship with Wales and Scotland as each team won three games. Scotland fell 13-4 at Twickenham in their final game of the season, costing them the Grand Slam and an outright title.

ONE OF THE GRANDEST GRAND SLAMS

England marked the 50th anniversary of the founding of the RFU with their third Grand Slam (and one of their sweetest). English rugby historian Barry Bowker, writing in 1978, claimed this was possibly England's finest season. Captained by Dave Davies, they scored 61 points to just nine against and ran in 13 tries while allowing just one.

1921 GRAND SLAM

MATCH ONE: England 18 Wales 3 (Twickenham)
For once, the English pack was smaller than the Welsh one.

England decided to rely more on mobility than strength and size and it paid off. Forwards such as the great Wavell Wakefield (Harlequins/RAF), debutant Reg Edwards (Newport) and Tom Woods (Devonport Services) won praise for their work as individuals and as a unit. Combined with smart back play, England ran out comfortable winners with four tries, a conversion and a drop goal. Winger Alastair Smallwood (Leicester) bagged a brace of tries. Rugby historian Huw Richards notes that eight of this English side were born outside England.

MATCH TWO: England 15 Ireland 0 (Twickenham)

Despite losing the great Dave Davies early on to injury, England won with plenty to spare. The versatile Wavell Wakefield came out of the pack to fill in the gap in the threequarters caused by Edward Myers (Bradford) moving to the fly-half slot.

MATCH THREE: Scotland 0 England 18 (Inverleith)

England kept another clean sheet as they dismantled the home side and claimed the Triple Crown. The English half-backs, Dave Davies and Cecil Kershaw (United Services), controlled the match with a superb kicking display. England scored four tries, but there is dispute in some sources as to whether one score came from Reg Edwards or Ernest Gardner (Devonport Services).

MATCH FOUR: France 6 England 10 (Stade Colombes)

France continued to grow as an international side and ran England close in front of 40,000 fans. The visitors were hugely challenged by the home forwards (who had some stars unavailable due to a domestic dispute). England's tries came through Cyril Lowe and forward Freddie Blakiston (Northampton).

BACK DOWN TO EARTH

After a fine Grand Slam, England, missing Dave Davies, began 1922 by suffering a 28-6 beating in Cardiff to eventual champions Wales. It was the highest score England had ever shipped at that point in history. The Arms Park was a swamp and the English players could barely stay on their feet. The Welsh had less of a problem. They had changed into longer (and illegal) studs after the referee had checked players' boots. This was the first time both England and Wales had worn numbers in this fixture.

Ireland were defeated in the next game and England beat Scotland in the final match. But the most remarkable result of the campaign came in the French game.

1922 – England 11 France 11 (Twickenham)

France looked set to shock everyone with their first win over

England but were cruelly denied in the dying moments. A late long-range penalty from England was off target, but the French got into a mess trying to gather and forward Tom Voyce (Gloucester) scored a critical try. If France's luck had held out, they would have been the only side other than South Africa to have beaten England at Twickenham since it opened in 1910.

Three of England's forwards in this match were born in Cardiff. They were Geoffrey Conway (Cambridge University), Ernest Gardner (Royal Navy) and Robert Duncan (Guy's Hospital).

ROSELESS BEFORE THE KING

England winger Harold Day (Leicester) had a torrid day ahead of the 1922 French match. His kit had been stolen during lunch and he had to play in 'boots that pinched, shorts like tights, and a jersey that cramped my breathing'. Rubbing salt into his wounds, there was not time to sew a rose on to his shirt before he met the King, who attended the game. Nonetheless, Day still kicked one conversion and two penalties to deny the French a famous win.

GRAND SLAM CHAMPIONS AGAIN

England achieved their second Grand Slam in three seasons. Once again, Dave Davies was the captain. Interestingly, from 1923 onwards only three players were allowed to form a front row under new laws.

1923 GRAND SLAM

MATCH ONE: England 7 Wales 3 (Twickenham)

England's first try here was apparently clocked in at ten seconds. Wavell Wakefield kicked off into a wind that kindly blew the ball back into the hands of his teammate and fellow forward Leo Price (Leicester). After charging downfield, Price attempted an ambitious drop goal. His kick missed, but instead of going dead as expected, it stayed in play and Price himself chased up and scored! Wales never recovered from what *The Times* claimed was as remarkable a thing as anyone had ever seen in rugby. England's only other points came from a drop goal from Alastair Smallwood.

MATCH TWO: England 23 Ireland 5 (Welford Road, Leicester)

Only 20,000 spectators turned up in Leicester to see England comfortably dispatch Ireland. The disappointing crowd confirmed the RFU's belief that Twickenham should host all home games. It was the last home Test played away from Twickenham until 1992 when England played Canada at Wembley due to construction work at HQ.

MATCH THREE: Scotland 6 England 8 (Inverleith)

The Triple Crown and Championship lay on the line in this tense and classic Calcutta Cup match which went to the wire. England took the lead thanks to superb speed and footwork from winger Alastair Smallwood dazzling several home defenders and earning him a try. The second try came from forward Tom Voyce following up on a kick from debutant centre Harold Locke (Birkenhead Park). England had to hold off a determined late rally from the home side, but just did enough.

MATCH FOUR: France 3 England 12 (Stade Colombes)

This was the final match for several key England players: the great Dave Davies (who had won 21 of his 22 Test matches), winger Cyril Lowe (his 18 tries for England were a record until 1989) and scrum-half Cecil Kershaw (who also competed in the Olympics as a fencer). This Grand Slam was achieved on a Monday and it was said that the score flattered England somewhat and marked a major development in the progress of French forward play. Davies, who kicked one drop goal, was playing whilst on his honeymoon.

A WISE OLD ROOKIE

In the 1923 Championship, England gave two caps to Frederick Gilbert (against Wales and France). The Devonport Services full-back was a sprightly 39. Or so it was said. His exact birth date is a subject of debate.

THREE OUT OF FOUR

England's extraordinary Championship run continued as they followed up the 1921 and 1923 Grand Slams with another in 1924. Wavell Wakefield was the man at the helm for this latest clean sweep.

Wavell Wakefield led England to the 1924 Grand Slam.

1924 GRAND SLAM

MATCH ONE: Wales 9 England 17 (St Helen's)

England's hero for this first win in Swansea since 1895 was Tom Voyce, who played on with broken ribs. The wet conditions would traditionally have suited the home side, but this England pack were far too strong for a Welsh pack with six new caps. England powered over for five tries, two of which came from debutant winger Carston Catcheside (Percy Park).

Wavell Wakefield took a nasty shoeing from one Welsh forward who, realising he had stamped on the wrong Englishman, then promptly apologised.

Catchy catches scoring habit

Howard Carston Catcheside, nicknamed 'Catchy', not only scored two tries on his Test debut against Wales, he scored a try in every game of the Grand Slam. No player had scored in every round of the Five Nations before.

MATCH TWO: Ireland 3 England 14 (Ravenhill, Belfast)

This was the first international at Ravenhill and the only one England ever played in Belfast. A fired up and bothersome Irish set of forwards had England on the ropes until the final quarter, when it is said the greater stamina of the defending champions saw them pull away. Carston Catcheside scored his most spectacular try of his spectacular season, gathering the ball on his own line and running the length of the field.

MATCH THREE: England 19 France 7 (Twickenham)

The home pack always had the edge as England claimed five

tries, three of which came from winger Jake Jacob (Oxford University).

MATCH FOUR: England 19 Scotland 0 (Twickenham)

England's total of 69 points and 17 tries for the Championship was hugely impressive for the era. This was their 33rd win from 40 games. Catcheside completed his own personal Grand Slam with his try three minutes from time (running in from halfway and twice handing off the same player) meaning he had at least one try in each game.

THROWING OUT A WINNING FORMULA?

The history of England international rugby is littered with strange selection decisions. The controversy around the 1925 match with New Zealand is perhaps one of the most difficult to understand. As it was the first meeting with the All Blacks since 1905, to say it was a big game is an understatement. The tourists arrived at Twickenham having won all 27 games to date on their tour and the hosts were Five Nations champions. Yet, instead of relying on the core of the team that had delivered the 1924 Grand Slam, the English selectors opted to bring in seven players from a trial game, displacing recent starters. They also blooded four new caps. It did not go well.

WALKING OFF AND WALKING AWAY

1925 – England 11 New Zealand 17 (Twickenham)

A crowd of 60,000 packed into the stadium for this match, a record for the time, and they saw a piece of rugby history.

Before the game, captain Wavell Wakefield encouraged his men to front up to the notoriously tough All Black pack. After a series of early scuffles and brutal plays, New Zealand forward Cyril Brownlie became the first ever player to be sent off in international rugby. There were no red cards then, just a finger from the referee pointing to the sideline. Brownlie had stamped on an opponent in the eighth minute. It was quite a feat to be dismissed back then and the crowd were stunned into silence. No other player was sent off in any Test match again until 1967 (Colin Meads of New Zealand at Murrayfield). After the game, debutant England prop Ronnie Hillard (Oxford University) retired from Test rugby. He famously said: 'If that is international rugby, I want nothing of it.'

The All Blacks, whose squad included the great George Nēpia at full-back, finished their tour with 32 wins from 32. Hilariously, Scotland refused to meet them as they were still in a huff over gate money from the 1905 clash (in which the SRU was entirely at fault anyway).

TWELVE YEARS OF SUCCESS

The loss to New Zealand was only the third English defeat since the 1913 loss to South Africa. In that time (which included the break caused by the First World War) England had played 28 games, won 25, lost two and drawn one.

NEW LAWS, NEW ERA

In 1926 it was finally put in the laws that a game should last

80 minutes. Before then it had never officially been codified. In 1925 it was also written into law that the ball must be thrown at least five yards in a line-out. Historian Barry Bowker wrote: 'A side effect of the change was that wingers, not scrum-halves, began throwing the ball in.'

Also in 1925, there was a change to the kicking laws. Goalkickers could now place the ball themselves and did not need a teammate to hold it. In addition, the defending team could no longer charge penalties. These changes helped make penalty attempts at goal far more frequent.

TWICKENHAM FALLS TO NORTHERN INVADERS

The 1926 Championship started with a lucky 3-3 draw in Cardiff and was followed by the first defeat to Ireland since 1911 (losing 19-15 in Dublin). France were dispatched 11-0 in London, but *The Times* labelled the English forwards as 'poor decrepit veterans' and concluded ' . . . if England disappointed, France never looked like winning – which, perhaps, was worse. The season finished with a historic low as Scotland earned their first win at Twickenham with a 17-9 victory. It was the first time a Home Union side had won at the ground.

LIVE RADIO COMES TO BRITISH SPORT

The 1927 England v Wales clash was the first ever British sporting event to be broadcast live on radio. It was an innovation inspired by American sport and feared by newspapers, who thought it would lead to fewer papers being bought, and sporting authorities, who worried it would lower attendances. The commentary was provided by Henry 'Teddy' Wakelam, a former Harlequins player. Before the match, the *Radio Times* magazine, and a couple of newspapers, published an image of the playing field divided up into numbered squares. These were then referenced in the commentary to help listeners know where the action took place. As radios became more affordable and popular, such innovations helped raise the profile of the sport and increased the fame of players.

YOUNGEST ENGLISH CAP

The 1927 Welsh game also saw Colin Laird win the first of his ten caps. The Harlequins fly-half was just 18 years and 134 days old. He is still the youngest England international.

1927 – France 3 England 0 (Stade Colombes)

The French gained their first victory over England in the 17th meeting of the two nations. A try after just ten minutes by French winger Edmond Vellat was the difference between the sides.

1928: A YEAR OF YOUTH AND VICTORY

England, led by lock Ronald Cove-Smith (Old Merchant Taylors) with a young back division in place, won five out of five games in 1928. This many wins would not occur in a calendar year again until 1988 when far more fixtures were played annually than in the 1920s.

1928 – England 18 New South Wales 11 (Twickenham)

This win over the 'Waratahs' was England's first triumph over a touring side since 1899 when they had defeated the New Zealand Natives team in a non-cap match. This match is now recognised as a full Test with Australia. At the time, Queensland had broken away from the Australian Rugby Union, so only players from New South Wales were considered for the tour.

1928 GRAND SLAM

MATCH ONE: Wales 8 England 10 (St Helen's)

Despite being dominated in the tight play in a wet and windy Swansea, heroic defence and some superior back play saw England home. Full-back Kenneth 'Monkey' Sellar of the Royal Navy/United Services was particularly praised for his work in keeping the Welsh at bay with all manner of brave play.

MATCH TWO: Ireland 6 England 7 (Lansdowne Road)

This was the game that ultimately gave England the title. Ireland won all their other matches and even scored twice as many tries as England over the tournament. In horrific wind and rain, England again produced a masterful defensive performance to stay close to Ireland until the dying moments when a drop goal from centre James Richardson (Birkenhead Park) allowed England to take the spoils.

MATCH THREE: England 18 France 8 (Twickenham)

Winger Godfrey Palmer (Richmond) and wing-forward Joe Periton (Waterloo) bagged two tries apiece.

MATCH FOUR: England 6 Scotland 0 (Twickenham)

England claimed their sixth Grand Slam with a first win over

Scotland since 1924. Despite the successful season, six of the England team never again played in the Championship.

GO FORTH (AND DON'T SPREAD THE WORD)

In 1928 the Home Unions stopped the increasingly common practise of players and officials publishing articles or giving special insight to newspapers and magazines. Promoting the game in this way was, according to the blazers that ran the game, simply not on!

IRISH CUSHIONS OF VICTORY

Irish fans celebrated their first win at Twickenham in 1929 (6-5) by throwing seat cushions 'high into the air'. *The Times* wrote: 'The Twickenham legend of England invincibility and good fortune in equal proportions thus is dying, or rather fading away, slowly but surely.'

FLYING TO THE TITLE

England's two wins (Wales and France) and a draw (Scotland) were enough to give them the title in 1930. However, the most memorable moment of the Five Nations occurred in the hours before the first game in Cardiff and mainly took place in the air.

SAM TUCKER'S FAMOUS FLIGHT TO CARDIFF
1930 – Wales 3 England 11 (Cardiff Arms Park)
On the morning of the Welsh game in Cardiff, 22-time capped

hooker Sam Tucker was enjoying a drink in Bristol as he had not been selected for the opening game of the Five Nations. After his liquid refreshment he returned to his office to work. His phone rang at 12.25 p.m. The English selectors pleaded with him to get to Cardiff as Exeter hooker Henry Rew had withdrawn at the last moment.

Sam Tucker had probably the most remarkable day in the history of international rugby union.

However, the last train to Cardiff had already departed and driving by car on the roads back then was not a viable option as it would take too long. Encouraged by the RFU, Tucker rang the local airfield to see if he could source a plane. Tucker (who had never flown before and admitted to being somewhat nervous) later explained:

The only thing I could do was call Filton Aerodrome, as there was no landing strip in either Bristol or Cardiff in those days. A lady answered the phone [and] said there was a certain 'Captain Somebody' in the air and she would try to get a signal to him to come down. By a stroke of luck she succeeded and the 'Captain' phoned me at 1 p.m. He said if I went out at once he would get me to Cardiff between 2 p.m. and 2.15. I was [there by 1.50] and there was the pilot with a small bi-plane two-seater already revved up. He stuck a helmet on my head, strapped me in and, with a roar, we were off. We arrived over Cardiff at roughly 2 p.m. and after circling around he thought he could land in a field. I thanked him, raced over the field on to the road and waved the driver [of a coal lorry] down [who] did the journey [to the Arms Park] in under ten minutes.

It didn't end there either. Tucker had to persuade officials that he wasn't a spectator trying to get in the ground for free and was due to line up for England. By pure luck he spotted a police officer he knew and was able to get inside. While all this was happening, reserve hooker Norman Matthews was all kitted up and ready to play and had even been part of the team photograph. Tucker arrived moments before the match started, took his place and had a stormer. By the end of the season he was England captain. Many thought he was man of the match. As for poor old Matthews? He never won an English cap.

ONE RULE FOR ALL

It may be hard to believe, but 1930 was the first year that IRFB laws were applied to all rugby games around the world. Until then, variations had existed regionally. In 1931 new laws were also passed on the exact shape of a rugby ball, making it smaller and heavier than was previously allowed.

BRITAIN AND ITS 'PLACE' IN THE WORLD

A criticism that has always been launched at British and English sport (certainly until the 1990s in the case of rugby) is that players often didn't have the ruthless streak and competitive nature other nations had. In particular, the media and fans often put too much praise on giving a 'jolly good show' or losing with honour. A great example of this in action can be found in a quote from 1930 in a book entitled *The Theory of Modern Rugby Football* by Ian Stuart, a teacher, author and broadcaster:

We have taught the world games, we have taught the world the true spirit in which to play those games, and if we no longer hold pride of place as players of the game, it matters nothing so long as we Britishers always continue to be looked up to as the truest 'players of the game' in the world . . . the 'Spirit of the game' is the prize.

We wonder why it is that other countries can defeat us at most sports, and the answer is to be found, not in that they are physically more endowed than we are, but that they have the temperament to practise doggedly their weakness, and endeavour to improve before they proceed any further. The Englishman, on the other hand, refuses to identify his weakness and practise assiduously to correct it. For this reason, the average Rugby footballer cannot place-kick. He refuses to practise, what he calls 'drudge work', except just now and then.

AN IMPROVED STATE OF THE GAME

Rugby historian Huw Richards has noted that in the 1930s, 11 per cent of English internationals had come through grammar schools, demonstrating that rugby had successfully expanded into state schools in the previous decade and, as a result, was no longer as socially exclusive as it had once been.

FAREWELL TO FIVE

The 1931 Five Nations saw England finish rock bottom, with only a draw against Wales (who still could not win at Twickenham) saving them from a whitewash of four defeats. England finished the season, their first without a win since 1905, with a loss in Paris. It was to be the last time the sides met until 1947. The Home Unions had lost their patience with the inability of the French Rugby Federation to stop blatant player payment in French club rugby. The following season the Championship reverted to the Four Nations and England shared the title with Wales and Ireland.

BY HOOK OR BY HOOK OR BY HOOK
1932 – England 0 South Africa 7 (Twickenham)

England picked three hookers in the front row for their third clash with the Springboks. Once again, they came up short and fell to a dull, but powerful group of tourists.

WALES END THE CURSE
1933 – England 3 Wales 7 (Twickenham)

Wales finally recorded a win at Twickenham after ten attempts thanks to a magnificent performance from Welsh winger Ronnie Boon who scored all the visitors' points with a try and a drop goal. The defeat meant that all England's Home Union rivals had now tasted success at HQ since it opened in 1910.

WHY SHOULD YOU BE SO SPECIAL?

The 1930s was a period of tight, defensive rugby with very little room for backs to strut their stuff. Former Welsh star Rowe Harding wrote: 'In the late twenties, the blind side wing-forward in the 3-2-3 formation stopped the scrum-half moving around the blind side . . . while the open side wing-forward drove the opposing outside-half across field. The [number eight] broke from the scrum and moved across behind his backs as an extra defender . . . kicking [out on the] full was allowed.'

In an attempt to stop the game becoming so regimented, the IRFB tried to stop the progress of forward play in 1933. Not keen on the specialisation that had developed in that area of the game, the board decided that once again (as had been the way decades before) the first forwards to arrive at a scrum would be the first to pack down. Former Welsh international Horace Lyne agreed, saying specialist forwards 'distressed him for they were spoiling football in all the countries'. The idea lasted two seasons and was then thrown out.

A CLEAN SWEEP, BUT NO GRAND SLAM

England, captained by scrum-half Bernard Gadney (Leicester), won all their games in 1934 to win the Championship. With France no longer part of the tournament, it meant a Triple Crown, but no Grand Slam.

1934 – Wales 0 England 9 (Cardiff Arms Park)

A visiting team of seven new caps beat a home side with 13 debutants. England had only won twice at the Arms Park before, so when they were travelling to Wales the day before and a black cat walked in front of their coach, they slowed down to allow it to cross the road. After all, you never know what help you need to win.

SOUTH AFRICAN CRICKET AND ENGLISH RUGBY: A FRUITFUL CONNECTION

England's full-back in 1934 was Harold (or Tuppy) Owen-Smith. Born in Cape Town, he was selected for England as he was studying at Oxford University. He would later successfully captain England. The RFU saw no issue in selecting overseas students in this period. Owen-Smith won ten England caps and would later captain them on three occasions. He also won five caps in cricket for South Africa and was even the Wisden Cricketer of the Year in 1930.

This dual sport and nationality combination was nothing new.
• William Milton won two England rugby caps (1874–75) and three South African cricket caps.
• Frank Mitchell won six England rugby caps (1895–96), two cricket caps for England and three cricket caps for South Africa.
• Reginald Schwarz won three England rugby caps (1899–1901) and 20 cricket caps for South Africa (he died in the First World War).
• Reginald Hands won two England rugby caps (1910) and one cricket cap for South Africa (died in the First World War).

OBOLENSKY'S MATCH: THE FLYING SLAV DEFEATS THE ALL BLACKS

1936 – England 13 New Zealand 0 (Twickenham)

England's first win over the All Blacks is famous for the contribution of a 19-year-old Russian prince. Winger Alexander Obolensky was born in Petrograd (now Saint Petersburg) in 1916, the son of Prince Alexis Obolensky. His family fled the revolution in 1917 and relocated to London. Blessed with incredible speed, his selection in 1936 against the All Blacks was the first of just four caps. But his performance that day secured his place in rugby folklore.

Prince Obolensky raced into rugby folklore against the All Blacks.

Few gave England hope in this game, but two spectacular tries from the debutant (one of which involved a run that covered three-quarters of the field) saw England home. Prior to the game some questioned his right to play for England as he had only been naturalised earlier that year. On matchday the teams were introduced to the Prince of Wales (later to become King Edward VIII). Without a hint of irony (seeing as he was Prince of Wales, a country he was not from himself and also part of the House of Windsor), the Prince of Wales asked Obolensky: 'By what right do you play for England?' Obolensky, who no doubt felt little need to grovel to royalty, simply replied: 'I attend Oxford University . . . Sir.'

A crowd of 73,000 saw England win comfortably with the forwards in particular dominating their opposites. The *New*

Zealand Herald wrote of England's 'superiority in the rucks', a term, according to historian Barry Bowker, unknown in British rugby at the time. The home side's only preparation for this game, in the days before proper training, was a somewhat disastrous meet-up the day before in the centre of London.

This was just the fourth defeat the All Blacks had suffered in 91 tour matches since 1905 and the last time they would lose on English soil until 1972. Obolensky, a pilot in the RAF, was to die tragically in 1940 during the Second World War in a training exercise. He was just 24.

FILM STUDY BRINGS RUSSIAN REWARD

Wales and England battled to a scoreless draw in the opening match of the 1936 Championship. Welsh full-back Vivian Jenkins was praised for the way he handled the threat of England speedster Alexander Obolensky. A short clip of the Russian prince's performance against the All Blacks had been shown on newsreel films in cinemas. Jenkins apparently spent four hours in the cinema waiting for repeats of the few seconds of film which showed Obolensky in action. It paid off. When the England winger tried to repeat a similar move to one that had worked against the All Blacks, he found himself stopped dead in his tracks by the analytical Jenkins.

TRIPLE CROWN GLORY

England won a Triple Crown in 1937 to take the spoils in the Home Nations Championship. It was the 50th edition of the tournament and England's 13th title. Harold 'Tuppy' Owen-Smith led the side to glory from full-back.

1937 – England 4 Wales 3 (Twickenham)
Wales scored the only try of this game as England managed only a first-half drop goal from winger Hal Sever (Sale). However, under the scoring system of the day it was enough for a victory.

1937 – England 9 Ireland 8 (Twickenham)
Hal Sever was again the difference in a one-point victory. This time the winger grabbed a try in the final five minutes of a hugely entertaining match. Ireland almost stole victory in the final minute, but a penalty attempt failed to hit the spot.

1937 – Scotland 3 England 6 (Murrayfield)
This was England's first ever win at Murrayfield (they had failed on their first six successive visits since the ground was first used for the fixture in 1925). The visitors benefited from Scotland

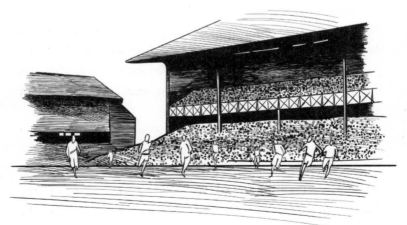

Twickenham in the late 1930s.

being reduced to 14 men through injury. Once again, Sever got his name on the scoresheet with a try and debutant and fellow winger Jimmy Unwin (Army) claimed England's only other try.

TELEVISION AND LAW AMENDMENTS CHANGE THE GAME

In 1938, two major developments would both impact the game in major ways. The first was a law change. It was now required that when a penalty was given, an offending team must retreat ten yards back from the spot of their offence. Before this change, the team being penalised did not have to move back from the mark. This meant that more penalties became kickable as it was no longer necessary for the kicker to retire from the spot the penalty was given so that he had more space to operate.

The other change was off the field. The 1938 Calcutta Cup at Twickenham was the first international rugby match to be televised. Due to the limitations of the technology of the day, the signal that beamed from the ground only had restricted reach. Combined with very few people owning a television at this time, it is likely only a few thousand people would have been able to see the game live. It was an incredible feat nonetheless and the start of something that would transform the sport forever.

The limited broadcasting signal meant Scottish fans missed out on what was only their side's second ever win at Twickenham. Their 21 to 16 win also gave the visitors a Triple Crown and tournament title.

ONE LAST HURRAH

In July 1939, it was agreed that France (who were made to give assurances that they had sorted out the troublesome aspects of their domestic game) could return to the tournament in 1940. But the Second World War meant the 1939 Home Nations Championship was to be the last until 1947.

England won two of their games in this final season before the war. Narrow victories over Wales (3-0) and Scotland (9-6) home and away respectively, along with a poor 5-0 loss at home to Ireland, meant England shared the title with Wales and Ireland. The win over Scotland saw England score three penalties to Scotland's two tries. This was an example of how penalty goals were taking an increasing role in the sport. Historian Barry Bowker wrote of this match: 'Thus, to the anger of the purists, three penalties beat two tries, and enabled England to share the international championship with Ireland and Wales who had also won two games each and lost one. In fact England reached this exalted position having scored only one try in their internationals.'

THE HORROR OF WAR RETURNS

The outbreak of war saw the Home Unions cease official internationals until 1947. However, unlike the First World War, where organised sport was halted, this time sport was seen as a way to boost morale among both the armed forces and civilian population. Club sides and international teams took part in many unofficial games during the conflict, often using the games to boost recruitment or raise money for war funds in the process. In 1942, 20,000 spectators watched unofficial England and Wales teams meet.

There was even an amnesty for rugby league players, who were allowed to play alongside union players during this time (except in Scotland, to the eternal shame of the SRU).

The match programme for one armed services match said: 'It must stagger our enemies to think that while Britain is engaged in the most momentous struggle of our existence, in the sterner game of war, the sporting community in its midst find time and facilities for participation in its favourite games and pastimes . . . [it is hoped spectators] . . . follow their rugby idols into khaki, in which outfit more undying glory can be won than in an international jersey.'

Twickenham was adapted for use by the War Office as a civil defence depot. As before, the rugby community signed up in huge numbers to fight in the conflict. In fact, Wavell Wakefield and Norman Wodehouse were two internationals that took part in both world wars.

14 England internationals died in the Second World War:

- Brian Henry Black (10 caps, aged 33)
- Lewis Alfred Booth (7 caps, aged 32)
- Paul Cooke (2 caps, aged 23)
- Vivian Gordon Davies (2 caps, aged 42)
- Hubert Freakes (3 caps, aged 28)
- Ronald Gerrard (14 caps, aged 30)
- William Luddington (13 caps, aged 46)
- Robert Marshall (5 caps, aged 27)
- Alexander Obolensky (4 caps, aged 24)

- Ernest Parsons (1 cap, aged 27)
- Henry Rew (10 caps, aged 34)
- Christopher Tanner (5 caps, aged 32)
- Derek Teden (3 caps, aged 24)
- Norman Wodehouse (14 caps, aged 54)

1919–39: THE STAR PLAYERS

WAVELL WAKEFIELD
Clubs: Harlequins, Leicester
Position: Flanker
Caps: 31 (1920–27)
Points: 18 (6 tries)

The 1st Baron Wakefield of Kendal, or Sir William Wavell Wakefield, was present in every England Test match from 1920 (the first game after the war) until 1926. This record of 29 consecutive appearances stood until 1971 when it was overtaken by John Pullin. During this period England won three Grand Slams – he was captain for the latter. Overall, he led England on 13 occasions and is ranked among the great England forwards. His smart thinking and athletic play influenced the way back-row play developed in the British game.

Historian Barry Bowker wrote of him: 'A complete footballer, he had all the attributes – strength, weight and speed – of a great forward. He was a master of the art of dribbling at pace, was up with his backs to share in attack and took and gave passes well . . . a tight forward with a tremendous shove . . . yet he was as fast as any winger and if a back were injured it was Wakefield who would probably be pulled out of the scrum.'

Off the field, Wakefield played a significant role in the founding of the Royal Air Force and served in two world wars. He had been around aircraft since a young age and was an exceptional pilot. He served as RFU president later in life and was also a Conservative MP.

WILLIAM 'DAVE' DAVIES

Clubs: Royal Navy, United Services, Harlequins
Position: Fly-half
Caps: 22 (1913–23)
Points: 24 (4 tries, 3 drop goals)

William 'Dave' John Abbott Davies may not be a name known by many modern fans, but he comfortably belongs among the pantheon of England greats. In 22 caps, he was on the losing side just once (his first match against South Africa). Born in Wales, Davies said that until he left Wales he 'knew nothing about rugby' and that as he really learnt to play rugby in England, that would be the nation he wished to represent. The only times Wales beat England during his career (1920 and 1922), Davies was absent.

Davies captained England 11 times, encompassing the 1921 and 1923 Grand Slams. He often played for England in a half-back partnership with his good friend and naval comrade Cecil Kershaw.

The RFU chairman of selectors, James Baxter, said of Davies: 'Not only is W.J.A. Davies the greatest match-winner who ever put on a football boot, but as captain of the national XV he was essentially the right man in the right place. Idolized by the men under him . . . his lovable personality and intense enthusiasm for the game marked him out as the ideal captain. No player was ever more closely marked . . . but nothing ever ruffled him. All he did was done at express speed – his drop at goal, his cut through, his kick to touch, his passing, all happened so quickly that the opposing forces were often left standing in sheer bewilderment. Internationals of more than one country have expressed their opinion that they would never beat England as long as Davies played, and they spoke the truth.'

The First World War robbed him of more glory on the field. He served his nation as Lieutenant Commander Davies before returning to the Test arena in 1920.

His commitment to England was shown by his decision to play against France in Paris in the 1923 Grand Slam campaign while on his honeymoon. It was his last cap. History does not record if the two things are connected.

CYRIL LOWE
Clubs: Cambridge University, Blackheath
Position: Wing
Caps: 25 (1913–23)
Points: 58 (18 tries)

If scoring 18 tries in 25 caps, winning 21 of his 25 matches in an England shirt and being a war hero isn't impressive enough for you, Cyril Lowe is also said to be part of the inspiration for the popular fictional character Biggles.

Despite being just 167cm (5ft 5in) and weighing approximately 54kg (8st 7lb), Lowe dazzled on the rugby field. Considered a 'complete footballer', he grabbed an astonishing eight tries in the 1914 Grand Slam alone. It was said it wasn't just his speed that made him such a lethal finisher, but his heart and determination.

In the First World War he was a fighter pilot and shot down nine enemy aircraft, winning the Distinguished Flying Cross and Military Cross in the process. His record number of tries was finally surpassed in the 1990s by Rory Underwood who, ironically, was also an RAF pilot.Um quae ipsa quo berit offic temqui as ati officim olorro cone nis deliquias doluptur?

1919–39 NOTABLE EVENTS IN ENGLISH HISTORY

- 1920: Women are finally eligible to be full members of Oxford University (established in the late 11th century) and study for full degrees.
- 1921: The British and Irish armed forces agree a truce and officially end the Irish War of Independence.
- 1922: The Irish Free State is created.
- 1923: The *Radio Times* magazine is published for the first time.
- 1924: Ramsay MacDonald becomes the first ever Labour prime minister.
- 1926: Major strikes take place among British workers over potential pay reductions and martial law is declared before the strike is resolved.

- 1927: An Act of Parliament renames the United Kingdom of Britain and Ireland to the United Kingdom of Great Britain and Northern Ireland (as the Irish Free State is no longer a part of the kingdom).

- 1928: After 70 years, the *Oxford English Dictionary* is completed.

- 1929: The Age of Marriage Act raises the age of marriage to 16. Previously those who had reached puberty could marry (aged 14 for males and 12 for females).

- 1930: On 18 April, the 8.45 p.m. evening bulletin on BBC radio simply said: 'Today is Good Friday. There is no news.' Fifteen minutes of piano music followed.

- 1931: *The Highway Code* is issued for the first time.

- 1932: The BBC World Service begins to broadcast (originally known as the 'BBC Empire Service').

- 1934: A rally of the British Union of Fascists in Birmingham attracts 10,000 people.

- 1935: With Germany rearming itself, the UK government reveals plans to triple the size of the Royal Air Force.

- 1936: The first Butlin's holiday camp is opened.

- 1937: The 999 emergency service is introduced.

- 1938: *The Beano* comic is launched.

- 1939: The Second World War begins.

1947–69: POTENTIAL AND PROMISE

	PLAYED	WON	DRAWN	LOST
FIVE NATIONS	92	41	17	34
TESTS	12	2	0	10
TOTAL	104	43	17	44

Championships (4)

1953, 1957 (Grand Slam), 1958, 1963

Shared Championships (3)

1947, 1954 (Triple Crown), 1960 (Triple Crown)

'Winning the Grand Slam was a landmark, but we didn't hug each other. It had happened, and that was it.'

GEORGE HASTINGS (ENGLAND PROP, 13 CAPS BETWEEN 1955 AND 1958)

FROM BOOM TO BEATLES

The rugby community marked the ending of the Second World War with a series of 'Victory Internationals'. These were six matches played in 1945 and 1946 ahead of the resumption of regular international rugby (the 'Kiwis', Wales, Ireland and Scotland made up the opponents). But these were not capped games.

Fittingly, France returned to the fold after being exiled from the Championship in 1931 to once again allow a return to the Five Nations format and offer the tantalising possibility of a Grand Slam to all teams.

Away from the playing fields, the years that followed the nightmare of the Second World War saw England suffer a period of austerity and hardship, with rationing of food, scarcity of certain goods and economic difficulty due to crippling national debt. There was hope, among many, that the sense of 'togetherness' the nation had felt during the war was going to lead to significant shifts in the social and class make-up of society. Alas, less was swept away than was hoped.

In the first post-war general election Winston Churchill, generally perceived today as a hero of the war effort, was repaid by the electorate with a crushing defeat that saw the Labour Party win its first outright majority. Prime Minister Clement Attlee set about creating the modern welfare state. Revolutionary for the period, it gave birth to a system of benefits which offered social security from 'cradle to grave' for all. In 1948, Aneurin Bevan spearheaded the founding of the National Health Service, so that all citizens, regardless of wealth, would have access to medical care.

The 1950s were a far more positive economic time, with Conservative Prime Minister Harold Macmillan stating in 1957 that 'most of our people have never had it so good'. Living standards had dramatically risen for most English people. This 'post-war boom' saw huge growth in production in areas such as car manufacturing, steel and coal and a rise in wages. Television was changing the way people lived and spent their social time. It is claimed that at the start of 1953 fewer than two million people in Britain owned a television set. However, over half a million sets were sold that year when it became known the coronation of Elizabeth II was to be televised. Some believe an average of 17 people watched each TV during the coronation.

By the 1960s, the 'winds of change' had led to a major decline in the role, influence and size of the British Empire as many colonies broke away and other nations, such as the USA and Russia, became more influential in directing world politics.

The Swinging Sixties also saw the rise of youth-driven popular culture that gave birth to everything from The Beatles to the miniskirt and helped put England and Britain at the heart of world culture and creativity. Thanks to an explosion in the birth rate after the war, more opportunities for women, increased educational prospects and the ending of 'dreary' and 'stifling' things like national service (until 1960 all healthy young adult males had to spend a period of time serving in the armed forces), young people had more chance to do the things they loved.

While the post-war period saw many advances in women's rights, progress was still frustratingly slow. Until the 1970s, many employers would sack women if they got married. It was not until 1946 that married women could work in the Civil Service and women were still barred from the Foreign Service until 1973. Even until 1944, married women could not be teachers. The 1960s at least saw a rise in the number of women in higher education and the laying of stronger roots in the belief that women were more than just mothers and wives.

ONE MAN LEFT STANDING
1947 – Wales 6 England 9 (Cardiff Arms Park)
When England resumed official Tests for the first time since 1939, only winger Dickie Guest (Waterloo) had been capped before for the visitors. Cardiff Arms Park had been damaged by enemy bombs and had not yet been repaired, meaning only around 40,000 spectators were able to attend.

Although they lost centre Edward Scott (St Mary's Hospital) in the opening quarter, 14-man England pulled off a win with Micky Steele-Bodger (Cambridge University) being pulled out of the pack and into the threequarters.

Despite beating Wales, a 22-0 thrashing in Dublin meant England ultimately finished on three wins in the restored Five Nations and had to share the title with the Welsh.

WALLABIES BOUNCE BACK TO LONDON
1948 – England 0 Australia 11 (Twickenham)
The Wallabies were the first tourists to visit Twickenham after the war and 70,000 fans saw the visitors put three tries past the home side. None of the Home Union sides were able to score a try against this strong Australian team during their 1947–48 tour.

POST-WAR TRAINING
'I worked in a factory, so I used to run every night, even in the snow. Round the streets, more or less in the dark. With England, in my time in the team after the war, the only training session we had was on the Friday before the game. We used to

go to Rosslyn Park for about an hour. We just had a few scrums and the backs mucked about a bit.'

Harry Walker, English prop who
won nine caps in 1947 and 1948.

A FOOT IN THE GAME

England endured a miserable 1948 Five Nations, managing only a home draw against Wales and losing every other game (including a 15-0 humiliation in Paris). The 3-3 draw against the Welsh was made up of a try for the visitors and a penalty for the home side. The offence, which gave England their penalty, came from Wales's Bleddyn Williams failing to play the ball with his foot after the tackle. This was a penalty offence until 1958.

'IT'S JUST A SCRATCH, OLD CHAP'

The 1948 Calcutta Cup was a brutal affair. Played in Edinburgh, Scotland won by 6 (two tries) to 3 (one penalty goal). England were hampered by losing scrum-half Richard Madge (Exeter) with torn knee ligaments in the opening exchanges. It meant England had just 14 men for most of the game. Back-rower Micky Steele-Bodger left the pack to take Madge's role on, but he too suffered a nasty concussion in the first half (although he played on).

Even worse, centre and captain Edward Keith Scott (Redruth) fractured his jaw in the first forty minutes. He still finished the match. Steele-Bodger later said of Scott's injury:

'You could see instantly what had happened. He had a crack right down the symphysis where the two jawbones meet, upper and lower – but for the time being there was no displacement. I remember to this day one of our chaps running on with lemons at half-time and Keith calmly asking him to order a taxi to be waiting outside the England changing room on the final whistle to take him directly to Edinburgh Infirmary, where he would need his jaw wired. And with that he turned back to his team and gave a stirring half-time talk before leading us back into battle. I was rather impressed . . . The war was a very recent memory and there was an understated toughness about players. Everybody had seen so much worse [in the war] and we were reluctant to make a fuss over "minor" injuries.'

SHIFTING POWER

In 1948, there was a significant development off the field. The IRFB was no longer dominated by the RFU, as it had been for almost 60 years, and English voting rights were reduced to two in line with the other founding nations.

THE ROSE, THE PUMA AND TRAGEDY

As they had done before the war, the RFU continued to pick overseas students studying in England. One of these was Barry Holmes from Argentina. A full-back, he won four caps for England in 1949 after arriving at Cambridge University to study agriculture. In that same year he returned back home and won two caps for his native Argentina. Tragically, just one week after his wedding, he died of typhoid fever. He was 21 years old. His mother is said to have laid a place at the dinner table for him every night for the rest of her life.

STUDENTS, COMING OVER HERE, TAKING OUR CAPS . . . ETC

England's continued selection of 'non-English' players studying in the country remained a source of controversy. It was also seen by some as unfair, as the internationals attracted to top universities like Oxford and Cambridge gave the RFU access to a real stream of talent. When England selected Ian Botting (a former touring All Black) on the wing against Wales in 1950, many felt this was taking things too far.

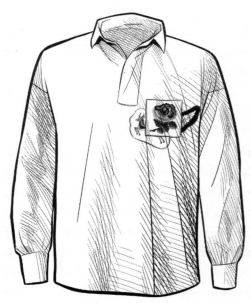

England's approach to picking international students did not sit well with many.

The Pathé newsreel from the 1950 home loss to Wales opened with a title screen saying: '15 WELSHMEN HUMBLE ENGLAND'S "FOREIGN LEGION"' and the voiceover goes on to say: 'Three South Africans and a New Zealander are playing in a team officially labelled England.'

In response to these selections, the Four Home Unions Committee ruled against dual nationality at international level.

WE'LL KEEP A WELCOME IN THE HILLSIDES . . . AND LONDON

After the 1950 Welsh match (the visitors won 11-5 and went on to win the Grand Slam), *The Times* highlighted the huge presence of Wales supporters, estimating a third of the crowd were cheering on the men in red. It also referenced one English supporter who, with 'grim humour', worried that 'unless the Rugby Union are careful, Twickenham will end up as one of the more famous Welsh grounds'.

A LAUGHABLE SET OF CHOICES

For most of the first century of international rugby, England's selectors were often criticised for inconsistent and, often, incoherent selection. However, in some ways the breadth, width and depth of the English club game was a hindrance. With so many clubs spread so widely across the nation (and in an era before television and match video availability) it was tough for selectors to see all the rugby they needed. It also meant that playing talent was spread thinly, unlike in, say

Wales where the top players played within a relatively small geographical area and for a smaller number of clubs. County rugby failed to address this issue and, as a result, trial matches were key to the selection process for England.

It didn't always work. One Welsh international, Clem Thomas, once said: 'The leading forwards in Wales used to fall about laughing every time England picked a team. All of us could have picked a far better team.'

TWICKENHAM FALLS TO THE FRENCH

1951 – England 3 France 11 (Twickenham)

France first played at HQ in 1911, but this was their first win there and a major moment in the history of French rugby. England were reduced to 14 men early in the game, but no one made a serious argument against France being deserved winners. The visitors' star player was the legendary flanker Jean Prat, who snatched a try, conversion and drop goal. The result contributed to England claiming the wooden spoon for the second year in succession.

BOKS WIN AGAIN

1952 – England 3 South Africa 8 (Twickenham)

The Springboks made it three wins and a draw in their four games against England (all in London). This was a formidable South African team who lost just one game (to London Counties) in 31 matches, including a clean sweep over all sides from the Five Nations.

A VICTORY OVER FATHER TIME

Blindside flanker Alec Lewis of Bath won his first England cap in the 1952 South African game. An injury in the war had prevented him from playing rugby for many years and he did not return to the playing field until he was 28. He was 31 when he made his debut and went on to win ten caps in total. Lewis lost his father at a young age to a tiger attack in India.

TELEVISION MONEY COMES . . . TRICKLING . . . IN

The BBC provided the RFU with the princely sum of £150 to show the 1952 clash with Wales (won by the visitors). According to rugby historian Huw Richards, England were more enthusiastic about rugby being televised than the other Home Unions (Scotland, true to form, were against any kind of progress). There was concern that live coverage would impact on attendances. But by the start of the sixties it had become the norm and fees from the BBC were over £2,000 per game.

DEATH AND SNOW

1952 – England 3 Ireland 0 (Twickenham)

This match had to be postponed due to the death of King George VI. When it was due to be played again over a month later, blizzards hit London and, if it were not for the fact Ireland had already travelled, the game would have been postponed again. In heavy snow and on a rock-solid pitch, England won thanks to a try from centre Brian Boobbyer (Rosslyn Park).

SUCCESS AT LAST

England won the 1953 Five Nations (their first title since 1937) but missed out on a Grand Slam due to a 9-9 draw in Dublin. That year also saw the arrival of centre Jeff Butterfield in national colours (see 'Star Players' section). Rugby historians consider Butterfield one of the finest centres in English rugby history and he was to win 28 consecutive caps and play a key role in many of the side's successes.

THE ALL BLACKS RETURN

1954 – England 0 New Zealand 5 (Twickenham)

England were unable to repeat their success from their last meeting with New Zealand in 1936, as the tourists won with a converted try. The fixture went ahead thanks to the efforts of ground staff who had piled 17 tons of straw over the turf in the previous week to ensure the pitch didn't completely freeze in bitterly cold weather.

This game is a classic example of how much the sport has changed. Not only was this just one match in a 36-match tour by New Zealand, but this encounter was also sandwiched between England's opening Five Nations games. New Zealand lost four games on this tour, with Cardiff, Wales, France and South West France all beating the men in black.

THE FIRST FALL AT THE FINAL HURDLE

Despite winning the Triple Crown in 1954, an 11-3 loss in

Paris in the final game of the season meant England had to share title honours with both France and Wales. This was the first occasion when an English team lost a game in which a Grand Slam was on the line.

PLAYING WHAT'S (VISIBLE) IN FRONT OF YOU
1956 – England 3 Wales 8 (Twickenham)

England picked ten new caps to face a Welsh team packed with players from the recent British Isles team that toured South Africa the previous summer. Despite the risky selection, the English pack did enough to win but were let down by poor goal kicking and back play. Winning his first and only cap for England was fly-half Mike Smith (Oxford University). Smith may have never won another rugby cap, but he won 50 for the England cricket team (and was captain for half of them). He was to be the last of England's dual internationals.

Ahead of the Welsh game, he told his half-back partner, Dickie Jeeps, that he shouldn't throw the ball too far in front of him as 'I don't see very well without my glasses'.

The game was also the first international for full-back Fenwick Allison (Coventry) who was described by Barry Bowker as 'a perfect catcher of the ball, aided if conditions required them by mittens'.

A PARTNERSHIP SECOND TO NONE

Among the debutants in Cardiff were second rows David Marques (Cambridge University) and John Currie (Oxford

University). This pairing would become the engine of the English pack and go on to make an astonishing 22 consecutive appearances together. The remarkable sequence ended after the 1961 South Africa match when Currie had to pull out of the opening game of the Championship due to illness. By this time both players were Harlequins.

David Marques and John Currie formed a legendary partnership in the second row.

1957 GRAND SLAM

This was England's seventh Grand Slam and 13th Triple Crown. However, this is believed to be the first time that the term 'Grand Slam' was coined in *The Times* and it soon became the term used to describe a clean sweep. In winning their first

Grand Slam since 1928, England were captained by hooker Eric Evans (Sale). He was 34 when named captain, making him the oldest player to lead the national side (he played on for England until he was 37).

MATCH ONE: Wales 0 England 3 (Cardiff Arms Park)

Selection consistency was a key factor in England's success this season. The RFU were frequently guilty of going into Welsh games (usually the first of the season) with bucketloads of new caps. This time only Harlequin fly-half Ricky Bartlett was receiving his international baptism. England's Fenwick Allison kicked the winning penalty goal after Welsh winger Keith Maddocks was deemed offside under his own posts as a line-out was taking place. The distraught Maddocks was never capped again.

MATCH TWO: Ireland 0 England 6 (Lansdowne Road)

Although England played almost three-quarters of the match a man down after winger Peter Thompson (Headingley) suffered a rib injury, they hung on to eke out a narrow win. England's scores came through a try from the excellent winger Peter Jackson (Coventry) and a penalty by full-back Robert Challis (Bristol). The latter was the only change from the victorious team that won in Cardiff.

Peter Jackson was one of the crucial players of the era and of this title win. His dazzling footwork earned him the nickname 'Nijinsky' after a celebrated Russian ballet dancer.

Kicking to touch

Bob Challis, the England full-back, would often kick to touch using a place kick when England were awarded a penalty. This unusual method was still employed by some teams and players as late as the 1980s.

MATCH THREE: England 9 France 5 (Twickenham)
An unchanged English side burst into a strong lead in the first half on a wet day in London thanks to a brace of tries from Peter Jackson. France rallied to within a point before a smart piece of dribbling and agility from captain Eric Evans, after a loose ball spilled out of a line-out ten metres from the French line, allowed him to squeeze in at the corner and give his side a vital score. Robert Challis was praised for some excellent last-ditch defence at full-back. This try by Evans made him the oldest ever English try scorer at 36 years and 22 days. England flew to Paris for this match, the first time they had ever done so.

MATCH FOUR: England 16 Scotland 3 (Twickenham)
England claimed what was to be their last Grand Slam until 1980 with three tries from centre Phil Davies (Harlequins), flanker Reg Higgins (Liverpool) and Peter Thompson. Bob Challis added two conversions. Interestingly, the Pathé newsreel for this game spoke only of England winning the Triple Crown and Championship, rather than a 'Grand Slam'. The phrase had still not yet come into common usage.

FLAT-FOOTED WALLABIES
1958 – England 9 Australia 6 (Twickenham)
After failing to beat New Zealand and South Africa since the Second World War, this was England's first post-war win over a southern hemisphere side (or a 'Dominion' side as per

the terminology of the day). While it was a poor Australian side (they lost 16 of their 36 games on an eight-month tour, including all five Tests), this game is famous for a spectacular solo try from Peter Jackson.

With just minutes remaining and the game tied, 'Nijinsky' took a pass on his right wing just outside the Australian 22 and handed off his opposite number Rod Phelps. Next, he indicated he planned to step inside full-back Terry Curley, before stepping him on the outside, somehow beating a desperate diving tackle. The move slowed him down, allowing Phelps a second stab at him. This time the Wallaby caught him and dragged him down, but Jackson had the strength to take his defender with him as he reached out, narrowly avoided the corner flag (which would have been in touch) and touch line to just ground the ball.

Peter Jackson's try is still discussed by today's rugby fans.

The home spectators were incensed by what they saw as dirty play from the Wallabies and vented their frustration on the visitors. This led to a cartoon in the *Daily Express* in which it was said 'the Twickenham crowd went all common and booed'.

The match also saw a series of nasty injuries. England had to play 50 minutes with only 14 men due to fly-half Phil Horrocks-Taylor (Cambridge University) leaving with a leg injury. Jeff Butterfield moved from centre to cover his loss, but was laid out three times with head knocks (some sources say four times). Debutant full-back Jim Hetherington (Northampton) also suffered a major concussion, but was still able to kick a crucial penalty. After the match he collapsed and needed to be assisted off the field.

PLACING YOUR OWN PLACE KICK

In 1958 a series of new laws were introduced to try and help the game flow more. One change was the abolition of the need to play the ball with your foot after a tackle and another was hookers now being allowed to strike with their 'near foot'. It was also no longer required that when a conversion was to be taken the ball had to be placed by a player other than the kicker. Now it was possible for the kicker to place the ball for his own kick.

UNDEFEATED CHAMPIONS WITH ONLY TWO WINS

England won the 1958 Five Nations with just two wins (coming against Ireland and France). As England drew against

Wales and Scotland, they remained undefeated and did enough to claim an outright title. However, starting with the Calcutta Cup game that ended England's 1958 season, England were to go five consecutive games without scoring a single try.

FRANCE FINALLY ARRIVE AS A MAJOR POWER

After two consecutive titles, England fell to fourth in the 1959 Five Nations. More significantly, France finally won an outright title. The French had celebrated a famous win over the South Africans at Ellis Park in 1958 and had now firmly arrived as a major rugby power. The *Observer* wrote that France's emergence to the top tier of rugby was 'like finding the All Blacks or Springboks on your doorstep'. The French combined fearsome forwards with 'scintillating' play in the open from both the backs and the pack.

After winning the 1959 title, France shared the spoils with England in 1960 and then won the Five Nations outright again in 1961 and 1962.

SOCIAL CHANGES

The 1960s saw a change in the social make-up of the England side. Historian Huw Richards, in his book *The Red and White: The Story of England v Wales Rugby*, wrote: 'A degree of social change was evident, though, in the England teams of the 1960s. They had more grammar than public school products (35 per cent to 26 per cent) for the first time.'

VISITING LIONS LACK BITE

1960 – England 14 Wales 6 (Twickenham)

England made an excellent start to the 1960s. A team with seven new caps beat a confident Welsh team who arrived at Twickenham with seven players from the 1959 British Isles team. The home side also ended their try drought with debutant winger Jim Roberts (Old Millhillians/Sale) bagging two. The victors racked up all their points in the first half, leaving Wales shell-shocked.

1960 – France 3 England 3 (Stade Colombes)

This dull draw was the only game either side failed to win during the season, meaning the Five Nations title was shared. England, led by scrum-half Dickie Jeeps, would go on to beat Scotland 21-12 in Edinburgh and win the Triple Crown.

SAME AGAIN . . . AND AGAIN?

The 1960 Five Nations saw England select the same XV for every single match. The selection was as follows:

Don Rutherford (Percy Park); John Young (Harlequins), Malcolm Phillips (Oxford University), Mike Weston (Richmond), Jim Roberts (O Millhillians/Sale); Richard Sharp (Oxford University), Dickie Jeeps (Northampton, captain); Ron Jacobs (Northampton), Stan Hodgson (Durham City), Peter Wright (Blackheath), David Marques, John Currie (Harlequins), Peter Robbins (Moseley), Derek Morgan (Medicals), Ron Syrett (Wasps).

NUMBERING UP

The 1961 season saw England players numbering up in the modern system, with full-backs as 15 and loose-head props as number 1. Prior to this, it seems England utilised the reverse system, with full-backs as 1 and loose heads as 15. This is incredibly useful to know when watching old footage on YouTube, if you are confused why all the 'wingers' seem so round and slow. Around this time other teams, like Wales, often wore letters, rather than numbers. Something that clubs like Bristol and Leicester did until the 1990s.

SUITED AND BOOTED

1961 – England 0 South Africa 5 (Twickenham)

The touring South Africans ran out on to the green grass of Twickenham wearing tracksuits, an unusual occurrence at the time. After stripping down to their playing kit, they proceeded to tear strips off England in an ugly encounter full of stray boots and fists. *The Times* reported one English forward after the match looked as if his face had been 'put through a mincing machine'. The Boks were criticised for dull play and elements of the home crowd were lambasted for jeering the visiting side. A day to forget all around.

A FIXTURE THAT DRAWS ATTENTION

England and France drew three times on the trot from 1959 to 1961. The results were 3-3 (Twickenham), 3-3 (Stade Colombes) and 5-5 (Twickenham).

CHAMPIONS AGAIN . . . BUT
ABOUT TO GO OUT IN THE COLD

England won the 1963 Five Nations, with only a scoreless draw in Dublin preventing a clean sweep. Other than the anomaly of a five-way shared title in 1973, this was the last time England were to be top of the pile until 1980.

1963 – Wales 6 England 13 (Cardiff Arms Park)

This was England's last win in Cardiff until 1991. Conditions were so bitterly cold, Wales wore special underwear in an attempt to combat the chill. England scored tries through second row John Owen (Coventry) and centre Malcolm Phillips (Fylde). Captain and fly-half Richard Sharp converted both scores and also slotted over a drop goal. Winning in Cardiff was a good sign for England, as whenever they had done so they went on to top the table.

1963 – Ireland 0 England 0 (Lansdowne Road)

An Irish fly-half called Mick English used his kicking boots to frustrate England in the rain of Dublin and hold them to a scoreless draw. This was England's 11th and final 0-0 result in their history.

SHARP'S MATCH

1963 – England 10 Scotland 8 (Twickenham)

England needed to win to claim the Championship, but Scotland also had hopes of winning the tournament and stormed into an 8-0 lead on a glorious spring day. Despite the poor start from the home team, the day was to ultimately

Richard Sharp etched his name into the history books with his 1963 Calcutta Cup performance.

belong to England captain and fly-half Richard Sharp. First Sharp combined with Peter Jackson (it was the winger's last appearance for the national side) to help send over prop Nick Drake-Lee (Cambridge University) in the right-hand corner. The try was superbly converted by full-back John Wilcox (Harlequins).

The moment that bestowed rugby immortality on Richard Sharp came in the second half. After an England scrum on the Scottish 22 (out on the right), Sharp took the ball deep and at pace. With the ball held in two hands, he effortlessly sold a dummy to beat one inside defender and two outside defenders before adding some swerve and an injection of pace. The ball was quickly tucked under his left arm as he crossed the 22. Then, with the Scottish full-back Colin Blaikie arriving to cover him, the ball was transferred back into both hands, another dummy was offered (and bought), and he swung inside, outraced Scottish scrum-half Stan Coughtrie and was over the line. England survived a few late scares to claim the Calcutta Cup and Championship. This was Scotland's 13th consecutive failure to beat their 'Auld Enemy'.

The newsreel footage of the game described Sharp's 'rare genius' as the 'finest thing to happen to English rugby since the war'. In later years, the England captain reflected on the day and on playing at Twickenham saying: 'There was a thunderous noise from the crowd, the old Twickenham was a wonderfully noisy stadium when full, but the reaction on the pitch was very understated and English. In those days everybody would always look to congratulate other people rather than accept any plaudits themselves which was still considered rather poor form.'

Remarkably, Sharp would only win one further cap and that was not to be until 1967.

LEAVING FOR DISTANT SHORES, FINALLY

In 1963, England became the first of the Home Unions to travel to New Zealand. Prior to this, the furthest place England had travelled to was France. England played two matches against the All Blacks, one against Australia and non-capped matches against Wellington, Otago and Hawke's Bay. Their only victory was to be in the opener, where they triumphed 14-9 over Wellington. The RFU were criticised for the scheduling, which saw England play six matches in 17 days after a demanding journey. Making matters worse, several top players were unable to travel, leaving the tourists understrength.

1963 – 1st Test – New Zealand 21 England 11 (Eden Park, Auckland)

England led 6-0 after seven minutes thanks to two penalties from full-back and new cap Roger Hosen (Northampton), a lead they held, against the odds, until half-time. Indeed, five minutes into the second half, the tourists led 11-3 after right wing John Ranson (Rosslyn Park), another player making his first Test start, scored a try. For a moment it looked like a major shock was on the cards, but New Zealand ended up with three tries after wearing down the weary English pack. New Zealand full-back Don Clarke finished with a try, three conversions, one penalty and a drop goal.

'THE DADDY OF ALL KICKS'

1963 – 2nd Test – New Zealand 9 England 6 (Lancaster Park, Christchurch)

An impressive performance from the Red Rose forwards took this one to the wire, before England lost cruelly in the dying minutes in a very unusual fashion. With minutes remaining, Don Clarke called a mark just inside his own half. There had not been a successful goal from mark in an English game for

32 years and they were so rare that there was confusion among the English team over how to defend against it.

The Times wrote: 'For the next couple of minutes, while the crowd yelled, [Clarke] made his mark at one place and then retired to make it at another. His older brother . . . was called in as ball holder. There were four Englishmen on the mark and during all this inordinate delay they question Mr. Murphy, the referee, on their rights as to charging. By one of those unhappy strokes which turn matches, Judd and Jacobs misunderstood these rights. They set off too soon and so presented Clarke with a free kick at the distant goal.'

A New Zealand paper labelled the winning goal the 'Daddy of All Kicks'. It was a cruel way to lose. This was the last time a game involving England had a successful goal from mark. The method of scoring was removed from the sport in 1977. The goal from mark meant that in the two Tests, Clarke had scored via every possible method in the game against England: a try, penalty, conversion, drop goal and goal from mark.

During the first half, England's second row Mike Davis (Torquay Athletic) dislocated his shoulder. It didn't stop him later returning to the field after a painkilling injection and winning one-handed line-out ball, even though his other arm was completely out of action. Historian Barry Bowker called it a 'display of courage unsurpassed in England's annals'.

'THE BIG WET'
1963 – Australia 18 England 9 (Cricket Ground, Sydney)

Just under 8,000 people turned out in grim conditions to

see Australia dispatch England. The home side outscored the tourists by four tries to three. England would not beat Australia on their own patch until 2003. The atrocious weather led the locals to dub the game 'The Big Wet'.

A CHANCE FOR REVENGE GOES BEGGING
1964 – England 0 New Zealand 14 (Twickenham)

After such strong efforts with an understrength and weary team the previous summer down in New Zealand, many felt England had a very good chance of getting revenge over the All Blacks in January 1964. Alas, it was not to be. England were never at the races as the tourists grabbed two tries (including one from the legendary Colin Meads) to go with two penalties and a conversion from Don Clarke.

THE GREATEST HYPHEN STORY IN RUGBY

England's fly-half at this time was Phil Horrocks-Taylor. Born in Halifax, he represented Cambridge University, Leicester, Middlesbrough, Yorkshire and the British Lions in his career. Horrocks-Taylor's name gave birth to one of rugby's most amusing anecdotes. After one match against Ireland, his opposite number, Mick English said: 'Horrocks went one way, Taylor the other and I was left holding the bloody hyphen.'

NEW LINES DRAWN IN THE GRASS

For much of the 1950s and early 1960s, rugby had become a

cluttered, claustrophobic game with often little room available for creativity and dazzling back play. To combat this, law changes were made around the offside line. It was now required that players not involved at the line-out (excluding the half-back) had to retreat ten yards. The offside line at scrum and maul was moved from the centre of the formation to the back foot, as it is still today. There was also a new law allowing the team throwing into the line-out to decide how many players could compete in it.

HANCOCK'S FINEST HOUR
1965 – England 3 Scotland 3 (Twickenham)

In 1964 Scotland beat England for the first time since 1950. In 1965, Scotland looked set to retain the Calcutta Cup as, with just a minute remaining, they had England pinned in their own 22. Then, winger Andy Hancock (Northampton) took the ball ten metres from his own line. This is how *The Times* reported what happened next:

When Hancock set out from his own 25 he was on a routine mission, and one could tell, from his running, how the various stages of awareness of great opportunity gradually dawned on him. First there was the look of a sleepwalker waking: then the dazed incredulity of a man suddenly told that he had won a huge football pool; but he kept going all the time, and finally we saw the hope exultant of that man in his determination to pocket his fortune before a recheck could possibly take it from him. All or nothing, lungs by now at bursting point, ecstatic legs acting automatically, and he reached his El Dorado in the corner where Obolensky had gained immortality nearly 30 years before. A magnificent effort . . .

Full-back (and later RFU president) Don Rutherford (Gloucester) was unable to add the extras to win it though. After the match, hero Hancock said he was too tired to feel elated after his score. RFU historian Barry Bowker claims there were 'no fewer than 119 line-outs' in this game. However, if this is true, it is not mentioned in most match reports and is far less famous than the 111 line-out game Wales and Scotland had played out a couple of years before.

PREPARING TO PLAY IS . . . TAKING IT TOO SERIOUSLY

England's captain in 1966 was Bedford's Budge Rogers. The flanker would win 34 caps, then a record for England, and would become the first English rugby player to be honoured by Queen Elizabeth II.

When he was named as captain, he was keen to make sure that his team got to know each other and had some time running through some moves by meeting up occasionally on a Wednesday night in Richmond. The day after he proposed his first session, he got a call from the RFU secretary, Bob Weighill, who insisted that such sessions would not go ahead. As a result, Rogers had to cancel his plans to try and make England a better team. England's best result in the 1966 Five Nations was a home draw with Ireland and the Red Roses finished bottom of the table. It was England's worst finish since 1948 when, fittingly, Bob Weighill was in the squad.

A CHANGE OF TUNE

England's miserable campaign persuaded some in the corridors of power that some form of coaching need to take place. Former international and RFU man Micky Steele-Bodger began taking 'tentative steps' towards helping England players prepare. RFU historian Barry Bowker wrote:

> *Initially this merely took the form of holding Sunday 'teach-ins' after the trials, but at least an attempt was made to impose a pattern of play, no easy task when Cornishmen and Lancastrians have to be blended with Londoners and Midlanders. Set moves were practised and policy laid down. From this time onwards team work has become all important, though the insistence on eliminating risks has led to a loss of spontaneity and England were no longer likely to run in many tries from their own 25. Indeed, a preference for playing their Rugby thirty yards from the opponents' line seems to have led to the selection of some backs who are quick over that distance, but not necessarily over a hundred yards . . .*

WALLABIES JUMP ALL OVER THE RECORD BOOK
1967 – England 11 Australia 23 (Twickenham)
This was the biggest score England had conceded since

Twickenham opened in 1910. It was not a particularly successful tour for the Wallabies, who lost 14 and drew 3 of their 36 games, but England simply had no answer for their innovative fast and short passing game. The tourist's captain, Ken Catchpole, was praised for his passing ability. He tended to stay on his feet rather than employ the more traditional dive pass. With heavier balls and no pimples for grip, unlike on modern balls, long accurate passing from a set piece under pressure was an incredibly difficult skill at the time.

This game saw Richard Sharp (England's 'unsecret weapon') return to the line-up for the first time since his famous performance over Scotland in 1963. The press labelled his recall, as captain no less, as a 'whopping gamble'. It didn't pay off and he never pulled on the white shirt again.

POINTS MACHINE

In the 1967 Five Nations, full-back Roger Hosen became the first England international to score 50 points. Born in Helston, Cornwall, Hosen possessed a powerful boot. In his ten caps he scored six conversions and 17 penalties for a total of 63 points.

TEEN CAUSES TRIPLE CROWN HEARTACHE
1967 – Wales 34 England 21 (Cardiff Arms Park)

England headed to Cardiff with a Triple Crown in their sights. Wales, meanwhile, were desperate to avoid a first ever Five Nations whitewash. Bizarrely, Wales picked uncapped 18-year-old Keith Jarrett at full-back. A centre, the teen had never played full-back before. The week before his club side Newport had wanted to help the teenager out so they picked him there for one game. He was so poor he was switched back to centre at half-time. So what happened when he faced England in front of a packed Cardiff Arms Park?

He scored an epic solo try, kicked five conversions and two penalty goals to score 19 points as Wales notched up their highest ever total against England. His personal points tally equalled a Welsh record set in 1910. The try was only the second ever by a Welsh full-back (the last coming in 1934) and he had run in alone from 80 metres out. His kicks? Three came off the posts and still went over.

Teenager and novice full-back Keith Jarrett broke English hearts in Cardiff.

BLACK AND WHITE CLASH IN FULL COLOUR
1967 – England 11 New Zealand 23 (Twickenham)

This was the first rugby game to be broadcast in colour in the UK. The 1967 All Blacks were a fearsome side led by Brian Lochore and coached by the astute Fred Allen. Coaching was in its infancy at this point in rugby history and many traditionalists shuddered at the concept. The tourists won all but one of their 17 matches – only a draw with Newport blemishing their record.

At HQ, after performing the haka to the Queen, rather than the English team, the Kiwis stormed ahead to an 18-point lead after just 35 minutes. England were never in the game and conceded five tries. Danny Hearn, one of England's first choice centres, tragically broke his neck and was paralysed the week before this match when making a tackle for Leicester against the same opponents.

EYE'VE BLOWN MY CHANCE

On the eve of the 1968 England v France match at Twickenham, England captain and flanker Dick Greenwood (Waterloo) injured his eye playing squash. The five-times capped Greenwood never played for England again. Greenwood would eventually coach England in the 1980s and his son Will Greenwood would go on to lift the World Cup with England.

CHA-CHA-CHA-CHANGES

The 8-3 win over Scotland at Twickenham in 1969 was

memorable for the first use of a replacement by England when Timothy Dalton (Coventry) came on for an injured Keith Fielding (Moseley).

For almost the entire first century of rugby union, the authorities had not permitted replacements for injured players. As often seen in this book, players would either have to struggle on through injuries (often as bad as fractured jaws or broken

Bob Hiller scored 138 points for England, a massive number for the era he played in

limbs) or depart the field and leave their team short. The law was finally changed after a series of high-profile incidents involving injured players heroically playing on and suffering even more severe injuries. In 1966, for instance, England number eight David Perry (Bedford) ended his career by staying on with damaged knee ligaments against France. Plenty of traditionalists, however, did not approve of replacement players being awarded caps. Tactical substitutions, however, would not come into play until the 1990s.

Another change in the late 1960s was that the ball could only be kicked directly into touch from the 22. If the ball was kicked outside the 22 and left the field of play without bouncing, the line-out would take place from where the ball was kicked. This law was designed to try and limit negative kicking and encourage attackers. Many felt it was an immediate success as there was an increase in Test tries after it was introduced.

GETTING THE GUYS TOGETHER AT LAST

In 1968, the IRB finally officially permitted training sessions for national teams. Then in 1969, ahead of the match with South Africa, the RFU followed 'a cricket precedent' and named a 30-man squad for the first time and also nominated a captain, full-back Bob Hiller (Harlequins) in advance of the team announcement. Under this new approach, the England squad would meet for several Sunday training sessions before their meeting with the Springboks. This may not seem much now, but for amateurs who had full-time jobs, and who had likely played for their clubs the day before (and drunk heavily afterwards), travelling to and taking part in these sessions was a serious step up in commitment.

While the IRB had permitted training sessions for teams, they were not supposed to be held more than 48 hours before a match. It is claimed England got around this by making sure more than 15 players were in attendance. After all, only 15 players make a team. So anything more than that was not seen by the RFU as a 'team' session.

FIRST COACH ARRIVES

England, inspired by the actions of other nations such as New Zealand, appointed Don White, a flanker who won 14 caps for England from 1947 to 1953, as their coach. Don Rutherford (a former England full-back) was appointed as the RFU's technical director. The times were certainly a-changing.

FALSE DAWN

1969 – England 11 South Africa 8 (Twickenham)

After a 30-9 stuffing from Wales in the final game of the 1969 Five Nations, England played their first game under the coaching of Don White and within the framework of the new squad system. The impact was instant as England claimed the scalp of the Boks for the first time.

The 1969–70 Springbok tour of Britain and Ireland was hugely controversial. In South Africa at the time there was a system of institutionalised racial segregation known as apartheid. This system saw black people oppressed while white people ran and controlled politics, culture, economics and all aspects of life. Non-whites were not permitted to play for the South African rugby side, for example, and visiting teams were usually encouraged (or ordered) to leave non-white players at home.

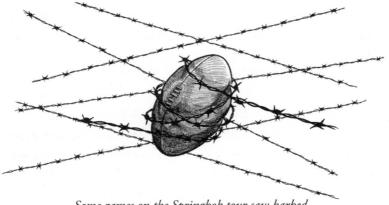

Some games on the Springbok tour saw barbed wire deployed to keep fans off the pitch.

Throughout the tour the Springboks were greeted by protests and direct action. Often there were clashes between protesters, police and fans. Some players took a personal stand too. John Taylor of Wales, who had seen apartheid first-hand with the Lions in 1968, refused to be considered for selection for the Welsh game and even attended protests. Unfortunately, many in the rugby community didn't want to consider politics or human rights, and just wanted to play against, or watch, the famous Springboks.

This first win over South Africa, combined with the new coaching and squad system, seemed to offer hope for a fresh, strong start to the approaching decade. What was to follow over the next ten years though was more often than not a horror show.

At Twickenham, England won through tries from hooker John Pullin (Bristol) and lock Peter Larter (Northampton), with a conversion and penalty from captain Bob Hiller. The South Africans almost didn't make it to the match as a protester had stolen their team bus in the morning . . . with the players on it! He was overpowered once the team twigged what was happening and he crashed the bus into some parked cars.

BLAZERS UPSET ABOUT MISSING BLAZER

During the 1969 official dinner following the Wales v England game, England's second row Nigel Horton (Moseley) fell foul of officialdom. In the book *Behind the Rose* he said:

I had a bit of a chip on my shoulder because I was working class, whereas the majority of people playing rugby were middle-class . . . I also had issues with the selectors. One of them cost me two years of my England career . . . I was young and not worldly when England played their last game against Wales at Cardiff Arms Park. At the post-match dinner, Wales were one of the few countries that went for suits rather than black-tie, mainly because many of the players were working-class and black-tie was something that they would rarely use. I only had one suit, but it was heavy, and it had been a beautiful day so it was quite warm. The Welsh and English players sat on mixed tables that evening, and because it was hot I took my jacket off.

A selector came up to me and said, 'Nigel, I think you should put your jacket on, it's upsetting a few people, and they are talking about it.' I turned to the other players on the table and asked if it was upsetting them, and they said it was no problem. That wasn't good enough, so I said, 'Are you telling me as a selector to put my jacket on?' He said, 'Yes', and so I did it.

Then, at two o'clock in the morning when I wandered into the players' room, the selector in question was in there having a drink and wanted to discuss it further – and I didn't. He was insistent, and I told him where to go. I didn't play for England again until 1971, which was the same season that selector left the panel.

1947–69: THE STAR PLAYERS

JEFF BUTTERFIELD

Club: Northampton
Position: Centre
Caps: 28 (1953–59)
(British Lions, 4 caps, 12 points)
Points: 15 (5 tries)

Not only was Jeff Butterfield a gifted athlete with superb handling and ball skills and the owner of a sharp rugby brain, he was a fitness fanatic. His commitment to staying in tip-top shape meant he had the stamina to maintain performance for a full 80 minutes, something many internationals were unable to do at the time. Butterfield is ranked among the great English centres and his 28 caps were won in one consecutive streak. He was part of one Grand Slam, two Triple Crowns and four Championship titles and led England on four occasions. Barry Bowker wrote of him: 'Perfectly balanced, he ran with the ball in front of him in both hands so that he could either give a model pass for the receiver to run on to or use the ball to effect a break through by means of a dummy . . . wonderful sense of timing in everything he did – including a tackle that took both man and ball out of the game.'

ERIC EVANS

Club: Sale
Position: Hooker, prop
Caps: 30 (1948–58)
Points: 15 (5 tries)

No biography of Eric Evans seems to leave out the term 'inspirational leader'. Yet Evans did not captain England until 1954 when he was 34. However, he was still captain when England won the 1957 Grand Slam and 1958 Five Nations. His ability to lead a Test team at 37 was helped by his supreme fitness and, perhaps, his job as a schoolteacher. He didn't agree with coaching, however, once saying the only place for a coach was transporting the team.

Praised for his technical ability as a hooker, he took an innovative approach to the game and his physical conditioning. He said of training: 'You can't make yourself ten foot tall, but you can make yourself fit. It needs guts and discipline to go to bed early, particularly over Christmas.'

Born in Droylsden, Greater Manchester, he often trained with Manchester United's 'Busby Babes'. He is commemorated by a statue in Audenshaw, Manchester and at the time of his retirement held the record for captaining England (13 times) and caps for a hooker (29).

BUDGE ROGERS

Club: Bedford
Position: Flanker
Caps: 34 (1961–69)
(British Lions, 2 caps)
Points: 9 (3 tries)

Fit and destructive, Budge Rogers caused countless problems for the backlines of England's opponents thanks to his ability to drift across and disrupt attacking threequarters. He was also a great link player, his conditioning helping him arrive at the breakdown to continue English attacks.

His 34 caps were an English record at the time and he also made an astonishing 485 appearances for Bedford. Rogers led England on seven occasions and toured with the British Lions to South Africa. Away from the playing field he held several prominent roles in the RFU, including chairman of selectors and RFU president. He was the first English rugby player to be honoured by the Queen.

1947–69 NOTABLE EVENTS IN ENGLISH HISTORY

- 1947: Harrods of London begins to sell soft toilet paper.

- 1948: The NHS begins operating.

- 1949: Winston Churchill gives a speech which supports the concept of a European Union.

- 1950: India becomes a republic and is no longer tied to the British Empire.

- 1951: The popular radio show *The Archers* begins broadcasting.

- 1952: After 13 years, tea is no longer rationed due to shortages.

- 1953: Ian Fleming published *Casino Royale*, the first James Bond novel.

- 1954: Roger Bannister becomes the first person to run a mile in under four minutes.

- 1955: Ruth Ellis is hanged for murder, the last woman to be executed in Britain.

- 1956: Double yellow lines are introduced on roads.

- 1957: John Lennon and Paul McCartney meet for the first time.

- 1958: The Notting Hill race riots occur (29 August to 5 September).

- 1959: Robert Smith (lead singer, writer and guitarist of The Cure) is born.

- 1960: *Coronation Street* begins broadcasting.

- 1961: Betting shops are allowed to operate, thanks to changes in British law.

- 1962: *The Sunday Times* begins to print a colour supplement, the first of its kind in the UK.

- 1963: The Sindy doll is introduced by a British toy firm in an attempt to rival Barbie.

- 1964: The infamous Great Train Robbery trial takes place.

- 1965: Cigarette advertising is no longer permitted on British television.

- 1966: Pickles the dog finds the Jules Rimet Trophy, the original World Cup trophy which had been stolen ahead of the 1966 tournament and England's victory.

- 1967: The UK applies for membership of the European Economic Community.

- 1968: London Bridge is sold to Robert Paxton McCulloch, a businessman from Missouri, who then had it transported to the USA.

1970–79: DISASTER AND GLORY

	PLAYED	WON	DRAWN	LOST
FIVE NATIONS	40	11	3	26
TESTS	11	4	0	7
TOTAL	51	15	3	33

Championships

None

Shared Championships (1)

1973 (Five-way tie)

'I never understood what the selectors were trying to do;
I am not sure the selectors did either.'

ROGER UTTLEY (ENGLAND SECOND ROW/BACK ROW,

23 CAPS BETWEEN 1973 AND 1980)

HARD TIMES ARE HERE AGAIN

The 1970s are possibly the most depressing decade in the history of the English national team. Wasted talent, ineffective (and laughable) selection and humiliation after humiliation on the playing fields of Europe. Yet, oddly, among the terrible results stand a handful of exceptional performances, including away wins in New Zealand and South Africa that rank among the most impressive results in the long annals of Test rugby.

Times were tough off the field too in England. In 1974, the Labour Party's James Callaghan (who would serve as prime minister from 1976 to 1979) said: 'Our place in the world is shrinking: our economic comparisons grow worse, long-term political influence depends on economic strength – and that is running out. If I were a young man, I should emigrate.'

The 1970s were far from England's and Britain's finest years. It wasn't just the questionable fashion that made things grim (it's often labelled the 'decade that fashion forgot'), the seventies were plagued by economic hardship, political strife, industrial turmoil and domestic terrorism (the IRA's bombing campaign in England reached previously unseen levels).

In 1972, the UK signed the Treaty of Accession, bringing the country into what would become the European Union. The decade also saw a major recession in large parts of the Western world and inflation rises that outpaced pay rises. In 1973 and 1974, the Conservative government needed to conserve electricity levels (due to the impact from striking workers) by introducing the 'three-day week'. Commercial enterprises could only operate for three consecutive days in a week. Even pubs were forced to close and television broadcasts stopped at 10.30 p.m.

In 1978 and 1979 the country (now under a Labour government) experienced what would be known as the 'Winter of Discontent'. In a bitterly cold period, amidst inflation, supply shortages and pay disputes, thousands of workers, led by trade unions, went on strike. With everyone from gravediggers to factory workers to sewage workers taking part in industrial action, the country effectively came to a halt at times. Bodies went unburied and rubbish piled up in the streets. The fallout led to the election of the Conservative Party's Margaret Thatcher, the nation's first female prime minister.

There were also positives to the 1970s. Working-class people were able to travel to far-off lands in a way that had never been possible previously as package holidays made travel cheaper and easier. In 1971 around four million British tourists ventured abroad. But by 1973 that number was nine million.

At the start of the decade, 91 per cent of families owned a television set and there were now three stations to choose from – all broadcasting in colour too, although many people still only owned black-and-white sets. By the end of the decade the Sony Walkman had emerged to transform the way people consumed the music they loved. What were people listening to? English acts that enjoyed major success in this period included Kate Bush, Elton John, David Bowie, Elvis Costello, the Police, the Bee Gees, Queen and Wings, along with punk acts like The Clash and the Sex Pistols.

A DECADE OF FIVE NATIONS DESPAIR

England's record in the Five Nations during the 1970s makes brutal reading. Here's the sequence of finishing positions: joint 4th, joint 3rd, 5th, 1st (shared), 5th, 5th, 5th, 3rd, 3rd and 4th.

And that first place is not as impressive as it seems. In the 1973 Championship, each team won its home games and lost its away games. With points difference still not used as a tie-breaker, it meant there was a five-way tie for the title.

THE DAY OF THE SUBS

1970 – England 13 Wales 17 (Twickenham)

Following a win over South Africa in England's first game of the 1969–70 season, fans were hopeful a good Five Nations lay ahead. After dispatching Ireland 9-3 at home, things looked good against Wales too. In the first half, winger John Novak (Harlequins) scored on his debut and the great David Duckham (Coventry), playing in the centre, also crossed the line. With two conversions and a penalty from captain Bob Hiller, England had a commanding 13-3 lead at the break.

Then, halfway through the second half, things got even worse for the visitors. The legendary scrum-half Gareth Edwards (still considered by some as the best player of all time) had to leave the field injured. He was replaced by new cap Chico Hopkins. What happened next has gone down in rugby folklore. Hopkins had a magical 20 minutes, setting up one try for J.P.R. Williams and claiming another himself. He turned the game and Wales had won. Hopkins never played for Wales again, but his 20 minutes of glory will never be forgotten.

Edwards wasn't the only key person to depart the field that day either. The referee broke his leg and dislocated his shoulder in a collision. The replacement referee was an RFU referee.

1970 – France 35 England 13 (Stade Colombes)

The heartache inflicted by the Welsh was followed up by a 14-5 loss at Murrayfield. But far worse was to come in Paris as England conceded more points than they had ever done before. In the warm Paris air, France breached England's line six times, an almost unheard of tally for Test rugby at the time and something that hadn't happened to England since 1931. It also equalled a record losing margin that had occurred back in 1922.

NOT A FAN OF THE HOME FANS

John Pullin, one of the great England hookers and captains, was not a huge fan of the Twickenham experience. He once said: 'Ninety per cent of the people were there because it was Twickenham. They were not really there to watch the rugby, whereas in Wales it was 90 per cent the other way. If you took one against the head at Cardiff Arms Park, a big noise would go up from the crowd because they understood and appreciated what was happening . . . at Twickenham, nobody would know. They wouldn't have a clue what was happening.'

UNHAPPY BIRTHDAY

England's centenary season was not much cause for celebration. It began with a 22-6 stuffing in Cardiff, then limped on with a narrow 9-6 win in Dublin, before a thrilling 14-14 draw with the French in London. This match was also notable for captain Bob Hiller scoring all 14 points, which was then the highest total by an English player in an international. Hiller also became the first England player to break the 100-point barrier in Tests. What came next though was to put a real dampener on the birthday celebrations: two losses to their oldest rivals in the space of a week.

1971 – England 15 Scotland 16 (Twickenham)

It may have been both England and Scotland's centenary, but

the Scots were determined to make England choke on the birthday cake while they enjoyed extra cream on top of their half. The visitors managed it by choosing 1971 as the first time to win at Twickenham since the Second World War.

1971 – Scotland 26 England 6 (Murrayfield)

In front of the prime minister and Prince of Wales, Scotland carried on their domination of the birthday party mood from the week before in this non-Championship match arranged to mark exactly 100 years since the first international rugby match and the first meeting of these two teams. Scotland got things going from the kick-off and Bob Hiller spoke memorably of the opening moments:

'Somebody decided that we were going to run everything that day, and that included if Scotland kicked long from the kick-off. Anyway they did kick off long. I caught it and passed it inside to Jeremy Janion and on to Cowman. Cowman passed to Spencer, who promptly dropped it, and John Frame picked it up and scored under the posts. The recording afterwards showed us that the score came in the 13th second of the match, but I can tell you we looked at the clock and it hadn't even reached 3 p.m. We had kicked off a minute early so we were five down before the game had even started!'

Other than three penalties from the ever-reliable Hiller, England had nothing to offer and with their pack on the back foot all afternoon, could not generate anything for the travelling supporters to get excited about. This was Scotland's biggest win over England since 1931 and they outscored the visitors five tries to one. The Calcutta Cup was not on the line for this game.

1971 – England 11 RFU President's Overseas XV 28 (Twickenham)

This was a special centenary match and, despite it not being against an international team, caps were awarded. The opposition was made up of some of the biggest names in rugby outside of the Home Unions. Players like Colin Meads, Brian Lochore, Ian Kirkpatrick, Jo Maso, Pierre Villepreux, Frik du Preez and Bryan Williams were more than a match for an English team who probably just wanted the birthday party over with at this stage. The scratch side outscored England six tries to one.

A 'FULL' TRY COUNT

Bob Hiller scored three tries from full-back for England in 1971. The last full-back to score a try for England before this was in 1880 when Thomas Fry scored at Manchester against Scotland. Hiller scored 138 points in 19 games, more than twice as many as the previous record-holder Roger Hosen.

TALENT APLENTY

Although results in the Five Nations did not show it, there was plenty of quality in the England team at this time. Sadly, due to a combination of poor preparation, odd selection policies and a weak domestic club set-up, England continued to be less than the sum of their considerable parts. David Duckham, a winger and centre for England, was so beloved in Wales for his flair and skill, they nicknamed him 'Dai'. If Welsh fans were affectionate for him, then it says a heck of a lot for how good he was. Alan Old (Middlesbrough) at fly-half was another player who would get thrown in and out of the side and never get the credit he deserved. He would still play a part in some famous wins.

Andy Ripley (Rosslyn Park) made his debut at number eight in 1972 and was not just a world-class rugby player but was a world-class athlete. He was a cornerstone of the English pack in many a game, as was hooker John Pullin. Yet, as this chapter will show, these and many other quality players had little to celebrate in a grim decade for the national side.

A TRYING TIME

By the 1972 Five Nations the value of the try had been increased to four points. It wasn't much help to England. For the first time they lost all four Five Nations matches to get whitewashed. They conceded 88 points, an amount boosted by the newly increased try worth. After losing at home to Wales (12-3) and Ireland (16-12), England dropped their captain Bob Hiller and took a 37-12 hiding in Paris in the final Test at the Stade Colombes stadium. It was at the time the highest points total England had conceded and the worst ever losing margin to France (it was equalled in 2006). The dismal season was rounded off with a 23-9 drubbing in Edinburgh. The win meant Scotland had beaten England four times on the trot for the first time since 1896.

THE MIRACLE IN AFRICA

After a first ever whitewash and a terrible run of seven defeats, England headed to South Africa with their tails firmly between their legs. Everyone and their dog predicted a severe hiding in the Test in Johannesburg. Led by John Pullin and coached by John Elders, England played a Herculean seven matches in just two weeks and three days (the final three were played at altitude too). The six tour matches ahead of the Test saw England win five and draw one. This sequence included a match with the

South Africa (Bantu) XV. This game was the first time that a non-white South African side had faced a European side on home soil.

1972 – South Africa 9 England 18 (Ellis Park, Johannesburg)
England's form in the pre-Test matches had impressed South Africa, but it was still felt by most that England would be unable to win this international. The fact the game was being played at 1,724 metres above sea level (meaning just 82 per cent of the oxygen available compared with sea level) only seemed to make the tourists' chances thinner. No Home Union side had even played at altitude before. What's more, England were on the back of seven straight Test losses, and had won just once in 13 games since a win over Ireland in 1970. In contrast, the Boks had won eight of their previous nine internationals (including two wins over the All Blacks and one over France). They were widely considered the best team in the world.

England not only shocked the rugby world, but the home side didn't even score a try, having to settle for three penalties. John Pullin's men controlled the match, with his pack of forwards keeping the Springbok pack in check the whole game. Scrum-half Jan Webster (Moseley) was universally praised for being a thorn in the side of the home team and controlling the game superbly. One South African rugby publication said that Webster 'deserved a medal'. Fly-half Alan Old was also singled out for praise.

Full-back and debutant Sam Doble (Moseley) kicked four penalties and a conversion to finish on 14 points, equalling the record set by Bob Hiller in a single match (1971 v France). The English back row unit of Andy Ripley, Tony Neary (Broughton

Park) and John Watkins (Gloucester) was rated by rugby historian Barry Bowker as one of the best ever English combinations.

The only try of the game came from winger Alan Morley (Bristol) after the South African full-back was unable to deal with a Webster kick. In later years, England prop Mike Burton (Gloucester) said: 'The Test was one of the greatest ever England wins, but in the middle of a Test match you thought that life could not get any worse. You were playing this game against the monsters, we were thousands of feet above sea level on the baked hard pitches, and there wasn't a single supporter on the trip, so there was no one shouting for England. There was kikuyu grass and the referee was a South African, no neutral refs in those days. And your mouth was as dry as dust because in those days they never even ran on with a drink of water.'

Afterwards, the Springboks came in for some criticism after failing to attend the post-match function with England. However, an apology was given, and it was claimed it was a timing mix-up rather than an unsporting response to defeat. The victory meant England became the first international touring side to complete an undefeated tour of South Africa. *The Times* wrote after the win that 'everyone will feel that the tide in English rugby has turned at last'.

BACK TO MEDIOCRITY

So how did England build on this historic win? By losing the next three games. Defeats followed to the All Blacks (9-0 at Twickenham), Wales (25-9 in Cardiff) and Ireland (18-9 in Dublin). However, England managed home wins over France

(14-6) and Scotland (20-13) to allow England to share the Championship with . . . well . . . France, Scotland, Wales and Ireland. Remarkably, each team won their home games and lost their away games, tying the table in five ways!

THE GREATEST OPENING LINE IN AFTER-MATCH DINNER HISTORY

In the 1972 Five Nations, Wales and Scotland had declined to travel to Dublin due to rising political tension and terrorist action concerning Northern Ireland (it was a period of significant violence as Unionists and Irish Republicans waged bloody campaigns for and against British rule). In 1973, England elected to ignore threats on their lives and travel. They were met at Dublin airport by armed soldiers and police and escorted to their hotel. David Duckham decided to take his wife on the trip with him. His reasoning was 'if we're going to die, we're going to die together'.

When they emerged on to the field at Lansdowne Road on matchday they were given a standing ovation by the home crowd. It was the best moment of the afternoon for the men in white as Ireland overwhelmed them 18-9. At the post-match function, John Pullin stood up to give his captain's speech and opened with the immortal line: 'We may not be very good but at least we turn up.' It brought the house down.

THE RATHER SPLENDID SEVEN

In 1973 the SRU held a 'world' sevens tournament involving

all eight members of the IRB (the Home Unions, France, New Zealand, Australia and South Africa, who played as a 'President's VII). England, who included the likes of Fran Cotton (captain), David Duckham, Roger Uttley and Andy Ripley, beat Ireland 22-18 in the final after dispatching Wales 24-10 in the semis. While it was not officially a World Cup, many newspapers of the day declared England world champions.

MORE UNEXPECTED GLORY ON FOREIGN FIELDS

After another middling Five Nations, little was expected of John Pullin's men for their hastily arranged tour to New Zealand (a planned trip to Argentina was cancelled due to kidnapping threats from terrorist groups). The tour began in Fiji with a narrow 13-12 win in a non-capped match in which jet-lagged players struggled to get over the finish line. It was followed by defeats to Taranaki (6-3), Wellington (25-16) and Canterbury (19-12). Once again, England were seen as lambs to the slaughter. Rugby writer and Kiwi Terry McLean previewed the match by saying: 'England are being asked to play a team principally made up of players who have been competing in the quasi-professional atmosphere of touring for almost two years.'

ENGLAND 'CONFOUND THE PROPHETS OF WOE AGAIN'
1973 – New Zealand 10 England 16 (Eden Park, Auckland)
Nine of the players who had lost to New Zealand at Twickenham the previous season lined up at Eden Park. A couple of the

England players drank sherry before the game to calm their nerves. When the All Blacks took an early lead with a well-worked try from winger Grant Batty, it seemed the writing was on the wall. But not long after, Jan Webster, who had been a hero in South Africa, picked up a loose ball from Andy Ripley, accelerated and stepped through a couple of All Black defenders before drawing the final man and putting centre Peter Preece (Coventry) into space. Preece's pass to his Coventry teammate and winger Peter Squires was behind him, but Squires gathered (possibly knocking on) and dabbed it down for the score.

Webster had a hand too in England's two other scores, tries from flanker Tony Neary and loose-head prop Stack Stevens (Penzance-Newlyn). There were two conversions from Peter Rossborough (Coventry). The home press marvelled at Webster totally outplaying legendary Kiwi scrum-half Sid Going. Alan Old at fly-half worked superbly with Webster to control the game through classic ten-man rugby tactics, something they were able to do thanks to an excellent display from the pack, in particular the back row.

Steven's second-half try was a thing of beauty. After a poor clearance from New Zealand, Webster took the ball at dazzling speed up to just outside the All Black 22. He passed inside to Stevens, who gave a lovely ball to second row Chris Ralston (Richmond) who took on two defenders before slipping back to Stevens who charged over from ten metres out to put England ahead. Neary's try came from incredible work from Webster after a New Zealand fumble and England held on to beat New Zealand for the first time in 37 years. *The Times* described the result as 'one of the greatest – and most unexpected –

Tony Neary was at the heart of the shock win away to New Zealand.

achievements in rugby history'. Terry McLean wrote: 'The All Blacks were hammered . . . And this, I tell you, is no fairy tale'.

There were four Coventry players in the backline and one more in the forwards (Fran Cotton). The referee for this game was Frank McMullen, a New Zealander who had won 11 caps for the All Blacks.

AND NOW . . . THE WALLABIES
1973 – England 20 Australia 3 (Twickenham)
In November 1973, just two months after the Kiwi win, John Pullin took his men to victory over a disappointing Australia. It meant that despite all the mediocrity on the fields of Europe in recent years, England had beaten all three of the big southern hemisphere teams in 18 months (two of them away from home, too).

BACK TO THE BOTTOM
So how did England follow up on the famous wins over New Zealand and Australia? Why, by finishing bottom of the 1974, 1975 and 1976 Five Nations. Here's a summary of some of the key moments and events from these fallow seasons.

1974 – France 12 England 12 (Parc des Princes)
England managed an unexpected draw in Paris on the occasion of the first trip to France's new home ground (it had been rebuilt since England's visits in previous years). Tragically, a large number of England supporters were among the 176 UK citizens who died after the game in a Turkish Airlines disaster that saw 346 people lose their lives in all. Eighteen of the dead came from the Bury St Edmunds rugby team. England played France just over a month later in a non-capped match to raise money for dependants of those who lost their lives in the crash; £87,557 was raised on the day, France won 26-7 and, sadly, a streaker saw fit to run across the field at half-time.

TIMES ARE A-CHANGIN'

In the 1970s, the regular fixtures started to rotate in the Five Nations. For most of the history of the tournament, going back to the 19th century, it generally occurred that the order England played the Home Unions in was Wales, followed by Ireland and then Scotland. The rotation idea was a Welsh one, and also included 'doubling up' games, so two games were played on the same weekend. One of the reasons there had been long opposition to the change of fixtures was that the RFU and SRU didn't want to move their traditional golf outing around the Calcutta Cup.

1974 – England 16 Wales 12 (Twickenham)

Although England finished last in the 1974 Five Nations, they beat Wales in controversial circumstances to claim their only win over the Welsh between 1964 and 1979. 'Dai' Duckham and Andy Ripley claimed the English tries. There was much anger after the game at a disallowed try Wales had suffered (and video indicates it was a legitimate try) and the RFU's failure to play the Welsh national anthem. The Welsh players had expected to sing it and were baffled when the referee signalled the game was to begin. A fierce row broke out afterwards and the RFU secretary said: 'My committee is firmly of the opinion that when countries of the four Home Unions play at Twickenham we play "The Queen" only. We are all part of the United Kingdom and the national anthem . . . is "The Queen".'

*'Dai' Duckham was one of the few England
players of the era adored by international fans.*

SWAP, CHANGE, PUT BACK AGAIN

In the 1974 Five Nations the English selectors used 27 players, an astonishing amount for the era (first-choice sides were always picked and only injured players could be replaced; there were still no tactical substitutions).

1975 – England 20 France 27 (Twickenham)

In the second game of the Five Nations, full-back Peter Rossborough scored 16 points from a try and four penalties. At the time it was the second highest ever score by an England player in a single Test (Alan Old had scored 17 against Ireland in 1974). Yet Rossborough never played for England again. England's only win this campaign was a 7-6 win in the final match to deny Scotland a Triple Crown. England still had to take the wooden spoon though.

BOOTS AND FISTS IN THE LAND OF OZ

In the summer of 1975 England, captained by Tony Neary and coached by John Burgess, headed to Australia. The tour was labelled by rugby historian John Griffiths as an 'unmitigated disaster'. The RFU decided to send a party leaning more towards youth than experience. They paid badly for it. Both Tests were lost and England fell in two of the six provincial games. But the loss in the two-game Test series came with a shocking amount of violence, most of it initiated by the home side.

1st Test: Australia 16 England 9 (Sydney Cricket Ground, Sydney)

Australia's young backs played some excellent rugby that the inexperienced and injury-ridden tourists were simply unable to cope with. It could have been a much higher score if England hadn't shown tenacity in the face of the overwhelming Aussie attack. Despite the dominance of the Wallaby attack, both sides only managed a single try apiece. The game concluded with a few bouts of boots and fists. This was to continue, quite literally, at the start of the next match.

THE BATTLE OF BALLYMORE

2nd Test: Australia 30 England 21 (Ballymore, Brisbane)

The opening of this match has to be seen to be believed. Australia piled in from the kick-off with tighthead prop Barry Nelmes (Cardiff) in particular getting a bashing as the home side just began attacking anything in white. Some reports listed Oz prop Stuart Macdougall as one of the worst offenders. It's worth noting, perhaps, that the referee for this match was Australian. At the first line-out fists flew and a mass punch-up took place, seemingly started by Macdougall (according to some sources) and England second row Bill Beaumont (Fylde) had to leave the field for seven minutes for stitches (leaving the visitors down a man as there were no blood subs back then). Gloucester loose-head prop Mike Burton was warned for using his head in the same fight. Not long after followed another line-out punch-up. Straight after, Burton made a late tackle on Australian winger Douglas Osborne and, just three minutes into the game, Burton was dismissed. He was the first English international ever to be sent off. Unsurprisingly, a short-handed, relatively inexperienced England side were unable to hold on to their 15-9 half-time lead and lost 30-21.

Years later, in the book *Behind the Rose*, Burton said:

The first thing to say about the Battle of Ballymore when I became the first Englishman to be sent off – and this was after 103 years of international rugby – is that I never, ever had any regrets about what I did. It was the second Test of a brutal series in which Australia set out to treat us like dogs; the opening stages of the second Test were like a war, they were kicking and punching everything as if it was a war – as if on a pre-arranged signal. The scenes were astonishing.

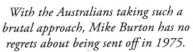

With the Australians taking such a brutal approach, Mike Burton has no regrets about being sent off in 1975.

PLAYING UNDER BURGESS

Number eight Andy Ripley was well known for his sense of humour and unique approach to the game. One interview he gave revealed both the lighter side of him and his view on England coach John Burgess. In an interview with the *Rothmans Rugby Yearbook* he once said:

We had [a penalty move] called 'Dam Busters' where we all stood in a horseshoe facing the opposition singing the Dam Busters *theme. Then the ball would be tapped and passed into the circle and suddenly everyone would wheel off with their arms outstretched. I remember once trying it against Newport but just as we were about to tap the ball the referee blew us up for time wasting. But if you think that was stupid, I remember playing for England when John Burgess was coach and you should have seen some of his penalties. They were a cross between Morris dancing and formation dancing, except instead of being done as a lark, it was all taken very seriously.*

REVENGE COMES SWIFTLY,
BUT ANOTHER POOR SEASON FOLLOWS

Under new coach Peter Colston and captain Tony Neary, a stronger England XV got revenge over a troubled Australian team in January 1976, winning 23-6 at Twickenham. Yet this was followed by a second Five Nations whitewash in five years. England conceded 13 tries and managed a measly two in response. In the 13-12 loss to Ireland at Twickenham, England opted to kick a penalty in the final minute (which was successful), rather than go for a try to win the match. Years later Bill Beaumont spoke of how terrified England players were of making a mistake. He claimed backs would often just pass on the ball so that they were in no danger of making an error themselves. It summed up so much of what was wrong with the national set-up. The RFU's Alec Lewis (chairman of selectors) resigned at the end of the Championship.

GETTING GIDDY IN MID TABLE

The 1977 and 1978 seasons saw England reach the heady heights of third in the Five Nations (both campaigns saw wins over Ireland and Scotland). One key aspect of the relatively successful season of 1977 was consistency. England selected the same team for each Five Nations game.

1977 – England 26 Scotland 6 (Twickenham)

This Calcutta Cup win ranks as one of the few true Championship highlights for England in the 1970s. Tries came through captain and number eight Roger Uttley (Gosforth), winger Mike Slemen (Liverpool), centre and debutant Charles Kent (Rosslyn Park) and scrum-half (and also a new cap) Malcolm Young (Gosforth). The English pack bossed the Scottish around all afternoon and the result was the biggest win England had recorded over their oldest rivals.

1977 – Ireland 0 England 4 (Lansdowne Road)

This win, thanks to a try from fly-half Martin Cooper (Moseley) was England's first away win in the Championship in six years and the first over the Emerald Isle since 1971. It also marked the first occasion in 17 years that England had won both of their opening matches in the Five Nations. Many fans dared to hope something special was on the horizon, but a 4-3 home loss to France and a 14-9 defeat in Cardiff left England in the middle of the table.

NO MORE GOALS FROM MARK

For the 1977–78 season, it was no longer possible to score a goal from mark. England had only managed four in 345 games (the last coming in 1927) and conceded five.

1978 – England 6 New Zealand 16 (Twickenham)

Remarkably, this was the first New Zealand side to win all four of its internationals while touring the Home Unions. Led by the great Graham Mourie at flanker, the All Blacks were never in trouble. In fact, they were much criticised for their dour approach and lack of creativity. Some felt with a bit more adventure, Bill Beaumont's side would have been well and truly swept away.

1979 – Wales 27 England 3 (Cardiff Arms Park)

England stumbled into the final year of a terrible decade with a fourth-place finish in the 1979 Five Nations after a 7-7 draw with Scotland at home, a 12-7 loss in Dublin and a surprise 7-6 win at Twickenham over France. It meant that when England travelled to Cardiff for their final game they had a shot at the title. However, Wales, in the final year of a golden era (in the 1970s they won five outright titles, shared two more, claimed three Grand Slams and five Triple Crowns) dismantled

England. Wales ran in five tries while racking up their biggest winning margin over England since 1905.

THE END OF THE DECADE THAT SUCCESS FORGOT FINALLY COMES

1979 – England 9 New Zealand 10 (Twickenham)

The All Blacks returned to the UK for a short tour a year after their last one (an unusual occurrence for the time) and just managed to sneak past Bill Beaumont's England. It was a poor game and new cap Les Cusworth (Leicester) at fly-half was, not for the last time, criticised for the amount of ball he kicked away. England had a chance to steal it late on, but a penalty from full-back William 'Dusty' Hare was unsuccessful.

1970–79: THE STAR PLAYERS

ANDY RIPLEY

Club: Rosslyn Park
Position: Number eight
Caps: 24 (1972-76)
Points: 8 (2 tries)

Andy Ripley is one of the great characters and players in English rugby history. The *Daily Telegraph*'s Brendan Gallagher once wrote that Ripley had held or held the following roles in life: 'England No.8, author, church warden, triathlete, British Superstars champion, city banker, 400 metres hurdler, motorcycle enthusiast, British canoe instructor, lecturer at the Sorbonne and . . . youngest ever president of Rosslyn Park'.

Amazingly, Ripley did not play rugby until he was 18 and at university. A Liverpool-born man, he preferred football until taking up rugby. He was a product in many ways of the 'Swinging Sixties' and, with his long hair, far from a typical English rugby player. He loved travelling and undertook a 'hippie tour' of the USA and even visited places like Afghanistan. A man of contrasts, his day job was working as a chartered accountant.

At 195.58cm in height (6ft 5in), he was a towering, yet athletic presence in the rugby of the 1970s. He was a great sevens player and competed on the celebrity TV show Superstars, where his athletic prowess made him a household name. When Ripley was approached by Puma and Adidas to wear their boots he wore both — one on each foot!

Ripley wrote a successful rugby book but gave all the profits to charity. The great French flanker Jean-Pierre Rives said of Ripley that he was a 'great player' and that 'unlike many people he has never made the mistake of taking himself too seriously'.

DAVID DUCKHAM

Club: Coventry
Position: Centre, winger
Caps: 36 (1969–76)
(British Lions, 3 caps)
Points: 36 (10 tries)

David Duckham was a bright gem of creativity in a stodgy

era of English play. Originally a centre – he announced his arrival on the Test scene with a 40-yard score against Ireland – Duckham's reputation would be built mainly as a winger. Thanks to his wonderful side-step, pace and flair, Duckham even won over Welsh supporters who affectionately nicknamed him 'Dai' after his performance in the 1973 Barbarians match against New Zealand at Cardiff Arms Park (considered by some as the greatest game of all time). He wasn't just a graceful player either, he had a mean hand-off and wasn't shy of contact.

Born in Coventry, he remained loyal to his home town and played 12 years for his local club. Upon retirement he was the most capped England threequarter of all time. He was awarded an MBE and wrote a rugby biography he entitled *Dai for England*.

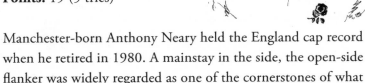

TONY NEARY
Club: Broughton Park
Position: Flanker
Caps: 43 (1971–80)
(British Lions, 1 cap)
Points: 19 (5 tries)

Manchester-born Anthony Neary held the England cap record when he retired in 1980. A mainstay in the side, the open-side flanker was widely regarded as one of the cornerstones of what little success England had in the 1970s. Neary played in the famous North Western Counties win over the All Blacks in 1972 and the Northern Division victory over the same opposition in 1979. He was also key to England's celebrated away wins over New Zealand and South Africa. While he had to endure a torrid time in the Five Nations for most of his career, he got to be part of England's 1980 Grand Slam in his final season in the white of England. Few fair-minded rugby folk begrudged him this long-awaited taste of European success.

Neary led England on seven occasions and toured twice with the British Lions. In 1998 he was jailed for stealing money from the trust fund of a friend.

JOHN PULLIN

Club: Bristol
Position: Hooker
Caps: 42 (1966–76)
(British Lions, 7 caps)
Points: 3 (1 try)

John Pullin is one of the true legends of English rugby and will be remembered for leading England to extraordinary wins over South Africa, New Zealand and Australia in just 18 months (only the latter game was at home). A farmer by profession (and nicknamed 'Piggy'), he was immensely strong and fit and a solid technical striker of the ball at scrum time. His training for rugby included running back and forth over the Severn Bridge.

Pullin played 298 times for Bristol and his 42 caps for England were a record for the time and included 36 consecutive appearances, which was also a record. Many of his fellow players felt he never had a bad game. Pullin beat New Zealand

THE EVOLUTION OF THE ENGLAND JERSEY

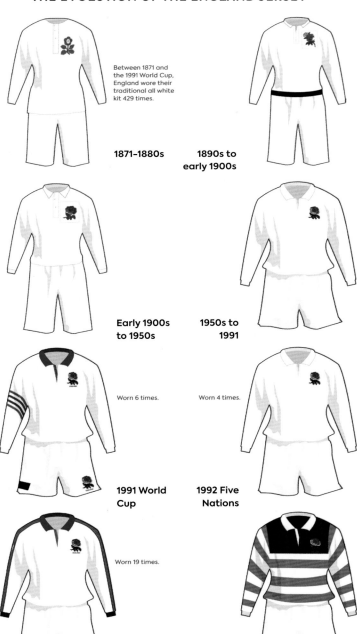

Between 1871 and the 1991 World Cup, England wore their traditional all white kit 429 times.

1871–1880s

1890s to early 1900s

Early 1900s to 1950s

1950s to 1991

Worn 6 times.

1991 World Cup

Worn 4 times.

1992 Five Nations

Worn 19 times.

1992 to 1995

1992 to 1996
(Change kit – not worn)

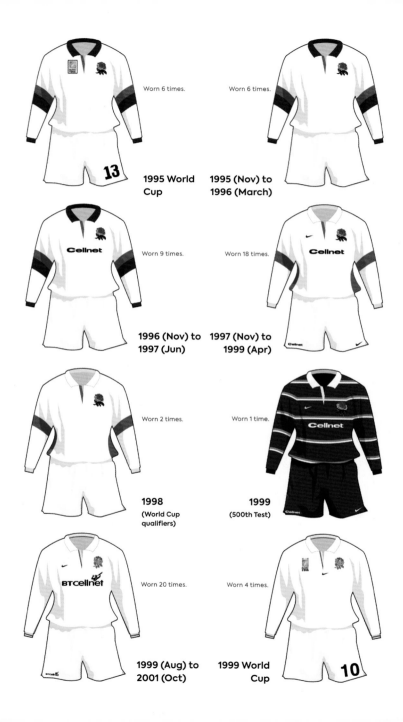

Worn 6 times.

1995 World Cup

Worn 6 times.

1995 (Nov) to 1996 (March)

Worn 9 times.

1996 (Nov) to 1997 (Jun)

Worn 18 times.

1997 (Nov) to 1999 (Apr)

Worn 2 times.

1998
(World Cup qualifiers)

Worn 1 time.

1999
(500th Test)

Worn 20 times.

1999 (Aug) to 2001 (Oct)

Worn 4 times.

1999 World Cup

Worn 1 time.

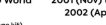

1999 World Cup
(Change kit)

Worn 8 times.

2001 (Nov) to 2002 (Apr)

Worn 12 times.

2002 (Jun) to 2003 (Aug)

Worn 39 times.

2003 (Aug) to 2007 (Jun)

2003 (Sep) to 2007 (Jun)
(Change kit – not worn)

Worn 7 times.

2003 World Cup

2003 World Cup
(Change kit – not worn)

Worn 19 times.

2007 (Aug) to 2009 (Jun)

Worn 2 times.

2007 (Aug) to 2009 (Jun) (Change kit)

Worn 7 times.

2007 World Cup

2007 World Cup (Change kit – not worn)

Worn 8 times.

2009 (Nov) to 2010 (Jun)

Worn 1 time.

2009 (Nov) v Argentina

Worn 1 time.

2010 v Wales (100th anniversary of Twickenham)

Worn 8 times.

2010 (Nov) v 2011 (Mar)

Worn 1 time.

2010 (Nov) v Australia

Worn 1 time.

2011 (Aug) v Wales

Worn 10 times.

2011 (Aug) to 2012 (Jun)

Worn 4 times.

2011 World Cup

Worn 1 time.

2011 World Cup
(Change kit)

Worn 8 times.

2012 (Nov) to 2013 (Mar)

Worn 3 times.

2012 (Nov) to 2013 (Jun)
(Change kit)

Worn 11 times.

2013 (Nov) to 2014 (Jun)

Worn 8 times.

2014 (Nov) to 2014 (Mar)

Worn 1 time.

2014 (Nov) v Samoa

Worn 12 times.

2015 (Aug) to 2016 (Jun)

2015 to 2016
(Change kit – not worn)

Worn 3 times.

2015 World Cup

Worn 1 time.

2015 World Cup
(Change kit)

Worn 7 times.

2016 (Nov) to 2017 (Mar)

Worn 4 times.

2016 (Nov) to 2017 (Jun)
(Change kit)

Worn 10 times.

2017 (Nov) to 2018 (Jun)

Worn 1 time.

2017 (Nov) v Argentina

Worn 8 times.

2018 (Nov) to 2019 (Mar)

Worn 1 time.

2018 (Nov) v Japan

Worn 7 times.

2019 (Jun) to 2020 (Mar)

Worn 1 time.

2019 (Sep) v Italy

Worn 4 times.

2019 World Cup

Worn 2 times.

2019 World Cup
(Change kit)

Worn 10 times.

2020 (Oct) to 2021 (Jul)

Worn 1 time.

2020 (Oct) v Georgia

Worn 1 time.

2021 (Feb) v Scotland

(150th anniversary)

Worn 10 times.

2021 (Nov) to 2022 (Jul)

Worn 1 time.

2021 (Nov) v Tonga

Worn 3 times to date.

2022 (Nov) –

Worn 1 time to date.

2022 (Nov) –

(Change kit)

playing for England, the Lions and the Barbarians. His after-dinner speeches were legendary and he wasn't afraid to upset officialdom when he had something to say.

1970–79 NOTABLE EVENTS IN ENGLISH HISTORY

• 1970: Eighteen-year-olds are allowed to vote in a general election for the first time.

• 1971: Margaret Thatcher (then education secretary) succeeds in her campaign to end free milk for schoolchildren over the age of seven (her government would later reduce the age again).

• 1972: The first official game by the England women's football team takes place.

• 1973: Women are now allowed to work on the London Stock Exchange.

• 1974: Ceefax is launched on BBC television. It is the world's first teletext information service.

• 1975: Forty-three people die in a Tube crash at Moorgate.

• 1976: Britain appoints its first female ambassador (Anita Roddick to Denmark).

• 1977: The England football team fail to qualify for the World Cup for the second successive time.

• 1978: Nicolae Ceaușescu, the notorious Romanian dictator, visits the UK and is made a Knight of the Order of the Bath. His wife is honoured by the Polytechnic of Central London.

• 1979: Margaret Thatcher becomes the first female prime minister.

1980–94: TWILIGHT OF THE AMATEURS

	PLAYED	WON	DRAWN	LOST
FIVE NATIONS	60	33	4	23
TESTS	29	18	1	10
WORLD CUP	10	6	0	4
TOTAL	99	57	5	37

Championships (3)

1980 (Grand Slam), 1991 (Grand Slam), 1992 (Grand Slam)

Shared Championships

None

World Cups

Quarter-final (1987), Runners-up (1991)

'It is never a great deal of fun attending a funeral and this was no exception as England rugby once again entered a state of mourning.'

BBC RUGBY SPECIAL ANNUAL ON ENGLAND'S 1987 WORLD CUP EXIT

YUPPIES AND POLL TAXES

The 1980s are now often associated with excess, wealth and the arrogance of 'yuppies' (yuppies were well-off, middle-class professionals obsessed with money and material goods). Yet the decade started with the impact of the recession of the 1970s still echoing on. The growing divide between rich and poor led to major polarisation in society, often within the same community or families.

Margaret Thatcher's hard-line approach to the trade unions (the 'enemy within') was praised and condemned depending on which side of the political fence you sat. The bitter battle between the establishment and striking miners in 1984–85 was one of the defining moments of the era, as those working in the coal industry tried to fight off colliery closures. Violent clashes between miners and the police tore communities apart and marked the beginning of the end of the coal industry in the UK. Thatcher also privatised many industries. When she left power in 1990, over 40 previously state-owned businesses had been handed over to private interests. Her introduction of the controversial Poll Tax in 1989 (a change in how people could be taxed by local authorities) further split public opinion and led to public rioting.

Thatcher also steered Britain into the Falklands War in 1982, defending two territories in the South Atlantic from Argentina. The rights and wrongs of this were fiercely debated and many felt British soldiers died and suffered injuries in a needless conflict, while others felt it showed Britain was still a major global power.

Thatcher was kicked out by her own ruthless party in 1990 as her popularity plunged, but even then Labour couldn't take advantage and in 1992 the Conservatives won another election with John Major at the helm.

The 1980s is famous for its often bombastic music (as often wonderful as it was ridiculous). Major English acts included bands like the Cure, Dire Straits, Wham!, Duran Duran, New

Order and The Smiths. Home computers became affordable for many and computers such as the Amstrad 464, Commodore 64 and ZX Spectrum (all with games loaded via cassette tape) transformed the social habits of children and teenagers forever. By the 1990s consoles were all the rage and Sega and Nintendo, with Sonic the Hedgehog and Mario at the forefront, battled to become the most popular devices.

On the rugby field, though, the decade began with elation as England claimed their first Grand Slam since 1957. But after the champagne had worn off, England regressed to mediocrity for most of the 1980s, until a young centre named Will Carling arrived on the scene and took a core of quality, dedicated players to continued Five Nations success and, almost, to the top of the world too.

THE WAIT IS OVER
1980 GRAND SLAM

Second row Bill Beaumont was captain and Mike Davis (former England second row) the man in the coaching tracksuit when England put the sorrows of the 1970s behind them with a first Grand Slam since 1957. Davis was a brave call as coach from the RFU. A hugely successful schools coach, he had not operated at senior level before. Despite the English players initially having reservations over his appointment, he was a breath of fresh air for the national set-up and soon proved he was worth his weight in gold.

After the narrow loss to the All Blacks in late 1979, the England team asked for more squad sessions. Not only did

Davis agree, he made them intense affairs and even invited the public to attend, figuring it was good for the players to get used to being under the public gaze when performing.

MATCH ONE: England 24 Ireland 9 (Twickenham)

As if the 1970s had never happened, a rejuvenated England burst out of the blocks in the 1980s with a big win over Ireland. This England team had a tough, powerful pack including a formidable front row of Fran Cotton, Peter Wheeler (Leicester) and Phil Blakeway (Gloucester). Tony Neary, Roger Uttley and John Scott (Cardiff) forged a quality back row and with Dusty Hare at full-back (who still holds the record for total career points in rugby with 7,337), England had a constant threat with the boot. England scored three tries in this opening fixture of the Championship. John Scott, scrum-half Steve Smith (Sale) and winger Mike Slemen were the men who crossed the whitewash for points. Future England coach Clive Woodward (Leicester) made his debut in this match, coming on as a replacement.

Blazers show their man management ability

After the win over Ireland, England's second row Nigel Horton (who was in for the injured Maurice Colclough) was enjoying a drink with his wife, teammates and opposing players. Suddenly, he got a tap on the shoulder. It was from an RFU selector who told him he had been dropped for the next match. Charming. Horton never added to his 20 caps.

MATCH TWO: France 13 England 17 (Parc des Princes)

England's impressive forwards took the visitors to a first win in Paris since 1964. It wasn't just raw power Beaumont and his pack were praised for, but their ability in the loose too. Despite conceding a try in just two minutes, England kept their cool to take control for large parts of the match and wear the French down. Both sides grabbed two tries, with England's coming through winger John Carleton (Orrell) and centre Nick Preston (Richmond). As well as a Dusty Hare penalty, England slotted two drop goals thanks to the boot of outside-half John Horton (Bath). Suddenly, there was genuine hope that something special was happening.

MATCH THREE: England 9 Wales 8 (Twickenham)

Ahead of the 1980 Championship, England had only beaten Wales once since 1963 (they had managed draws in 1964 and 1968 at Twickenham). It seemed at times the men in white would never get the Welsh monkey off their back. Wales came to Twickenham with lots of media talk about rough play, especially concerning players like flanker Paul Ringer. After both teams had been told off by the referee for fighting, Ringer hit England's John Horton high and late in the 14th minute and was sent off. It was the first time an international player had been sent off at Twickenham since New Zealand's Cyril Brownlie in 1925.

Despite being a man short, Wales outscored England two tries to none. And although they missed five penalties, Wales led 8-6 with just minutes remaining. It seemed to English fans that the barren run against the Welsh was set to continue. But a last-gasp penalty from Dusty Hare not only helped England take the glory on the day, it set them up for a Grand Slam and Triple Crown opportunity in Edinburgh. It may have been ugly and a little fortunate, but a win was a win.

Telegraphing a win

England's master kicker Dusty Hare never had a kicking coach. He used to practise his goal kicking by aiming at a telegraph pole in a field on his family farm.

MATCH FOUR: Scotland 18 England 30 (Murrayfield)

England claimed their long-awaited Grand Slam in some style, with both sides praised by the press for their performances. The visitors came storming out of the blocks, with Clive Woodward in particular shining as England quickly racked up a 16-point lead after half an hour. John Carleton claimed a hat-trick (the first English player to do so since 1924) and Mike Slemen and Steve Smith bagged the other tries, with Dusty Hare slotting two conversions and two penalties. The tries may have come from backs, but the donkey work was done by a fine pack. It was noted by coach Mike Davis that the forwards for this Championship contained six players who had captained England.

Scotland had a late, exciting rally, but, as *The Times* wrote, 'England held out and the sound of no side, blown by an excellent French referee, must have been sweetness to the ear.' Bill Beaumont was chaired off the pitch and can probably thank his team's winning of the Grand Slam for him getting the *A Question of Sport* gig on the BBC years later.

This was to be a fitting Championship send-off for Tony Neary and Roger Uttley, two consistent and excellent servants to England through troubled times.

*John Scott was criticised for lifting the ball
above his head after scoring a try.*

CAESAR PLAYS TO THE MOB OF TWICKERS!

In the 1980 win over Ireland, England number eight John Scott scored his first (and only) try for his country. He raised the ball above his head in celebration. The RFU was not happy at this display of emotion, neither was rugby correspondent John West of *The Times*, who wrote:

I concede that Scott has special reason to be pleased, because it was the first try he has scored for his country. But he struck a gladiatorial pose, ball held aloft in his hand, like some Caesar back from the wars taking his plaudits from the populace. I hope he will consider, on reflection, that he was not just failing to conform to the ethos aforesaid but encouraging every impressionable young player who was watching, whether at Twickenham or through the eyes of television, to believe that this was acceptable behaviour. Things were not much more appealing at Cardiff where one of the Welsh scorers, Graham Price, momentarily raised a clenched fist; David Richards had a colleague jumping on to his back after scoring, and every try was celebrated with sufficient song and dance to suggest that it may not be so very long before Rugby Special *begins to look like a poor man's* Match of the Day.

IF THE CAP FITS

England followed their 1980 Grand Slam with a disappointing second-place finish in 1981, winning just two games – Scotland (23-17) and Ireland (10-6).

Meanwhile, in 1981 it was announced by the International Board that its members may 'accord full international status to matches with other countries whose sustained quality of play obviously justifies it'. The RFU's Micky Steele-Bodger used the opportunity to suggest that caps therefore could be awarded for England's Test series in Argentina in the coming summer. It was the beginning of a major, if slow, shift in the global rugby community about what Test rugby could be.

1981 SUMMER TOUR

England undertook a seven-match trip to Argentina, becoming the first of the Home Unions to visit the country (England's plan to tour in 1973 had to be abandoned due to terror threats). The tourists remained undefeated, with five wins over club or regional outfits, one Test win and one Test draw.

1st Test: Argentina 19 England 19 (Ferro Carril Oeste Stadium, Buenos Aires)

This was the first time an International Board country awarded caps against a non-member. The Pumas made the most of their elevated status and almost claimed a famous win in the Buenos Aires sunshine. The home side were impressive and led for most of the game. England trailed by six points with five minutes left and it took a late Clive Woodward try (his second) to spare England's blushes.

2nd Test: Argentina 6 England 12 (Ferro Carril Oeste Stadium)

Captain Bill Beaumont ranks this win as his best in an England shirt outside of the Grand Slam triumph. On a drizzly day, England had to dig deep to conjure up the goods in an often brutal match and claim the series. Fly-half Huw Davies (Cambridge University) bagged the only English try and the trusty Dusty Hare added the extras, along with two penalties. Still, the great Argentinian outside-half Hugo Porta captained his men well and they almost stole a try at the death, but in the slippery conditions the ball got away from Argentina's winger and Beaumont's men claimed the win.

FAREWELL TO BILLY

After leading England to a win at Twickenham over Australia (15-11) and a draw with Scotland (9-9) in the opening Five Nations match of 1982, Bill Beaumont was forced to retire aged just 29 due to repeated concussions. He had won 34 caps (33 of them consecutively), a then record for an English lock, and led England 21 times (also a record at the time). In his absence England finished joint second in the Championship, with Ireland winning their first title since 1974 and their first Triple Crown since 1949.

SMART CELEBRATIONS

After a somewhat unexpected win in Paris (27-15) in 1982, one of the most notorious pranks in rugby history took place. In the post-match function, gift bottles of aftershave were left on the players' tables. England second row Maurice Colclough (Angoulême) decided to play a cruel prank on prop Colin

Smart (Newport). Colclough secretly emptied his bottle and filled it with wine and then drank it in front of everyone, pretending it was aftershave. Smart, no doubt wanting to show he too was game for a laugh, subsequently downed his bottle of the real stuff. He had to be rushed to hospital and have his stomach pumped. Teammate Steve Smith later said that Colin had been in a bad way but that his breath 'smelt lovely'.

BAD TIMES ARE HERE AGAIN

Just three seasons after Grand Slam glory, England were back on the bottom of the table. The 1983 Championship saw England manage nothing more impressive than a 13-13 draw in Cardiff. Which was, at least, their best result in the Welsh capital since 1963. England would finish in the bottom two of the Five Nations every year between 1983 and 1987. After the 1983 campaign, departing coach Mike Davis remarked: 'I have turned wine into water.'

BUZBY DISHES OUT THE CASH

The 1983 clash with Wales was the first Home Union international to be sponsored, with British Telecom paying to be associated with it. It was such a poor game that newspapers mentioned hardly any fans even bothered invading the pitch at the end (it was common for mass pitch invasions in Cardiff at the time).

TAKING NOTES FOR FUTURE REFERENCE

Clive Woodward has often spoken of how poor he thought the preparation of England was in the 1980s. He once said that the 'environment of England was wrong. It didn't challenge us as players. It didn't give us the preparation we needed . . . the coaches insisted on a style from the Stone Age, focusing almost exclusively on forward play.' He also admitted that he failed to understand why winning a Grand Slam should have been so hard, saying: 'We had an amazing team, a mighty forward pack and many of them had been around for years. Why had winning a Grand Slam taken so long? It really wasn't that difficult.'

THE ALL BLACKS FALL AGAIN IN LONDON
1983 – England 15 New Zealand 9 (Twickenham)

England notched up their third win in 12 games over the All Blacks and the second London win since 1936. The match was part of a short eight-match programme for the tourists in England and Scotland. New Zealand's only other Test was with Scotland and it ended 25-25, which to this day is the best result (along with the 1925 tie) the Scots have ever had in the series. Hooker Peter Wheeler (Leicester) captained England for the first time and his team were coached by Dick Greenwood. It was an ill-disciplined game and multiple England players needed stitches to keep playing on.

England's only try came from second row Maurice Colclough who worked his way over from a line-out yards from the Kiwi line after good work from his pack. It was his only Test try. Dusty Hare kicked the extras and added three penalties as well. Making his debut at loose-head prop was Colin White (Gosforth). He was 34 years old and had lost three of his fingers five years previously in a work accident.

After the win, English supporters once again raised their hopes that another successful era was fast approaching. They would have to wait.

REVERSION TO THE NORM
1984 – Scotland 18 England 6 (Murrayfield)

With New Zealand freshly defeated, what did England go on to do in their next game? Lose 18-6 to Scotland at Murrayfield. This was the 100th meeting between the two sides and it was a painful one for the English pack who had no answer to the home side's power and control. England's Dusty Hare kicked his 50th penalty in this game, the first Englishman to reach such a figure. England would finish fourth in the Championship, with only a narrow win at home over Ireland (12-9) to keep them off the bottom.

ANOTHER TOUR TO APARTHEID SOUTH AFRICA

Despite condemnation from the British government, leading exiles from South Africa, the World Council of Churches and countless political and social groups in the UK and around the world, the RFU voted in large numbers to tour South Africa in 1984. In a statement that would have been laughable (if it were not so tragic), the RFU said it hoped that by retaining contact with the Springboks, it would encourage further reform in the nation.

While England had to travel with several top players unavailable, only a couple refused to tour on moral grounds. Ralph Knibbs, a highly rated Bristol centre, had the opportunity to become the first black player to be capped since James Peters in 1908. He phoned the South African embassy after he was selected for the tour and was told he would be an 'honorary white person' while with England so he would be permitted to go into hotels with his teammates. Knibbs was also advised to have a bodyguard to avoid being shot if he was to leave the main party and be somewhere alone. Taking his mother's advice to be true to himself, Knibbs declined to tour. He didn't feel it was the right thing to do on a moral level. Sadly, he never played for England at senior level.

In his book *Endless Winter*, rugby writer Stephen Jones wrote of an incident involving one RFU committee man that sums up the ignorance that existed about the awful state of affairs in South Africa. Arriving late on tour, the blazer met with the English touring party on the train and said: 'Do you know something? I believe the problems of South Africa have been exaggerated. When we came down . . . we waved at blacks in the fields and they all waved back. They seemed happy enough.'

England had 18 senior players unavailable for the seven-match tour (which included two Tests). Of the five non-international games, England won four and drew one. The Tests, however, were grim affairs, with England suffering two heavy defeats. It's more than arguable, however, that the 33-15 and 35-9 defeats were far less shameful than the decision to tour

*England did little good for the reputation
of rugby by travelling to South Africa.*

itself. One England player, flanker Chris Butcher (Harlequins),
enjoyed the country so much he moved there not long after.

A LONG WINTER

England played eight Tests in the 1984–85 season: two touring
games against Australia and Romania, four in the Five Nations
and two internationals in the seven-match tour to New
Zealand. It was a poor year with just two wins and a draw in
England's credit column and a fourth-place finish in the Five
Nations. Here are a few highlights from the season.

1984 – England 3 Australia 19 (Twickenham)

Hot on the heels of the whitewash in South Africa, England

suffered what was then their worst defeat to the Wallabies and also their worst result at HQ since the war. England had five new caps, including both half-backs. Scrum-half Nigel Melville (Wasps) was also captain, the first man since 1947 to lead England on his debut (when Joe Mycock captained that 1947 side, he was one of 14 new caps in an England team playing its first game since the war). Stuart Barnes (Bristol) was the new fly-half. However, the success of the man who would occupy the number ten shirt in the next match with Romania would limit his career with England.

1985 – England 22 Romania 15 (Twickenham)

Debutant outside-half Rob Andrew (Cambridge University) scored a record 18 points on his debut against a strong, if limited, Romanian side. Andrew received the ball from the kick-off and launched a thrilling attack that ended in the Romanian 22. From the line-out he kicked a sweet drop goal, just 45 seconds into his first start. He added another later and landed four penalties. Another debutant, winger Simon Smith (Wasps) got the only try of the match. Rob Andrew would go on to become the main source of England's points until his final cap in 1997.

The Romanian team of this era, made up largely of military personnel, were a tough proposition. They had recently beaten Wales and Scotland, drawn with Ireland, had regularly beaten France and even scared New Zealand.

1985 Five Nations

This was another poor year for England, whose only success

was a 9-9 draw with France and a 10-7 win over Scotland, both at home. Other than a try from winger Rory Underwood (RAF/Leicester), all England's points came from the same pair who scored in the Romanian game: Rob Andrew and Simon Smith. Andrew racked up 50 points in his first five caps and Smith had three tries after just five caps (although he never scored again in his final four caps). Underwood, a pilot with the RAF, would also become one of the key figures in England's attack in the following decade.

THE CALENDAR BEGINS TO MUSHROOM

The six games England played between November 1984 and April 1985 were the most they had played in a single domestic season (this does not include summer tours). The higher fixture count was a hint of the changes that were to come and the arrival of the first World Cup in 1987 was to transform the length and intensity of fixture lists forever.

OUT OF THE WOODS AND INTO THE GREEN

England travelled to New Zealand in the summer of 1985 with a new coach, Martin Green, as Dick Greenwood was no longer able to give enough time to the team due to employment commitments. Green was assisted by Brian Ashton, who would become head coach 21 years later. England were led by Paul Dodge (Leicester), a centre who, with 30 caps to his name before the tour, was one of the more experienced players to travel. The tourists won four of their five non-Test matches, only falling to Auckland (who had won 15 straight games against touring teams).

FROM BLACK TO WHITE

Among the six uncapped players named for the tour to New Zealand was Jamie Salmon (Harlequins). The centre had previously won three caps for the All Blacks. His appearance in the first Test made him the first player to play for both England and New Zealand.

1st Test: New Zealand 18 England 13 (Lancaster Park, Christchurch)

England led at half-time thanks to tries from number eight Mike Teague (Gloucester) and new cap and winger Mike Harrison (Wakefield). Stuart Barnes at fly-half added a conversion and a penalty goal. Despite the two tries, England ultimately lost to six penalty goals from All Black full-back Kieran Crowley. England full-back Huw Davies (Wasps) became the very first English player to get capped in three different positions after previously starting at outside-half and centre.

2nd Test: New Zealand 42 England 15 (Athletic Park, Wellington)

Both teams named the same line-ups and even the man with the whistle was the same as the previous week. Yet that was about all that was similar to the first Test as England were humiliated in an often ill-tempered affair. Stuart Barnes said it was one of the most violent matches he had ever played in.

Despite a try from flanker John Hall (Bath) after two minutes, the men in white succumbed to what was then their worst defeat ever (biggest losing margin and highest score conceded). In all, the All Blacks grabbed six tries to the tourists' two. Mike Harrison got his second interception try in two weeks and was nicknamed 'Burglar Bill' by the TV commentator.

ALWAYS THE BRIDESMAID

With today's packed international fixture lists and rotating squad system, the vast majority of players who spend time in the national squad will likely pick up a handful of caps, even if they are nowhere near first choice. Spare a thought then for players like Andy Simpson (Sale). The unlucky hooker sat on the bench 18 times for England and was never capped. Worst of all, one of the non-cap games he played in was against Italy and Italy awarded caps to their players!

1986 – Scotland 33 England 6 (Murrayfield)

England finished joint third in the 1986 Five Nations, with Twickenham wins over Wales (21-18, with all points from the boot of Rob Andrew) and Ireland (25-20). However, they were utterly taken apart north of the border by their oldest rivals. England were so poor that many felt the scoreline flattered the visitors. The second half saw the Scots claim 21 unanswered points and to this day this is Scotland's biggest win in the history of the fixture. England conceded 100 points in the tournament for the first time ever.

THE FIRST PENALTY TRY

In the 1986 win over Ireland, England were awarded a penalty try by Clive Norling (Wales) for Ireland kicking the ball out of a scrum as the English were approaching the try line. It was the first penalty try ever in an England Test.

1986 – England XV 39 Japan 12 (Twickenham)

At half-time in this non-capped match the visitors led 12-6. England recovered and got three late tries to end with a flattering winning score. But the fact a 'minnow' like Japan could cause England such problems at HQ was a sign that the rugby world order was beginning to evolve, even if the fact caps weren't awarded here was another sign the pace of change was glacial.

POOR SHOW IN EUROPE BEFORE
FIRST GLOBAL JAMBOREE

Ahead of the first ever Rugby World Cup, England finished joint bottom with Wales in the Five Nations. After a 17-0 thrashing in Dublin (their worst loss to Ireland in 40 years), England lost to France, Wales (see below) and ended with a 21-12 win over Scotland at home. Around this time, Tony McNab, a fitness coach who had worked with legendary Olympian Daley Thompson, came in to do some conditioning work with the England squad. He was horrified at what he saw and set a summer fitness programme for players to follow.

THE BATTLE OF CARDIFF
1987 – Wales 19 England 12 (Cardiff Arms Park)

England's loss to Wales in Cardiff in 1987 easily ranks among the low points when compiling a history of the national team. Fed up with continually being bullied on Welsh soil and not having won in the Welsh capital since 1963, England decided that they would no longer be intimidated in the cauldron of Cardiff Arms Park. It was a game so violent that the RFU banned four English players afterwards.

Before the game, scrum-half and captain Richard Hill (Bath) gave a speech so fiery and inflammatory to his charges that reserve hooker Brian Moore later said it was 'almost ludicrous'. Fired up and ready to rumble, England were looking to set down a marker and in the first minute came the first punch-up. Moments later it kicked off again and amid a flurry of punches, England second row (and police officer) Wade Dooley (Preston Grasshoppers) swung a punch that connected so well it fractured the cheekbone of Welsh number eight Phil Davies. In the days afterwards it was asked by several in the media how a police officer could get away with an assault that he would arrest someone for if he saw it on the street. In the sludge and damp of Cardiff, the game continued in a similar fashion. And while Wales were no angels, even the English media laid the brunt of the blame on the visitors. In the end, the tough-guy tactics didn't even work as Wales, inspired by their half-backs, Robert Jones and Jonathan Davies, once again triumphed in Cardiff. Rory Underwood was one of the players who made a mistake that led to the Welsh try. He was to have many unhappy days in Cardiff, being involved in key scores for Wales in the losses in 1989 and 1993 too.

The RFU were under huge pressure to take action and in response banned Richard Hill, hooker Graham Dawes (Bath), prop Gareth Chilcott (Bath) and Wade Dooley. Shortly after the game, RFU secretary Dudley Wood spoke about the relationship between Wales and England, saying: 'Our relationship is based on trust and understanding . . . they don't trust us and we don't understand them.'

THE RED ROSES ARE BORN

1987 – Wales Women 4 England Women 22 (Pontypool Park, Pontypool)

On 5 April 1987, the first international match for the England and Wales women's teams took place in Pontypool. England were led by back rower Carol Isherwood and it was a historical moment for women's sport in Britain. Isherwood had also captained Great Britain in 1986 against France. Isherwood was a key figure in the founding of the women's game and was later inducted into the World Rugby Hall of Fame.

1987 WORLD CUP (NEW ZEALAND & AUSTRALIA)

Today, the World Cup is seen as the pinnacle of the sport. Back in 1987, it was opposed by as many as it was welcomed by. All the Home Unions were against the idea (as was the body that is now World Rugby). The traditionalists feared it would lead to professionalism. The tournament hung in the balance to the very last moment, with constant talk of it being cancelled or some teams not attending. Early in the year, the RFU refused to allow the World Cup mascot, Mr Drop, to appear on the field at Twickenham on matchday.

Any worries that England would be tainted by anything close to professionalism in the first World Cup soon faded away. Many of the English players treated the World Cup like a glorified end of season tour and drank the corresponding amount of beer for such a trip. Number eight Dean Richards (Leicester) said that the squad had 'a hell of a party'.

South Africa did not take part as they were still rightly ostracised due to the apartheid regime, leaving New Zealand to win on home soil at a relative canter.

Captain: Mike Harrison

Coach: Martin Green

POOL GAMES

Australia 19 England 6 (Concord Oval, Sydney)

Many had Australia, not New Zealand, as favourites for the tournament, and England's performance was described as 'heartening'. While there was little doubt the hosts were the better side, the Wallabies got one try through David Campese that was such a 'non-try' the winger was too embarrassed to celebrate. In reaching out to touch down, Campese lost control on the knee of outside-half Peter Williams (Orrell) (which was about a foot from the ground). Frustrated, Campese buried his head in the grass only for the referee to award a try. England were praised afterwards for not bringing the incident up in the post-match interviews. The men in white lost first choice full-back Marcus Rose in the opening ten minutes to concussion. His replacement, Jon Webb, was taken by surprise as at the time of the injury he was sitting down with a chocolate éclair in his mouth.

England 60 Japan 7 (Concord Oval)

England banked ten tries against Japan in the first capped match between the nations. Captain and winger Mike Harrison grabbed a hat-trick.

England 34 USA 6 (Concord Oval)

This was also a first capped match between the two nations. England scored four tries, flanker Peter Winterbottom claiming half of them.

QUARTER-FINAL

England 3 Wales 16 (Ballymore, Brisbane)

This quarter-final horrified and bored the rugby world in equal measure. Wales outscored England three tries to nil in a match that was widely agreed to be the worst of the tournament. Former England captain Bill Beaumont wrote: 'Almost by tradition [Wales's] presence on the same field . . . seemed to paralyse England.' Wales ruled the roost in the scrums, the line-outs and the thinking department as the Welsh half-backs manipulated the game. It was the final match in charge for coach Martin Green. Afterwards he said, 'I wish the Scots and Irish luck in the cup, but I am afraid I cannot say the same to the Welsh.'

Dean Richards revealed that England's preparations for the game took place in an area with no rugby fields and included scuba diving, waterskiing, tennis and golf.

*England didn't take the best approach to
trying to conquer the world in 1987.*

DREAM BIG

England may not have set the world alive in the first World Cup, but the tournament did spark inspiration in a little boy back home who would later take England to the top of the world. One eight-year-old boy was so thrilled by the tournament he wrote down a series of personal goals in a notebook of his. These included playing for England, captaining them, kicking for them and winning a World Cup. The boy's name? Jonny Wilkinson.

A NEW DAWN (SLOWLY) RISES

Geoff Cooke was appointed to coach England after the 1987 World Cup. Described as being as comfortable in a tracksuit as he was dealing with officialdom, Cooke played a huge role in breaking down some of the conflict between the playing squad and the blazers on the committee of the RFU. As Cooke saw his strength training and developing the backs, he brought in former England back rower Roger Uttley to lead the forwards. The pair recognised they had a huge task to undertake that involved trying to change the very culture that not only seemed to run through English rugby, but English society in general. Brian Moore wrote of this trait in his award-winning autobiography, saying that 'anyone who approached his task with anything approaching dedication was viewed with suspicion. If you publicly avowed such dedication you were the object of ridicule . . . It has never been the English way to publicly show dedication. Far better to embrace the cult of the amateur: try your hardest, but never take a professional approach.'

THE SWING LOW YEARS BEGIN

The 1988 Five Nations was not spectacular for England, but at least England put together two wins, beating Scotland at Murrayfield (9-6) and Ireland at home (35-3). There were small signs the Cooke era may well take England up a level.

1988 – France 10 England 9 (Parc des Princes)

Future England captain and key figure for the Cooke years, Will Carling (Harlequins), made his debut in the centre as England took the World Cup finalists to the wire in Paris. England's back row were impressive, most notably England legend and openside Peter Winterbottom (Headingley) and new cap and blindside Mickey Skinner (Harlequins). England were unable to build on this in the next game as they fell 11-3 to Wales at Twickenham.

FANCY A GAME OF CALCUTTA CUP BALL?

After England's Calcutta Cup win in Edinburgh, two opposing players took it upon themselves to take the historical trophy out for a kickabout . . . literally. England's Dean Richards (who was a policeman) and Scotland's John Jeffrey removed the cup from the post-match function and proceeded to play rugby with it in the street. Some say it was kicked like a football, others that it was dropped. Either way, it suffered a fair bit of damage. Richards was banned for a game by the RFU and Jeffrey for six months by the SRU.

SWEET CHARIOT

1988 – England 35 Ireland 3 (Twickenham)

This game has become a key moment in English rugby history. England had not scored a try in their first three Championship games and when they went 3-0 down at half-time, it didn't seem likely their try drought was going to end. Even worse, captain Nigel Melville suffered a dislocated ankle.

In one of the biggest turnarounds in Five Nations history, England scored six second-half tries and 35 unanswered points to blast Ireland out of contention. Three of those tries came from winger and new cap Chris Oti (Cambridge University). Oti was the first black player to play for England since James Peters 80 years earlier. In response to this remarkable debut, the crowd began singing 'Swing Low, Sweet Chariot', an African-American spiritual song with strong links to slavery. Until 2020, it was generally believed this was the first time this had been sung at Twickenham. However, World Rugby Museum historian Phil McGowan discovered a video that revealed it had been sung in 1987 at the Middlesex Sevens (an annual club sevens tournament) when another black winger (and future rugby league star), Martin Offiah played some spectacular rugby. Even Offiah did not realise he had inspired the first singing of the song at HQ. It is thought the song was chosen as Offiah's nickname was Chariots. Why was that his nickname? Because his surname, when pronounced badly by commentators, sounded like 'of fire' (as in *Chariots of Fire*, the famous Olympic movie).

The song would go on to become the only song sung by

England fans during games (excluding the singalong that happens with the tragic music played on the PA after games) and become a key part of England marketing campaigns. However, over time, use of the song and its origins in rugby became increasingly controversial (see page 391 for more on this).

THE COOKE AND CARLING ERA BEGINS

After the Five Nations, England played Ireland in the 'Dublin Millennium' celebrations to mark the city's 1,000th year (England won 21-10) before heading out on a nine-match tour to Australia and Fiji. England lost both Tests against the Wallabies, but beat Fiji in Suva (25-12) in what was the first capped match between the nations.

Coach Geoff Cooke had made some major progress in laying the foundations for a stronger national set-up. In particular he had managed to reduce the selection panel from the unwieldy seven it had been and clipped it down to just three (including his manager Roger Uttley). Alongside implementing better training and preparation, Cooke was starting to see success in introducing a smarter brand of rugby. While there were to be a few hiccups along the way in 1989 and 1990, the building bricks for what was going to be a major period of success were being put firmly in place.

Cooke's decision to make Will Carling captain was not greeted with universal acclaim at the time. The appointment was a bolt out of the blue for everyone. When Cooke rang the Harlequins centre to appoint him captain, Carling thought he was getting dropped. Aged just 22, there had been no younger captain of the national side for 57 years (Peter Howard in 1931). It turned out to be a master stroke.

Early on in his reign, Cooke told his squad: 'If you just want to be failures and under-achievers, just carry on as you are going. But if you want to be part of a successful England team you have to get thinking of yourselves as international athletes, as the elite of your sport, and not traditional players.'

Will Carling would lead England through one of its most celebrated eras.

1988 – England 28 Australia 19 (Twickenham)

Will Carling's first match as captain could scarcely have gone any better. A vintage performance and a convincing win over a team they had lost to twice that summer delighted the home crowd who were beginning to believe England had turned a corner. Carling's men even played some wonderful running rugby, something that had not been seen too often at Twickenham in the previous few years. Rory Underwood scored twice, making it six consecutive games in which he had crossed the line.

CARDIFF ARMS GRAVEYARD

1989 – Wales 12 England 9 (Cardiff Arms Park)

A dreadful Wales team looked set for a first ever Five Nations whitewash and England arrived with high expectations of finally winning over the Severn Bridge for the first time since 1963. England had drawn with Scotland (12-12), beaten Ireland (16-3) and defeated the French (11-0). It meant they turned up in Cardiff with a chance to win the title for the first time since 1980 (or at least share it). But once again, Cardiff was the graveyard of English dreams.

From the opening kick-off England lost flanker Mike Teague to a vicious elbow and it was soon clear they were not going to have things all their own way. They were kicked around the park by Wales's Robert Jones and bossed in the line-out by Bob Norster. Jon Webb and Rory Underwood had shockers in defence and under the high ball. A scrambled try after a dreadful loose pass from Underwood allowed Wales to claim the only try. It meant the long wait for a win in Cardiff and a Championship title would have to go on.

England's scrum-half Dewi Morris (Liverpool/St Helens), sang both national anthems at Cardiff. Morris was born and raised in Wales to a Welsh father and English mother. He revealed years later he received lots of abuse from Welsh supporters who resented him choosing to play for England. 'Sometimes I wish I had been known by the first name of Colin,' he admitted. 'I'm sure, if I'd have been called Colin rather than Dewi there would have been a lot less focus on my Welsh family and we wouldn't have had the same level of abuse.'

TRYING TIMES WITH DRAGONS

Rugby historian Huw Richards has noted that in 11 meetings with Wales in the 1980s, England scored a grand total of just five tries. None of these tries came after 1984 either. On the other side of the ledger, Wales logged 16.

ONE STEP FORWARD . . .

After big wins away to Romania (58-3) and at home to Fiji (58-23), England entered the 1990 Five Nations as legitimate contenders. England's pack was beginning to harden with some serious talent who were a handful for any team from north or south of the equator. It was made up of players like Brian Moore, second rows Paul Ackford (Harlequins) and Wade Dooley, and back rowers like Peter Winterbottom, Mike Teague and Dean Richards. Will Carling and Jeremy Guscott

(Bath) were a fine centre partnership who provided plenty of opportunity for the deadly finisher that was Rory Underwood. Guscott scored six tries in his first four caps, so Underwood wasn't the only potent scorer in the side either. In full-back Simon Hodgkinson (Nottingham) and fly-half Rob Andrew, England had a pair of deadly marksmen to punish teams that conceded penalties under the pressure their forwards were able to create. Many tipped England for the Championship and Grand Slam in 1990.

1990 – England 34 Wales 6 (Twickenham)
England dispatched Ireland 23-0 at home and comprehensively dismantled France 26-7 in Paris (the biggest winning margin over the French in 74 years) in their opening games of the 1990 Five Nations. This triumph over Wales, however, was a major turning point in the series between the nations. Since 1964 England had only won four of 27 matches between the sides (with three draws occurring too). After this four-try dismantling of an abject Welsh side, England would dominate the fixture until 2005. Wales would only win in 1993 and 1999 during this period. At the time this was England's biggest ever score and winning margin over Wales and Welsh coach John Ryan was forced to step down in response. The victory made England overwhelming favourites for the final game with Scotland.

THE SLOW WALK
1990 – Scotland 13 England 7 (Murrayfield)
Never before had two Home Union sides met in the final

match of the Championship with a Grand Slam on the line for both sides. The game has gone down in tournament folklore. An intense and biting atmosphere greeted the visitors with the home side determined to bring down their cocky Auld Enemy. Scottish captain David Sole walked his team out (generally teams ran out back then) into a fiery cauldron of Scottish nationalism, inflamed in part it is said by a resentment towards Margaret Thatcher's government (a symbol of England, not Britain, to Scots) and policies they saw as being unfair to Scottish people, such as the trialling of the hated Poll Tax. Jeremy Guscott wrote that games against Scotland in this period became a 'nastier experience'.

As soon as the match kicked off, it became clear that Sole's men had no intention of letting the script laid out earlier in the week by English journalists play out. In the second half, Tony Stanger gathered a kick by Gavin Hastings to score perhaps the most famous try in Scottish history and drive a killer nail into English hopes.

The loss was a key turning point in the Cooke/Carling era and several players identified it as the moment England decided to tighten up and play a far more focused power game with emphasis on strangling the life out of opponents rather than playing a more complete 15-man game. Guscott later wrote in his autobiography: 'That was the end of an era . . . England teams came to value victory over everything from that point on and performance and style became secondary considerations. We could beat teams through the power of our forwards so why worry about anything else? Why concern yourself about the development of the game when the only thing that meant anything was winning? It was a powerful argument at the time and one I bought into . . . England became cussed and determined. They did occasionally break free, but only for the blinkers to come on as soon as defeat loomed.'

Carling admitted English arrogance had 'come back to bite us' and ranked the loss as even worse than the 1991 World Cup final.

SAVAGED BY PUMAS

England, with eight senior players unavailable due to personal and work commitments, undertook an unhappy seven-game summer tour to Argentina in 1990. It was a tense trip in many ways as this was the first English side to play in Argentina since the Falklands War. Not helped by awful home refereeing in the non-Test matches, England won just three games. One bright spark though was the international debut of prop Jason Leonard (Saracens). It was to be the first of an epic 114 caps before his retirement in 2004.

2nd Test – Argentina 15 England 13 (Jose Amalfitani Stadium, Buenos Aires)

Despite outscoring their hosts by two tries to none, England lost their first game to a national team outside of the 'big eight' (the Home Unions, France, South Africa, New Zealand and Australia). It meant the series ended one win each after England had won the first by a comfortable 25 points to 12. England had their revenge a few months later, smashing the Pumas 51-0 at Twickenham after Argentinian prop and teenager Federico

Mendez had been sent off for a sickening blind-side punch on Paul Ackford.

1991 GRAND SLAM

The first major success of the Cooke/Carling era was achieved as England embarked on one of their most successful periods in their long history. After the heartbreaking failure of 1990, the men in white took no chances and ground their way to Grand Slam glory, the first clean sweep since 1980. Thinking back to the failure in Edinburgh, Carling reflected: 'We were in business mode. We had let a Grand Slam go begging through arrogance and that wasn't going to happen again.'

THE CARDIFF BOGEY IS FINALLY LAID TO REST

MATCH ONE: Wales 6 England 25 (Cardiff Arms Park)

After 28 years of trying, England finally won at Cardiff Arms Park. Coach Geoff Cooke felt a huge reason for England's constant failure was the passion of the home crowd and the noise and singing they generated. To counter this, for three days before the match he blasted out the Welsh national anthem everywhere from the training pitch to the team bus. He also had the team stay at a hotel right next to the stadium and made the team walk through the bustle of the home fans to get into the ground. By the time the anthems were sung for real, the English players claimed to be utterly bored by it.

England's pack steamrollered the Welsh and the relentless pressure allowed Simon Hodgkinson to kick a then record seven penalties. Mike Teague, whose last appearance in Cardiff in 1989 had ended after three seconds, scored the only try of the game. Teague, Dean Richards and Paul Ackford were in commanding form. The *Daily Telegraph* described England's efforts as 'exciting as watching the tide turn in Swansea Bay'. English fans, starved of success on Welsh soil, quite rightly couldn't have cared less. Jason Leonard was astonished to see English fans crying after the game in joy.

Simon Hodgkinson's boot was critical to the 1991 Grand Slam.

THE SOUND OF SILENCE

The late 1980s and early 1990s was a period of extreme conflict between those who wished to retain the amateur status of rugby and those who saw professionalism as inevitable. The latter argued that the time demanded from top players while holding down a job was just too great. The introduction of the World Cup had only heightened that pressure, especially when British players saw that New Zealand players were blatantly breaking all sorts of amateur regulations by doing paid television adverts or other commercial activities. In the background of all this, the union were getting more money from ticket sales, sponsorship and television deals. More games also meant more travel, jaunts and functions for blazers to enjoy too. It's worth noting that in the early 1990s, committee members got more tickets for games than players, who would obviously wish to give tickets to family, friends and understanding employers who gave them the time off to play and train.

By the 1991 Five Nations, the IRB had relaxed certain rules around commercial activity by players but, with classic conservatism, the RFU did not choose to implement these new interpretations. The English players – often losing money or limiting their career opportunities to the demands of year-long fitness programmes, increased squad sessions and more games – were rightly furious. When the BBC agreed to offer £500 for media duties (to be split among the entire squad), the RFU vetoed it. The players agreed to make a stand and after the win in Cardiff refused to talk to the media. Unfortunately, it meant the post-match coverage was not all about the Cardiff curse being ended, but about 'player power'. The old guard took every opportunity to put the boot into the 'greedy' players and the media narrative was, on the whole, grossly unfair to the players.

MATCH TWO: England 21 Scotland 12 (Twickenham)

The England line-up contained 12 of the players who had lost the Grand Slam showdown in 1990 and all of the XV from the previous game in Cardiff. Will Carling handed out press cuttings from the 1990 loss to Scotland to his team, reminding them of what had gone before. Revenge wasn't just served cold, but dully. Again, the English forwards dominated proceedings and Simon Hodgkinson slotted over the resultant penalties (five this time). The winners' only try was from winger Nigel Heslop (Orrell), and that at least contained some running rugby.

MATCH THREE: Ireland 7 England 16 (Lansdowne Road)

The same XV travelled to Dublin and while they won, they faced the toughest test of their Triple Crown success. The Irish were limited, but full of heart, harassment and hope. Rory Underwood and Mike Teague got two key tries, important on a day when Simon Hodgkinson's kicking radar lacked its usual precision.

MATCH FOUR: England 21 France 19 (Twickenham)

For the second successive season, England were in a Grand Slam showdown. Once again, England named an unchanged XV, the first time since 1960 that the team had been stable for all four Championship games. The contest was an absolute classic. France outscored England three tries to one and two of their scores were as good as any ever seen in London. In fact, Philippe Saint-André's try (which began in the French in-goal area), is considered by many as the greatest score ever at Twickenham. Nonetheless, to the frustration of neutral rugby romantics, England won thanks to the power of their excellent pack, a quality Rory Underwood try, a Rob Andrew drop goal and four penalties and a conversion from Simon Hodgkinson. It meant England would head into a home World Cup later in the year as champions of Europe.

Jeremy Guscott later discussed the downside of this era of England success, writing: 'We are down in the record book as winners and that is no mean achievement. But in terms of developing the sport and playing exciting rugby, it was a backward step.'

RETURN TO OZ

As in 1988, England toured Australia and Fiji. The seven-match tour was controversial as many saw it as overdoing things in a World Cup year. Taking place in July, some said it was too far out from the October World Cup, others that it was too close. It wasn't the most successful one, either way. England won three games and lost four (including a 27-13 loss to Fiji B).

Australia 40 England 15 (Sydney Football Club, Sydney)

A week after dispatching Fiji 28-12 in Suva, the Grand Slam champions came unstuck in Sydney. This was a huge disappointment for the Five Nations champions and a major dent in the confidence many had in England to win the World Cup. The Australian pack, led by the magnificent second row John Eales and inspired by the play of flanker Willie Ofahengaue, ran England around the park. Australia scored five tries to England's one. The manner of the defeat would have major repercussions just a few months later at Twickenham.

RUN, RUN WITH THE BALL

Ahead of the 1991 World Cup, England released a record that, if you've ever heard it, you will not want to be reminded of. An official RFU butchering of 'Swing Low, Sweet Chariot', originally a beautiful spiritual, the song contained a wonderfully ironic chant from the England side that said 'You've gotta run, run with the ball, you've gotta run with the ball'. Coming on top of a Grand Slam that seemed to contain 141 kicks for every pass, it was a further indignation to heap upon the poor victims forced to endure what must be one of the most painful four minutes of popular culture ever created.

GETTING SHIRTY

The 1991 World Cup was the first time England wore a shirt that was anything other than plain white with a rose. To the horror of traditionalists, a deal had been struck with Cotton Traders (set up by former England internationals Fran Cotton and Steve Smith) to produce replica shirts for the England side. The traditional England shirt could not be copyrighted and could therefore be made and sold by anyone. Producing officially licensed shirts was a smart move commercially, even if the designs would often turn out to be as attractive as a three-month old egg sandwich. For the 1991 World Cup, England's traditional cotton shirts had a blue collar with four hoops (two red, two blue) on the right sleeve.

1991 WORLD CUP (UK AND FRANCE)

The 1987 World Cup had broken new ground in rugby but had not been the most well-run of events. Far too many teams, such as England, had treated it with limited respect when it came to preparation and fitness. The 1991 version was different. This time it was full on for all that took part. The matches were spread out among the lands of the teams that made up the Five Nations, but the final was to be at Twickenham. Coming off the back of a Grand Slam and with the strides made under the guidance of Geoff Cooke and the leadership of Will Carling, English hopes were high indeed.

ITV covered the tournament, the first time major rugby had been on Britain's commercial channel and some players, such as Jerry Guscott, felt the increased access of television crews to off-field activity had a negative impact on the squad at times. The 1991 World Cup raised rugby's profile to previously unscaled heights. Almost every newspaper in the UK produced special supplements and devoted far more print and pictures to rugby than had ever been allocated to the sport before. And with England almost going all the way to glory, it was a huge boost for the English game.

Captain: Will Carling
Coach: Geoff Cooke

THE POOL GAMES

England 12 New Zealand 18 (Twickenham)

At this point in the tournament's history, all group games were held over the space of just seven or eight days. Despite being a prime opportunity to spread the gospel of rugby, this huge opener between hosts and defending champions took place in the afternoon when kids were still in school and adults at work. There were no floodlights at Twickenham at the time, so although the game was scheduled for midweek, they had to kick off as usual in the afternoon as if it were a weekend game. Michael Jones, New Zealand's godlike flanker, got the only try of a flat, penalty-strewn match. The loss meant England would likely have to travel to Paris for the quarters.

England 36 Italy 6 (Twickenham)
A crowd of 30,000 trickled into Twickenham as England scored four tries (two from Jerry Guscott) in an uneventful win in which Italy conceded 37 penalties. With no yellow cards back then, they happily slowed down the game as much as possible.

England 37 USA 9 (Twickenham)
Rory Underwood bagged two of England's five tries in a match that saw Will Carling lead England for a record 22nd time.

QUARTER-FINAL
France 10 England 19 (Parc des Princes)
England triumphed in one of the most full-blooded (and dirty) clashes in World Cup history. The English pack were magnificent in keeping a rabid French pack in check. Hooker Brian Moore in particular needled the French forwards into a state of frenzy, smartly making them press their own self-destruct buttons.

The game generated several iconic moments: Flanker Mickey 'the Munch' Skinner's crunching tackle on Marc Cécillon; winger Nigel Heslop shoulder-charging French captain Serge

Blanco and getting felled by a retaliatory punch from the full-back; a sweet try from Rory Underwood after a Jerry Guscott break; and a captain's try from Will Carling which involved him ripping the ball out of French hands and powering over.

The home crowd were furious at the result and refereeing and French coach Daniel Dubroca grabbed referee David Bishop in the tunnel after the game and, as a result, was forced to resign.

SEMI-FINAL

Scotland 6 England 9 (Murrayfield)

Scottish captain and full-back Gavin Hastings missed a sitter in front of the posts in the final quarter of the game that would have put his team ahead. It is perhaps the most famous miss in rugby union history. There was no try from either side in a tense game with more passion than skill on display. Not long after Hastings' missed kick, Rob Andrew slotted the winning drop goal and England had done enough to make their first ever final.

FINAL

England 6 Australia 12 (Twickenham)

There exists a well-established narrative that England lost this final because Australia's David Campese tricked England into playing a wider game by calling them boring in the build-up. The hosts had marched to the final (and their 1991 Grand Slam) with effective, if hugely uninspiring play. Yet Will Carling's men tried a more open approach in the biggest game of their lives and came up short. Many argue that England were shamed into throwing the ball about and lost because of it. However, in the summer tour before the World Cup, England had played a tighter game against the Wallabies and been convincingly beaten 40-15 and several players have claimed it made no sense to play the same way again in the final. Others, such as Brian Moore, bemoan the failure of the English half-backs to test the Wallaby back three under the high ball, especially after the only early test put up to Oz full-back Marty Roebuck almost led to a score. After that, England bizarrely abandoned the tactic.

For all Campese's talk of flowing rugby, the only try of the game came from Oz prop Tony Daly crashing over from a line-out just two metres out (line-outs could be anywhere right up to the try line back then). England frequently troubled the Australians with clean line breaks and created several chances, but lacked the precision to finish them off.

There was a huge moment of controversy near the end involving, you've guessed it, David Campese. With Underwood open out on the left in the Australian 22, Campese deliberately knocked on a pass from Peter Winterbottom which would have put the English winger away. It was a smart, if cynical, move and gave away a penalty rather than a try. And with no yellow cards at the time, it didn't even reduce the Wallabies to 14 men. The men in gold hung on and took 'Old Bill' back down under with them.

The England XV that played that day was the oldest team England had ever fielded (with an average age of 30 plus). There were also seven Harlequins in the English side: Brian Moore,

'The Hand of Campo.'

Simon Halliday, Jason Leonard, Paul Ackford, Mickey Skinner, Peter Winterbottom and captain Will Carling. Australia's Troy Coker also represented the London side, making it a record eight players from one club in the final. Remarkably, Leonard was able to get his revenge over the Wallabies in the 2003 World Cup final!

ENGLAND ALMOST CAUGHT SHORT

The World Cup final in 1991 was arguably the biggest game in English rugby history up until that point. Yet on the morning of the match (according to Brian Moore) it was found that the shorts from kit suppliers Cotton Traders didn't fit. RFU officials had to run to a sports shop in Richmond to find replacements.

A patch was then added to cover up a branded logo on one leg and an English rose patch was added to the other.

1992 GRAND SLAM

England bounced back from the disappointment of the World Cup final by winning a second successive Grand Slam. A legal dispute between the RFU and Cotton Traders saw England revert to their traditional white playing kit for this Championship. The kit manufacturers threatened England with legal action seeking £20 million in damages if England did not honour an eight-year deal. By the time England played again the following season, the two were back working together again.

MATCH ONE: Scotland 7 England 25 (Murrayfield)

The scoreline didn't tell the full story here as England were in trouble for large parts of this game. Most shockingly, considering the dominance of the English pack at the time, the home side scored a pushover try and, in the first half at least, ruled the line-out. The turning point came when an injury to flanker Tim Rodber (Northampton/Army) allowed Dean Richards to enter the field and change the game as he produced a display which steadied the English ship and allowed England to pull away. It almost didn't happen though. When Richards was summoned to the fray, he had to travel down from the grandstand in a lift with Dick Best (part of the coaching set-up) and the lift got stuck. The door had to be forced open and Richards had to crawl through a three-foot gap to get out. Rory Underwood and Dewi Morris scored tries.

MATCH TWO: England 38 Ireland 9 (Twickenham)

This rout saw England rack up their highest total in the Five Nations since the Second World War. Jon Webb scored 22 points (including two tries) as England ran in six tries in a display of power and pace that Ireland simply had no answer for.

MATCH THREE: France 13 England 31 (Parc des Princes)

France were so fired up to get revenge over England for recent World Cup and Grand Slam defeats, they ended up boiling over and conceding a penalty try and having two players sent off. England wisely exploited France's rage and players like Brian Moore cleverly wound up the hotheads in the French team at every opportunity. Dean Richards later said: 'The policy was that if they hit you, you smiled and then gave them a wink to wind them up even more. And, hey presto, they had two people sent off on the day.'

Jon Webb had another fine day with 19 points (including a try) and Rory Underwood and Dewi Morris bagged the other tries.

MATCH FOUR: England 24 Wales 0 (Twickenham)

Will Carling scored in the opening minute and that was about as close as Wales got. It said a lot for how far England had come that it was felt they had underperformed in this game and not won the Grand Slam in the style that people had hoped for. Once again, the players were carried off the field in triumph. England's 118 points over the tournament was a Five Nations record at the time.

NEW SHIRT, NEW STADIUMS AND NEW POINTS

1992 – England 26 Canada 13 (Wembley Stadium, London)

Due to improvements being made at Twickenham, England played their first ever game at Wembley. They were also wearing new shirts with a red stripe on the sleeve, after the legal dispute with Cotton Traders was put to bed. Canada caused England a lot of problems, which was even more impressive than it seems as several first-choice players could not get time off to travel and play. This was also the first time England had played since the value of tries had been increased to five points. Winger Ian Hunter (Northampton) scored two tries on his debut.

THE GRASS IS ALWAYS . . . SHORTER

English players were hugely impressed by the quality of the grass at Wembley and, in particular, the shortness of it. The RFU's management of the playing field at HQ had always been a source of frustration and black humour among England players. It was said by some it felt like you couldn't even see your boots when playing at Twickenham.

RFU BOW DOWN TO THE SHAMEFUL OLD GUARD IN SOUTH AFRICA

1992 – England 33 South Africa 16 (Twickenham)

Thanks to political and social changes in South Africa and the ending of apartheid, the Springboks were allowed to return from international exile. The return to Twickenham was not a happy one as they conceded the most points they had ever done to that point in their history.

The RFU did not play the English national anthem for this game as, shamefully, they didn't want to upset the old reactionaries in the South African rugby union. The Springboks were no longer allowed to sing the anthem 'Die Stem'. The song was seen as a symbol of white supremacy and of apartheid and the SARFU had agreed not to use it any more (something they ignored in their first game back after exile). The RFU, for some bizarre reason, were worried about upsetting a few dinosaurs and decided, therefore, that if the Springboks had no anthem, they wouldn't sing one either. #rugbyvalues

FALLING AT THE THIRD HURDLE

England's attempt to make history with a third consecutive Grand Slam fell short after a shock defeat in Cardiff in the second round. The upset came thanks to a sleepy Rory Underwood allowing Welsh captain Ieuan Evans to score a try against the run of play. It got even worse in the final match when England, who were still in with a chance to win the tournament on newly introduced points difference, collapsed to defeat in Dublin by 17-3.

Lock Martin Johnson (Leicester) made his England debut in the 1993 Five Nations, playing in the opening win over France.

SEVENTH HEAVEN

England won the first ever official World Cup Sevens at

Murrayfield in April 1993. Captained by Andy Harriman (Harlequins), the squad contained future full World Cup winners such as Matt Dawson (Northampton) and Lawrence Dallaglio (Wasps). England beat Fiji in the semis and Australia in the final – shocking fans who had seen them lose to the Wallabies in the group quarter-final stage.

1993 – England 15 New Zealand 9 (Twickenham)

Will Carling's men put the disappointment of the previous season behind them with a famous November triumph over New Zealand. The victory meant Carling had now led England to wins over all the 'traditional' rugby nations. The game wasn't pretty, with neither scoring a try, but it was absorbing. Rob Andrew was praised for his control of the game and the English back row of Tim Rodber, Ben Clarke and Dean Richards won plenty of plaudits. Full-back Jon Callard (Bath) kicked four penalties and Rob Andrew struck a trademark drop goal. It was England's fourth win over New Zealand.

IRELAND UPSET THE (BOOZY) CHARIOT

Hot off the win over New Zealand, most pundits thought England would win another Five Nations title. Yet after a late win over Scotland, England were pipped 13-12 by a fiery Irish side in Dublin. It ultimately cost England the title. Years later Will Carling discovered some of the English team had enjoyed a few beers the evening before the game.

Wales won an unexpected title on points difference, but England denied them a Grand Slam with a 15-8 win on the final day at HQ. It was a sign of the limited rugby Will Carling's men were employing that Rory Underwood's try in the first half was England's first try in six games! England also won in Paris (18-14) to make it seven victories on the trot over France.

THE COOKE ERA ENDS

Geoff Cooke stood down after the Five Nations. He had brought England from the depths of post-1987 World Cup humiliation to the highs of two Grand Slams, wins over the All Blacks, Australia and South Africa and a World Cup final appearance. His resignation was linked with his frustrations with the RFU on a range of matters. He was replaced by Jack Rowell, the hugely successful Bath coach. It was hoped Rowell would expand the way England played as it was increasingly felt by many in the game that England's style would bring Five Nations success, but not be enough for World Cups.

Brian Moore said of Cooke: 'Few remember how awful England were when he took the position . . . some, like Clive Woodward, subsequently doubted his achievements and claimed he produced dull rugby. I and the rest of English rugby should be grateful for what he did.'

RETURN TO AFRICA

England undertook an eight-match tour to South Africa in the summer of 1994. With the third World Cup due to be held in the country the following year, it seemed like smart preparation. England lost five games but did win the first Test by two tries to nil (32-15), before falling 27-9 a week later. Tim Rodber – defending his teammate Jonathan Callard who had been viciously raked across the face in a game against Eastern Province – became the second player to be dismissed in an England shirt (but luckily for him this was a non-cap game).

1st Test – South Africa 15 England 32 (Loftus Versfeld, Pretoria)

Some said this was as fine a performance as ever given by England in Test history. The tourists, who had lost four of the five previous tour games, stormed into a 20-0 lead to the horror of the proud home supporters. Rob Andrew scored an astonishing 27 points in a full house of one try, five penalties, two conversions and a drop goal. Remarkably, the second Test swung completely in the opposite direction with the Springboks winning 27-9.

MINNOW MASHING

England rounded off the calendar year with wins at home over Romania (54-3) and Canada (60-19). The latter was the highest score England had ever managed at the time at Twickenham and Rob Andrew broke his own national record with 30 points (six penalties and six conversions).

BILL BEAUMONT

Club: Fylde
Position: Second row
Caps: 34 (1975–82)
(British Lions, 7 caps)
Points: 0

Bill Beaumont will forever be remembered as the man who took England to the 1980 Grand Slam, the first since 1957. A quality jumper at the front of the line and a physical and feisty presence, he was also known as an exceptional leader and motivator. He led England on 21 occasions, a record for the time, and won 33 of his caps in consecutive games.

He toured twice with the British Lions and was captain of the North of England side that defeated the 1979 All Blacks. Sadly, his career was ended by injury far too early and he retired in 1982 aged just 29. His profile was so high that he became a fixture on the BBC quiz show *A Question of Sport* for many years. He went on to become one of the sport's leading administrators as chairman of World Rugby.

WILL CARLING

Club: Harlequins
Position: Centre
Caps: 72 (1988–97)
(British Lions, 1 cap)
Points: 54 (12 tries)

Will Carling had planned a career in the military, like his father, and joined the Army. However, when he became aware that it would impact his freedom to pursue his rugby dreams, he left. He was named captain aged just 22, making him the youngest player ever to lead England. He overcame the doubters and took England to three Grand Slams, the only Englishman to have managed this feat. He was part of four outright Championship wins and four Triple Crowns, as well as steering England to the 1991 World Cup final. He won 44 of his 59 games as captain.

Known primarily for his leadership, his playing abilities have unfairly been overlooked by many. He was praised by many of his partners in the centre, especially Jeremy Guscott who labelled him world class. Carling was a fast and forceful runner who also had the agility to avoid unnecessary contact and the handling ability and timing to put his partners into space.

Arguably, his assault on the obnoxious television character Mr Blobby (from Noel Edmonds's TV show *Noel's House Party*) was his finest moment.

BRIAN MOORE

Club: Nottingham, Harlequins
Position: Hooker
Caps: 64 (1987–96)
(British Lions, 5 caps)
Points: 4 (1 try)

Brian Moore's nickname 'Pitbull' was perfectly suited to his tough, abrasive and relentless approach to the game. He was a cornerstone of England's pack during their domination of European rugby in the first half of the 1990s. Excellent both tactically and technically, he inspired those around him while often upsetting those he faced. Moore refused to accept second best and threw his World Cup runners-up medal into the River Thames.

Smart as a button, his ability to wind up opponents wasn't limited to the pitch either. His well-aimed barbs in the press, particularly in relation to the French, helped to distract and infuriate opponents who should have spent more time focusing on their own game. France's Philippe Saint-André admitted that, despite his pleas, his teammates in the French pack would make a point of going after Moore in contests. This, of course, was Moore's plan.

He wasn't afraid of the committee men that so often can blight rugby either and was a central figure in the movement to protect the interests of players as the game went professional. He was known to split fees he got for commercial activities, even when he was entitled to keep the payment for himself.

PETER WINTERBOTTOM

Club: Headingley, Harlequins
Position: Flanker
Caps: 58 (1982–93)
(British Lions, 7 caps)
Points: 13 (3 tries))

Peter Winterbottom is still rated by many as not just one of England's finest number sevens, but one of the world's best. The Yorkshireman and former farmer was as tough as they come too. Jeremy Guscott said you could 'put six bullets in him and Wints would just keep getting back up'. The blond-haired back rower seemed to have an engine that allowed him to never get tired. He hit like a train and was a constant annoyance to any side he lined up against. His early career was spent in lacklustre English teams, but he was durable enough to keep going and played in every match of the 1991 and 1992 Grand Slams.

ROB ANDREW

Club: Oxford University, Nottingham, Wasps, Toulouse, Newcastle
Position: Outside-half
Caps: 71 (1985–97)
(British Lions, 5 caps, 11 points)
Points: 396 (2 tries, 33 conversions, 86 penalties, 21 drop goals)

Rob Andrew smashed multiple England point-scoring records. He started as he meant to go on too, with a drop goal in the first minute of his Test career (the first three of 18 points on his debut). His 396 points was a massive total for the era, especially as he was not always even the main goalkicker for the side.

A very solid ten, rather than a flair man (supporters of the day were usually divided between Andrew's effective style and the sparkle of his arch-rival Stuart Barnes), Andrew was one of the lynchpins of the success in the Carling and Cooke era. Steady and sure were the qualities he offered. The fly-half for the 1991, 1992 and 1995 Grand Slams, England fans will always remember him for his dramatic late drop goal in the win over Australia in the 1995 World Cup quarter-final.

Andrew's influence extended beyond his playing days as he went on to mentor Jonny Wilkinson at Newcastle and held senior positions at the RFU, including the role of director of elite rugby. He sits in the World Rugby Hall of Fame.

1980–94 NOTABLE EVENTS IN ENGLISH HISTORY

- 1980: Unemployment hits the two million mark, its highest point since the 1930s.

- 1981: Rupert Murdoch purchases *The Times* newspaper.

- 1982: Johnny Marr and Morrissey form the Smiths.

- 1983: Seat belt usage is now mandatory for front seat passengers in cars.

- 1984: Police officer Yvonne Fletcher is shot and killed by a gunman shooting from the Libyan embassy.

- 1985: In the aftermath of the Heysel Stadium disaster, in which 39 people died, English football clubs are banned from European competitions.

- 1986: Over 30 million people watch the Christmas Day episode of *EastEnders*.

- 1987: Boris Johnson is dismissed from his role at *The Times* (created thanks to a family connection) for inventing a quote and falsely attributing it to historian Colin Lucas (his godfather).

- 1988: Health Minister Edwina Currie resigns after claiming most British eggs are infected with salmonella bacteria.

- 1989: The Cure release their masterpiece *Disintegration*.

- 1990: In reaction to the horrors of the Hillsborough disaster in which 95 Liverpool supporters died (later increasing to 97), Lord Justice Taylor recommends that all top division stadiums become all-seater.

- 1991: Cosmonaut Helen Sharman becomes the first British person in space (and the first Western European woman).

- 1992: The satirical magazine *Punch* ceases publication. It had been in print since 1841.

- 1993: The political party UKIP is formed.

- 1994: In March, the IRA carry out mortar attacks on Heathrow Airport on three occasions.

1995–2003: TO THE TOP OF THE WORLD

	PLAYED	WON	DRAWN	LOST
FIVE/ SIX NATIONS	40	33	0	7
TESTS	35	21	2	12
WORLD CUP	18	14	0	4
WORLD CUP QUALIFIERS	2	2	0	0
WORLD CUP WARM-UP GAMES*	5	4	0	1
TOTAL	100	74	2	24

*Listed separately due to their experimental nature and mass substitutions. Full caps were awarded, however, and they are considered full internationals.

Championships (5)

1995 (Grand Slam), 1996 (Triple Crown), 2000, 2001, 2003 (Grand Slam)

Triple Crowns (without winning Championship) (3)

1997, 1998, 2002

World Cups

Quarter-final (1995, 1999), Winners (2003)

'What I am proud of is I have searched for the best of me and I have been a team man without fail.'

JONNY WILKINSON (ENGLAND FLY-HALF/CENTRE, 91 CAPS BETWEEN 1998 AND 2011)

BRITPOP, COOL BRITANNIA AND THE RISE OF THE RUGBY 'MERCENARY'

Almost exactly 100 years to the day since rugby had mutated into two codes in 1895 over the matter of payments to players, rugby union became a professional sport. When it was announced by the IRFB that the game was now 'open', it is said that one committee member was so distraught at the decision he repeatedly banged his head on the wall while groaning.

By the mid-1990s, fighting off professionalism was both pointless and hypocritical. Elite rugby was raking in millions in cash for everything from television sponsorship to ticket sales to merchandising deals and hospitality boxes. Ahead of the 1995 World Cup, South Africa, New Zealand and Australia announced that a US$555 million deal had been struck with Rupert Murdoch's News Corp for television rights. With so much money in the sport, and players being asked to effectively give up months out of their working lives each year to represent their countries (and plenty more time to play for their clubs), no one could reasonably expect players to do things for free. There were, of course, plenty of blazers in rugby union committees around the world that did want players to do it for nothing. Many of these officials no doubt bemoaned the corrupting influence of professionalism while flying around the world first class and staying in five-star hotels, all paid for from the money coming into the sport. Indeed, the RFU members who attended the meeting that decided the future of the game had been told to vote against turning the game professional.

The 1995 World Cup was the final nail that splintered the rickety coffin of amateurism. Once the game went pro, amateur committees and volunteer officials were suddenly arranging massive player contract deals with no idea what they were doing. There was a period of madness in which huge sums of money flowed into the game as certain players and clubs got very rich. Eventually, the Devil came to collect his dues and some famous clubs went bust or dropped out of the top tier of the game before some level of order was restored.

For the England rugby team, of course, the period covered in this chapter includes the finest moment in the national side's history. Yet the 2003 World Cup win came after bitter disappointments in the 1995 and 1999 tournaments and several setbacks in the Six Nations. Whilst, in hindsight, Martin Johnson's men seemed destined to claim the Webb Ellis Cup, the ride was a lot rockier than is often remembered.

Off the field, the late 1990s saw economic growth in England and restored pride in British and English culture during a period often dubbed 'Cool Britannia'. London was cited by many as once again being the cultural capital of the world amidst an explosion of music, fashion and art. Tony Blair led Labour back to power in 1997 after 18 years of Tory rule. The new prime minister boasted he had been in a punk band in his youth and enjoyed inviting rock and pop stars to Downing Street for photo opportunities.

English artists like Oasis, Blur, the Spice Girls, Pulp, the Verve and Robson & Jerome (!) dominated the airwaves in what some hailed another golden era for popular music. The end of the millennium also brought great drama as the 'millennium bug' (also known as the Y2K problem) caused major panic around the world due to fears computer systems could crash as a result of the way dates were stored and programmed (many worried there would be confusion in some computers with the year 2000 being read as the year 1900). To this day, debate continues as to how significant this problem really was.

1995 GRAND SLAM

Jack Rowell (who had dismissed Dick Best from the coaching staff after the summer tour) oversaw his first Five Nations and guided England to their third Grand Slam since 1991. While the opposition in the tournament at this time was often weak, Will Carling's men played far more stimulating rugby at times than they had for large chunks of the two previous Grand Slams. Critics remained, however, with some saying England still lacked an adequate 'plan B' if things did not go well and that the likes of New Zealand would not be troubled by the type of rugby needed to win a Grand Slam. Nonetheless, it meant England again entered a World Cup as Five Nations champions.

MATCH ONE: Ireland 8 England 20 (Lansdowne Road)

Flanker Ben Clarke (Bath), who got caught stamping on Irish winger Simon Geoghegan, became the first international to be yellow-carded after the IRB introduced the new disciplinary system to Test level. England, nonetheless, triumphed in grim conditions to end a two-game losing run against Ireland. Will Carling, Ben Clarke and Tony Underwood (Leicester) got the English tries.

MATCH TWO: England 31 France 10 (Twickenham)

Despite another spectacular near length of the field try at Twickenham by France, England made it eight on the trot against their Gallic rivals in a thrilling game. Unlike in the epic 1991 clash though, England outscored their opponents three to one on the try count with five-pointers from Jeremy Guscott and Tony Underwood (who bagged two). The back row of Tim Rodber, Ben Clarke and Dean Richards was superb. French flanker Laurent Cabannes was a remarkable player who, four years earlier, had spent a year in a wheelchair after a car crash.

Dean Richards was a key figure in the success of the 1990s.

MATCH THREE: Wales 9 England 23 (Cardiff Arms Park)

After the blip in 1993, England again showed Cardiff no longer held the fear over them it once had with a comfortable dispatching of a spirited, but mediocre, Welsh side. England's cause was helped by the sending off of Welsh prop John Davies for stamping. Prop Victor Ubogu (Bath) got the game's opening try and Rory Underwood, who had played a critical part in the key scores for Wales in the 1987, 1989 and 1993 clashes, went some way to exorcising his Cardiff ghosts with a brace of tries in the second half.

The prop who bet on himself (or thought he had)

Before the 1995 clash with Wales, Victor Ubogu gave a friend £100 to lay a bet that he would be the game's first try scorer (a rare thing for a prop). He got odds of 18/1. So, when Ubogu did get the opening try, he was of course, over the moon. After the game he was in the mood to celebrate and splash the cash and spent hundreds of pounds on drink. Unfortunately for him, it turned out his buddy had not actually placed the bet.

MATCH FOUR: England 24 Scotland 12 (Murrayfield)

England got to claim the Championship, Grand Slam, Triple Crown and Calcutta Cup in a tougher than expected win over Scotland. Rob Andrew scored all of England's points with a drop goal and seven penalties. His winning tally also took him to the top of the English international point scoring list. Before the match, former Scotland flanker John Jeffrey said England fans at Twickenham looked like 'Barboured yobs'.

History of a different kind was made when Dewi Morris became the first blood replacement for England when he temporarily replaced scrum-half Kyran Bracken (Bristol). Blood subs had been introduced in 1993. Once again, as in 1991, England had gone unchanged throughout the whole campaign.

57 BLAZERS GET A NEW NICKNAME

Ahead of the 1995 World Cup the pressure for the game to go professional was all but irresistible. There were even rumours that rich businessmen like Rupert Murdoch and Kerry Packer were planning to sign up players to a rival professional version of the sport during the World Cup. The RFU, however, continued on the whole to stick a finger in the dam and try to resist the oncoming flood. RFU secretary Dudley Wood's action – or lack of action – around the inevitable move to professionalism made him an unpopular figure with players. Brian Moore later wrote: 'That Wood was prepared to destabilise his own team so close to a World Cup illustrates his priorities. There was no tactic he would not use, no depth to which he would not sink, in a battle that, by that stage, he knew had been lost, it was unadulterated spite.'

Wood himself remarked that on certain topics, such as amateurism, he was 'not too fussed about being labelled a dinosaur or King Canute'. However, he and his fellow committee men were less impressed by what captain Will Carling called them just ahead of the World Cup.

Carling had been recording an interview for a documentary when, unaware his interviewer Greg Dyke still had a microphone on, he was asked what he thought would happen if the game went professional. The England captain said that if the game went pro it would no longer need the '57 old farts' in the RFU to run it. Dyke used the answer in his programme and a scandal was born. The RFU president Dennis Easby had Carling fired as captain. However, the RFU hadn't counted on the players backing their leader. Rob Andrew and Dean Richards said they would refuse the captaincy if offered it and it soon became clear the squad would stand by Carling. The RFU was forced into a humiliating climbdown.

Brian Moore summed up the whole story well, writing in his excellent autobiography: 'Will's old fart comments were neither here nor there – they were clearly off air, not for use and not particularly offensive. In fact they bordered on the generous in my opinion. What was absolutely incredible is that some of those in power – a very small minority, not the majority – chose this moment, five or six weeks before a World Cup in which we were well in the frame, to sack the England captain over something so utterly trivial.'

1995 WORLD CUP (SOUTH AFRICA)

The only rugby World Cup to be made into a Hollywood movie, the 1995 edition was spectacular. This was the first edition to feature South Africa who, due to the sporting boycott of apartheid era South Africa, were not included in 1987 and 1991. The hosts made up for lost time by winning the Webb Ellis Cup at the first time of asking. Nelson Mandela, the revolutionary turned president, wearing a Springbok shirt as he handed the trophy over to Francois Pienaar, is perhaps the most famous moment in all of rugby. For 27 years, Mandela had been imprisoned by the South African government and there he was, wearing what many saw as the ultimate symbol of white South Africa. The symbolism of the moment reverberated throughout the world and still echoes in history now.

For England though, their 1995 World Cup was to be forever associated with one man. And he wasn't wearing a white shirt.

Captain: Will Carling

Coach: Jack Rowell

POOL GAMES

England 24 Argentina 18 (Kings Park Stadium, Durban)

England's first match ever under floodlights was a close-run thing. The Pumas scored the only two tries of the game and if Argentina had possessed an accurate goalkicker they would quite likely have won. Rob Andrew – as he had in the final contest of the Five Nations – kicked 24 points (including two drop goals) to spare the blushes of the Grand Slam champions. After the game, the UK media dubbed England coach Jack Rowell as 'Jittery Jack', implying all was not well on the coaching front.

England 27 Italy 20 (Kings Park Stadium)

Led by Rob Andrew, England laboured past Italy with a try each from brothers Rory and Tony Underwood on the wings. The captain added a conversion and five penalties.

England 44 Western Samoa 22 (Kings Park Stadium)

Rory Underwood grabbed a brace, Neil Back (Leicester) at

flanker added another and England also won a penalty try in a much-improved display over the Samoans. Thanks to brutal Samoan tackling (and only five replacements being allowed in those days), a battered English side finished with Brian Moore and Kyran Bracken on the flanks.

QUARTER-FINAL
England 25 Australia 22 (Newlands, Cape Town)

'One flipping kick,' said centre Jerry Guscott later. 'That's all we managed to do really well during the 1995 World Cup quarter-final.' But what a kick it was. Andrew's winning drop goal came in the dying moments of the match, with the encounter heading to extra time. He struck it on the Australian ten-metre line, direct from a line-out-turned-maul out on the left. It was a peach of a shot and flew over with plenty of room to spare. Guscott's statement on this quarter-final is perhaps a little harsh. Rory Underwood finished off a great counter-attack after the Wallabies fumbled in the English 22 in the first half to get England's only try.

SEMI-FINAL
England 29 New Zealand 45 (Newlands)

As anyone who witnessed this extraordinary contest will attest, the scoreline of this game spins a very false tale. This was the match which created rugby's biggest ever superstar: Jonah Lomu. Not only was the Kiwi wing 196cm (6ft 5in) and around 125kg (19st 9lb), his pace off the mark was frightening

The rugby world will never forget Jonah Lomu's 1995 performance against England.

and his power and aggression almost unmatched. Just 20, he'd already set the tournament alight with some bursting runs and scores against the other Home Union sides. But nothing like what he unleashed against England had happened before. Four minutes into the game and Lomu took a bouncing pass about 30 metres out from the English line. He simply shrugged off a despairing Tony Underwood, survived an ankle tap from Will Carling and then, while stumbling, ran OVER Mike Catt. It was the first of four tries from Lomu. New Zealand were two tries up after six minutes. Late in the game, All Black number eight Zinzan Brooke even smashed over a long-range drop goal. With the match in the bag, New Zealand uncharacteristically relaxed, allowing some late scores from Rory Underwood and Will Carling (two apiece). Carling later dubbed Lomu a 'freak'. The Kiwi went on to be rugby's first millionaire. Amazingly, he was never even fully fit during his career due to a kidney problem. He sadly died aged just 40.

THIRD PLACE PLAY-OFF
England 9 France 19 (Loftus Versfeld, Pretoria)
A game described by one England player (correctly) as 'utterly pointless'.

UNDERWOOD FINALLY GETS A PIZZA THE ACTION
Tony Underwood's failure to get to grips with Jonah Lomu in the 1995 World Cup led to him making a Pizza Hut commercial. In the advert, a tiny Underwood is desperately trying to get

a taste of Lomu's pizza. After the comically oversized Lomu knocks down the English winger, Tony's brother, Rory, and his mother burst in. Mrs Underwood proceeds to perform a chop tackle on Lomu and the brothers steal the pizza. A classic in the genre of adverts turning sporting failure into a nice income stream.

THE PROFESSIONALS

Rugby finally turned professional after the World Cup. England's first game as pros was against the newly crowned Springboks in November 1995.

1995 – England 14 South Africa 24 (Twickenham)

England were never really in this match and Will Carling's men could be thankful that the Boks left plenty of points on the field rather than the scoreboard. Coach Jack Rowell was again widely criticised for failing to produce the 15-man expansive style of play that many felt had been promised. Over 78,000 fans packed into the newly renovated Twickenham for this encounter.

1995 – England 27 Western Samoa 9 (Twickenham)

Poor old Paul Grayson (Northampton) making his debut at outside-half with his club partner Matt Dawson inside him, was booed by his own crowd thanks to England's reliance on the boot in this match. The debutant slotted five penalties before Lawrence Dallaglio (winning his second cap) and Rory Underwood claimed tries.

PRO FIVE NATIONS CHAMPIONS

England recovered from an opening day last-minute loss to France (15-12 in Paris) to become the first champions in the professional era of the Five Nations thanks to wins over Wales (21-15), Scotland (18-9) and Ireland (28-15). England won the title on points difference, the first time they had done so since the system had been introduced as a tie-breaker.

LIMP FAREWELL FOR A GREAT CAPTAIN
1996 – England 28 Ireland 15 (Twickenham)

England took the Triple Crown in Will Carling's final game as captain. The Harlequins centre had decided to step down as captain, but was not retiring. While England won, Carling had to leave the field in the first half after damaging his knee ligaments. Wales's unexpected win over France on the same day gave England the title. The Five Nations trophy was in Cardiff and had to be rushed back to London for the post-game dinner. It meant Carling could only hobble up the Twickenham steps to lift the barely known Millennium Trophy (the pointless trophy created in 1988 for the winners of this fixture).

NEW CENTRE OF LEADERSHIP
1996 – England 54 Italy 21 (Twickenham)

New captain Phil de Glanville (Bath) partnered former captain Will Carling in this November Test. England ran in seven tries in an unmemorable game played in a stadium that was one third empty. A month later, de Glanville was injured and the captaincy was given to Jason Leonard against Argentina. The prop saved England with a try six minutes from time to avoid a humiliating home defeat and give England a 20-18 win.

TACTICAL THINKING

In the 71st minute of the win over Italy, prop Rob Hardwick (Coventry) became the first tactical substitution for England when he replaced Jason Leonard. The decision to change the law to allow non-injured players to be replaced was controversial and, to some people, is still a blight on the game today. Jack Rowell was criticised for his poor employment of tactical substitutions throughout the 1996–97 season, with critics claiming he wasted opportunities to introduce fresh players at key times.

A GRAND SLAM GOES BEGGING

With Jack Rowell's future already under a cloud, the 1997 Five Nations saw England dispatch Scotland 41-13 in London, Ireland 46-6 in Dublin and Wales 34-13 in Cardiff to take the Triple Crown at a canter. The win over Ireland was, to that point, England's largest Five Nations win and the first time in half a century they had scored six tries away from home. The Cardiff win was particularly painful for Welsh fans as it was the final international played at the 113-year-old Cardiff Arms Park before it was knocked down and rebuilt into today's Principality Stadium.

But in between the away wins over Ireland and Wales, Phil de Glanville's men suffered a disappointing home loss to France.

1997 – England 20 France 23 (Twickenham)

England coach Jack Rowell had promised running rugby and while his side did try to play with ambition, the backline rarely clicked. However, Phil de Glanville's men did enough to command a 20-6 lead after 60 minutes thanks to a 30-metre try from Lawrence Dallaglio and four penalties and a drop goal from Paul Grayson. Then, in classic French style, everything clicked for the men in blue and they stormed back with two splendid converted tries and a penalty to sneak the game and shock the Twickenham crowd into silence. It would ultimately cost England the title and increase the pressure on Jack Rowell. France would go on to win the Grand Slam.

THE PUMAS MEET THE ENGLISH SHORN OF THEIR LIONS

The summer of 1997 saw England take a six-match tour of Argentina while the British Lions toured South Africa with 18 Englishmen. While standard practice now, the RFU's decision to award caps during a Lions tour was not deemed a popular one and many claimed it devalued the worth of an international cap. Phil de Glanville had not made the Lions and led a squad with 16 uncapped players.

The tour ended with four wins and two losses. The Test series was tied at one win each after England's 46-20 win in the opener was met with a strong response from the Pumas who won 33-13 the following week.

THE ROWELL AND DE GLANVILLE
ERA ENDS IN A COOKED-UP FARCE

1997 – Australia 25 England 6 (Sydney Football Ground)

Despite the fact the two nations had first met on the rugby field in 1909, it was decided that when England and Australia met outside of a World Cup, they would do so for the honour of lifting the Cook Cup (imaginatively named after Captain James Cook). Originally it was agreed that the two sides would meet every year home and away to decide who held the cup. Thankfully, apart from 1997, this has only happened once, so complete overkill in this fixture was avoided.

This first Cook Cup game took place in July, just three days after the British Lions tour. Absurdly, and with no regards for player welfare, 12 tired English players were flown straight over from South Africa to face a far fresher home side.

It also turned out to be the final game with Phil de Glanville as captain and Jack Rowell as coach. It had been a tough gig for de Glanville who had to partner with previous captain Will Carling in the centre for many of his eight games in charge, while a sizeable majority of fans and critics felt Jeremy Guscott should have been inside centre instead of de Glanville. Rowell had tried to give his England more freedom than Geoff Cooke had allowed, giving players input into how they played. But he was unable to fully get the team on board (or perhaps there were not enough players capable of taking control). When his contract ended after the Australia game, Rowell, who was not a full-time coach, resigned.

THE 'MARGINAL GAINS' ERA BEGINS

When former England centre and Grand Slam winner Clive Woodward became head coach in the autumn of 1997, he turned up at Twickenham to begin work from his office. Except, there wasn't one.

'What do you need an office for?' had been the response to Woodward from Don Rutherford, the RFU's director of rugby and former England international. Woodward, an obsessive follower of new trends and techniques in business, immediately began rebuilding everything in English rugby to create a truly elite environment. He brought in a New Zealander, John Mitchell, to help with coaching. At the time, bringing in a non-native coach was not the done thing and it caused a fair few moans of annoyance in the rugby community. There were even more when he then brought Phil Larder, a rugby league coach, into the set-up. The concept of a rugby league man even being at Twickenham had been unthinkable for over a century and now, two years after the game went pro, Woodward was inviting one into the heart of the coaching squad. Quite rightly though, the England head coach couldn't have cared less.

Woodward also believed in giving players the best of everything, so that they could focus on nothing but improving. Jason Leonard, who had been around a fair few England set-ups, said: 'What Clive created was a no-excuses set-up. You'd always have some excuse in the early days. The food was bad, you'd trained badly because you'd been working all day, the bed was too small, you were stiff from the journey. Now, all that was taken away. We were pampered. But to get all these perks we had to perform, and there was no comeback whatsoever if we didn't.'

BAPTISM OF FIRE

Clive Woodward appointed 25-year-old Lawrence Dallaglio as his captain. The new captain and coach were thrown in at the deep end as the RFU had set up an autumn fixture list unlike any played before. They would face Australia, New Zealand, South Africa and New Zealand again on consecutive weekends. England picked up two draws (the first and last games) and two losses, but showed moments of promise, even if they lacked poise.

1997 (1st Test) – England 8 New Zealand 25 (Old Trafford)

Two moments from this day have become etched into rugby folklore and neither occurred during the actual game. Before the match, England hooker Richard Cockerill (Leicester) infamously marched up to the haka to eyeball Norm Hewitt in a fierce stand-off. On the way there he kicked New Zealand flanker Josh Kronfeld's scrum cap across the field after seeing it lying on the grass. After the match, in which England were outscored three tries to one, the All Blacks trudged off somewhat frustrated with themselves for what they felt was a poor performance. The home side, meanwhile, performed a lap of honour. The *Independent* called it 'embarrassingly deluded' and the New Zealand press went to town on the incident. To this day the moment is brought up as an example of English sport often being accepting of mediocrity. The follow-up match two weeks later saw a thrilling 26-26 draw (England had led 20-3 at one point).

The first Test had been played in Manchester as an attempt by the RFU to take England out of London and closer to their northern fans. It was a symbolic moment in the new professional era, in light of how much northern talent had been lost or neglected after the great split of 1895.

CLOSE, BUT NO CIGAR

Clive Woodward's first Championship in the hot seat ended with a Triple Crown, but not a title. England lost their opening match in Paris 24-17 to the eventual Grand Slam champions. Ironically, the match only went ahead thanks to the technical skills of English pitch experts who helped French groundsmen see off a potential frozen pitch. While the score looked close, even the England management admitted that the scoreline flattered the visitors. Nonetheless, it wasn't a bad championship for Lawrence Dallaglio's men and a few key players were blooded or began to find their feet.

1998 – England 60 Wales 26 (Twickenham)

This was a crushing defeat of a poor Welsh side, even if the visitors scored two early tries through centre Allan Bateman (including one near length of the field team try that rates among Twickenham's finest). England ran in eight tries to humiliate the Welsh. Results like this prompted some in the media to propose that it may be better for England to break away from the Five Nations and join an annual tournament including

South Africa and New Zealand. Former international Paul Ackford suggested that France and England looked set to run up over 100 points over a Celtic team.

THE (FUTURE) GOLDEN BOY ARRIVES ON STAGE
1998 – England 35 Ireland 17 (Twickenham)

After a 34-20 win in Edinburgh, England secured a Triple Crown at home with a hard-earned win over a fired-up Irish side. Captain Lawrence Dallaglio refused to shake hands with Ireland's David Corkery after the final whistle, he was so upset with some of the Cork man's play and niggle. But the big talking point in this game was the debut of Jonny Wilkinson aged just 18 years and 314 days. The future World Cup hero came on two minutes from the end of normal time at full-back. He narrowly missed out on the record for youngest England international (which still belongs to Colin Laird aged 18 years and 124 days in 1927). Sadly for Wilkinson, his first start was shortly to come for England and, for reasons beyond his control, it was going to be awful.

THE SUMMER OF 1998 AND THE TOUR OF HELL

For many, the summer of 1998 represents the lowest point in England's rugby history. Many of England's top players were exhausted from the 1997 Lions tour and a lengthy international and domestic season. With a World Cup year coming up, players desperately needed a break for recovery (those who weren't already injured that is). The RFU, in its infinite wisdom, scheduled a seven-match tour that included two Tests against New Zealand and one-offs against South Africa and Australia. There was also a major power struggle between clubs and the RFU, with concern about burnout, injury and compensation. As a result, the clubs advised many of the players to make themselves unavailable. Twenty uncapped players were involved in the tour, as mainstays of the side like Martin Johnson, Lawrence Dallaglio, Jason Leonard and Richard Hill (the Saracens flanker, not the scrum-half and captain of the 1980s) did not travel. As you can imagine, it didn't go well.

'I'm sure I was chosen because I had two working legs,' said prop Phil Vickery (Gloucester). The average number of caps per player in the squad was less than four and only six players of the 37 had more than ten caps to their name. Scrum-half Matt Dawson was given the dubious honour of taking his English cubs, rather than lions, to battle.

Dick McGruther of the Australian Rugby Union (ARU) was disappointed in the squad that travelled that summer, saying it was 'probably the most underequipped group of Englishmen to be sent to Australia since the first Fleet'. He invited local fans to come and enjoy a 'Pommie thrashing'. Things weren't helped by a drinking culture that, according to players like flanker Lewis Moody (Leicester), developed as soon as the tour began when management encouraged players to bond over drinking sessions at the start of the tour.

England, unsurprisingly, lost all seven games. Outside of the Tests they lost to New Zealand A (18-10), New Zealand Rugby Academy (50-32) and New Zealand Maori (62-14).

Australia 76 England 0 (Lang Park)

'This is not what international rugby is about,' said John O'Neill of the ARU. 'It was not a contest.' This was perhaps the darkest day in 150 years of English international rugby as a side with five new caps shipped 11 tries (despite the fact it was only 6-0 after 30 minutes). It remains the worst England defeat to this day. Number eight Tony Diprose (Saracens) was captain in the absence of an injured Matt Dawson. On the sidelines

for this game there were a bunch of lads doing press-ups for charity. The idea was for every single point scored they would have to do a set of press-ups. By the end they were so exhausted they had to start doing sit-ups instead.

1st Test – New Zealand 64 England 22 (Carisbrook, Dunedin)

Not only was this another record defeat, second row Danny Grewcock (Saracens) became just the second England international to be sent off. He was given his marching orders in the first half for stamping.

ALWAYS DARKEST BEFORE THE DAWN

After the loss in Dunedin, the following week England lost 40-10 to the All Blacks in Eden Park and then lost their final Test match 18-0 to South Africa. Despite the poor planning, preparation and understrength team, many players should be given credit for never giving up on this ridiculous tour. And the scorelines of the four internationals show that England actually improved as the tour progressed. Manager and former England star Roger Uttley praised the work of the coaching team of Phil Larder, Brian Ashton, John Mitchell and Dave Alred.

Woodward won over many players when he was so horrified at the hotel England were put in at one stage of the tour he paid for an upgrade on his own credit card. While the RFU were unhappy at this, the coach had shown his players he had their best interests at heart. Woodward reflected on the tour in his autobiography, saying: 'We never looked back. Less than two years later we went back and beat South Africa in Bloemfontein. The Tour of Hell was really the making of me. And it was the making of many of the players.'

Jonny Wilkinson later mused: 'I thought I was getting somewhere in the game until I went on that tour. It was as if someone was saying to me: 'You think you've done well, but hold on. You've got a long way to go to even get close to this level.' I raised my standards. In one respect I spent years trying to distance myself from the experience, but I have always maintained that it taught me more than anything else I have gone through, or ever will.'

QUALIFICATION FOR THE WORLD CUP

It's a relatively forgotten footnote in English rugby history that England played two qualifiers for the 1999 Rugby World Cup and both games were played at the McAlpine Stadium in Huddersfield.

1998 – England 110 Netherlands 0 (McAlpine Stadium, Huddersfield)

The brave amateurs of the Netherlands were unable to offer anything but heart as the white-shirted pros of England swept in for 16 tries with Paul Grayson kicking a national record of 15 conversions. In what was at the time England's biggest ever win, Neil Back scored four tries, the first time an English forward had done so since 1881 when George Burton (Blackheath) managed the same tally against Wales. The following week England had a tougher task as they only got past Italy by 23-

15, with the Italians angry about a disallowed try that may have helped them pull off a huge shock. Either way, both teams qualified for a 20-team World Cup in 1999.

A 50/50 CHRISTMAS

England played two more games at Twickenham in December of 1998 to make it a dozen games in a calendar year. The arrival of the modern era's congested international calendar had truly begun. England lost the Cook Cup game with Australia 12-11 thanks to four penalties from Australian legend and second row John Eales. However, the year finished on a high with a 13-7 win over the Springboks.

CELTIC GRAND SLAM HEARTACHE (PART I)

England looked set to make it a clean sweep in the final ever Five Nations in 1999 (Italy were waiting in the wings to join in 2000 and create the Six Nations). Everything went smoothly with Lawrence Dallaglio's men triumphing 24-21 at home to Scotland, winning 27-15 in Dublin and squeaking past France 21-20 at Twickenham. In the latter game, Jonny Wilkinson kicked all the points. Wales, coached by future New Zealand coach Graham Henry, were all that stood between England and a Grand Slam.

1999 – Wales 32 England 31 (Wembley)

England were overwhelming favourites to beat a mediocre Welsh side who had lost to Ireland and Scotland, but pulled off a seemingly freak win in Paris. The fact this 'away' game was being played in London, not Cardiff (the Millennium Stadium was being built for the upcoming World Cup later in the year), only seemed to help England more.

In the first half, England were all over Wales and had scored three tries without conceding any. Yet, Welsh fly-half Neil Jenkins punished England for every infringement within kickable range and when the teams broke for the interval it was only 25-18 to the men in white. Jonny Wilkinson had missed a conversion from almost in front of the posts, but it didn't seem like it would matter. Late in the second half, leading 31-25, Dallaglio turned down a kick at goal to go for a fourth try. It didn't pay off.

With minutes remaining, England led 31-25 and Clive Woodward, unfamiliar with the set-up at Wembley, was asking officials where the team needed to head to claim the Five Nations trophy. Two minutes into injury time, Welsh centre Scott Gibbs earned his place in Welsh folklore by dancing through one third of the English team to score. Jenkins kicked the extras to consign England to defeat. In one cruel minute England had lost the title, the Grand Slam and the Triple Crown. It meant Scotland would win the last ever Five Nations instead.

BOASTS, STINGS AND NEWSPAPERS

England's World Cup preparations were rocked when captain Lawrence Dallaglio appeared on the front page of the newspaper rag known as the *News of the World*. The paper claimed Dallaglio had dealt drugs and had boasted about taking drugs on tour with the Lions. Undercover reporters had posed as potential sponsors and while socialising, Dallaglio made all sorts of claims about drug-taking. He later claimed he had been stupid and foolishly made up the stories to impress them. Whatever the truth, he lost the captaincy and Martin Johnson, by now a globally respected second row, took over.

SUMMER BLUES

England played three summer Tests ahead of the World Cup. One was a 106-8 rout of the USA and another a 36-11 victory over Canada (both games were at Twickenham). The other match was a 22-15 loss to Australia in Sydney. The most interesting thing about this encounter was that it was the first time England hadn't played in white. A blue kit with thin white and red hoops and blue shorts was worn to mark both the fact it was the 500th England Test match and a century since the first Wallabies game. Australia, meanwhile, wore light blue. The shirt colours were picked to represent the colours worn in the first ever Australian representative match when the Aussies faced a British Isles team in 1899.

1999 WORLD CUP (WALES)

While Wales were the official hosts, the other Home Unions and France held multiple matches in the 1999 edition of the World Cup. Indeed, both semi-finals were held at Twickenham (which is why England supported their neighbours' bid to host it). If England were able to win over all their pool opponents, including tournament favourites New Zealand, they wouldn't even have to play away from their home ground until the final in Cardiff. As it turned out, neither they nor the All Blacks would make the final as Rod McQueen's watertight Australians (they conceded just one try all tournament) took the trophy for the second time in three World Cups.

Captain: Martin Johnson
Coach: Clive Woodward

POOL GAMES

England 67 Italy 7 (Twickenham)

Jonny Wilkinson kick-started England's World Cup campaign with 32 points from a try, five penalties and six conversions.

England 16 New Zealand 30 (Twickenham)

Lawrence Dallaglio really got in the face of England's greatest foe Jonah Lomu in this quarter-final, shoving the ball into the winger's head and throwing his weight into the big man and causing a cut lip. Sadly for England fans this was as Lomu lay on the ground moments AFTER the scourge of England had scored the game's key try after taking the ball from 60 metres out and running around or through Jerry Guscott, winger Austin Healey (Leicester), Matt Dawson and Dan Luger (Saracens). The try came in the 58th minute with the scores tied at 16-16. Woodward later admitted that he should have played young prodigy Jonny Wilkinson in the centre with Paul Grayson at fly-half, as the former had not yet developed enough leadership and experience.

This match was the first occasion England had conceded 30 points at Twickenham. Even worse for England, by losing this game they were destined to play in a quarter-final play-off, just days after their final pool match and just days before the quarter-final. The good news, not that England knew it, was that this was to be their last Twickenham loss for four years.

England 101 Tonga 10 (Twickenham)
A game that summarised all that was wrong with international rugby. Two sides mismatched in everything from funding to preparation time. The home side collected 13 tries, the islanders not being helped by being reduced to 14 men in the first half when prop Ngalu Taufo'ou hit England's Richard Hill with a forearm smash. This was the third time England had scored over 100 in less than 12 months, having never done so before in their entire history.

QUARTER-FINAL PLAY-OFF
England 45 Fiji 24 (Twickenham)
England, clad in a new blue change kit, led 21-3 at half-time in a game that was never really in serious doubt. The main issue was that the loss to New Zealand had forced them to have to play this game in the first place and they would travel to Paris to face a rested Springbok team having played an extra game and with little time to recover. Tries came from winger Nick Beal (Northampton), Dan Luger, Neil Back and hooker Phil Greening (Sale)

QUARTER-FINAL

England 21 South Africa 44 (Stade de France)

England dropped out of the World Cup to the repeated sound of South Africa's second-choice fly-half, Jannie de Beer, hitting five second-half drop goals. Four of the drop goals came from on or beyond the English ten-metre line. He also scored five penalties and two conversions. His 12 out of 12 successful attempts with the boot gave him 34 points. Before de Beer's drop goal masterclass, Martin Johnson's men had trailed at half-time by just 16-12. Indeed, with nine minutes left on the clock, they were still only behind by 25-21. The *Guardian* declared that England had fallen victim to 'a freak performance never before witnessed in international rugby'.

*Kick, kick, kick,
kick and kick.*

NO MORE COMPROMISE

After the World Cup loss, the English press gleefully jumped on remarks Clive Woodward had supposedly made to 'judge him' on the World Cup. However, he claims the newspapers simplified a statement he made into a snappy headline. Either way, several journalists and pundits pushed heavily for a new head coach.

But in response to the disappointment of Paris, Woodward swore he would no longer compromise on how he did things. He continued to introduce new ideas and concepts, many of which were fantastic, some of which were ludicrous and some of which were abandoned (one of his strengths was the ability to admit something wasn't working). One particular innovation, which has now become fairly routine, was having players change into fresh kit at half-time. The idea being it was both a physical and a mental restart. Woodward was committed to sparing no expense in making sure his squad and coaches had everything they could possibly need.

Another boost to England was the opening of their Pennyhill Park training facility. The facilities on offer at the venue covered everything from training pitches to recovery rooms and swimming pools. It was another example that no expense would be spared in the quest to win a World Cup.

CELTIC GRAND SLAM HEARTACHE (PART II)

Injury to Martin Johnson meant Matt Dawson led England for the 2000 Six Nations. Big home wins over Ireland (50-18) and Wales (46-12), as well as a 15-9 win in Paris, meant once again England headed into the final weekend with a Grand Slam there for the taking. Scotland had lost their four previous games, including a stunning opening day loss to newcomers Italy, so were staring a whitewash in the face. Meanwhile, Neil Back kicked the first (and only) drop goal by an English forward in the win over Italy (59-12)

2000 – Scotland 19 England 13 (Edinburgh)

England's title dreams were washed away in the Edinburgh rain as Woodward again saw a Grand Slam slip from his grasp. An inspired Scotland upset the odds thanks to a display of passion and guts as fly-half Duncan Hodge scored a try, a conversion and four penalties.

England utterly failed to adapt to the wet conditions and were mocked afterwards when some players and coaches suggested they had been caught out by the weather. Quite why rain in a Scottish winter was such a surprise has, to this day, never been made clear. Making it all even worse, due to a mix-up in communication, the England team failed to collect the Six Nations trophy and left a member of the royal family waiting in the cold in the vain hope of presenting a trophy. Well, there are sadder stories, to be fair.

TURNING POINT IN AFRICA

Martin Johnson was back at the helm for a five-match tour of South Africa in the summer of 2000. England won all three non-internationals and, after losing the first Test 18-13, they

Martin Johnson is a giant figure in rugby history.

bounced back to win 27-22 in Bloemfontein. Johnson was inspiring in the way he carried out the grunt work and Jonny Wilkinson kicked all of his side's points (eight penalties and a drop goal). It was one of the great away wins for England and it launched an 11-game winning streak.

2000 – England 22 Australia 19 (Twickenham)
England opened their autumn with a famous win over the Wallabies that Clive Woodward saw as a turning point, saying: '18 November 2000 is an important day in England's rugby history because it was on that day that our team psychologically broke Australia's back . . . [it was the] start of an unparalleled five-match winning streak against the Wallabies.'

The game was won in the eighth minute of injury time thanks to winger Dan Luger touching down an Iain Balshaw (Bath) kick. It took the use of the relatively new television replay technology to confirm the score. Twickenham went wild. England rode the momentum to claim further autumn wins over Argentina (19-0) and South Africa (25-17).

A STRIKE . . .
After the win over Australia, tensions came to a head between the RFU and the players over player payments. The players felt the RFU had not fully adapted to professionalism and, to a degree, took advantage of the fact that playing for England was an honour by short-changing the players in other areas. In particular, there was conflict around match fees and how much of these payments should be linked to wins and how much just

to playing. The RFU refused to budge and, in the end (and to Woodward's fury), the players threatened to strike and not play in the next game against Argentina. Phil Vickery described it as drawing 'a line in the sand separating the old amateur game from the new professional one. There had to be a change in the way things were being done.'

In reaction to the strike, Woodward told the players they could not stay at the team hotel. By the next day a compromise was reached and the players came back into the fold. Some of the squad even felt like the whole thing had bonded them a little more as they had had to stick together. Woodward's failure to outright back his players was not seen in the best light by all.

CELTIC GRAND SLAM HEARTACHE (PART III)

After the last-day failures against Wales (1999) and Scotland (2000), England were determined to finally win another Grand Slam and avoid falling at the final hurdle. Huge favourites, they swept aside Wales (44-15), Italy (80-23), Scotland (43-3) and France (48-19 in Paris). It all looked set to be third time lucky. But . . .

2001 – Ireland 20 England 14 (Lansdowne Road)

An outbreak of foot and mouth disease prevented Ireland from finishing their fixtures in the 2001 Six Nations, meaning three of their games were delayed until later in the year. England had undertaken a short tour of North America in the summer, beating the USA and Canada (the latter twice). They had done so without their British & Irish Lions players who had been in Australia. When the Irish match was rearranged for October, however, England had lost all the momentum and sparkle that had been in evidence in the first four games of their campaign.

A passionate Dublin crowd created an electric atmosphere and Martin Johnson's men never recovered after Ireland's captain and hooker Keith Wood powered over for a try after 15 minutes. The shock loss ended an 11-game winning streak and, to the amusement of fans from the other Home Unions, England had once again had their Grand Slam chariot rammed off the road yards from the finish line. Neil Back, who was upset with referee Paul Honiss, said it was the lowest point of his career.

SWINGS AND ROUNDABOUTS

Ahead of the 2001 clash with Wales in Cardiff, Jonny Wilkinson and his kicking coach, Dave Alred, were struggling to find some green space to do some kicking practice. On the morning of every game, the pair had a short kick-around to get game ready. However, the England team were staying in Cardiff Bay and they were unable to find anywhere suitable. In the end, the determined duo jumped over the fence of a local school and the famous fly-half used the swings and play animals as obstacles to kick to and over. The somewhat childlike approach did England no harm. A few hours later, England won 44-15 and Wilkinson kicked four penalties and a conversion.

BILLY WHIZZ RUSHES IN

The 2001 Six Nations saw rugby league legend Jason Robinson (Sale) make his international union debut. Brought back to union in 2000 after a previous spell in 1996, Robinson quickly became a fan favourite with his incredible acceleration and an ability to sidestep at a speed that seemed to rewrite the laws of physics. Playing as both a winger and a full-back, he would go on to join the pantheon of English greats and ultimately captain the side too.

ONCE MORE THE BRIDESMAID

The 2002 Triple Crown

After the October edition of Celtic Grand Slam Heartache, England got back to winning ways with a 21-15 win over Australia, a cruel 134-0 victory over Romania and a 29-9 triumph over South Africa. It meant they again headed into a Six Nations with pressure on to win a Grand Slam. But there was to be no final day heartache this time around. Instead, England suffered their solitary loss in round four, falling to France 20-15 in Paris. Clive Woodward said this was one of Jonny Wilkinson's poorest games for England. The tenacious French flanker Serge Betsen had a stormer against the fly-half and Wilkinson, never one to back down from a challenge, sought out Betsen at rucks and in contact to show he wasn't intimidated. It may have proven his toughness, but it didn't help England's cause. Once again England had missed out on a Grand Slam, but at least had a Triple Crown as it wasn't a Celtic nation upsetting them this time.

TRYING TIME

Between November 2001 (during the win over Australia) to the win over Ireland, England scored a mind-blowing 31 tries without conceding one. Twenty of those came in the 134-0 win over Romania, a game in which outside-half Charlie Hodgson (Sale Sharks) scored 44 points.

THIS TRAIN IS BOUND FOR GLORY

After the Triple Crown in 2002, England embarked on what is by far the most glorious period in their history. After the loss in Paris, England would win their next 14 games, only losing their record narrowly after putting out a weakened team in a World Cup warm-up match in 2003. Here are the other highlights from 2002.

2002 – Argentina 18 England 26 (Estadio Jose Amalfitani, Buenos Aires)

An England team without several key members of their pack and led by Phil Vickery overcame a nine-point half-time deficit away to a tasty Puma side – it was the biggest comeback in English rugby history to that point.

2002 – England 31 New Zealand 28 (Twickenham)

England faced the big three from down south on successive autumn weekends and began with a bang. Jonny Wilkinson scored 21 points (including a quality solo try) and Lewis Moody and winger Ben Cohen (Northampton) grabbed five-pointers. Even England's old nemesis, Jonah Lomu, couldn't help New Zealand get a win (although he scored two tries of his own). The All Blacks rallied late on to come back from 31-14, but it was too late.

2002 – England 32 Australia 31 (Twickenham)
This week Ben Cohen grabbed a brace of tries (the rest of the scoring came from the boot of Wilkinson) as England made it three consecutive wins over the Wallabies for the first time ever.

2002 – England 53 South Africa 3 (Twickenham)
England humiliated a petty and violent Springbok side with a record win that included seven tries. In a game packed with thuggery, second row Jannes Labuschagne was dismissed after 23 minutes for a late tackle on Jonny Wilkinson. England punished them with a humiliating beating on the scoreboard. After the November series, England sat atop the official world rankings for the first time ever.

WOODWARD FINALLY GETS HIS SLAM
2003 GRAND SLAM
After four years of falling a game short, England finally won a Grand Slam – their first since 1995 and the start of the professional era. With the 'monkey' finally removed from their back, Martin Johnson's men could charge into a World Cup as top dogs in Europe.

MATCH ONE: England 25 France 17 (Twickenham)
Jason Leonard won his 100th cap as England navigated what

was seen by many as the biggest challenge to their Grand Slam ambitions. To avoid Serge Betsen again bottling up Jonny Wilkinson as in 2002, Woodward moved his man to centre and put Charlie Hodgson at fly-half. The day before this win the England squad learned of the devastating death of Nick Duncombe, a 21-year-old scrum-half who had won two caps in the 2002 Six Nations. The Harlequins player had died after contracting meningitis.

MATCH TWO: Wales 9 England 26 (Millennium Stadium)

Wales, fresh off a humiliating loss to Italy, tried hard but had little to offer as tries from centre Will Greenwood (Harlequins) and flanker Joe Worsley (Wasps) helped them home. Greenwood always seemed to enjoy his clashes with Wales: in six career games he scored seven tries against them.

MATCH THREE: England 40 Italy 5 (Twickenham)

With Martin Johnson injured, Jonny Wilkinson took charge in a game much tighter than the score suggested and in which England spent more time defending than the visitors. It was 33-0 after 20 minutes, and then Italy dominated possession until the end.

MATCH FOUR: England 40 Scotland 9 (Twickenham)

Jason Robinson bagged two tries in this romp against a Scottish side who never looked like ending a losing streak in London that had begun in 1983.

MATCH FIVE: Ireland 6 England 42 (Lansdowne Road)

For only the sixth time in Championship history, two sides met in a Grand Slam showdown. This is by far the most one-sided of such 'winner takes all' contests and the first time an away side in the fixture prevailed. Ahead of the game the media focused on England's failure to carry out a clean sweep in each of the previous four seasons. Martin Johnson's men knew a failure to win here would put a serious dent in their confidence ahead of the World Cup later in the year.

Before the match, Martin Johnson led his men out on the field in Dublin and stood next to the red carpet, always in place for the ever so exciting meeting before each Dublin game with the Irish president. However, Johnson had mistakenly gone to the Irish side of the red carpet. When he was asked to move so the Irish team could stand there instead, he refused, suggesting the home side simply go to the other side of the carpet across the halfway line. Rather than stand in front of the English (as several players suggested to their captain Brian O'Driscoll) or push them back, after a tense stand-off the Irish instead lined up alongside the English on the same side of halfway, forcing their own president to walk over the grass to greet them. It was seen as a psychological victory for the visitors before the game even began. Afterwards the RFU wrote an apology to the IRFU and the IRFU apologised to the president.

The match itself was tight for 60 minutes, but Johnson's England weren't going to let a fifth Grand Slam go begging and scored most of their points in the final quarter. Tries on the day came from Lawrence Dallaglio, centre Mike Tindall (Bath), Dan Luger and Will Greenwood (two tries). The Grand Slam ghost was buried at last.

SUBLIME SUMMER OF THE STEROID ORCS

England prepared for the World Cup with two Tests away to

Australia and New Zealand. Clive Woodward was determined to push his team as hard as possible in preparation for a tournament that would take place in Australia. After a 23-9 win over the New Zealand Maori in an uncapped match, England headed to Wellington to face the All Blacks.

2003 – New Zealand 13 England 15 (Westpac Stadium, Wellington)

England won for the second time away over the All Blacks in what is still one of the most remarkable results in the national side's history. Five years after the humiliation of the Tour from Hell and 30 years since John Pullin shocked the All Blacks on Kiwi soil, England triumphed again away from home against New Zealand. The result was all the more impressive as at one point England were reduced to 13 men after Neil Back and Lawrence Dallaglio received yellow cards. Despite only having six forwards, England held off the All Blacks close to their own line and, during this spell, even added a drop goal from Jonny Wilkinson (who scored all the visitors' points).

It was a genuine humiliation for the proudest of rugby nations and positioned England as outright favourites for the World Cup. The following week England won 25-14 over Australia in Melbourne. The results prompted one New Zealand journalist to write: 'The rest of the [English] pack were simply giant gargoyles, raw-boned, cauliflower-ear monoliths that intimidated and unsettled. When they ran on to the field, it was like watching a tribe of white orcs on steroids. Forget their hardness – has there ever been an uglier forward pack?'

England may have been labelled 'orcs on steroids', but they just laughed it off.

THE LONG FOOT OF THE LAW

After this match New Zealand second row Ali Williams was cleared of stamping on the head of full-back Josh Lewsey (Wasps). Clive Woodward was furious and vowed to always travel with legal representation in future, a decision that was to pay off in the World Cup.

ENGLAND ALMOST GO ALL IN ONE

Today, tight rugby kits are the norm. But when England first dressed in their skin-tight kit in 2003, it was a source of amusement and laughter to many. Clive Woodward had claimed that the baggy cotton shirts of the era had prevented Jason Robinson bagging a hat-trick in one match and wrote to Nike to ask them to design tighter shirts. However, when they made the shirts they also had to give them to France and South Africa as they were kit suppliers for England's rivals too.

While traditionalists tutted, it could have been much worse: England even trialled out an all-in-one kit. Dan Luger suffered the indignity of having to try it out to the amusement of his teammates. But luckily for him and the squad, the International Rugby Board would not sanction such a kit.

2003 WORLD CUP (AUSTRALIA)

Glory. Quite simply, the 2003 World Cup is the highest point in the history of the English national side. The first major team trophy won by the nation since the 1966 football World Cup, the reaction to the victory took interest in rugby across the land to stratospheric levels. England now had as many world titles as New Zealand, who had still not won one since 1987. The tournament confirmed the sporting immortality of players like Jonny Wilkinson, Martin Johnson and Jason Robinson.

England flew into Australia as the number one team in the world and with 15 wins from the previous 16 Tests (the only loss being a near irrelevant World Cup warm-up by the second XV to France). The English pack were feared across the rugby world, with players like Phil Vickery, Trevor Woodman, Jason Leonard, Martin Johnson, Ben Kay, Neil Back, Richard Hill, Lawrence Dallaglio, Steve Thompson, Lewis Moody and others giving opposing forwards many sleepless nights.

The Aussie media, desperate to upset England's march to glory, led a ferocious campaign against England, labelling them 'white orcs on steroids' or 'Dad's Army'. The Wallaby camp joined in too. Clive Woodward noted that future England coach Eddie Jones and his team were happy to harp on about how slow and boring England were.

Captain: Martin Johnson
Coach: Clive Woodward

POOL GAMES

England 84 Georgia 6 (Subiaco Oval, Perth)
Rugby World Cup pool stages always involve cruel mismatches, and this was one of two for England in their group. The men in white blasted over for a dozen tries.

England 25 South Africa 6 (Subiaco Oval)

In a bruising battle in Perth, a well-taken try from Will Greenwood in the 63rd minute was key to sending England to victory. Lewis Moody charged down a kick from Springbok number ten Louis Koen just inside the South African ten-metre line. Will Greenwood pounced, hacked ahead with precision and dived on the ball to open up a little daylight. Wilkinson added two further drop goals to take his tally to 20 and seal the match. The game was notable for both sides losing several shirts. The skin-tight technology used at the time was still experiencing teething troubles and shirts and numbers regularly went AWOL from their owners' backs.

After the win, one Australian newspaper, referring to Wilkinson's boot, asked, 'Is that all you've got?'

England 35 Samoa 22 (Docklands Stadium, Melbourne)

Tournament favourites England may have been, but they experienced some incredibly scary moments against the proud Islanders who possessed but a fraction of the playing budget and preparation time their opponents enjoyed. After just six minutes Samoa led by ten points, number eight Semo Sititi rounding off a superb team try that had started inside their own half. England replied after 24 minutes with a try from Neil Back after a prosaic line-out catch and drive from five metres out. Samoa led at half-time by 16-10. Again, England's forwards had to respond, forcing a penalty try after a collapsed scrum in the 54th minute. Amazingly, the huge underdogs came back, thanks to inspired play and the boot of Earl Va'a. After regaining the lead they held on to it until the 65th minute, when the superior fitness of the favourites began to come through. Tries from Iain Balshaw and Phil Vickery (his first for England) eventually pulled a nervous England clear.

England prop Trevor Woodman admitted there were some 'twitchy backsides' for England during the match. They got twitchier afterwards too. It was discovered that England briefly had 16 players on the field due to a mix-up with replacements. There was (admittedly daft) talk of them being thrown out of the tournament or docked group points. But defended by the QC they had brought with them, the fallout was just a £10,000 fine.

England 111 Uruguay 13 (Suncorp Stadium, Brisbane)

Cruel. Five Josh Lewsey tries and 12 for his teammates in a depressing day for rugby.

QUARTER-FINAL

England 28 Wales 17 (Suncorp Stadium)

Once again, as in the Samoan pool match, the rugby world was briefly turned on its head. Wales, whose first team had been humiliated by the England reserves in the summer, outscored England by three tries to one and gave Goliath a huge scare. Wales's first try, started and finished by wonder winger Shane Williams, was a peach. When the Welsh pack drove the English pack back from a five-metre line-out for the second try, England fans once again began to nibble on their nails. However, a fantastic substitute appearance from Mike Catt helped relieve the pressure on Jonny Wilkinson, with Catt adding another kicking dimension to his side's game. Then came another moment of magic from Jason Robinson in a career overflowing with sparkle. Early in the second half, Robinson took the ball inside his own ten-metre line and took off. Beating exactly a third of the Welsh team with his acceleration and footwork, he carried it 50 metres and fed Will Greenwood (who seemed to be addicted to scoring against Wales) who ran in from ten metres out to score. Wilkinson finished with 23 points as England avoided a repeat of their inglorious 1987 quarter-final loss to the Welsh and marched onwards.

SEMI-FINAL

England 24 France 7 (Stadium Australia, Sydney)

It was Wilkinson 24, France 7 in appalling conditions in Sydney. France's Serge Betsen grabbed the game's solitary try, but wet and windswept English fans cared not a jot as their metronomic fly-half slotted five penalties and three drop goals. England had another shot at Australia in a World Cup final – this time away from home. One squad player, Jason Leonard, even had a personal score to settle, having played in the 1991 final.

FINAL

Australia 17 England 20* (Stadium Australia)
(*After extra time)

England finally made it to the top of the world and became the first (and still the only) northern hemisphere side to lay their hands on the Webb Ellis Cup. But despite being heavily favoured by most rugby observers, England had to dig deep for it. The Wallabies, defending champions and on home soil, heroically tried to resist the white wave of destiny.

On a rainy night in front of 82,000 fans, Australia drew first blood when winger Lote Tuqiri out-jumped Jason Robinson in a competition for a Stephen Larkham cross kick. With just six minutes gone, the home side were 5-0 up. But England didn't panic. After 30 minutes they led 9-5 thanks to the relentless boot of Jonny Wilkinson and the power of their experienced and feared pack. Shortly before half-time, Ben Kay tidied up some loose ball from an English line-out and England worked it out left via some smart interplay between Jonny Wilkinson and Lawrence Dallaglio. The fly-half fed it to right winger Robinson (popping up on the left wing) and, from 20 metres out, 'Billy Whizz' put on the burners and skinned the cover defence to score in the corner. At the break, England led 14-5. They had one hand firmly on the trophy.

But the Wallabies had not read the script. They smartly ground their way back into the match, with centre Elton Flatley chipping away at England's lead as Martin Johnson's men's discipline slipped. Even worse for English fans, their side failed to add to their total in the second half. In the last play of regular time, England were penalised at the scrum and Flatley kept his cool to equal the scores and take it to extra time, where a further 20 minutes had to be played.

In the latter stages of the match, England's scrum had begun to concede regular penalties and Clive Woodward sent for his most experienced player: Jason Leonard. The front rower used all the know-how he had gained in his long career (after all, he had played in the 1991 final too) and decided to NOT scrummage. The wily veteran had realised that Phil Vickery was continually getting penalised unfairly and thought it better to 'stop' scrummaging so that the Australians wouldn't get awarded an easy penalty.

Two minutes into extra time, Wilkinson put England 17-14 ahead after Australia infringed at a line-out. Exhausted players from both sides began falling, with several players getting treated for aching muscles. Richard Hill was one key player to have his involvement curtailed by cramp and was replaced by an excellent Lewis Moody. In the fatigue of battle, even simple things were hard to execute. England's line-out, usually utterly dependable, became a source of concern. With just three minutes remaining, a poor tap down from an English line-out led to a mad scramble to recover a loose ball. Strong Wallaby pressure forced Dallaglio to concede a penalty and Flatley again kicked the points to equalise matters. With so little time left, it looked like the final was heading to ten minutes of sudden death.

The drive to glory

Yet, the dreaded sudden death bout did not come, thanks to the most famous drive in English rugby history. With just over a minute of extra time left, England had a line-out on the right-hand side, ten metres out from the Australian 22. Martin Johnson revealed after the game that Ben Kay called a long line-out throw, even though he knew hooker Steve Thompson was nervous about it. Thompson had missed a few long throws earlier, so the home side stacked the front of the line-out, 'daring' Thompson to go long.

Kay, sensing Thompson's nerves, reassured his hooker that he would take the blame if it went wrong, saying: 'Underthrow it, you've gone too big before now . . . if they steal it, don't worry, that's our problem.' The bold call paid off and the Wallabies were unable to react in time. Dawson spun out the resultant ball a bit haphazardly, but Wilkinson took it and fed a charging Mike Tindall to set up a ruck. Just a few metres outside the Oz 22, Australia expected a Wilkinson drop goal, but Dawson, realising this, cleverly sneaked through a gap and made vital extra yards. Brought down 15 metres out, the position was perfect, but with their scrum-half and best passer on the floor, England needed to set up another phase – which they duly did through captain Johnson. He made not a single yard, but it didn't matter, it freed up Dawson.

The whole world knew what was coming next and the Australian defenders were ready for it. But stopping it was another thing. The ball flew back to Wilkinson, standing just outside the 22, and using his 'weaker' right foot, he calmly slotted his way to immortality. Amazingly, Wilkinson had missed three earlier attempts during the game with his preferred left foot. With 26 seconds left, England led by three and there was no coming back for the defending champions. England were on top of the world.

The immortal team that day were:

Josh Lewsey (London Wasps); Jason Robinson (Sale Sharks), Mike Tindall (Bath), Will Greenwood (Harlequins), Ben Cohen (Northampton Saints); Jonny Wilkinson (Newcastle Falcons), Matt Dawson (Northampton Saints); Trevor Woodman (Gloucester), Steve Thompson (Northampton Saints), Phil Vickery

(Gloucester), Martin Johnson (Leicester Tigers, capt), Ben Kay (Leicester Tigers), Richard Hill (Saracens), Lawrence Dallaglio (London Wasps), Neil Back (Leicester Tigers).

Replacements used: *Jason Leonard (Harlequins), Lewis Moody (Leicester Tigers), Mike Catt (Bath), Iain Balshaw (Bath).*

Glory, at last.

A NATION CELEBRATES

England partied hard on the night of their World Cup victory. Later, Jonny Wilkinson revealed: 'I did have a couple of beers, but that was a solidarity thing with the other guys. There are times for letting yourself go, but Saturday night I just wanted to let it all soak in.'

But the party had only just started. Despite arriving back in London just after 4 a.m. on the Tuesday after the final (on a plane called 'Sweet Chariot'), they were greeted by thousands of fans at Heathrow Airport. The centre of London came to a standstill as the conquering heroes were wined and dined at Buckingham Palace and 10 Downing Street, paraded about on two open-top buses to an estimated 750,000 delirious fans. Dallaglio was quoted as saying: 'This is quite a humbling experience.' To round it all off, the Mayor of London, Ken Livingstone, granted the team the Freedom of the City of Greater London, declaring: 'You are the first and only people to be awarded that distinction.'

1995–2003: THE STAR PLAYERS

JONNY WILKINSON

Club: Newcastle Falcons, Toulon
Position: Fly-half, centre
Caps: 91 (1998–2011)
(British Lions, 6 caps, 67 points)
Points: 1,179 (6 tries, 162 conversions, 239 penalties, 36 drop goals)

Jonny Wilkinson was so good that he ended his club career being hero-worshipped by rugby fans in France. Born in Frimley, Wilkinson showed an obsessive approach to improving his skills from a young age. He would not even skip kicking practice on Christmas Day and often his mother would have to drag him away from the rugby field when it was so dark he couldn't even see the posts. He made his international debut under Clive Woodward in Dublin aged just 18. His first World Cup was 1999, and he appeared in the 2003, 2007 and 2011 versions too – his famous drop goal, of course, winning the second of those tournaments (he also played in the 2007 final). He did all this despite a horrific run of injuries, including a run of bad fortune that kept him out of the England team for over three years.

More than just a double-footed kicker, Wilkinson loved defending and coaches often had to plead with him to stay out of rucks and mauls and let the forwards do the grunt work. Always humble, he was awarded the Lifetime Mike Pyke Nonchalant Try-Scoring Award by *The East Terrace* website for his cool, calm and unfussy responses to scoring tries.

Wilkinson was the holder of the international points record for several years and his 36 Test drop goals are still an international record and eight more than his nearest rival in that regard (Hugo Porta of Argentina). His final club years were spent at Toulon where he became a huge favourite of French rugby followers and enjoyed European glory.

MARTIN JOHNSON

Club: Leicester Tigers
Position: Second row
Caps: 84 (1993–2003)
(British & Irish Lions, 8 caps)
Points: 10 (2 tries)

Martin Johnson was almost an All Black. A promising youngster, in 1989 he was invited by Kiwi legend Colin Meads to develop his skills and gain some experience in New Zealand. During his time there he was capped by New Zealand U21s. But Johnson turned down further chances to wear a silver fern for the pursuit of wearing the red rose. Thirty-nine of his caps were as captain and he was the victor in 34 of them. A huge and intimidating presence, one reason Clive Woodward picked him to lead England was the psychological advantage he could offer at the captain's coin toss when the opposing captain saw the sheer size of the man. An uncompromising character, Johnson was certainly not afraid to put himself about and never took a backward step in a confrontation.

A three-time Lions tourist (twice as captain), for all his world-class forward skills, his most important asset seemed to be his sheer force of will and influence on teammates – a giant in more ways than one. Fittingly, his final act in an England shirt was to lift the Webb Ellis Cup. Sadly, his time as England coach was almost a complete contrast to his time on the field, but his legacy will always live on as long as England play rugby.

JASON ROBINSON

Club: Sale Sharks
Position: Full-back, wing
Caps: 51 (2001–07)
(British & Irish Lions, 5 caps, 10 points)
Points: 140 (28 tries)

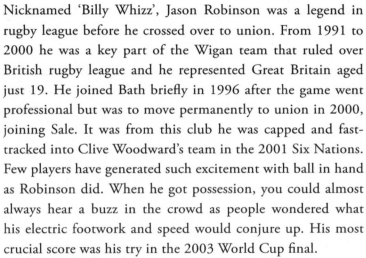

Nicknamed 'Billy Whizz', Jason Robinson was a legend in rugby league before he crossed over to union. From 1991 to 2000 he was a key part of the Wigan team that ruled over British rugby league and he represented Great Britain aged just 19. He joined Bath briefly in 1996 after the game went professional but was to move permanently to union in 2000, joining Sale. It was from this club he was capped and fast-tracked into Clive Woodward's team in the 2001 Six Nations. Few players have generated such excitement with ball in hand as Robinson did. When he got possession, you could almost always hear a buzz in the crowd as people wondered what his electric footwork and speed would conjure up. His most crucial score was his try in the 2003 World Cup final.

Robinson originally retired from the Test arena in 2005 but was tempted back for the 2007 Six Nations and appeared in that year's World Cup. He was the first black captain of England, leading the side on seven occasions. He said of his career: 'I look back now and think, "How has little me from a council estate in Leeds gone on to play not only rugby league for England but to play rugby union and to be captain as well?"'

RICHARD HILL

Club: Saracens
Position: Flanker
Caps: 71 (1997–2004)
(British & Irish Lions, 5 caps)
Points: 60 (12 tries)

Richard Hill is probably the most sung about unsung hero in rugby history. Nicknamed the 'silent assassin', he was widely admired by teammates and opponents across the world. Clive Woodward never dropped him, the only player not to fall foul of the coach during his whole reign. Best known as a blindside flanker, even though he preferred being a number seven, Hill was a ruthless, tireless, uncompromising soldier. When it came to the hard work like rucks, tackles and mauls, he just kept going and going. He formed the 'Holy Trinity' back row with Lawrence Dallaglio and Neil Back. He is not to be confused with scrum-half Richard Hill who took part in the Battle of Cardiff in 1987.

JASON LEONARD

Club: Harlequins
Position: Prop
Caps: 114 (1990–2004)
(British & Irish Lions, 5 caps)
Points: 5 (1 try)

Jason Leonard's magnificent career spanned the amateur and

professional eras. Indeed, he appeared in World Cup finals as both a pro (2003) and an amateur (1991). His career also spanned both sides of the scrum. Capped against Argentina when he was just 21 (often mistakenly listed in the media as 22), he became the youngest English Test prop in history. He was a key building block of the powerful packs that brought England success in the twilight of the amateur era under Will Carling, but was also adaptable and skilled enough to thrive in the professional game. His career almost came to an end in 1992 when serious injury threatened to end it all. Leonard had a piece of his hip bone used to repair a ruptured vertebra in the top of his neck and was playing again half a year later. His introduction as a replacement in the 2003 World Cup final for Phil Vickery has been hailed by many (including Clive Woodward) as a key turning point. Recognising that the referee was unsympathetic to English scrummaging efforts, Leonard decided to effectively 'not scrummage' so as to not give the official a reason to penalise his side.

His 114 caps were at one point a world record and he was the most capped English player ever until 2022 when his record was claimed by Ben Youngs. Leonard served in four Grand Slam teams, one World Cup win, three Lions tours and captained England twice. He averaged one try every 114 games for England.

1995–2003 NOTABLE EVENTS IN ENGLISH HISTORY

• 1995: Manchester United's Eric Cantona attacks a thug in the stands for verbally abusing him after being sent off against Crystal Palace.

• 1996: Dolly the sheep is born. She is the first mammal ever to be cloned from an adult cell.

• 1997: The Conservative tabloid the *Sun* switches allegiance to the Labour Party ahead of the general election.

• 1998: The UK and Irish governments sign the historic Good Friday Agreement, ending the majority of the violence of The Troubles.

• 1999: The England football manager, Glenn Hoddle, is fired for his comments that imply people born with disabilities had committed sins in a previous life.

• 2000: After 77 years, Wembley Stadium closes so that it can be demolished and rebuilt to serve modern needs.

• 2001: Sixty-seven UK nationals die in the terrorist attacks by al-Qaeda on 11 September in the USA.

• 2002: Joe Strummer, co-founder of the Clash, dies aged 50.

• 2003: UK forces take part in the invasion of Iraq.

2004–22: PEAKS AND TROUGHS

	PLAYED	WON	DRAWN	LOST
SIX NATIONS	95	60	2	33
TESTS	85	44	2	39
WORLD CUP	22	16	0	6
WORLD CUP WARM-UP GAMES*	13	8	0	5
AUTUMN NATIONS CUP	4	4	0	0
TOTAL	219	132	4	83

*Listed separately due to their experimental nature and mass substitutions.
Full caps were awarded, however, and they are considered full internationals.

Championships (4)

2011, 2016 (Grand Slam), 2017, 2020 (Triple Crown)

Triple Crowns (without winning Championship) (1)

2014

World Cups

Runners-up (2007, 2019), Quarter-finals (2011) Pool stages (2015)

Autumn Nations Cup

2021

'You will never do it again. Your country is incapable of sustained success. You will win it and you will drop off.'

STEVE HANSEN ON ENGLAND AFTER THEIR 2003 WORLD CUP WIN

BACK AMONG THE CHASING PACK

After the summit came the inevitable descent. And

unfortunately for English fans, the descent after the World Cup triumph was rapid, bumpy and painful. Yet after the dramatic victory in Sydney, all the right noises came out of the England camp. Clive Woodward proclaimed: 'We are still a long way from the finished article and I don't want this to be a small blip in history. I want the success of England to go on forever so that we become the leading force in world rugby and take over the mantle of the All Blacks and the South Africans.'

In the years that followed, however, England collapsed like no other previous world champion team had. They would not win another Six Nations title until 2011. As world champions their Six Nations finishing positions were: third, fourth, fourth and third. Martin Johnson had retired after lifting the World Cup and his presence was sorely missed. After a horrific summer tour in 2004 to New Zealand and Australia (which was planned terribly by the RFU), the recently knighted Sir Clive Woodward quit. Retirements and injuries also frustrated England. Wilkinson, plagued by injuries, would not wear the white of his nation again after the World Cup until February 2007.

Although England somehow bravely scrambled to the 2007 World Cup final, their 2011 and 2015 World Cups were unmitigated disasters. After years of feasting at rugby's top table, England had been reduced to trying to catch the eye of the head waiter and failing miserably.

Like their rugby team, the nation was to dramatically transform too in this period. Most notably, the Brexit referendum saw 53.4 per cent of English voters vote to leave the European Union. The Brexit vote – and the political squabble around it – divided the country in a way perhaps not seen for centuries.

AFTER THE PARTY, THE LONG HANGOVER

After climbing rugby's Mount Everest, England fell off the other side. The years that followed the World Cup were grim and the places the national team visited at times made older fans feel they were back in the 1980s. Arguably, England's approach to victory had been 'all or nothing', and once the trophy was claimed, everything that had helped support England in getting to the top seemed to crumble away. Some, like Clive Woodward, felt that despite the success of 2003, too few RFU officials and too few English clubs were willing to continue to make the sacrifices and changes needed to keep England at the top of the international game. Since the day Jonny Wilkinson kicked his most famous drop goal, the England national team have lived a somewhat Jekyll and Hyde existence. Two World

After the victory party, the hangover.

Cup final appearances were achieved, but an inglorious pool stage exit at home in 2015 and the embarrassment of 2011 (on and off the field) have left English fans frustrated, confused and hungry for global success.

BACK TO EARTH WITH A BUMP

Fresh from the celebrations of the World Cup win, England returned to the more traditional battleground of the Six Nations. Led by new captain Lawrence Dallaglio (and with Jonny Wilkinson injured), relatively routine wins were earned in Rome (50-9) and Edinburgh (35-13). Then, to borrow one of rugby writing's most tired clichés, the chariot wheels came off.

2004 – England 13 Ireland 19 (Twickenham)

Before this match, Irish captain Brian O'Driscoll had spoken about giving 'the prawn sandwich brigade something to choke on'. His side did just that. England's 22-match victory streak at home came to a stunning end as the visitors outplayed and overpowered the home side. English fans had not witnessed a home loss since the defeat to New Zealand in the 1999 World Cup. The *Guardian* called aspects of the world champions' performance a 'shambles', especially the line-out.

Irish fly-half Ronan O'Gara kicked 14 points (Girvan Dempsey grabbed a try too) and he spoke after the game about how much Jonny Wilkinson was missed: 'Maybe the leadership of [Martin] Johnson would have helped, but I think Wilkinson was probably a bigger loss in terms of how creative he can be.' England didn't know it then, but it would still be years before

Wilkinson would return to the international fold. England rounded off the 2004 Six Nations with a 24-21 loss in Paris. For a team that had lost once in its last 25 games (and that with a second-string side in a near meaningless World Cup warm-up), two losses in five games was officially a crisis. But the summer was to bring further horrors.

THE TOUR FROM HELL: PART II

After a relentless few years on the treadmill of international rugby, the last thing England needed was another tour down under. So, the RFU sent them to New Zealand (for two Tests) and Australia.

2004 Summer Tour
1st Test: New Zealand 36 England 3 (Carisbrook, Dunedin)

The only positive for England from this disaster in the 'House of Pain', was they rallied to only concede six points in the second half, having trailed 30-3 after 40 minutes. Tries from Carlos Spencer, Joe Rokocoko and Doug Howlett effectively put the tourists on the canvas in the first half. England's only points came from fly-half Charlie Hodgson.

2nd Test: New Zealand 36 England 12 (Eden Park, Auckland)

England conceded the exact same number of points as the week before, scored nine more themselves, but finished with one man fewer than they started with. Second row Simon Shaw (London Wasps) was dismissed for a knee to the back of

Kiwi lock Keith Robinson after ten minutes. It was England's first sending off since the 1998 'Tour from Hell', when another English second row, Danny Grewcock, had also been sent off for inappropriate use of his legs against New Zealand.

Australia 51 England 15 (Suncorp Stadium, Brisbane)
This horror show was to be a sad and limp bookend to the Clive Woodward era. While the head coach tried to put on a brave face, defence coach Phil Larder admitted it was 'a massive embarrassment' and that England were clearly 'running on empty'. The home side scored six tries to England's two. The Wallabies even opted to kick a last-minute penalty to rub salt in the wounds and cross the half-century mark.

FAREWELL, SIR CLIVE
The summer of woe brought down the curtain on Clive Woodward's time nurturing the rose of England. After returning from Australia, speculation dragged on for weeks about whether he could hold on to his position. It seemed at first Woodward would hang on for the autumn series, but it was not to be. After negotiations with the RFU, he announced his resignation. His position was taken by Andy Robinson, the former England flanker who had won eight caps between 1988 and 1995. Robinson was a key part of the World Cup win, having been forwards coach under Woodward and for many it at least felt like a natural progression.

On the sudden fall from grace, Woodward later wrote: 'The thought in November 2003 that in nine months I wouldn't be coaching that team, well I would have just laughed. I would have gone: "What do you mean? I have just won the World Cup. We have won 44 out of 50 games – how could I not be coaching the team next September?"' He departed to give his 'first love' football a go, heading to Southampton FC as their performance director in 2005. By August 2006 he was no longer working there.

In the same week the head coaching role changed hands, Lawrence Dallaglio retired from Test rugby. The legendary forward was unhappy with the structure of the English game and the volume of matches played. Although he later changed his mind about stepping away from the national side, he did bring an end to his role as captain. Lewis Moody, who had played in the 2003 World Cup, wrote in his autobiography: 'Everything had been geared to winning the World Cup. After that? Well, nobody had given it much thought.'

ROBINSON AND ROBINSON

Andy Robinson appointed Jason Robinson as his captain. It was the first time a former rugby league player had been appointed captain of the England team. The bodies of countless Victorian and Edwardian administrators and officials are no doubt still spinning in their graves. The Sale Sharks winger and skipper started out with two wins from two as his team saw off Canada (70-0) and South Africa. Meanwhile, behind the scenes, some experienced players felt the RFU were cutting corners on funding, resources and planning in a way they never would have under Clive Woodward.

2004 – England 32 South Africa 16 (Twickenham)

Outside-half Charlie Hodgson scored a massive 27 points in England's sixth successive win over the Springboks. He bagged a try, two conversions, five penalties and a drop goal in a result that reassured many that England were back on track. They were not.

2004 – England 19 Australia 21 (Twickenham)

The absence of Jonny Wilkinson haunted England as three goal-kickers were used in a disappointing loss to the Wallabies. There was a wave of criticism for new coach Andy Robinson as centre Henry Paul (a controversial import from rugby league) was substituted after just 24 minutes. It was felt Paul had been thrown in far too early. Robinson's apparent struggles with selection were to be even more obvious in the next game England played.

MID-TABLE MEDIOCRITY
AND A MIDDLING AUTUMN

The 2005 Six Nations

The world champions, who finished the championship captained by second row and back rower Martin Corry (Leicester), were to lose three of their 2005 Six Nations matches, consigning themselves to a lowly fourth place. The Championship started with England losing in Cardiff for the first time since 1993. Andy Robinson had taken a huge gamble on picking 18-year-old Mathew Tait (Newcastle Falcons) for his debut in the Celtic cauldron. It backfired badly as Tait's opposite number, Gavin Henson, twice humiliated the teenager by picking him up in the tackle and carrying him back several yards. Nonetheless, England led until the 77th minute, when a silver-booted Henson kicked a monster penalty to send Wales on their way to a first Grand Slam in 27 years.

An 18-17 home loss to France followed (the first loss to the French at HQ since 1997). The defeat came despite a 17-6 half-time lead. Hopes of bouncing back in Dublin were crushed as Ireland won in a fixture that produced an identical score (19-13) to its 2004 counterpart. The 43-22 home win over Scotland in the Calcutta Cup did little to ease the seemingly unshakeable gloom over the national side.

A NOT TOO BAD AUTUMN

England wisely did not tour in the summer of 2005, briefly stepping off the monotonous treadmill of Test rugby. It was a move they should have made in 2004 after a World Cup cycle. In the autumn they defeated a poor Australia (26-16), lost narrowly to New Zealand (19-23) in a spirited display, and then rounded off the year with a big win over Samoa (40-3), albeit one that saw England's Lewis Moody sent off (along with his club teammate Alesana Tuilagi who was playing for Samoa). Moody had responded furiously, if somewhat understandably, to a dangerous tackle by Tuilagi on leaping winger Mark Cueto (Sale).

THE SORROWFUL SEVEN

Any hope that the brakes on England's fall from the top of the rugby world had been successfully applied were ended by the horrors of 2006. England again ended sitting dismally in fourth at the conclusion of the Six Nations. This was followed up with a double battering in Australia on the summer tour – losing 34-3 and 43-18 – and an autumn so poor that, just two years after his appointment, Andy Robinson was forced to step down. After seven straight losses (equal to their run of defeats in 1905 and 1906), including a home loss to Argentina, the calls for his resignation were deafening. It meant England would go into a World Cup year having to defend their crown with another new coach. Here are some of the key moments from that year.

2006 SIX NATIONS

Scotland 18 England 12 (Murrayfield)

After convincing wins over Wales (47-13) and Italy (31-16) some began talking of a Grand Slam for England. But the Scots ended that dream. Once again, a wet and windy Murrayfield was to be a graveyard for English hopes and in a tryless encounter, the home side outfought the visitors. Charlie Hodgson kicked four penalties for England, but the amount of penalties his own side conceded meant Scotland were able to kick themselves home and dry. There was also controversy when captain Martin Corry was replaced by Lawrence Dallaglio (who had come back from international retirement) after 64 minutes. It suggested to some that Robinson didn't back his own leader.

France 31 England 6 (Stade de France)

France, who would go on to win the title, dismantled England in a record-equalling victory. Thanks to a try from Florian Fritz (in the opening minute), and a pair from Dimitri Yachvili, the visitors lost by an amount that equalled the margin of loss in their 37-12 defeat in Paris in 1972. The defeat was littered with errors and effectively ended England's title hopes.

England 24 Ireland 28 (Twickenham)
A last-minute stretch and score in the corner from Irish winger Shane Horgan meant Ireland had now won three on the bounce against their rivals – with two of those wins coming in London. Before that, Ireland had only beaten England once in the previous nine meetings.

A CRUEL SUMMER

With Martin Corry being rested by Andy Robinson, Worcester's Pat Sanderson was chosen to lead England in the two-Test series in Australia. Unfortunately for the flanker, it was to be a case of a career highlight mixing with a personal nightmare as England were comprehensively beaten. With rugby seasons seemingly blending into one another, more and more players were choosing to skip summer tours or were being advised to miss them by their own coaches. Other players rested or unavailable included Steve Thompson, Ben Cohen, prop Andrew Sheridan (Sale), prop Matt Stevens (Bath), Lawrence Dallaglio and Josh Lewsey.

There were more changes behind the scenes too, with coaches Joe Lydon (backs), Dave Alred (kicking) and Phil Larder (defence) all swept away. Larder claimed later that Robinson wanted the players to have more input, something he strongly disagreed with for this group of players who he thought needed more of a firm hand. In their place came Brian Ashton, Mike Ford and John Wells.

1st Test: Australia 34 England 3 (Stadium Australia, Sydney)
Even simple goal kicks were missed in a game in which England barely showed up. The result raised few eyebrows back home as no one seriously expected the tourists to compete.

2nd Test: Australia 43 England 18 (Docklands Stadium, Sydney)
This fifth straight loss made it England's worst run of defeats since 1984. England were now ranked sixth in the world.

AN AGONISING AUTUMN

The only chance Andy Robinson had of keeping his job was a massively successful autumn campaign. But bar a win in the first of two encounters with South Africa, all other games were lost. Robinson was doomed.

England 20 New Zealand 41 (Twickenham)
This was not only a sixth consecutive loss, but England's biggest ever defeat at home.

England 18 Argentina 25 (Twickenham)
If defeats to New Zealand were painful, they were not unexpected. A first home loss to the Pumas, however, was

beyond the pale for the Twickenham faithful. It also took England's run of defeats to seven. Realistically, Robinson was now doomed as coach, whatever the result of the final two games of 2006. The home crowd booed at the game's conclusion.

1st Test: England 23 South Africa 21 (Twickenham)

Phil Vickery powered over from short range seven minutes from time to rescue England, who had trailed 18-6 in the second half. It wasn't going to be enough to save Robinson his job, but it was enough to bring a huge smile to captain Martin Corry's face and even prompted what seemed like words of thanks to a higher power from Joe Worsley.

2nd Test: England 14 South Africa 25 (Twickenham)

Despite leading 14-3 at the interval, England crumbled. The *Guardian*'s match report led with the words: 'Oh dear'.

WHERE HAVE YOU GONE, MR ROBINSON?

After such a torrid year it was inevitable that Andy Robinson was to fall on his sword. Under his watch England had lost 13 of 25 games. The coach did not want to leave, but as world champions it simply wasn't good enough and he was shown the door.

Brian Ashton was promoted from the ranks to become head coach. A hugely respected man who was seen as one of rugby's great thinkers, one of his first actions was to consign to history the famous 'black book' that Clive Woodward had put such emphasis on. Phil Vickery says that in his first team meeting,

Ashton said, 'You write in this book if you want to write in it. We don't need all these codes of conduct and dos and don'ts. It's up to you as individuals now. And we won't be having half so many meetings either.'

FROM FOURTH TO . . . THIRD

Brian Ashton's first Six Nations (with prop Phil Vickery now captain) saw England finish in their best position for three years. They rose up to the heights of third again (as they had in 2004). But for glum England fans, there was one big thing to be happy about: the saviour of 2003 was finally back in an England shirt.

THE WOE OF WILKINSON
AND HIS WONDER RETURN

2007 – England 42 Scotland 20 (Twickenham)

After 1,169 days, Jonny Wilkinson again wore the red rose of England. Since he had kicked the winning drop goal against Australia in 2003, the Newcastle fly-half had not been able to pull on the national shirt due to an extraordinary run of injuries, illness and bad luck (although he did play for the British & Irish Lions on the disastrous Clive Woodward tour of 2005).

So what had kept him out of Test rugby?

• Fractured facet in his right shoulder (December 2003)

• Damaged nerves and tissue in shoulder and neck requiring surgery (February 2004)

- Deep bruising in bicep muscle (October 2004)
- Medial ligament damage in left knee (January 2005)
- Recurrence of knee injury (March 2005)
- Stinger injury in shoulder/neck during 2005 Lions tour (July 2005)
- Inflamed appendix which required removal (September 2005)
- Sports hernia which required surgery (November 2005)
- Torn adductor (this groin injury was not connected to the earlier sports hernia) (January 2006)
- Medial ligament injury in his right knee (September 2006)
- Lacerated kidney (November 2006)

Wilkinson marked his return to national colours by scoring a fairy-tale-like 27 points from five penalties, two conversions, a drop goal and a try. It was the most scored by a single player in the history of the Calcutta Cup. The media and fans, of course, went wild. The number ten's return wasn't the only big story either. Jason Robinson was back too after not featuring for England since 2005 (and his 'retirement' from Test rugby), bagging two tries himself. It was like old times for the Twickenham faithful.

2007 – England 20 Italy 7 (Twickenham)
The comeback kids claimed all the points in a dour win over Italy which brought the home crowd back to earth with a bump after the joy of the Calcutta Cup match. A first-half try from Jason Robinson and five Wilkinson penalties were all England could manage.

CROKE PARK WELCOME
2007 – Ireland 43 England 13 (Croke Park, Dublin)

Ireland won their fourth on the trot against England. But the big story here was the venue and the reaction of local fans to the visiting team. With Lansdowne Road being rebuilt, Ireland were playing on the historic turf of Croke Park. The venue has been the traditional home of Gaelic sports in Ireland since the 1880s and holds a special place in the history of nationalism in Ireland. Indeed, one of the stands of the 82,500 capacity stadium contains rubble from the 1916 Easter Rising against British rule.

And in 1920, on what was to become known as Bloody Sunday, 14 people were killed during a Gaelic football match when the British Auxiliary Division and the Royal Irish Constabulary entered the ground and opened fire. Among the dead were 13 spectators and a player. The shooting was a reprisal for a series of IRA attacks earlier that day in which 15 people (mainly British Army officers) were killed or wounded.

Understandably, in light of the history of the stadium and the nation, many were reluctant to see 'foreign sports' like rugby played at Croke Park. Indeed, there was a specific rule in the Gaelic Athletic Association that forbade it. The idea of the English rugby team playing there (and singing 'God Save the Queen') was hugely controversial.

Amid much soul-searching and national debate, the GAA agreed to the fixture taking place. There were huge concerns about how crowds, fans and locals would react to the arrival of England on the field. A son of a former GAA player published a letter that typified many people's views on the situation:

'I cannot reconcile the provocative words of "God Save the Queen" being sung in the very stadium where Michael Hogan and others died at the hands of crown forces on Bloody Sunday.'

Yet, when England lined up at an electrically charged Croke Park, their anthem was greeted with complete respect by the home fans, even applauded. In response, the Irish belted out their anthem with as much pride as any team ever had. The Irish fans and players rightly received praise from around the world for embracing such a historic event with such dignity and pride. The warm welcome ended there though. The Irish went on to score four tries and dismantle England in a genuine battering. The win eclipsed the record 22-0 Irish winning margin of 1947.

AN AVERAGE TEAM OF
NO-HOPERS HEAD TO FRANCE

After the beating in Croke Park, England got their first win over France since the 2003 World Cup (winning 26-18 at home) but then fell to a poor Welsh side in Cardiff by 27-18. The Six Nations was followed by a 2-0 defeat in a Test series in South Africa (England lost by 58-10 and 55-22). The World Cup warm-ups saw a home and away loss to France and a 62-5 win over an embarrassing Welsh side in London. It meant England headed to France to defend their world crown off the back of four wins and six defeats in 2007. Combined with the poor results of the previous three years, it was fair to say that labelling England as 'no-hopers' was generous at best.

WELCOME BACK, IT'S BEEN A WHILE

During the summer tour of South Africa, prop Kevin Yates (Saracens) was called up to play after a combination of illness and injury had England's team sheet being rapidly amended. It meant that Yates had set a new record for the longest spell between caps for England. The front rower had last played international rugby nine years and 353 days previously, during the 1997 Argentinian tour.

2007 WORLD CUP (FRANCE)

Defending champions England hobbled into the 2007 World Cup as 33/1 outsiders. No world champion team had ever fallen so far from grace between tournaments. After a poor start against the minnows of the USA and a spectacular stuffing from South Africa, England, somehow, ended up in their second straight final – 2007 was, without doubt, England's strangest World Cup adventure.

Captain: Phil Vickery
Coach: Brian Ashton

POOL GAMES

England 28 USA 10 (Stade Félix Bollaert, Lens)

England were widely criticised for lack of width or attacking class in a poor opening game. Leading 21-3 at half-time, England could only add a further seven points in the second half with a try from flanker Tom Rees (Wasps) and a conversion from Bath outside-half Olly Barkley (their best player on the day). Lawrence Dallaglio picked up a late yellow card and captain Phil Vickery was subsequently cited and banned for two matches for a trip on USA's Paul Emerick.

England 0 South Africa 36 (Stade de France, Paris)

Depending on which newspaper you picked up the day after this game, England were humbled, humiliated, smashed, stuffed or annihilated in what remains their worst World Cup defeat. South Africa's scrum-half Fourie du Preez was a thorn in the side of the men with red roses on their shirts and the game was effectively over at half-time with the Boks 20-0 up. Making things worse, one of England's only bright sparks, the legendary Jason Robinson, departed with a hamstring injury. The 2003 World Cup winner had announced that his retirement would come at the end of the tournament. With England such a shambles and at risk of exiting in the group stage, it seemed that this would be his final World Cup appearance. Brian Ashton, however, felt that England had improved on their opening game.

After the match, the England squad had a major meeting to clear the air and some players claim that it was here things changed. Lewis Moody later wrote: 'A lot of the players had their say . . . We focused on our lack of structure. Every so often, I'd look across at Brian [Ashton], standing in the corner with his head bowed, and felt for him. He had the vision, but we needed the structure . . . His power eroded away during that meeting. The reality was from that point onwards, he had lost the players.'

England 44 Samoa 22 (Stade de la Beaujoire, Nantes)
Twenty-four points from Jonny Wilkinson (three conversions, four penalties and two drop goals) and a pair of tries each from flanker (and captain for the match) Martin Corry and winger Paul Sackey (London Irish) were enough to get at least one of England's World Cup-defence wheels back on track.

England 36 Tonga 20 (Parc des Princes, Paris)
Paul Sackey got another brace of tries and Jonny Wilkinson another couple of drop goals as England clinched a quarter-final spot.

QUARTER-FINAL
England 12 Australia 10 (Stade Velodrome, Marseille)
England dismantled the Australian scrum and wore down their pack to beat the low expectations set after the grim pool stages and earn a shock semi-final spot. While Oz's Lote Tuqiri claimed the game's only try, four penalties from the boot of Jonny Wilkinson put England through. The defending champions even added some width to their game to complement powerful displays from the likes of loose-head prop Andrew Sheridan, second row Simon Shaw and a back-row unit of Martin Corry, Lewis Moody and Nick Easter (Harlequins). Jason Robinson was also fit again, meaning his appearance in the 36-0 thrashing by the Springboks was not, thankfully, his final game.

SEMI-FINAL

England 14 France 9 (Stade de France)

After beating tournament favourites New Zealand in Cardiff the week before, it seemed that France were set to claim their destiny and finally get their hands on a World Cup. England's win over Australia was dismissed by many as an anomaly and few expected much in Paris. Yet France decided to play a tight, limited game – the exact type of style England would have welcomed. Josh Lewsey, playing on the wing, put England ahead after 90 seconds after a smart kick from scrum-half Andy Gomarsall confounded the French defence. However, France led 9-8 with five minutes remaining, but a Wilkinson penalty and sweet drop goal saw England snatch it at the death. Phil Vickery's men were, unbelievably, in the final and the hosts were out.

A load of odd balls

The 2007 World Cup was plagued by complaints by kickers about the match balls. Players were finding that while the training balls were great, there seemed to be huge inconsistencies in the way the match balls flew. Some would swerve one way and some fly off in the other direction. Wilkinson and Toby Flood (Leicester) had figured this out and took advantage of the fact that the day before a match, kickers could practise with some of the match balls which, luckily, were numbered. They would try to memorise the way each numbered ball flew and then make adjustments in the match accordingly (or if possible, switch balls). An example of this can be seen in the semi-final where Wilkinson swaps balls with a ball boy to find one of the more trustworthy balls before he kicks a successful penalty.

FINAL

England 6 South Africa 15 (Stade de France)

Just weeks after losing 36-0 on the same ground to the same opposition, England made South Africa work incredibly hard for their win. At 9-3, winger Mark Cueto went over in the left-hand corner, but television replays showed clearly he was in touch before grounding. Cueto has claimed since, bizarrely, that everyone in the ground and watching on television that day had seen he had scored. The cameras, however, did not lie. He still likes to claim the score.

Mark Cueto was unable to stay in play in his attempt to score.

South Africa's points all came from the boots of Percy Montgomery and Francois Steyn, with Wilkinson's feet supplying all of England's contribution to the scoreboard. While England may not have been good enough to get over the finish line in first place, they once again showed incredible resilience and spirit. Finishing as runners-up was, in the context of the previous few seasons, a huge achievement by Ashton's men and they could hold their heads up high.

AVERAGE SERVICE RESUMED
2008 Six Nations and the fall of Brian Ashton
England's bizarre 2007 World Cup campaign raised hopes that England were back as an elite team. Some, like former international Jerry Guscott, backed England to win the 2008 Six Nations. In the end, as they had in the World Cup, England had to settle for the runners-up spot. But despite it being the best finishing position since 2003, it wasn't enough to stop a change of head coach.

2008 – England 19 Wales 26 (Twickenham)
Wales, with 13 Ospreys in the starting line-up, triumphed at Twickenham for the first time since 1988. The Welsh had been knocked out of the World Cup by Fiji and, with just over 20 minutes remaining, England had led by 19-6. But thanks to multiple penalties against players like back rower James Haskell (Wasps), loose passing from Wilkinson and an inability to finish things off, England were swept away in a late avalanche of Welsh points. Wales, coached for the first time by Warren Gatland, would surprise everyone by going on to win the Grand Slam.

EVEN THE GREATEST GET NERVES

Despite his records, points, caps and glory, Jonny Wilkinson could still get extraordinarily nervous before a game. Ahead of the 2008 Six Nations opener against Wales, the outside-half claimed to have suffered the 'biggest bout of pre-match nerves I have ever experienced . . . an hour to go before the coach leaves for the game, an old thought process rifles through my mind. If you could offer me a way out now, would I take it? Right now, I probably would, I'd probably leg it.' Of course, Wilkinson didn't leg it and lined up a few hours later in the white shirt.

THE MEDIOCRITY CONTINUES

After the Welsh loss, England scrapped to a 23-19 win over Italy in Rome. Toby Flood and Paul Sackey grabbed first-half tries to put England 20-6 up at half-time. The visitors struggled to retain the ball and all England could manage in the second half was a Wilkinson penalty. In this match Wilkinson became the first English player to break the 1,000 points mark in international rugby. That was about all there was to celebrate as the pressure increased on head coach Brian Ashton.

Next up, England somehow grabbed a first Six Nations win in Paris since 2000 with tries from Paul Sackey and Richard Wigglesworth (Sale) helping them along the way in a match that finished 24-13.

2008 – England 33 Ireland 10 (Twickenham)

England ended a four-match losing streak to Ireland with this comfortable victory. The match was notable for the 18 points of 19-year-old Danny Cipriani (Wasps) on his third cap and first game as starter. The performance of the talented and controversial back ignited a national debate among fans and media over who was better between Wilkinson and Cipriani. The youngster won the man of the match award. During the live television post-match interview, he said the award should have gone to the 'f****** forwards'.

The hype from the English media was embarrassing at times. One prominent broadsheet journalist called for Cipriani to be made captain and one newspaper ran a picture of the two players standing together and had a body language 'expert' analyse the image to explain how Cipriani was the more confident, dominant player. In the long run, of course, most of the media changed tack and no doubt cynically enjoyed the off-field drama and issues Cipriani was to have later in his career.

ROB ANDREW BACKS BRIAN ASHTON

Prior to the Irish game, Rob Andrew (by then the RFU's elite rugby director) had said that Brian Ashton would remain as England head coach even if his side lost. The RFU, after all, had even given Ashton a long-term contract in December 2007. By April, Ashton was removed by the RFU and World Cup captain Martin Johnson (who had no experience of management at this level) was the head honcho. Former hooker Brian Moore said: 'What has happened to Ashton . . . is a disgrace.'

THE MARTIN JOHNSON ERA GRIMLY BEGINS
(UNDER ROB ANDREW)

The appointment of Martin Johnson continued an age-old British sporting tradition of throwing former great players into a top coaching position despite the fact they've not really done any coaching or managing. It is a tradition that pretty much always ends badly and the RFU patriotically decided to add another example to a long, long list of such sporting disasters. Former England star Dean Richards said: 'His appointment remains tribute to the deep-rooted British belief that character matters more than proven technical skill, a faith-based experiment in on-the-job training.'

The summer tour to New Zealand, however, was led by Rob Andrew as Johnson was unavailable due to family commitments. Captained by second row Steve Borthwick (appointed by Johnson in a decision journalist Stephen Jones called bizarre), a young England squad fell by 37-20 and 44-12 in the two-match series.

The tour was also overshadowed by serious allegations against four players for their behaviour after the game, leading to a ban on players bringing women back to their hotel rooms after matches. In a subsequent hearing, full-back and winger Mike Brown (Harlequins) and winger Topsy Ojo (London Irish) were found guilty of misconduct and fined. Ojo never played for England again and Brown was to wait four years for his next cap.

AUTUMN FALLS (AS DOES TWICKENHAM)

Martin Johnson's first four games at Twickenham offered precious little hope things would be changing for England. A 39-13 win over the scratch Pacific Islanders side (a combination of Fiji, Samoa and Tonga) was followed by losses to Australia (28-14), South Africa (42-6) and New Zealand (32-6).

2008 England 6 South Africa 42 (Twickenham)

This was England's worst ever home defeat. Ill-disciplined and careless, even the Boks having two men sin-binned did little to help stem the green tide.

2008 England 6 New Zealand 32 (Twickenham)

The *Guardian*'s Michael Aylwin described the All Blacks as only 'half interested' in this match. Yet they still played England off the park. The home side did their best to help them though, with four yellow cards. The roll of honour for this achievement was populated by James Haskell, Lee Mears (Bath), Toby Flood and Tom Rees (Wasps). It was the second heaviest home defeat England had ever suffered.

AND SO IT GOES ON
2009 SIX NATIONS

In the first Championship of the Johnson era, England won three of their five games – finishing in second place. Italy were dispatched first (36-11), then there were losses to Wales in Cardiff (23-15) and Ireland in Dublin (14-13). The campaign was salvaged somewhat with wins at home over France (34-10) and Scotland (26-12). A trademark of the Johnson era was a continually high penalty count against England. The *Guardian* asked: 'Is the great Martin Johnson out of his depth as an international manager and presiding over a bunch of dimwits who pay minimal attention to what he says? It is starting to look horribly like it.'

SUMMER UP NORTH (AND DOWN SOUTH)

The summer of 2009 saw a rather unusual Test series take place with Argentina. The first Test was played at home at Manchester's Old Trafford and the second Test was played in Salta, Argentina. The home side took the spoils on both occasions with England winning 37-15 before losing the return fixture 24-22. The reason for the odd set-up was that the Argentinian union desperately needed the cash a fixture in England could provide and a UK venue made it easier for them to access their European-based players.

ONE OUT OF THREE AIN'T GREAT

England's autumn series saw another win over Argentina (16-9) but two losses. England's cohesion, especially up front, was severely criticised. There was a general consensus that Lewis Moody was a standout performer, but also that a big reason he looked so good was that he was having to make up for a lack of support from others in his team. England fell to Australia (18-9) and New Zealand (19-6). At the end of 2009, England had lost 17 of their 36 games since the 2003 World Cup final.

MIDDLE OF THE MIDDLING ROAD AGAIN

England slipped back to third in the 2010 Six Nations, scoring just six tries in five games. Three of those five-pointers came on the opening day in a 30-17 win at Twickenham over Wales. Next was a nervy win in Rome over Italy, a Mathew Tait try and 12 points from Jonny Wilkinson just about getting England home by 17-12. Jerry Guscott wrote that captain Steve Borthwick was 'close to sounding delusional with his views on how he believed his team played because the team's performance was terrible'.

Next up, Ireland continued their dominance over England since 2003 with a 20-16 win at Twickenham, thanks to two Tommy Bowe tries. The bad results kept coming. There followed a 15-15 draw at Murrayfield and a 12-10 loss in Paris. For the final game Lewis Moody took over the captaincy with Borthwick injured. The 57 times capped second row, who first played for England in 2001, would recover from his injury but was never capped again. Meanwhile, the media knives for Martin Johnson were getting pretty sharp.

SEVEN YEAR DROUGHT ENDS

For the first time since the 2003 World Cup, England won a major match in the southern hemisphere during yet another (yawn) trip down under. After losing 27-17 in Perth in the first Test, Martin Johnson got the big result he needed to help kick his period at the helm into life.

2010 – 2nd Test – Australia 20 England 21 (ANZ Stadium, Sydney)

Ben Youngs (Leicester), in his first start, had a dazzling debut as England forced a drawn series with their Australian rivals. Powered by forwards such as Lewis Moody (captain), Nick Easter, Tom Croft (Leicester) and Courtney Lawes (Northampton), the visitors looked vastly improved and much sharper than they had in the Six Nations. The scores came from Youngs, Chris Ashton (a try each), Toby Flood (one conversion and two penalties) and his replacement from Toulon, Jonny Wilkinson (one penalty). Displaying the typical calmness of the English media, many pundits made comparisons with the 2003 team.

NOVEMBER MAGIC

2010 – England 35 Australia 18 (Twickenham)

England conjured up a 'scintillating' performance to overcome the Wallabies in the best game of their autumn campaign. A week after falling again to New Zealand (26-16), a double from winger Chris Ashton thrilled the home crowd. His second try, which began when the dark-shirted England countered from their own line, has gone down in English rugby folklore. Australia were turned over trying to breach the English line and Ben Youngs darted away from the breakdown and threw a pass to his right to Courtney Lawes who, 15 metres from his own line, offloaded to Chris Ashton just before he was hit hard. Ashton burned down the right wing, turned infield just before halfway and showed enough gas to go the rest of the way untouched and dive over the line.

Sadly, at this time, all English scores at Twickenham were accompanied by the crime against human ears that is the song 'Tom Hark' by the Piranhas (originally recorded by Elias and His Zig-Zag Jive Flutes). The RFU, who must feel 70,000 odd fans cheering is not atmospheric enough, insisted all home tries are greeted by this abomination. The other games in the autumn series saw a 26-13 win over Samoa and a 21-11 loss to the Springboks.

THE ASH SPLASH CONTROVERSY

Chris Ashton's long solo try was topped off by what was to become his trademark 'Ash Splash' dive. The celebration split opinion wildly. Some saw it as arrogant, unsportsmanlike, tacky and crass, others as just the type of thing Chris Ashton would do when scoring. Head coach Martin Johnson was not a fan. The celebration was brought up in a team meeting the following week where Johnson, citing examples in which such dives had gone wrong, argued it was not a risk worth taking. Ashton continued to do it though, even if it did look a bit daft when he scored against a second-rate team or, as on one memorable occasion, his try was disallowed for an earlier offence. Ashton was a player that attracted controversy in his career. Whether it was for hair-pulling, illegal contact with an opponent's eyes, shouting during an opponent's place kick attempt or biting, he was frequently in the news.

SIX NATIONS GLORY AGAIN

2011 was to end in disgrace, but it was to start with England's first Six Nations title since 2003. While a Grand Slam and Triple Crown were to prove elusive, Mike Tindall (captaining in the absence of Lewis Moody) led his team to some much-needed silverware.

MATCH ONE: Wales 19 England 26 (Millennium Stadium, Cardiff)

Under Friday night lights, England started their Championship campaign with a bang and two Chris Ashton tries. Before the match, Welsh coach Warren Gatland had identified England hooker Dylan Hartley (Northampton) as a potential weak link for England, saying: 'He's always got a lot to say, hasn't he? Let's see what he has got to offer and how he fronts up against us.' Unfortunately for Wales, he fronted up in an excellent performance. The visitors' man of the match, though, was Toby Flood. He kicked 13 points and excelled with both ball in hand and when kicking for position and pressure.

MATCH TWO: England 59 Italy 13 (Twickenham)

Chris Ashton grabbed four tries, adding to his two in Cardiff. It meant that after two rounds, he had equalled the Six Nations Championship individual try tally for a season (other players had scored more in the pre-Six Nations format).

MATCH THREE: England 17 France 9 (Twickenham)

England overcame the 2010 Grand Slam champions in a tightly fought match in London. It was 9-9 at the break, with all the points coming from the kickers (Toby Flood and Dimitri Yachvili). But in the second half, second row and man of the match Tom Palmer (Stade Français) charged down a Yachvili kick, leading to a try for full-back Ben Foden (Northampton). The win allowed England to start thinking of Championship glory.

MATCH FOUR: England 22 Scotland 16 (Twickenham)

Again it was 9-9 at the break, as it had been in the French game, and again England prevailed in the second half. A try from replacement Tom Croft, who burst over from almost 20 metres out, helped England again claim the Calcutta Cup and took them one step away from a Grand Slam.

MATCH FIVE: Ireland 24 England 8 (Aviva Stadium, Dublin)

Ireland smashed English Grand Slam hopes, meaning while England still won the Championship, they looked rather glum when collecting their trophy. Flanker Tom Wood said: 'It felt pretty much like we'd had our hearts ripped out in that game against Ireland. We didn't go to Dublin for scars or lessons. We went for a Grand Slam and we got it wrong. It was unacceptable and a bitter pill to swallow and brought us back down to earth, even though we ultimately won the Championship.'

While disappointing, a Championship was still a great achievement and English fans were happy again to be at the top of the European tree.

A WEIGHTY CHANGE

The loss to Ireland led to a shift in England's fitness and strength programme. Not everyone thought it was a good thing. Speaking in the book *Behind the Rose*, Nick Easter said: '[We] over-reacted to that defeat, and our style leading into the World Cup began to change . . . The general consensus was that we had over-played, and that opponents had worked out how we wanted to play – and that our style of a fast game was not going to win the World Cup. The training [afterwards] was geared more towards being big and strong but not mobile and fast. There was a big emphasis on weights, gym and wrestling.'

2011 WORLD CUP (NEW ZEALAND)

England's 2011 World Cup will forever be remembered more for what happened off the pitch than what happened on it. From supposed drunken nights out involving dwarves being thrown, to allegations of inappropriate behaviour to hotel staff and Manu Tuilagi being detained by police for jumping off a ferry into Auckland harbour, it was non-stop tabloid speculation and scandal. While the infamous British press overplayed and overhyped some of what happened, there was plenty to be furious about. England players did themselves no favours and Martin Johnson was left constantly tearing his hair out at the amount of time he had to spend dealing with non-rugby matters. Meanwhile, thanks to what some saw as rather generous refereeing in the final, New Zealand finally won another World Cup. The last one had come back in 1987 and was also on home soil.

Captain: Lewis Moody
Coach: Martin Johnson

POOL GAMES

England 13 Argentina 9 (Otago Stadium, Dunedin)
A black-clad England rallied from 9-3 down with just 14 minutes left to sneak past Argentina. Mike Tindall's men

(leading in the absence of the injured Lewis Moody) were undisciplined from the off, conceding eight penalties in the first 40 minutes alone. Prop Dan Cole also got shown a yellow as the referee grew tired of constant English infringements. Even Jonny Wilkinson had an off day with the boot. Luckily, replacement scrum-half Ben Youngs darted over after solid work from his forwards in the 66th minute and a tiring Pumas side were unable to recover from the blow. England got in a bit of bother with tournament organisers after several player numbers peeled off or got damaged during the game, making it hard for officials to identify players.

England 41 Georgia 10 (Otago Stadium)

Once again England suffered at the lips of the referee in a stop–start performance. Hooker Dylan Hartley was sin-binned as another referee tired of England infringements. Lewis Moody's men led by just 17-10 at the halfway stage against a team ranked 16th in the world. In the end the minnows tired and England ran in five tries. Chris Ashton was again criticised for his Ash Splash celebration dive. Many felt it was in poor taste for a player from an extremely well-funded and well-prepared tier one team to (effectively) mock a tier two team as he scored. Others were irritated that a winger would celebrate scoring a try against a team that had been exhausted by the work of his pack, rather than by his own efforts.

England 67 Romania 3 (Otago Stadium)

Mark Cueto and Chris Ashton both bagged hat-tricks as England scored ten tries. The former grabbed his triple in an

11-minute spell. About the only interesting thing from this game was England's kicking coach, Dave Alred, and their fitness coach, Paul Stridgeon, were found guilty of changing the ball that Jonny Wilkinson used to kick two of his conversions. The laws of the game state that the same ball must be used for the conversion as was used to score the try. It led to the pair of them being barred by the RFU from attending the next match at Eden Park.

England 16 Scotland 12 (Eden Park, Auckland)

England's oldest foe led by three points with just three minutes left on the clock when Chris Ashton dived over for the winning try. His late score wide out on the right was the first try in 157 World Cup minutes between these two sides (after the 1991 contest only saw points from the boot). It was wet, miserable and again England were constantly penalised. Once more England trailed at the break. This time they had to rally from 12-3 down.

QUARTER-FINAL

England 12 France 19 (Eden Park)

A week after falling to Tonga in a pool match, France sparked against their biggest rival and ended England's participation in the 2011 World Cup. True to form, England started badly and trailed at the break by 16-0. Although Lewis Moody's team had not set the world alight, hopes were high they could beat a French team in disarray. After losing badly to New Zealand and being upset by Tonga, the French camp was rumoured to be in pure chaos and the players allegedly began taking their own training sessions as they no longer trusted their coach, Marc Lièvremont. While England rallied in the second half with tries from Ben Foden and Mark Cueto, any hope England would repeat their World Cup wins over France from the 1991, 2003 and 2007 tournaments were effectively over after 40 minutes. The loss allowed the English media to fully dig its cruel claws into Martin Johnson's squad and, by mid-November, the former World Cup winner departed as coach.

For England fans, the events of 2003 seemed a lifetime ago.

THE AFTERMATH OF 2011

The post-tournament review held by the RFU, Premier Rugby and the Rugby Players Association was not pleasant reading for anyone involved in English rugby. *The Times* wrote: 'To watch England play has been excruciating, but to see the lack of development of some promising young men is sporting tragedy. Fine prospects such as Courtney Lawes, Dan Cole, Tom Croft, Dylan Hartley, Tom Wood, Chris Ashton, Ben Youngs and Ben Foden should be contenders for a place in any world team. But they are marking time, and the Johnson regime stands accused of standing in their path.'

Captain Lewis Moody announced his retirement from international rugby. Martin Johnson took all responsibility for the failings of his team and stood down. Those who had questioned the wisdom of appointing a head coach with no coaching experience got to say, 'I told you so.' So, once again, the throne of power at Twickenham had a new backside in it as fast as you could say 'Andy Robinson'. Oh, wait. He'd already been there. This time it was Stuart Lancaster in the hot seat.

THE RISE OF THE HOUSE OF LANCASTER

Stuart Lancaster began his England reign as an interim head coach, stepping up from his role overseeing the England Saxons (the development/second XV). Lancaster's coaching pedigree included Leeds Tykes and a role as the RFU'S elite rugby director. He immediately set about trying to fix the rotten culture the national set-up had developed. He promised to remove players who lacked the required character for England, introduce plenty of new blood and build firm and positive foundations. His assistants were Graham Rowntree (former England prop) and rugby league legend (and former union international) Andy Farrell.

His first squad, named for the 2012 Six Nations, saw 15 players from the Elite Player Squad replaced and eight uncapped players make the matchday group for the opening match at Murrayfield. He also named 25-year-old Chris Robshaw (Harlequins) as his captain. The flanker, with only one cap at the time, was a surprise appointment. Initially he was appointed for the opening two games. But just as his coach would soon become the long-term replacement for Martin Johnson, so would Robshaw retain leadership of the side.

A NEW ERA (AGAIN)
2012 – Scotland 6 England 13 (Murrayfield)

Chris Robshaw celebrated his first game in charge by leading England to a first win on Scottish soil since 2004. The build-up to the game had been heated. England teams being labelled arrogant by the opposition is nothing new, but this time the charge was laid by former England player and former England head coach Andy Robinson. The man who had only a few years previously been in charge of the national side in his home country was unhappy with the way certain players behaved towards Scotland in the 2011 World Cup, singling out full-back Delon Armitage (London Irish) in particular.

On the field, 20-year-old Saracens centre Owen Farrell (Saracens) made his debut. He was one of three new caps (Brad

Barritt of Saracens and Phil Dowson of Northampton being the others). The side also featured Charlie Hodgson at ten, starting his first Test in four years. Hodgson marked his return with the only try of the game as he collected a bouncing ball after charging down a kick from Dan Parks. The rest of the points came from the confident boot of the new cap Farrell. It wasn't pretty, but it was the win a new-look England needed.

A solid campaign

England were to finish second in the 2012 Six Nations. While they had won the Championship the year before, they had actually won the same number of games. The difference was Wales's win at Twickenham meant the Welsh were able to claim a Grand Slam and top the table. Despite a scare in Rome, after the horrors of the 2011 World Cup it all felt like progress and there was a distinct lack of off-field scandal and incidents of small people being thrown around. The campaign also included a 24-22 win in Paris (with tries from Ben Foden, Manu Tuilagi and Tom Croft) and a 30-9 win over Ireland. This win was significant too as Ireland had won seven of the previous eight clashes since the 2003 World Cup. It was to be the start of a four-match winning sequence over the men in green.

AN AUTUMN SURPRISE
2012 – England 38 New Zealand 21 (Twickenham)

After the moderate success of the Six Nations, England had a rather mediocre run of games. A three-Test tour of South Africa saw England lose the opening two Tests, while drawing

Owen Farrell immediately had an impact in the
England shirt and would become a key player for the side.

the third match. That was followed by an autumn campaign that began with a comfortable, if expected, 54-12 win over Fiji, but narrow losses to Australia (20-14) and South Africa (16-15). Just as the sound of sharpening knives began to emerge in the press, England shocked the rugby world with a totally unexpected win over New Zealand.

The Kiwis had been in fine form and were confident that they would claim a tenth successive win in the fixture and arrived at Twickenham unbeaten in 20 matches. *Rugby World* magazine went as far as to claim an English win would rank as their 'greatest victory'. While that status may be debatable, there is no doubt it turned out to be one of the great afternoons in English rugby history. New Zealand boasted 804 caps in their team, compared to just 221 in the home side, yet by the end the visitors were being run ragged. England scored tries through Manu Tuilagi, Brad Barritt and Chris Ashton and points from the boot were earned by Owen Farrell and Freddie Burns (Gloucester). The *Guardian* newspaper was full of praise for Tuilagi, writing, 'Manu Tuilagi left New Zealand in disgrace last year after being fished out of Auckland Harbour at the end of England's dismal World Cup campaign and fined £3,000. The All Blacks were left wishing he had been thrown back after the Samoa-born centre inspired a record England victory over the World Cup holders.'

As in the 1995 World Cup final, New Zealand pointed to illness as a major factor in the defeat, but few in HQ that day cared much for that reasoning.

FAVOURITES AGAIN

England's win over New Zealand had the bookies, and plenty of pundits, place England as favourites to win the 2013 Six Nations. After four games it looked like a wise bet too. Scotland were dismissed 38-18 at Twickenham; Ireland fell by 12-6 in a grim Dublin battle of the boot; and France were overcome 23-13 in a freezing London battle. With minds perhaps on a Grand Slam opportunity in Cardiff, England struggled past Italy in Twickenham. Italy grabbed the only try of the game, but Toby Flood kicked six penalties to get England home by 18-11.

2013 – Wales 30 England 3 (Millennium Stadium)

England were seen as favourites to claim their first Grand Slam in a decade. Wales were theoretically in the hunt for the title too, but needed to win by more than eight points to claim it. Few gave them a chance of that. Lancaster said in the build-up that winning would give England the inner confidence and belief that they could win big games and finals, referring to the 2015 World Cup in England.

Yet, once again, Cardiff was a graveyard for English hopes and, yet again, England fell at the final hurdle of a Grand Slam climb. But this was a true stuffing. Wales barged their way to what was then their biggest winning margin ever over their oldest enemy. Winger Alex Cuthbert scored two tries, Dan Biggar kicked the other 20 points and instead of winning a Grand Slam, Triple Crown and Championship, England lost it all. Wales had claimed the title.

Chris Robshaw later said: 'I don't know if we were quite ready for a Grand Slam game, and . . . a Championship game, in the heart of Wales. The animosity we felt towards us was definitely an experience that will stay with us a long time. We've asked ourselves some hard questions since then. Did we deal with that in the right way? Did we panic a bit? Yes, we did – and I'd include myself in that.'

BACK ON TRACK

After the Six Nations loss, England got back on track with a successful tour to Argentina (in which they won both Tests) and two wins from three in the autumn internationals. The victories came against Australia (20-13) and Argentina (31-12). However, there was to be no repeat of the New Zealand heroics of 2012, as the All Blacks got revenge with a 30-22 win.

ONCE AGAIN THE BRIDESMAID

2014 – France 26 England 24 (Stade de France)

England finished second again in the Six Nations as a 26-24 defeat to France in Paris on the opening weekend was enough to derail their title hopes. England conceded three tries, one after just 32 seconds. But after rallying from 16-3 down, England looked set to pull off the biggest comeback in their history, until winger Gael Fickou scored with just three minutes left to claim the spoils for France.

England went on to win all their other games and beat Ireland 13-10. But although the English and Irish both ended the Championship with four wins, the Irish claimed the title thanks to a superior points difference.

A BLACK SUMMER, A GREY AUTUMN

England followed up the disappointment of the Six Nations with a summer trip to ever-welcoming New Zealand. A gruelling three-match Test series saw Chris Robshaw's men fall by 20-15, 28-27 and 36-13. Despite the losses, England acquitted themselves well in the opening two Tests. The first match was the cruellest loss. Drawing 9-9 at Eden Park after 40 minutes, England were undone by a late Marland Yarde (Harlequins) yellow card which meant they had to play the last ten minutes a man down. Yet, a penalty from Danny Cipriani brought things level after 73 minutes. But with three minutes to go, All Black centre Conrad Smith went over in the corner after sustained pressure, to break English hearts.

The lost series was all the more frustrating when it was considered that England's preparations had been severely affected by the timing of the Premiership final. With the Northampton and Saracens final taking place a week before the tour was to begin, eight players were unavailable for the first Test due to jet-lag protocols.

The autumn series in Twickenham kicked off with New Zealand again the opposition. England could still not quite grab a victory over them and lost 24-21. It meant New Zealand had won five straight in the series since Stuart Lancaster had masterminded the famous win in 2012. With South Africa then consigning England to what was their fifth straight defeat since the Six Nations (winning 38-21), the English fans and press were again starting to feel gloomy ahead of the 2015 World Cup. The *Independent* suggested 'alarm bells' were beginning to ring for Robshaw's men as constant errors continually undermined their chances to eke out victories.

There were some positives in the November games though. A 28-9 win over Samoa was followed by a much-needed triumph over Australia. Number eight Ben Morgan (Gloucester) grabbed a brace of tries and outside-half George Ford (Bath) kicked 16 points to take a little pressure off Stuart Lancaster in a 26-17 triumph.

SECOND AGAIN!

England again finished the Six Nations with just one loss and again failed to win the title, with Ireland claiming back-to-back Championships for the first time since 1949. It meant that England had lost just four games in four years in the Six Nations but had not a single title to show for it. England's only loss this campaign was in Dublin (19-9).

PLAY IT FOR THE FIRST TIME, SAM

England played three warm-up games ahead of the World Cup. The most significant moment (and one that would have major repercussions a few months later), was the capping of Sam Burgess (Bath) in the centre. Burgess, a Yorkshireman, was a high-profile switch to rugby union from league, where he had been a big star down under. He made his debut for Bath in October 2014 and played mainly as a flanker for them.

Ten months later he was parachuted into the World Cup squad and was involved in the friendlies against France and Ireland. The move brought both praise and condemnation in almost equal measure. A stunning player and athlete, the major concern many had was whether he could adjust to the technicalities of Test rugby in such a short space of time.

THIS IS ENGLAND

It was hoped that with a World Cup on home soil, England would reap the advantage hosting offered and make a serious run at winning it. To do so, they were going to have to get out of the 'Group of Death' they occupied: which included Australia, Wales and Fiji. But despite the inconsistencies in results that Lancaster's reign had thus far provided, memories of big wins such as the 2012 one over New Zealand kept fanning flames of optimism among many of the England faithful. Even if, in reality, the result was an extreme exception to the rule when it came to facing the All Blacks over recent years.

2015 WORLD CUP (ENGLAND)

Following on from their off-field embarrassment in the 2011 World Cup, England suffered possibly the greatest humiliation in their rugby history as they crashed out of their own party in their own home in the pool stages of the 2015 edition. Losses to a sparkling Australian team and an injury-ravaged Welsh side in the 'Group of Death' meant that England had failed to reach the knockout stages for the first time ever. The results brought a swift guillotine down on the Stuart Lancaster era. The coach was damned for his selection in the centre of Sam Burgess over George Ford in the key match with Wales. Burgess had only converted from league ten months earlier and the combo that faced Wales had not played together before! It was also the 14th centre pairing in just four years under Lancaster.

It wasn't just the coach who came under fire: captain Chris Robshaw faced huge criticism for his captaincy, particularly his decision to go for a try late on against Wales, rather than take a possible draw with a penalty kick.

Flanker James 'The Brand' Haskell, meanwhile, got into a Twitter argument with 2003 World Cup winner Neil Back over a selfie stick. The retired flanker took exception to Haskell parading around the field with his camera ahead of the clash with Fiji. It was that kind of tournament.

Captain: Chris Robshaw

Coach: Stuart Lancaster

The Brand and Back got in an amusing spat during England's worst-ever World Cup.

POOL GAMES

England 35 Fiji 11 (Twickenham)

England, wearing an all-red kit, had a tough opening 60 minutes against a strong Fiji side before pulling away in the final quarter. The opening try of the tournament was a penalty try for the home side, but full-back Mike Brown added two tries in a man of the match performance. A score from powerful number eight Billy Vunipola (Saracens) in the final play of the match gave England a vital bonus point.

England 25 Wales 28 (Twickenham)

Few gave injury-depleted Wales much chance when they arrived in the hosts' backyard for this vital pool match. The Dragons came to London without several key players, including Jonathan Davies, Leigh Halfpenny, Cory Allen, Eli Walker and Rhys Webb. It only got worse for the visitors as Scott Williams, Hallam Amos and Liam Williams also departed during a brutal encounter. At one stage in the second half, a seemingly broken Wales side trailed by ten points. But, in the 71st minute, scrum-half Lloyd Williams, a replacement winger, made a spectacular infield kick to set up scrum-half Gareth Davies who picked up the ball with his fingertips and scored. Dan Biggar (who kicked eight from eight) soon added a penalty and put Wales in the lead. With a couple of minutes remaining, England were awarded a penalty in a very kickable position. In a decision that would go down in infamy, Robshaw opted to go for the corner and try for the win. Wales repelled the subsequent line-out drive and the captain's bold call was harshly criticised in the media.

England 13 Australia 33 (Twickenham)

For any hope of emerging from the 'Group of Death' and managing to avoid the ignominy of exiting their own World Cup on their own patch, England had to beat Australia. But the home side were never in the contest as Australian fly-half Bernard Foley ran them ragged as he clocked up two tries, three conversions and four penalties in a comfortable win. To round off the misery, Owen Farrell suffered a late sin-binning for a dangerous tackle.

England 60 Uruguay 3 (City of Manchester Stadium, Manchester)

England scored ten tries. It didn't matter. Nick Easter became the oldest England cap to score a try at 36 years and 56 days.

THE AXE FALLS ON THE HOUSE OF LANCASTER

On 11 November 2015, a month after England crashed out of the World Cup, Stuart Lancaster and the RFU agreed to part ways. His record was 28 wins in 46 games.

THE SAM BURGESS MONTHS END

After the World Cup exit, Sam Burgess appeared committed to the England and Bath set-up, with his coach at the club, Mike Ford, saying the player wanted to go to the 2019 World Cup. By December though, after 14 months in union, and five games for England, Burgess went back to league. Later, Burgess responded to criticism that his inclusion hindered England's World Cup efforts by saying: 'If people actually re-watched the games I participated in you will see I added to the team. What cost us an early exit was individual egos and selfish players not following our leader.'

BIG THANKS TO OUR SPONSORS

No World Cup campaign takes place now without England players forced to take part in major television and social media campaigns for sponsors. The quality and wisdom of these adverts vary. Poor old Chris Robshaw became the object of countless memes and mocking videos after one RFU sponsor ended their commercial with Robshaw looking directly into the camera saying: 'We're playing at home. We always back ourselves at home.' Unfortunately for England, these adverts continued to run even after England had lost at home to Wales and Australia. It got more painful every time they aired.

ENGLAND OPENS UP TO FOREIGN LEADERSHIP

Nine days after Stuart Lancaster departed, the RFU appointed its first ever overseas head coach. Eddie Jones, who had coached against England in the 2003 World Cup final, was brought in. The Australian was fresh from taking Japan to a shock win over South Africa in the World Cup and had an impressive CV at club and international level. His impact was immediate.

SWEET SEVENTEEN!

To say the arrival of Eddie Jones as head coach shook things up is an understatement on the same level as saying Chris Ashton likes the attention to be on him at the end of a successful team move. Jones, with his new captain Dylan Hartley, was to take the national team on an extraordinary 17-game winning streak (which was a total of 18 for the team if you throw in the win over Uruguay at the end of the World Cup).

Hartley's appointment was typical Eddie Jones. Although he held 66 caps already, no one expected the 29-year-old New Zealand-born hooker, who had a CV which included bans for biting, gouging, striking and verbally abusing a referee, to be team leader. Indeed, his career bans totalled 54 weeks if you added them all together. 'I admire his aggressive and uncompromising approach to playing rugby,' said Jones.

Eddie Jones would instantly transform
the fortunes of England at international level.

2016 GRAND SLAM

MATCH ONE: Scotland 9 England 15 (Murrayfield)

Eddie Jones resisted the opportunity to sweep out the old guard in his first match in charge, putting 512 caps of experience out on the field in Murrayfield. There had been calls for exciting talents like second row/flanker Maro Itoje (Saracens) and full-back Elliot Daly (Wasps) to be brought in and shake things up. But Jones was in no rush. The mischievous head coach also said Scotland, who had not beaten England since 2008, were favourites. The game was far from fancy, but England got the win they needed so badly. Tries came from lock George Kruis (Saracens) and winger Jack Nowell (Exeter), with Farrell adding a conversion and a penalty.

MATCH TWO: Italy 9 England 40 (Stadio Olimpico, Rome)

Outside centre Jamie Joseph (Bath) pulled out a second-half hat-trick in this five-try romp. There was also a debut for 21-year-old Maro Itoje, who would go on to have a fantastic campaign and become a firm fan favourite.

MATCH THREE: England 21 Ireland 10 (Twickenham)

Ireland were looking to make history by winning a third consecutive championship in 2016, but England put that dream to rest, consigning them to a second defeat of the campaign. Despite James 'The Brand' Haskell and scrum-half Danny Care (Harlequins) collecting second-half yellow cards, England did enough to keep control and keep on track for the title. Anthony Watson (Bath) and Mike Brown crossed for the home tries.

MATCH FOUR: England 25 Wales 21 (Twickenham)

England had to dig deep to prevent Wales stealing a famous

comeback win. Leading 19-0 after the interval, it seemed the home team were cruising. In the 72nd minute, it was 25-7. But Dan Cole was sin-binned and Wales rallied dramatically. A quick pair of tries from George North and Taulupe Faletau made it 25-21 with two minutes left. A late attack from Wales gave England a huge scare, but they just held on (although replays later showed that North was not in touch in the final play and the game should have continued on). The Dragons had scored three tries to one, but left things too late to sneak a win. The Twickenham faithful didn't care, they were now looking forward to a potential Grand Slam.

MATCH FIVE: France 21 England 31 (Stade de France)

A 13-year wait for the Grand Slam ended in Paris, with Eddie Jones and Dylan Hartley's men completing a dramatic turnaround in English fortunes since the World Cup. In the first half Danny Care sniped through the French defence to score a great try from 45 metres out. Dan Cole got a try too, although knowledgeable rugby fans were baffled by referee Nigel Owens's decision to ignore a blatant obstruction (clearly visible in the TMO process) on the French tackler who tried to tackle the English prop. But England were good value for their win with their pack in excellent form, especially when it came to spoiling the French line-out. At the end, Anthony Watson grabbed another try to cap off an excellent Six Nations for him and his team.

THE PRODIGAL SON RETURNS (AND WINS)

If critics worried that England's revival was another false dawn, the summer soon put paid to that. After a meaningless win over Wales in a friendly at Twickenham, England headed down under to face the Wallabies in a three-match Test series. Jones coached his adopted nation to a 3-0 series win over his native country – and the side he had taken so close to glory in the 2003 World Cup final himself. England won 39-28, 23-7 and 44-40 to stun Australia and send a signal out to the rugby world that England were again a force to be reckoned with.

A PERFECT YEAR

November saw convincing victories over South Africa (37-21), Fiji (58-15), Argentina (27-14) and Australia (37-21). The triumph over the Boks was the first victory in a decade in the fixture. It meant that 2016 had seen England win all 13 matches they played. After the final win of the year, *Times* journalist Stephen Jones wrote: 'All the southern-hemisphere nations should be worried. We in Europe are under no compulsion to grant them fixtures, and after this autumn, it could just be that the proud European teams decide that they are hardly worth playing. England completed their autumn in a riot of noise, passion, imperfections and excellence . . . '

LIKE WAITING FOR A BUS . . .
SIX NATIONS WINS COME IN TWOS

England put together back-to-back Championship wins for the first time since 2001. There was no clean sweep though. Just as in 2000, 2001, 2011, 2013 and 2017, England fell at the last hurdle and blew the Triple Crown and Grand Slam. This was the first time bonus points were used in the tournament, but they didn't impact the result, England's four wins were enough, with all other rivals losing at least two games.

MATCH ONE: England 19 France 16 (Twickenham)

England's pack wore down the French and centre Ben Te'o's (Worcester Warriors) try put the dagger in to get England's title defence off to a good start. This 15th consecutive win took England past the record set by Clive Woodward's team.

MATCH TWO: Wales 16 England 21 (Principality Stadium, Cardiff)

The English backs took advantage of a loose kick from Welsh centre Jonathan Davies with less than five minutes left on the clock to snatch a dramatic victory in Cardiff. Elliot Daly gassed Alex Cuthbert for pace and went over in the corner to break Welsh hearts.

MATCH THREE: England 36 Italy 15 (Twickenham)

One of the most fascinating and amusing games in years as Italy's early tactics baffled England so much the visitors led 10-5 at the break. The Italians refused to form rucks at the tackle, allowing them the freedom to stand next to and among the England backs as no offside line had been formed. It was not a new tactic, and smart observers had seen such things before and knew that pick and gos were the best technique to beat it. It seemed many 'top' pundits and players hadn't though. Total chaos reigned and it led to an amusing conversation between James Haskell and referee Romain Poite. When asked what they should do to form a ruck, the Frenchman replied: 'I am not the coach.' Later, Haskell asked for more information on what the 'rule' was.

While England eventually figured it out, Italy were in the game until the final quarter. But a late flurry somewhat distorted the scoreline. In the aftermath, Eddie Jones fumed at the Italian tactics, saying it was 'not rugby'. Even though, well, it was. It was just a bit different. Despite the fact such tactics had been used before in pro rugby, World Rugby quickly changed the law to prevent teams ever being challenged in this way again. The match is now referred to as the 'ruckgate' game.

MATCH FOUR: England 61 Scotland 21 (Twickenham)

This win meant England retained the title and also equalled New Zealand's record for consecutive wins. Scotland conceded seven tries in what was the biggest winning margin in Calcutta Cup history. Jonathan Joseph secured a hat-trick of tries.

MATCH FIVE: Ireland 13 England 9 (Aviva Stadium)

New Zealand's 18-match winning run had been ended in 2016 by Ireland. Now it was England's turn to be halted on a record 18 games by the Irish. Ireland's intensity, concentration and physical commitment rattled the visitors to again blow up an English Grand Slam. It was Eddie Jones's first reverse as head coach of England. The title, however, was England's.

ANOTHER WINNING RUN

After the loss in Ireland, England got back on track with a seven-match winning streak. It included a two-match series win in Argentina and an autumn hat-trick over Australia (30-6), Argentina (21-8) and Samoa (48-14). England also won the opening two games of the 2018 Six Nations.

UNEXPECTED FALL FROM GRACE

After two consecutive titles, England dramatically dropped to fifth place in the 2018 Six Nations – a spot they had last occupied in the 1987 season (which prior to Italy joining the tournament was bottom place). Italy were beaten in Rome (46-15) and Wales in London (12-6) before the wheels came off with the remaining three games lost. In fact, after winning 22 of his first 23 games as coach, Eddie Jones would lose five on the bounce, with two losses following in the three-match series with South Africa in the summer.

2018 – Scotland 25 England 13 (Murrayfield)

It had been a decade since Scotland had won the Calcutta Cup and an incredible 14 years since they had even scored a try against England at home. But as the old saying goes: 'You wait 14 years for a home try in a historic rivalry and then three turn up before half-time.' Thanks to a pair of tries from Huw Jones and another from Sean Maitland, the Scots were 22-6 up by the interval. A shell-shocked England were not able to do enough to pull things back. This was England's worst loss in the series since 1986 and the subsequent loss to France (22-16) meant Ireland were able to claim the title.

2018 – England 15 Ireland 24 (Twickenham)

This was England's first home loss since the 2015 World Cup and the first at home in the Championship since 2012. The victory gave Ireland just their third Grand Slam in their history.

A RARE MEETING WITH OLD RIVALS
2018 – England 15 New Zealand 16 (Twickenham)

England met the All Blacks in November for the first clash between the sides in four years. The 'rarity' made the occasion all the more special and the game all the spicier. In wet conditions, the home side burst into a 15-0 lead thanks to a try in the opening two minutes by Chris Ashton and another from captain Dylan Hartley after a driving maul shoved New Zealand back 15 metres. However, the tourists hit back to make it 15-10 at the break.

With five minutes left, the All Blacks led 16-15, when flanker Sam Underhill (Bath) gathered a charge-down ball from Courtney Lawes to finish impressively from 40 metres out. Frustratingly for the English fans, after replay review it was deemed (not without controversy) that Lawes was fractionally offside. A famous win was denied.

A NEW MAN WEARS THE CROWN

For the 2018 autumn series, and to the frustration of rugby statisticians everywhere, Eddie Jones had announced that Owen Farrell and Dylan Hartley would be co-captains. The hooker had been increasingly falling victim to injuries and some pundits began to question if he was still the right man for the job. As it happened, after three games of shared captaincy with Farrell, his last ever international was the 2018 November win over Australia (37-18). In his autobiography Hartley, who won 85 per cent of his games as captain, claims Eddie Jones revealed he had lost the captaincy by saying: 'You're f*****, mate.'

With Hartley injured, Owen Farrell was confirmed as the new (and only) England captain.

DISAPPOINTMENT AHEAD OF THE WORLD CUP

England's final Six Nations campaign ahead of the World Cup was a flat one. Despite a strong win in Dublin on the opening weekend (32-20), a third-round defeat by 21-13 away against Wales (who would go on to win the Grand Slam) effectively ended their title hopes. But the biggest twist in the season was the most bizarre match in Calcutta Cup history.

2019 – England 38 Scotland 38 (Twickenham)

Scotland had not won a Calcutta Cup match at Twickenham since 1983. When this was mentioned to Eddie Jones, he joked if they meant '1883'? After 31 minutes in this match, England had stormed to a 31-0 lead and it was all still a bit of a joke. At half-time, Scotland's fly-half Finn Russell had an argument about tactics with his coach Gregor Townsend. With nothing to lose, the visitors changed things up. What followed was one of the most extraordinary halves of rugby ever played. As the game entered injury time, Scotland led 38-31. They had blitzed England with six tries of their own and four conversions. It was beyond the scope of the most romantic Hollywood scriptwriter. Cruelly, the men in blue weren't quite able to complete the fairy-tale ending, as England battered the Scottish line to eventually work George Ford over in the 83rd minute to salvage an embarrassing draw.

2019 WORLD CUP (JAPAN)

England's 2019 World Cup was, in more ways than one, oceans apart from the horrors of 2015. Looking to bury the ghost of the group stage exit on home soil in the previous tournament, England went all the way to the final, convincingly knocking out the All Blacks along the way.

That semi-final win will live long in the memory of English fans, with the 19-7 scoreline flattering the men in black. Eddie Jones had prepared his squad brilliantly for the specific threat of the New Zealanders, and it was clear early on that England were the superior team. The glory of the win, however, glossed over the fact that South Africa would be a very different challenge in the final and require a totally different game plan. The inflated hopes of English media and fans were spectacularly burst in the final when the Springboks strolled home, once again claiming England's scalp in a final. While it was a bitter pill to swallow, in the end it was a welcome tonic after the nightmare of 2015.

Captain: Owen Farrell

Coach: Eddie Jones

POOL GAMES

England 35 Tonga 3 (Sapporo Dome, Sapporo)

Eddie Jones was frequently in a rage in the stands as England were consistently frustrated by Tonga. But a strong performance from Manu Tuilagi in the centre, including two tries, helped England overcome a rusty start and get a crucial first win. The powerful Leicester player had been absent in the 2015 World

Cup debacle due to ongoing injury issues. However, treatment from a witch doctor apparently helped rid him of three lady spirits who had 'married themselves' on to him and been the cause of his injuries.

England 45 USA 7 (Kobe Misaki Stadium, Kobe City)
The USA conceded seven tries and suffered a red card after flanker John Quill delivered a nasty Owen Farrell-like shoulder charge on Owen Farrell.

England 39 Argentina 10 (Tokyo Stadium, Tokyo)
An early red card for an Owen Farrell-like tackle by lock Tomas Lavanini on England captain Owen Farrell made England's task that little bit easier as they grabbed their third bonus point win in as many games, booking their place in the quarter-finals. It was the first time in 16 years the Pumas had failed to make the knockout stages.

England (0) France (0) (CANCELLED)
Thanks to the danger from Typhoon Hagibis, one of the most powerful storms to wreak havoc on mainland Japan in decades, England's match with France (along with two others in the tournament) was cancelled and the game recorded as a 0-0 draw. At least 98 people were killed by the typhoon – a sober reminder of how unimportant rugby really is in the greater scheme of things.

QUARTER-FINALS

England 40 Australia 16 (Ōita Stadium, Ōita Prefecture)

Winger Jonny May, winning his fiftieth cap, nabbed two tries in just three minutes as England bulldozed their way into the semi-final. Other tries came from prop Kyle Sinckler (Harlequins) and winger Anthony Watson as the men in white secured their biggest win ever in the knockout stages of the World Cup.

Manu Tuilagi was a key player in England's journey to the final.

SEMI-FINALS

England 19 New Zealand 7 (International Stadium Yokohama, Yokohama)

Manu Tuilagi scored a try, George Ford kicked four penalties and Owen Farrell bagged a conversion in a game destined to rank among England's greatest World Cup wins. The Kiwis were shell-shocked in the opening 40 minutes, a half in which the *Guardian*'s Lee Calvert accurately wrote that New Zealand were 'largely nowhere'. The three-time World Champions had won 15 of the previous 16 matches between the two teams, yet on this day in Yokohama they were never in the match. The scoreline flattered the All Blacks as a superb performance by the pack, especially from back rowers Sam Underhill and Tom Curry (Sale), guided England to their fourth final.

FINAL

England 12 South Africa 32 (International Stadium Yokohama)

South Africa had reached the final with a late three-point win over a hugely physical Welsh team. Smart rugby observers recognised that the Springboks were going to be a totally different challenge to the All Blacks, yet too many in the English media assumed England would breeze past the South Africans due to the way they took New Zealand apart. The Boks had England's scrum in all sorts of trouble and once the men in green took a 12-6 lead at half-time, it was hard to see Eddie Jones's men coming back. Fly-half Handre Pollard kicked 22 points and two second-half tries from Cheslin Kolbe and Makazole Mapimpi put paid to England's dreams.

Despite this being their third World Cup final, South Africa had never scored a try in a final before (which included extra time in 1995). The win made the Springboks the most successful side in tournament history. While they had the same number of titles as New Zealand, they were not part of the 1987 or 1991 World Cups, meaning they had reached that number in two fewer tournaments.

BACK ON TOP

England claimed their 29th outright Championship with four out of five wins in the 2020 Six Nations. France, too, had four wins and both teams, with bonus points taken into account, had accumulated 18 points in the table. However, England's superior points difference gave them the edge. The tournament was interrupted by the Covid outbreak and the final set of fixtures did not take place until late October.

MATCH ONE: France 24 England 17 (Stade de France)

On a rainy night in Paris, England fell 17-0 behind and never recovered, going down 24-17. Ultimately, France would suffer a surprise loss to Scotland and allow England to be the first team since Wales in 2013 to sneak the title after losing their first game of the campaign.

MATCH TWO: Scotland 6 England 13 (Murrayfield)

The BBC's Tom English called this match 'turgid'. Prop Ellis Genge (Leicester) was the scorer of the match's solitary try just ten minutes from the end. Captain Owen Farrell kicked the rest in the wind and rain that plagued the match.

MATCH THREE: England 24 Ireland 12 (Twickenham)

George Ford and Elliot Daly tortured the visitors with an excellent tactical kicking display and helped pin Ireland in their own half. Ford and Daly added a try each too before half-time, giving the home side a 17-0 interval lead. Replacement hooker Luke Cowan-Dickie (Exeter) scored England's third and Owen Farrell slotted all the kicks.

MATCH FOUR: England 33 Wales 30 (Twickenham)

England took the Triple Crown despite a late comeback from Wales. Winger Anthony Watson, Manu Tuilagi and Elliot Daly claimed a try each, and Owen Farrell and George Ford added three conversions and four penalties between them. But a late yellow card for replacement Ellis Genge (offside) and a red card for Tuilagi (dangerous tackle) allowed the Dragons to mount a final attack on the home side. Tuilagi was praised for his apologetic and calm response to the card, checking in on George North who had been the Welsh player on the receiving end.

MATCH FIVE: Italy 5 England 34 (Stadio Olimpico)

Ben Youngs got to celebrate his 100th cap with a brace of tries in a win that allowed England to claim the Championship. Hooker Jamie George (Saracens), who was winning his 50th cap, also got into the mood of things with a try of his own. With Tom Curry and Henry Slade (Exeter) also scoring five-pointers, England did enough to pop the victory champagne.

SWINGING OUT OF AN AWKWARD HISTORY

In October 2020 the RFU responded to an ongoing debate about the history and usage of England rugby's unofficial anthem 'Swing Low, Sweet Chariot' at Twickenham. The RFU announced that it would 'use its social media and event audiences to proactively educate fans on the history and provenance of the song'. Popular myth has it that the song had come to the fore for English rugby fans at Twickenham in 1988 when black winger Chris Oti made his debut or alternatively that it referenced Martin Offiah (see page 233). However, former players like Brian Moore highlighted that the song had a tradition in rugby circles that dated well before Oti and Offiah and that it was usually sung with very 'rude gestures'. Moore said 'Swing Low' was not suitable as a national song as it has 'no relevance to England' and that it 'should be celebrated in its rightful context'.

In June 2020, Maro Itoje revealed that the singing of the song at England games made him 'uncomfortable'. The RFU consulted players and fans and decided that while the singing of the hymn would not be banned, it would no longer feature in England's messaging, commercial activities or be used as motivational lyrics around the ground. As of 2022, England fans continued to sing it despite the feelings of Itoje and others being made public.

A POST-COVID WORLD
THE AUTUMN NATIONS CUP

With the coronavirus pandemic forcing cancellation of the traditional autumn internationals, England took part in the

Autumn Nations Cup: a tournament involving the Six Nations teams with the addition of Georgia and Fiji. It was an odd, one-off event created to ensure top level rugby could be played and much needed income from sponsors and television companies could continue to flow in. Adding to the strange feeling was that due to coronavirus preventative measures, almost all games were played behind closed doors in eerie silence (the final saw 2,000 fans in attendance, however). The tournament never quite shook off its makeshift feeling, not helped by the fact that even the official website failed to record the stats and data usually expected of modern Test rugby.

But winning is always better than losing and the title was claimed by England – but not without more than a little drama.

GROUP STAGE

England 40 Georgia 0 (Twickenham)

Hooker Jamie George made history with the first ever hat-trick by an English hooker. Sadly, there were no fans there to enjoy it with him. Flanker Jack Willis (Wasps) scored on his debut.

England 18 Ireland 7 (Twickenham)

Winger Jonny May scored such a good try that the RFU produced a commemorative T-shirt to celebrate it. Taking the ball inside his own 22 out left, he beat the first Irish defender with a step, burned past two others through pace, then just before reaching halfway he kicked over the full-back, beat the cover to the ball, hacked ahead and scored to the right of the posts. It was one of the great solo tries not just at Twickenham, but for England.

Wales 13 England 24 (Parc y Scarlets, Llanelli)

England played their first game in Llanelli since a 0-0 draw with Wales in 1887! This game was probably just as entertaining as the previous one 133 years before. In a flat encounter, tries from Henry Slade and Mako Vunipola, along with four penalties and a conversion from captain Owen Farrell, were enough to send England to the top of their group and into the final.

THE AUTUMN NATIONS CUP
England 22 France 19* (Twickenham)
(*After extra time)

A tournament that few had taken to in the group stages appeared to be fading to farce when France effectively put out a reserve XV due to a conflict with their domestic clubs over player release. Full of unknowns and new caps, France were expected to be crushed by a cricket score by most observers. Yet, in the final play they led 19-12 after an extraordinary display (particularly in defence) in which they held the lead from the 15th minute after a beautiful try from Brice Dulin. England benefited from a huge slice of luck in the 79th minute when a knock-on from Owen Farrell resulted in a penalty to England by referee Andrew Brace. From the kick to the corner, England managed to drive over with a try from Luke Cowan-Dickie to secure sudden-death extra time.

There was no score in the first half of extra time, but five minutes into the second half, France were pinged for sealing off in the tackle. Owen Farrell stepped up and slotted a kick over from about ten metres from the left touchline, bang on the

Maro Itoje is a superstar of the modern era for England.

French 22. It was cruel for the young French side, but few of the 2,000 in attendance cared. The trophy belonged to England and there was even merchandise produced to celebrate. But how much was actually sold is another matter.

AUTUMN CHAMPIONS TO SPRING CHUMPS

Defending champions England plummeted to fifth in the 2021 Six Nations table, repeating their grim finish of 2018 and equalling their 1987 calamity. The tournament, due to the difficult situation caused by Covid, began just three months after the 2020 version was completed and was played to empty stadiums.

The dreadful campaign kicked off with Twickenham falling to the Scots for the first time since 1983. Despite the close scoreline (11-6), England were barely in the match and Finn Russell's boot and a try from winger Duhan van der Merwe saw off a pair of Owen Farrell penalties. The home side conceded ten penalties in the opening half an hour and indiscipline was to be a factor for the whole campaign. The loss was followed by a routine 41-18 win over a poor Italy and a record 40-24 thumping in Cardiff.

There was a small highlight with a 23-20 win over France in London (thanks to a 77th-minute Maro Itoje try) but their Six Nations ended on a dismal note with a 32-18 loss in Dublin.

THE COVID ERA CONTINUES

Covid complications around travel and stadium safety meant England stayed at home rather than tour in the summer of

2021. Without their British & Irish Lions, England, led by flanker Lewis Ludlow (Gloucester), dispatched USA (43-29) and Canada (70-14) in front of restricted crowd numbers.

The autumn saw crowds back and a clean sweep with victories over Tonga (69-3), Australia (32-15) and world champions South Africa (27-26). The latter win was sealed by a last-gasp penalty from 22-year-old outside-half Marcus Smith (Harlequins). The youngster had lit up English club rugby in the previous season, taking Quins to the league title, and with this dramatic win he was all but anointed a messiah by a slavering media.

SIX NATIONS 2022

England again endured a disappointing Six Nations as coach Eddie Jones found his critics increasing in number and volume. Despite losing three of their games (20-17 to Scotland, 32-15 to Ireland and 25-13 to France), points difference allowed England to finish in third place in the table. England's wins came away to Italy (33-0) and narrowly at home to Wales. The game finished 23-19 and the visitors outscored the hosts three tries to one.

WINNING RETURN TO OZ

Eddie Jones had established himself as English coach by winning a three-match series against his native Australia back in 2016. He didn't quite engineer a clean sweep in 2022, but he did steer his men to a series win.

Marcus Smith quickly became a huge fan favourite and media star.

Led by Courtney Lawes, England recovered from a 30-28 reverse in the first Test to win 25-17 and 21-17 in the subsequent contests. The impressive series win helped remove some of the pressure that had been building on Jones. Ellis Genge and full-back Freddie Steward (Leicester Tigers) were two standout stars for England, winning plenty of praise from fans and critics.

ENGLAND FALL, FALL AND FALL IN THE FALL (AND SO DOES EDDIE JONES)

After the happy summer, England came crashing down to earth with a bump in London — falling 30-29 to Argentina in the opening match of the autumn. Despite 63 per cent possession, 60% territory, a metres gained advantage of 427 metres to Argentina's 157 metres, and all sorts of other small 'victories', the Pumas won at Twickenham for the first time. Captain Owen Farrell kicked five penalties and converted tries from Joe Cokanasiga (Bath) and Jack van Poortvliet (Leicester). But the tourists were inspired by winger Emiliano Boffelli who scored 25 points on his own and ended a ten-game losing streak in the fixture. Before the game, with an axis of Marcus Smith, Farrell and Manu Tuilagi, there had been much hope for not just victory, but a victory with style and power.

Eddie Jones had no problem though in guiding England to a rout of his old team, Japan, seven days later. The Brave Blossoms collapsed 52-13. Amazingly, this was only the third time the sides had met in a full cap international.

The All Blacks were the opposition for the third game of the autumn and it was an oddly compelling affair. It was the first clash between the sides since England's 2019 World Cup win and New Zealand were rounding off a strange year in which they had suffered several defeats — including losses at home to Argentina and Ireland (twice). Excitement was high as it was only the third time England had faced their old rivals under Eddie Jones. The rarity of the fixture added wonderfully to the spice around it. Unfortunately there was a disastrous start for scrum-half Jack van Poortvliet who threw a fourth-minute pass to Kiwi Dalton Papali'i' for a score. The tourists looked an utterly different side to the one that had stumbled through 2022 and England were 14-0 down within ten minutes.

With just ten minutes left on the clock, New Zealand led 25-6 and it seemed England were playing for pride. Then the 2022 All Blacks imploded once more, as they had been wont to do during the year, and an inspired England rallied. First a wonderful break from Marcus Smith took England close to the line and, after a powerful pick and drive from replacement prop Will Stuart (Bath), England had another try. A yellow card to New Zealand's Beauden Barrett offered another chink of light and full-back Freddie Steward went over followed, in the final minute, by Stuart claiming another. Unbelievably, it was 25-25.

Whatever slim hopes of a victory rally there were ended in some controversy a minute later, however, when Smith opted to kick to touch rather than risk a loss in running from his own half. Nonetheless, it had been one of the most extraordinary second halves seen at HQ.

The year ended on a crushing low as South Africa brushed England aside 27-13 in a dominant display. A red card for Springbok replacement prop Thomas du Toit after 60 minutes for a dangerous challenge did nothing but keep the score down as England were well and truly outplayed, outthought and outmuscled. Once again, as he had done for every other loss in the autumn and for most of England's 2022 losses (his team won just five of 12 contests), Eddie Jones took the blame for the team's shortcomings and sounded confident that all was on track for the 2023 World Cup. But as England rugby fans know, and as this book reveals, there is far more to the rich history of English rugby than just World Cups. All the matches matter and his continued dismissal of poor results was wearing thin with the media and supporters, many of whom openly booed England and Jones after the Bok loss.

A NEW ERA BEGINS

Alongside two years of mediocre results, there was a barrage of criticism around Jones's abrasive and demanding coaching style, which many labelled as out and out bullying. The rumour mill was fuelled by a revolving door of personnel which saw a seemingly never-ending stream of fresh faces having to be brought in as coaches, doctors, physios and analysts left in unprecedented numbers. By early 2022 Jones had, according to the *Times*, had 17 different direct coaching assistants during his reign. Many of the departed were rumoured to have left due to the incredibly demanding hours they were expected to work and the constant demands and unrelenting pressure from their boss. After huge media pressure and a formal review process, in the first week of December, Bill Sweeney, the Rugby Football Union chief executive, announced Jones was leaving his role.

The new era for England would be led by Steve Borthwick, coach of Leicester Tigers, who had worked with Jones both for England and Japan. A 57-times capped former England second row, Borthwick has an enormous task on his hands. A giant man in the flesh, and equipped with a formidable rugby brain, Borthwick, like all who have led England, has the privilege of shaping the history of a great rugby nation.

2004–22: THE STAR PLAYERS

OWEN FARRELL

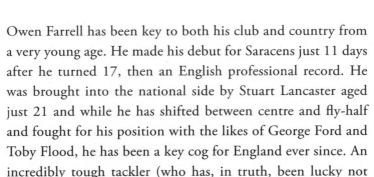

Club: Saracens
Position: Fly-half, centre
Caps: 101 (2012–)
(British & Irish Lions, 6 caps, 34 points)
Points: 1,125 (10 tries, 182 conversions, 234 penalties, 3 drop goals)

Owen Farrell has been key to both his club and country from a very young age. He made his debut for Saracens just 11 days after he turned 17, then an English professional record. He was brought into the national side by Stuart Lancaster aged just 21 and while he has shifted between centre and fly-half and fought for his position with the likes of George Ford and Toby Flood, he has been a key cog for England ever since. An incredibly tough tackler (who has, in truth, been lucky not to pick up a few more cards in his time), Farrell's accurate kicking boots have allowed him to rake in over 1,000 points for England. Eddie Jones turned to him to captain England after Dylan Hartley's era ended.

Farrell is the son of rugby league legend Andy Farrell (who also played union for England and coached in the national set-up while Owen played).

LEWIS MOODY

Club: Leicester, Bath
Position: Flanker
Caps: 71 (2001–11)
(British & Irish Lions, 3 caps, 5 points)
Points: 45 (9 tries)

Nicknamed 'Mad Dog', Lewis Moody was famous for his utter disregard for his own physical wellbeing. Playing in an era when awareness around concussion was much lower, he continually played on despite severe bangs to the head, always giving his all. His incredible engine and stamina made him a constant thorn in the side of opponents, particularly on kick-offs where he was known for his bravery in challenging for a high ball. He was involved in every game in the victorious 2003 World Cup campaign and played two key roles as a replacement for England in extra time in the final. Firstly, his chase from a restart forced Australia's Mat Rogers to slice his clearance and give England a line-out from ten metres outside the 22. Moments later he received the long line-out throw that set up the famous winning kick from Jonny Wilkinson. Moody was also a critical figure in England's surprise 2007 World Cup run and in the latter years of his international career he led England on 11 occasions (including the 2011 World Cup).

MAKO VUNIPOLA

Club: Saracens
Position: Prop
Caps: 74 (2012–)
(British & Irish Lions, 9 caps)
Points: 10 (2 tries)

Mako Vunipola has been described by Eddie Jones as one of the five truly world-class players he has coached during his career. 'He's probably the best loose-head in the world,' said Jones in 2021. 'He has ten carries a game and makes 15 tackles. You won't find any other loose-head who gets through those sorts of numbers.' Brother to another huge fan favourite for England, number eight Billy, Vunipola has been a rock of the modern England team, as well as the British & Irish Lions (he has made three tours). His work rate is the stuff of legend among teammates, despite accusations that early in his career he was a little less keen to put in the hard yards. As well as being a powerful ball carrier, the Saracens prop has been known to perform some lovely stuff with the ball in hand too. A truly class player.

MARO ITOJE

Club: Saracens
Position: Second row, flanker
Caps: 62 (2016–)
(British & Irish Lions, 6 caps)
Points: 20 (4 tries)

Oghenemaro Miles 'Maro' Itoje is one of the superstars of the modern game. Born in Camden to Nigerian parents, Itoje showed exceptional sporting ability from a young age and even represented his country in shot put (Under 17s). An imposing figure at 197cm (6ft 6in) tall and 110kg (17st 5lb), his athleticism and rugby brain make him a fearsome opponent and he has been one of the core players of Eddie Jones's England. Famed for his destructive qualities in defence and at the breakdown, he also possesses superb attacking skills and line-out ability. He made his debut for Saracens aged just 19 and has had huge success with the club, including four Premiership titles (while also picking up European Player of the Year for himself along the way). Itoje was key to both England's 2016 and 2017 Six Nations titles and the successful Test series in Australia (2016), playing at both lock and blindside flanker. His value to Eddie Jones's England team cannot be underestimated and the Australian coach considers Itoje one of the few genuinely world-class players he has coached.

He was first picked for the British & Irish Lions aged 22. Between May 2015 and September 2016, Itoje did not taste defeat once for club or country across an astonishing 31 games. Despite criticism about his tendency to give away needless penalties at times, Itoje's athleticism, strength, hard-working attitude and positional play combine to make him one of the greats of the modern era.

2004–22 NOTABLE EVENTS IN ENGLISH HISTORY

• 2004: Boris Johnson is sacked from his position as Conservative shadow minister for publicly lying about his personal life.

• 2005: A ban on hunting with dogs in England and Wales comes into force.

• 2006: The BBC announces that its main sports programme, *Grandstand*, will come to an end after 48 years.

• 2007: Following Wales, Scotland and Northern Ireland, England introduces a smoking ban in enclosed public places.

• 2008: Lewis Hamilton becomes Formula One World Champion, the youngest driver ever to claim the title.

• 2009: Harry Patch dies aged 111. He was the last British survivor of the trenches of the First World War.

• 2010: Cadbury is taken over by Kraft Foods, an American competitor, in an £11.5 billion deal.

• 2011: The 2011 England riots (often called the London riots) take place between 6 and 11 August. Five people die.

• 2012: Sarah West becomes the first female warship commander in the Royal Navy.

• 2013: The Nobel Prize in Physics is awarded to physicist Peter Higgs for his theory of the Higgs boson.

• 2014: The Met Office reveals that 2014 is the warmest year in the UK since records began.

• 2015: England finally follows the example of Scotland, Northern Ireland and Wales in introducing mandatory charges for plastic bags at supermarkets.

• 2016: Boris Johnson writes an unpublished newspaper article stating 'Britain is a great nation, a global force for good. It is surely a boon for the world and for Europe that she should be intimately engaged in the EU.'

- 2017: A suicide bomber kills 22 people at the end of a pop concert at the Manchester Arena.

- 2018: Professor Stephen Hawking dies aged 76.

- 2019: 11.7 million people watch England v USA in the FIFA Women's World Cup, the most viewed British television broadcast of the year.

- 2020: Minister Michael Gove admits Prime Minister Boris Johnson skipped five consecutive emergency meetings (COBRA) concerning the coronavirus crisis.

- 2021: 18-year-old British tennis player Emma Raducanu, ranked 150th in the world, shocks the planet and wins the US Open.

SHIRTS AND STADIUMS: WHERE THEY PLAYED AND WHAT THEY WORE

PLAYING KITS

[*See the centre spread for a representation of all official England shirts since 1871.*]

When England switched to wearing Umbro kits in 2020, many fans welcomed a return to an English kit manufacturer. More, however, complained that Umbro had no heritage in the sport. They could not have been more wrong. Umbro made kit for many years for everyone from England to Wales and the British Lions as well as many British club sides. The thing was that for most of the period they made official playing shirts for England, they were not allowed to display their logo on the shirt. It could usually only be seen on the inside label. It was, however, often visible in later years on training gear. Here's a list of official suppliers since the 1960s:

- Lillywhites (1960s and earlier)
- Umbro (approximately early 1970s to 1983)
- Bukta (1984–90)
- Cotton Traders (1991–97) (The 1992 Five Nations saw England briefly revert back to a traditional shirt due to a legal dispute with Cotton Traders.)
- Nike (1997–2012)
- Canterbury (2012–20)
- Umbro (2020–)

ENGLAND AND WALES HAVE
EACH OTHER'S NUMBERS

The 1922 Championship saw Wales and England agree to always number their teams for the first time. Before this, some teams had worn numbers on occasion in international rugby. The 1897 New Zealand team did so, as did later All Black touring teams. Wales and New Zealand both wore numbers in their epic 1905 game, for instance. But it is unclear if England wore numbers before their formal decision to do so from 1922. When numbers were worn, the system often varied. At first, England teams tended to label the full-back number one and work up to the forwards so that a loose-head prop was 15. Some teams, such as Wales, used letters or even missed out the number 13 to avoid bad luck. According to rugbyfootballhistory.com, sometimes unions changed player numbers to fool pirate printers of unofficial rugby programmes.

Numbering players was distasteful to the Scots at first. During the 1920s, Scotland asked visiting teams not to number players. When King George V attended a Calcutta Cup match and asked why the players were not numbered, he was told by the SRU president that 'this is a rugby match, not a cattle sale'.

ONLY ONE SHIRT REMAINS

Just one shirt survives from the original 20 jerseys from England's first game in 1871. It belonged to forward John Clayton (Liverpool) and is housed in the museum at Twickenham.

THRIFTY TIMES

Today's players get given (literally) bagfuls of kit and gear for every tournament or campaign. They even get as many as four shirts per match. Things weren't always like that:

> *'You got a cap – just one. We had to buy our own shorts, and as Coventry's shorts were blue I had to go and buy two pairs of white shorts. All they gave us were the socks and shirts, and after the games they'd even go through your kit to get the shirt back. They never gave us anything, which you could understand a bit, clothes were on coupon. I do know that in the two years I played every game and they'd come in afterwards and make sure they got jerseys 1 to 15 safely back.'*
> **Harry Walker (9 caps for England between 1947 and 1948)**

YOU'VE BEEN SELECTED . . . NOW GO SHOPPING

In the 1870s players would find out about selection through the post. As well as being told to get as fit as possible for the game, they would be sent the following information about playing kit:

> *'The uniform (which should be written for by the first mail) consists of white jersey with badge and ribbon, white flannel knickerbockers and dark brown stockings. It is obtainable from J Markham, Tailor, Rugby, as is the cap, which is of rose velvet with silver lace badge. In ordering a jersey, the size of your collar and measurement around the chest should be stated. If you can give Markham a London address where you can conveniently*

call, it will be the safer plan, as parcels are so frequently delayed in transmission through town to other Railways.'

A ROSE BY ANY OTHER DESIGN . . .

Until 1921, the rose on the England shirt was not standardised and in the early years of the national team players supplied their own crest to add to the shirt (and some northerners used a white rose). Old team photos show a surprising inconsistency in the roses worn by players.

SOCKS AND STOCKINGS

It wasn't just roses that were different in the early days – until around the early 1930s players wore club socks (or stockings as they were often called in the early years of international rugby) when playing for England.

YOU KNOW THEIR NUMBERS, HERE ARE THEIR NAMES

During the 2022 Autumn Nations Series, England players had their names featured on the back of their shirts. This was the first time ever England had done this. Wales had briefly experimented with this approach between 2005 and 2008. Many traditionalists feel this takes away the concept that the player does not 'own' his shirt, but is rather given the honour to wear it while he tries to live up to its legacy. Modern marketers, however, believe there are pounds to be made through the names on shirts approach.

STADIUMS

'To my ears the noise seemed an incessant high-pitched
wailing, weird and eerie, as though the sound came from
a congregation of lost souls hovering about the high stands.'
Rowe Harding, a Welsh international who played at
Twickenham in the 1920s

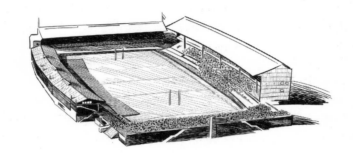

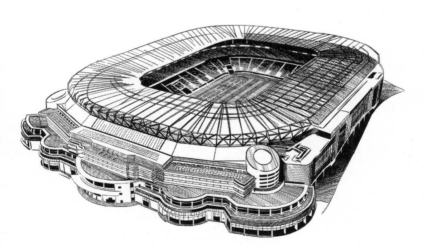

Twickenham has grown from humble
beginnings to one of the best stadiums in rugby.

A SHORT HISTORY OF THE CABBAGE PATCH

Prior to the purchase of land at Twickenham, England played their home internationals in a variety of venues in the north and south of England. One of the key drivers for the RFU to build their own stadium came after the New Zealand and South African Tests of 1905 and 1906. Both games were held at Crystal Palace and both attracted over 40,000 fans and as the RFU did not own the ground, large chunks of the profits did not come to them.

In the early days of Twickenham's use, many in the rugby community complained that the ground was too far from central London. With terracing in use in the early days and different seating arrangements to the present day, fans were advised to arrive early to avoid disappointment.

In 1912 *The Times* wrote: ' . . . those who wish to secure a good place at the fence will be well-advised to make an early start for the somewhat remote and inaccessible theatre of war.'

THE LONG, LONG, GREEN, GREEN GRASS OF HOME

'It was horrendous trying to kick off the floor; it was so soft and spongy. There didn't seem to be any grass management at Twickenham in those days whereas now it's the best playing surface in the world. Twickenham was a disgrace throughout most of my career. It was either a muddy mess or the grass was a foot tall and it was like playing in a meadow.'

Dusty Hare, England 1974–84 and scorer of 240 points.

STADIUM TIMELINE

- **1907:** William Williams and William Cail of the RFU drive the purchase of 10.25 acres of land in Twickenham for £5,500 12s 6d. Prior to purchase, the land was used to grow cabbages. This has led to the ground being nicknamed 'The Cabbage Patch' or 'Billy Williams's Cabbage Patch'.

- **1908:** The first stands are constructed on the east and west side of the playing field.

- **1909:** Harlequins beat Richmond 14-10 in the first game at the venue. Fewer than 2,000 fans attend. Harlequins also use the ground as it would otherwise lie empty for most of the year, so that makes it an ideal home for the London side.

- **1910:** England beat Wales in the first international game at Twickenham. It marks the first time England have beaten Wales in 12 years and the visitors do not win at the ground until 1933.

- **1925:** A North Stand is added to the ground, built by Archibald Leitch, famous for working on football stadiums such as Anfield and Hampden Park as well as rugby's Cardiff Arms Park. The capacity is upped to 60,000.

- **1927:** The East Stand is expanded (holding 12,000 spectators) and the South Terrace also has its capacity increased to 20,000.

- **1929:** The Rowland Hill Memorial Gates are built. George Rowland Hill was a member of the RFU in the 1880s, spent time as secretary and as president and served the union for 49 years. He was part of the committee that saw England exiled by the other Home Unions for refusing to join their proposed international union and he later helped ensure working-class players were refused 'broken-time' payments, leading to the Great Schism.

- **1931** and **1932:** New West Stand built, which includes offices for the RFU (the ground also has the nickname of 'HQ'). Extra land (six acres) is purchased and capacity is now 74,000. The ground will see very little change after this until the 1980s.

• **1933:** The RFU says that floodlights are not in the best interest of the sport and, as a result, there is no plan to install them at the stadium.

• **1937:** Permission is given to expand 'Rugby Road' which approaches the stadium to help with traffic management.

• **1939–45:** During the war the ground becomes a Civil Defence Depot and would have a key role to play as a decontamination centre if London suffered a chemical attack.

• **1950:** Twickenham's famous weathervane is installed on the South Terrace (it has been moved since). Crafted by Kenneth Dalgleish (a Scot), it stands 1.9 metres tall and depicts the Greek god Hermes (Mercury) passing a ball to a rugby player.

• **1950s:** The ground contains five tea rooms and 12 bars (one of which seats 400 people).

• **1954:** The Jehovah's Witnesses hold their first convention at the ground, something that still takes place today.

• **1963:** Harlequins move to their own stadium across the road from Twickenham. Their ground is named after former England international Adrian Stoop.

• **1965:** Structural issues lead to closure of the South Terrace.

• **1972:** The 'Coade' stone lion is installed at Twickenham. A gift from the Greater London Council, in 1991 it would be gilded in gold.

• **1978:** Planning permission is granted for extensive rebuilding of the ground.

• **1981:** The South Terrace is rebuilt as the South Stand and now includes 12 corporate boxes.

- **1983:** An informal rugby museum is built underneath the South Stand.
- **1990:** A newly extended North Stand is opened and, following the success of the South Stand, also includes corporate facilities.
- **1991:** The World Cup final is held at Twickenham. England lose 12-6 to Australia.
- **1992:** Development begins on improved East and West Stands.
- **1995:** Completion of the new stands increases capacity to 75,000 and gives Twickenham a 'horseshoe' shape.
- **1996:** The Museum of Rugby opens in the East Stand.
- **2000:** The first game of rugby league is played at Twickenham (England v Australia).
- **2003:** The Rolling Stones play the first concert at the venue (permission is given for three concerts a year).
- **2005:** The South Stand is demolished as part of a major new redevelopment which will increase capacity to 82,000.
- **2006:** The new South Stand is opened.
- **2016:** The Los Angeles Rams play the New York Giants in the first NFL game at HQ.
- **2016:** The Rose and Poppy Gates are unveiled as part of the Rowland Hill Memorial Gates. The players walk through them on matchday and the gates are a monument to help people remember the fallen from the First World War and include poppies built from shell casings from the Battle of the Somme.
- **2017:** The Museum of Rugby moves to the South Stand.
- **2018:** The East Stand undergoes improvements, including six floors dedicated to function and event space.
- **2020:** The West Car Park temporarily becomes an NHS national testing centre for coronavirus.

RESULTS AND RECORDS
All stats correct as of December 2022

CHAMPIONSHIPS (HOME NATIONS, FIVE NATIONS, SIX NATIONS)

OUTRIGHT TITLES (29)

1883, 1884, 1892, 1910, 1913, 1914, 1921, 1923, 1924, 1928, 1930, 1934, 1937, 1953, 1957, 1958, 1963, 1980, 1991, 1992, 1995, 1996, 2000, 2001, 2003, 2011, 2016, 2017, 2020

SHARED TITLES (10)

1886, 1890, 1912, 1920, 1932, 1939, 1947, 1954, 1960, 1973

GRAND SLAMS (13)

1913, 1914, 1921, 1923, 1924, 1928, 1957, 1980, 1991, 1992, 1995, 2003, 2016

TRIPLE CROWNS (26)

1883, 1884, 1892, 1913, 1914, 1921, 1923, 1924, 1928, 1934, 1937, 1954, 1957, 1960, 1980, 1991, 1992, 1995, 1996, 1997, 1998, 2002, 2003, 2014, 2016, 2020

WOODEN SPOONS (14)

1899, 1901, 1903, 1905, 1907, 1931, 1948, 1950, 1966, 1972, 1974, 1975, 1976, 1983

WORLD CUP RECORD

WINNERS (2003), RUNNER UP (1991, 2007, 2019), SEMI-FINAL (1995), QUARTER-FINAL (1987, 1999, 2011), GROUP STAGE (2015)

AUTUMN NATIONS CUP

WINNERS (2021)

WORLD RANKINGS RECORD

HIGHEST POSITION: 1st (2003, 2003–04, 2019)
LOWEST POSITION: 8th (2009, 2015–16)

MOST CAPS (ALL TIME)

AME	CAPS	DEBUT	FINAL GAME	WINS
EN YOUNGS	121	2010 (SCOTLAND)	–	81
ASON LEONARD	114	1990 (ARGENTINA)	2004 (ITALY)	86
WEN FARRELL	101	2012 (SCOTLAND)	–	68
YLAN HARTLEY	97	2008 (PACIFIC ISLANDERS)	2018 (AUSTRALIA)	66
OURTNEY LAWES	96	2009 (AUSTRALIA)	–	67
AN COLE	95	2010 (WALES)	2019 (SOUTH AFRICA)	66
ONNY WILKINSON	91	1998 (IRELAND)	2011 (FRANCE)	66
ANNY CARE	87	2008 (NEW ZEALAND)	–	55
AWRENCE DALLAGLIO	85	1995 (SOUTH AFRICA)	2007 (SOUTH AFRICA)	60
ORY UNDERWOOD	85	1984 (IRELAND)	1996 (IRELAND)	55

MOST CAPS (DEBUT BEFORE PROFESSIONALISM IN 1995)

NAME	CAPS	DEBUT	FINAL GAME	WINS
JASON LEONARD	114	1990 (ARGENTINA)	2004 (ITALY)	86
RORY UNDERWOOD	85	1984 (IRELAND)	1996 (IRELAND)	55
MARTIN JOHNSON	84	1993 (FRANCE)	2003 (AUSTRALIA)	67
MIKE CATT	75	1994 (WALES)	2007 (SOUTH AFRICA)	50
WILL CARLING	72	1988 (FRANCE)	1997 (WALES)	53
ROB ANDREW	71	1985 (ROMANIA)	1997 (WALES)	53
RICHARD HILL	71	1997 (SCOTLAND)	2004 (AUSTRALIA)	50
NEIL BACK	66	1994 (SCOTLAND)	2003 (AUSTRALIA)	52
JERRY GUSCOTT	65	1989 (ROMANIA)	1999 (TONGA)	51
BRIAN MOORE	64	1987 (SCOTLAND)	1995 (FRANCE)	45

MOST POINTS

NAME	POINTS	CAPS	CAREER	POINTS PER GAME AVG.*
JONNY WILKINSON	1,179	91	1998-2011	13.0
OWEN FARRELL	1,125	101	2012-	11.1
PAUL GRAYSON	400	32	1995-2004	12.5
ROB ANDREW	396	71	1985-97	5.6
GEORGE FORD	308	84	2014-	3.7
TOBY FLOOD	301	60	2006-13	5.0
JONATHAN WEBB	296	33	1987-93	9.0
CHARLIE HODGSON	269	38	2001-12	7.1
DUSTY HARE	240	25	1974-84	9.6
RORY UNDERWOOD	210	85	1984-96	2.5

*Rounded to one decimal place.

MOST TRIES

NAME	TRIES	CAPS	CAREER	TRIES PER GAME AVG.*
RORY UNDERWOOD	49	85	1984-96	0.6
JONNY MAY	35	72	2013-	0.5
BEN COHEN	31	57	2000-06	0.5
WILL GREENWOOD	31	55	1997-2004	0.6
JEREMY GUSCOTT	30	65	1989-99	0.5
JASON ROBINSON	28	51	2001-07	0.5
DAN LUGER	24	38	1998-2003	0.6
JOSH LEWSEY	22	55	1998-2007	0.4
ANTHONY WATSON	22	51	2014-	0.4

*Rounded to one decimal place.

RESULTS BY DECADE

DECADE	PLAYED	WON	DRAWN	LOST	WIN %
1871–1880	14	8	4	2	57.14
1881–1889	22	15	5	2	68.18
1890–1899	30	14	1	15	46.67
1900–1909	37	11	3	23	29.73
1910–1919	21	16	1	4	76.19
1920–1929	42	29	3	10	69.05
1930–1939	34	17	4	13	50.00
1940–1949	13	5	1	7	38.46
1950–1959	43	22	6	15	51.16
1960–1969	48	16	10	22	33.33
1970–1979	51	15	3	33	29.41
1980–1989	61	28	5	28	45.90
1990–1999	91	61	2	28	67.03
2000–2009	115	72	0	43	62.61
2010–2019	120	82	3	35	68.33
2020–2022	31	20	1	10	64.52
TOTAL	**773**	**431**	**52**	**290**	**55.76**

RESULTS BY TEST MATCH TYPE

TEST TYPE	GAMES	WON	DRAWN	LOST	WIN%
CHAMPIONSHIP (FOUR/FIVE/SIX NATIONS)	493	269	40	184	54.56
NON-CHAMPIONSHIP TESTS/ NON-WORLD CUP	**206**	**108**	**12**	**86**	**52.43**
WORLD CUP WARM-UPS	18	12	0	6	66.67
WORLD CUP (INCLUDES QUALIFIERS)	**52**	**38**	**0**	**14**	**73.08**
AUTUMN NATIONS CUPS	4	4	0	0	100.00
TOTAL	**773**	**431**	**52**	**290**	**55.76**

AMATEUR ERA RESULTS
BY TEST MATCH TYPE (1871 – JULY 1995)

TEST TYPE	GAMES	WON	DRAWN	LOST	WIN%
CHAMPIONSHIP (FOUR/FIVE NATIONS)	362	180	38	144	49.72
NON-CHAMPIONSHIP TESTS	**86**	**43**	**8**	**35**	**50.00**
WORLD CUP	16	10	0	6	62.50
TOTAL	**464**	**233**	**46**	**185**	**50.22**

PROFESSIONAL ERA RESULTS
(JULY 1995 – PRESENT DAY)

TEST TYPE	GAMES	WON	DRAWN	LOST	WIN%
CHAMPIONSHIP (FIVE/SIX NATIONS)	131	89	2	40	67.94
NON-CHAMPIONSHIP TESTS/ NON-WORLD CUP	**120**	**65**	**4**	**51**	**54.17**
WORLD CUP WARM-UPS	18	12	0	6	66.67
WORLD CUP (INCLUDES QUALIFIERS)	**36**	**28**	**0**	**8**	**77.78**
AUTUMN NATIONS CUPS	4	4	0	0	100.00
TOTAL	**309**	**198**	**6**	**105**	**64.08**

RESULTS PER OPPONENT
(CAPPED GAMES ONLY)

OPPONENT	GAMES	WON	DRAWN	LOST	WIN%
ARGENTINA	25	19	1	5	76.00
AUSTRALIA*	55	28	1	26	50.90
CANADA	7	7	0	0	100.00
FIJI	7	7	0	0	100.00
FRANCE	109	60	7	42	55.05
GEORGIA	3	3	0	0	100.00
IRELAND	139	80	8	51	57.55
ITALY	27	27	0	0	100.00
JAPAN	3	3	0	0	100.00
NETHERLANDS	1	1	0	0	100.00
NEW ZEALAND	43	33	2	8	18.60
NZ NATIVES	1	1	0	0	100.00
PACIFIC ISLANDERS	1	1	0	0	100.00
RFU PRESIDENT'S XV	1	0	0	1	0.00
ROMANIA	5	5	0	0	100.00
SAMOA	8	8	0	0	100.00
SCOTLAND	140	76	19	45	54.29
SOUTH AFRICA	45	16	2	27	35.56
TONGA	4	4	0	0	100.00
URUGUAY	2	2	0	0	100.00
USA	7	7	0	0	100.00
WALES	138	66	12	60	47.83
TOTAL	773	431	52	290	55.76

*Includes 1928 match with NSW Waratahs, now classed as an Australia team.

SCORING TOTALS 1871–2022

TEAM	TRIES	PENALTY TRIES	CONVS	PENS	DROP GOALS	GOALS FROM MARK	POINTS
ENGLAND	1,750	26	1,086	1,341	144	4	13,829
OPPONENTS	1,221	13	692	1,100	158	5	10,068

BIGGEST WINNING MARGINS

2001: ENGLAND 134 ROMANIA 0 (TWICKENHAM, NOVEMBER TEST)

1998: ENGLAND 110 NETHERLANDS 0 (HUDDERSFIELD, WORLD CUP QUALIFIER)

1999: ENGLAND 106 USA 6 (TWICKENHAM, WORLD CUP WARM-UP MATCH)

2003: ENGLAND 111 URUGUAY 13 (BRISBANE, WORLD CUP)

1999: ENGLAND 101 TONGA 10 (TWICKENHAM, WORLD CUP)

BIGGEST LOSING MARGINS

1998: AUSTRALIA 76 ENGLAND 0 (BRISBANE, SUMMER TOUR)

2007: SOUTH AFRICA 58 ENGLAND 10 (BLOEMFONTEIN, TEST SERIES)

1998: NEW ZEALAND 64 ENGLAND 22 (DUNEDIN, TEST SERIES)

2004: AUSTRALIA 51 ENGLAND 15 (BRISBANE, SUMMER TOUR)

2007: ENGLAND 0 SOUTH AFRICA 36 (PARIS, WORLD CUP)

RESULTS BY HEAD COACH

NOTE: The RFU have used various titles for the role of coach/manager over the years. 'Head Coach' has been chosen here.

COACH	PERIOD	GAMES	WON	DRAWN	LOST	WIN %
DON WHITE	1969–71	11	3	1	7	27.27
JOHN ELDERS	1972–74	16	6	1	9	37.50
JOHN BURGESS	1975	6	1	0	5	16.67
PETER COLSTON	1976–79	18	6	1	11	33.33
MIKE DAVIS	1979–82	16	10	2	4	62.50
DICK GREENWOOD	1983–85	17	4	2	11	23.53
MARTIN GREEN	1985–87	14	5	0	9	35.71
GEOFF COOKE	1988–94	49	35	1	13	71.43
JACK ROWELL	1994–97	29	21	0	8	72.41
CLIVE WOODWARD	1997–2004	83	59	2	22	71.08
ANDY ROBINSON	2004–06	22	9	0	13	40.91
BRIAN ASHTON	2007–08	22	12	0	10	54.55
ROB ANDREW*	2008	2	0	0	2	0.00
MARTIN JOHNSON	2008–11	38	21	1	16	55.26
STUART LANCASTER	2012–15	46	28	1	17	60.87
EDDIE JONES	2016–2022	81	59	2	20	72.84
TOTAL		**470**	**279**	**14**	**177**	**59.36**

*Caretaker coach

TEAM RESULTS BEFORE HEAD COACH POSITION
(1871–1969)

Note: England had no coach for the 1969 Five Nations. Don White became head coach in December 1969 (leading England to an 11-8 win over South Africa).

GAMES	WON	DRAWN	LOST	WIN %
303	152	38	113	50.17

RESULTS ACCORDING TO
NATIONALITY OF REFEREE (NEUTRAL)

REFEREE'S UNION	GAMES	WON	DRAWN	LOST	WIN %
ARGENTINA	4	4	0	0	100.00
AUSTRALIA	43	26	1	16	69.47
FRANCE	89	52	4	33	58.43
IRELAND	177	95	17	65	53.67
ITALY	2	2	0	0	100.00
NEW ZEALAND	70	38	1	31	54.29
SCOTLAND	133	62	10	61	46.62
SOUTH AFRICA	63	39	2	22	61.90
WALES	156	93	10	53	59.62
TOTAL	**737**	**411**	**45**	**281**	**55.77**

Note: On five occasions during England internationals the starting referee has been injured and replaced by another official. This table only considers the nationality of the starting referee.

RESULTS FOR GAMES WITH
NON-NEUTRAL REFEREES

REFEREE'S UNION	GAMES	WON	DRAWN	LOST	WIN %
AUSTRALIA	3	0	0	3	0.00
ENGLAND	14	10	2	2	71.43
FRANCE	1	1	0	0	100.00
IRELAND	3	2	1	0	66.67
NEW ZEALAND	3	1	0	2	33.33
SCOTLAND	3	0	2	1	0.00
SOUTH AFRICA	1	1	0	0	100.00
WALES	2	2	0	0	100.00
TOTAL	**30**	**17**	**5**	**8**	**56.67**

Note: This table looks at games where a match referee has been either from the RFU or the union of England's opponents. This mainly occurred in the early years of international rugby or in touring games in the amateur era.

RESULTS FOR GAMES WITH NO REFEREES

WITHOUT REFEREE	GAMES	WON	DRAWN	LOST	WIN %
TOTAL	6	3	1	2	50.00

Note: The first six England Test matches had no referees. Captains would solve disputes between themselves. If unable to do so, an appeal was lodged to two umpires who watched from the sideline. Both unions supplied one umpire each.

MOST GAMES AS CAPTAIN

NAME	GAMES	WINS	WIN %	TEST CAREER
WILL CARLING	59	44	74.6	1988-96
CHRIS ROBSHAW	43	26	60.1	2009-18
MARTIN JOHNSON	39	34	87.2	1993-2003
OWEN FARRELL*	35	22	62.9	2012-
DYLAN HARTLEY*	27	23	85.9	2008-18

*Eddie Jones appointed Owen Farrell and Dylan Hartley as joint captains on three occasions. The pair won two of these games and lost one. These statistics have not been included in the above table.

RESULTS: 1871–2022

Games 1 to 35 did not feature scoring (see 'History of Scoring' table on page 33).

G – Goal (a converted try)

T – Try

DG – Drop goal

GFM – Goal from mark

Abbreviations/Glossary

Test = refers to non-tournament/non-World Cup match

Test (1) or (2) or (3) – reference to first, second or third match in a 'Test series'

HN = Home Nations (earlier version of the Six Nations)

5N = Five Nations (earlier version of the Six Nations)

6N = Six Nations

WC = World Cup

WCQ = World Cup qualifier

WCW = World Cup warm-up

AUTC = Autumn Nations Cup

GAME	DATE	TYPE	H/A	CITY	CAPTAIN	OPPONENTS	RESULT	SCORE (FOR)	SCORE (OPP)	COACH
1	27/03/1871	TEST	AWAY	EDINBURGH	FREDERIC STOKES	SCOTLAND	LOST	1T	1G, 1T	N/A
2	05/02/1872	TEST	HOME	LONDON	FREDERIC STOKES	SCOTLAND	WON	1G, 1DG, 2T	1DG	N/A
3	03/03/1873	TEST	AWAY	GLASGOW	FREDERIC STOKES	SCOTLAND	DRAWN	NIL	NIL	N/A
4	23/02/1874	TEST	HOME	LONDON	ALFRED HAMERSLEY	SCOTLAND	WON	1DG	1T	N/A
5	15/02/1875	TEST	HOME	LONDON	HENRY LAWRENCE	IRELAND	WON	1G, 1DG, 1T	NIL	N/A
6	08/03/1875	TEST	AWAY	EDINBURGH	HENRY LAWRENCE	SCOTLAND	DRAWN	NIL	NIL	N/A
7	13/12/1875	TEST	AWAY	DUBLIN	FRANK LUSCOMBE	IRELAND	WON	1G, 1T	NIL	N/A
8	06/03/1876	TEST	HOME	LONDON	FRANK LUSCOMBE	SCOTLAND	WON	1G, 1T	NIL	N/A
9	05/02/1877	TEST	HOME	LONDON	EDWARD KEWLEY	IRELAND	WON	2G, 2T	NIL	N/A
10	05/03/1877	TEST	AWAY	EDINBURGH	EDWARD KEWLEY	SCOTLAND	LOST	NIL	1DG	N/A
11	04/03/1878	TEST	HOME	LONDON	EDWARD KEWLEY	SCOTLAND	DRAWN	NIL	NIL	N/A
12	11/03/1878	TEST	AWAY	DUBLIN	MURRAY MARSHALL	IRELAND	WON	2G, 1T	NIL	N/A
13	10/03/1879	TEST	AWAY	EDINBURGH	FRANK ADAMS	SCOTLAND	DRAWN	1G	1DG	N/A
14	24/03/1879	TEST	HOME	LONDON	FRANK ADAMS	IRELAND	WON	2G, 1DG, 2T	NIL	N/A
15	02/02/1880	TEST	AWAY	DUBLIN	LENNARD STOKES	IRELAND	WON	1G, 1T	1T	N/A
16	28/02/1880	TEST	HOME	MANCHESTER	LENNARD STOKES	SCOTLAND	WON	2G, 3T	1G	N/A
17	05/02/1881	TEST	HOME	MANCHESTER	LENNARD STOKES	IRELAND	WON	2G, 2T	NIL	N/A
18	19/02/1881	TEST	HOME	BLACKHEATH	LENNARD STOKES	WALES	WON	7G, 1DG, 6T	NIL	N/A
19	19/03/1881	TEST	AWAY	EDINBURGH	LENNARD STOKES	SCOTLAND	DRAWN	1DG, 1T	1G, 1T	N/A
20	06/02/1882	TEST	AWAY	DUBLIN	ALBERT HORNBY	IRELAND	DRAWN	2T	2T	N/A
21	04/03/1882	TEST	HOME	MANCHESTER	ALBERT HORNBY	SCOTLAND	LOST	NIL	2T	N/A
22	16/12/1882	HN	AWAY	SWANSEA	EDWARD GURDON	WALES	WON	NIL	2G, 4T	N/A
23	05/02/1883	HN	HOME	MANCHESTER	EDWARD GURDON	IRELAND	WON	1G, 3T	1T	N/A
24	03/03/1883	HN	AWAY	EDINBURGH	EDWARD GURDON	SCOTLAND	WON	2T	1T	N/A
25	05/01/1884	HN	HOME	LEEDS	EDWARD GURDON	WALES	WON	1G, 2T	1G	N/A
26	04/02/1884	HN	AWAY	DUBLIN	EDWARD GURDON	IRELAND	WON	1G	NIL	N/A
27	01/03/1884	HN	HOME	BLACKHEATH	EDWARD GURDON	SCOTLAND	WON	1G	1T	N/A
28	03/01/1885	HN	AWAY	SWANSEA	EDWARD GURDON	WALES	WON	1G, 4T	1G, 1T	N/A
29	07/02/1885	HN	HOME	MANCHESTER	EDWARD GURDON	IRELAND	WON	2T	1T	N/A
30	02/01/1886	HN	HOME	BLACKHEATH	CHARLES MARRIOTT	WALES	WON	1GM, 2T	1G	N/A
31	06/02/1886	HN	AWAY	DUBLIN	CHARLES MARRIOTT	IRELAND	WON	1T	NIL	N/A
32	13/03/1886	HN	HOME	EDINBURGH	EDWARD GURDON	SCOTLAND	DRAWN	NIL	NIL	N/A
33	08/01/1887	HN	AWAY	LLANELLI	ALUN ROTHERHAM	WALES	DRAWN	NIL	NIL	N/A
34	05/02/1887	HN	AWAY	DUBLIN	ALUN ROTHERHAM	IRELAND	LOST	NIL	2G	N/A
35	05/03/1887	HN	HOME	MANCHESTER	ALUN ROTHERHAM	SCOTLAND	DRAWN	1T	1T	N/A
36	16/02/1889	TEST	HOME	BLACKHEATH	FRED BONSOR	NZ NATIVES	WON	1T	0	N/A
37	15/02/1890	HN	HOME	DEWSBURY	ANDREW STODDART	WALES	LOST	0	1	N/A
38	01/03/1890	HN	AWAY	EDINBURGH	JOHN HICKSON	SCOTLAND	WON	6	0	N/A
39	15/03/1890	HN	HOME	BLACKHEATH	ANDREW STODDART	IRELAND	WON	3	0	N/A
40	03/01/1891	HN	AWAY	NEWPORT	FREDERICK ALDERSON	WALES	WON	7	3	N/A
41	07/02/1891	HN	AWAY	DUBLIN	FREDERICK ALDERSON	IRELAND	WON	9	0	N/A
42	07/03/1891	HN	HOME	RICHMOND	FREDERICK ALDERSON	SCOTLAND	LOST	3	9	N/A

GAME	DATE	TYPE	H/A	CITY	CAPTAIN	OPPONENTS	RESULT	SCORE (FOR)	SCORE (OPP)	COACH
43	02/01/1892	HN	HOME	BLACKHEATH	JAMES PYKE	WALES	WON	17	0	N/A
44	06/02/1892	HN	HOME	MANCHESTER	SAMUEL WOODS	IRELAND	WON	7	0	N/A
45	05/03/1892	HN	AWAY	EDINBURGH	FREDERICK ALDERSON	SCOTLAND	WON	5	0	N/A
46	07/01/1893	HN	AWAY	CARDIFF	ANDREW STODDART	WALES	LOST	11	12	N/A
47	04/02/1893	HN	AWAY	DUBLIN	SAMUEL WOODS	IRELAND	WON	4	0	N/A
48	04/03/1893	HN	HOME	LEEDS	ANDREW STODDART	SCOTLAND	LOST	0	8	N/A
49	06/01/1894	HN	HOME	BIRKENHEAD	RICHARD LOCKWOOD	WALES	WON	24	3	N/A
50	03/02/1894	HN	HOME	BLACKHEATH	RICHARD LOCKWOOD	IRELAND	LOST	5	7	N/A
51	17/03/1894	HN	AWAY	EDINBURGH	ERNEST TAYLOR	SCOTLAND	LOST	0	6	N/A
52	05/01/1895	HN	AWAY	SWANSEA	SAMUEL WOODS	WALES	WON	14	6	N/A
53	02/02/1895	HN	AWAY	DUBLIN	SAMUEL WOODS	IRELAND	WON	6	3	N/A
54	09/03/1895	HN	HOME	RICHMOND	SAMUEL WOODS	SCOTLAND	LOST	3	6	N/A
55	04/01/1896	HN	HOME	BLACKHEATH	ERNEST TAYLOR	WALES	WON	25	0	N/A
56	01/02/1896	HN	HOME	LEEDS	ERNEST TAYLOR	IRELAND	LOST	4	10	N/A
57	14/03/1896	HN	AWAY	GLASGOW	FRANK MITCHELL	SCOTLAND	LOST	0	11	N/A
58	09/01/1897	HN	AWAY	NEWPORT	ERNEST TAYLOR	WALES	LOST	0	11	N/A
59	06/02/1897	HN	AWAY	DUBLIN	ERNEST TAYLOR	IRELAND	LOST	9	13	N/A
60	13/03/1897	HN	HOME	MANCHESTER	ERNEST TAYLOR	SCOTLAND	WON	12	3	N/A
61	05/02/1898	HN	HOME	RICHMOND	FRED BYRNE	IRELAND	LOST	6	9	N/A
62	12/02/1898	HN	AWAY	EDINBURGH	FRED BYRNE	SCOTLAND	DRAW	3	3	N/A
63	02/04/1898	HN	HOME	BLACKHEATH	FRED BYRNE	WALES	WON	14	7	N/A
64	07/01/1899	HN	AWAY	SWANSEA	ARTHUR ROTHERHAM	WALES	LOST	3	24	N/A
65	04/02/1899	HN	AWAY	DUBLIN	ARTHUR ROTHERHAM	IRELAND	LOST	0	6	N/A
66	11/03/1899	HN	HOME	BLACKHEATH	ARTHUR ROTHERHAM	SCOTLAND	LOST	0	5	N/A
67	06/01/1900	HN	AWAY	GLOUCESTER	RICHARD CATTELL	WALES	LOST	3	13	N/A
68	03/02/1900	HN	HOME	RICHMOND	JOHN DANIELL	IRELAND	WON	15	4	N/A
69	10/03/1900	HN	AWAY	EDINBURGH	JOHN DANIELL	SCOTLAND	DRAW	0	0	N/A
70	05/01/1901	HN	AWAY	CARDIFF	JOHN TAYLOR	WALES	LOST	0	13	N/A
71	09/02/1901	HN	AWAY	DUBLIN	WILLIAM BUNTING	IRELAND	LOST	6	10	N/A
72	09/03/1901	HN	HOME	BLACKHEATH	WILLIAM BUNTING	SCOTLAND	LOST	3	18	N/A
73	11/01/1902	HN	HOME	BLACKHEATH	HARRY ALEXANDER	WALES	LOST	8	9	N/A
74	08/02/1902	HN	HOME	LEICESTER	JOHN DANIELL	IRELAND	WON	6	3	N/A
75	15/03/1902	HN	AWAY	EDINBURGH	JOHN DANIELL	SCOTLAND	WON	6	3	N/A
76	10/01/1903	HN	AWAY	SWANSEA	BERNARD OUGHTRED	WALES	LOST	5	21	N/A
77	14/02/1903	HN	AWAY	DUBLIN	BERNARD OUGHTRED	IRELAND	LOST	0	6	N/A
78	21/03/1903	HN	HOME	RICHMOND	PERCY KENDALL	SCOTLAND	LOST	6	10	N/A
79	09/01/1904	HN	HOME	LEICESTER	FRANK STOUT	WALES	DRAW	14	14	N/A
80	13/02/1904	HN	HOME	BLACKHEATH	JOHN DANIELL	IRELAND	WON	19	0	N/A
81	19/03/1904	HN	AWAY	EDINBURGH	JOHN DANIELL	SCOTLAND	LOST	3	6	N/A
82	14/01/1905	HN	AWAY	CARDIFF	FRANK STOUT	WALES	LOST	0	25	N/A
83	11/02/1905	HN	AWAY	CORK	FRANK STOUT	IRELAND	LOST	3	17	N/A
84	18/03/1905	HN	HOME	RICHMOND	FRANK STOUT	SCOTLAND	LOST	0	8	N/A

GAME	DATE	TYPE	H/A	CITY	CAPTAIN	OPPONENTS	RESULT	SCORE (FOR)	SCORE (OPP)	COACH
85	02/12/1905	TEST	HOME	LONDON	VINCENT CARTWRIGHT	NEW ZEALAND	LOST	0	15	N/A
86	13/01/1906	HN	HOME	RICHMOND	VINCENT CARTWRIGHT	WALES	LOST	3	16	N/A
87	10/02/1906	HN	HOME	LEICESTER	VINCENT CARTWRIGHT	IRELAND	LOST	6	16	N/A
88	17/03/1906	HN	AWAY	EDINBURGH	VINCENT CARTWRIGHT	SCOTLAND	WON	9	3	N/A
89	22/03/1906	TEST	AWAY	PARIS	VINCENT CARTWRIGHT	FRANCE	WON	35	8	N/A
90	08/12/1906	TEST	HOME	LONDON	VINCENT CARTWRIGHT	SOUTH AFRICA	DRAW	3	3	N/A
91	05/01/1907	TEST	HOME	RICHMOND	BASIL HILL	FRANCE	WON	41	13	N/A
92	12/01/1907	HN	AWAY	SWANSEA	BASIL HILL	WALES	LOST	0	22	N/A
93	09/02/1907	HN	AWAY	DUBLIN	JOHN GREEN	IRELAND	LOST	9	17	N/A
94	16/03/1907	HN	HOME	BLACKHEATH	ERNEST ROBERTS	SCOTLAND	LOST	3	8	N/A
95	01/01/1908	TEST	AWAY	PARIS	THOMAS KELLY	FRANCE	WON	19	0	N/A
96	18/01/1908	HN	HOME	BRISTOL	JOHN BIRKETT	WALES	LOST	18	28	N/A
97	08/02/1908	HN	HOME	RICHMOND	CURLY HAMMOND	IRELAND	WON	13	3	N/A
98	21/03/1908	HN	AWAY	EDINBURGH	ANDREW SLOCOCK	SCOTLAND	LOST	10	16	N/A
99	09/01/1909	TEST	HOME	BLACKHEATH	GEORGE LYON	AUSTRALIA	LOST	3	9	N/A
100	16/01/1909	HN	AWAY	CARDIFF	ROBERT DIBBLE	WALES	LOST	0	8	N/A
101	30/01/1909	TEST	HOME	LEICESTER	ROBERT DIBBLE	FRANCE	WON	22	0	N/A
102	13/02/1909	HN	AWAY	DUBLIN	ROBERT DIBBLE	IRELAND	WON	11	5	N/A
103	20/03/1909	HN	HOME	RICHMOND	ROBERT DIBBLE	SCOTLAND	LOST	8	18	N/A
104	15/01/1910	HN	HOME	LONDON	ADRIAN STOOP	WALES	WON	11	6	N/A
105	12/02/1910	HN	HOME	LONDON	ADRIAN STOOP	IRELAND	DRAW	0	0	N/A
106	03/03/1910	5N	AWAY	PARIS	EDGAR MOBBS	FRANCE	WON	11	3	N/A
107	19/03/1910	5N	AWAY	EDINBURGH	JOHN BIRKETT	SCOTLAND	WON	14	5	N/A
108	21/01/1911	5N	AWAY	SWANSEA	JOHN BIRKETT	WALES	LOST	11	15	N/A
109	28/01/1911	5N	HOME	LONDON	JOHN BIRKETT	FRANCE	WON	37	0	N/A
110	11/02/1911	5N	AWAY	DUBLIN	JOHN BIRKETT	IRELAND	LOST	0	3	N/A
111	18/03/1911	5N	HOME	LONDON	ANTHONY HENNIKER-GOTLEY	SCOTLAND	WON	13	8	N/A
112	20/01/1912	5N	HOME	LONDON	ROBERT DIBBLE	WALES	WON	8	0	N/A
113	10/02/1912	5N	HOME	LONDON	ROBERT DIBBLE	IRELAND	WON	15	0	N/A
114	16/03/1912	5N	AWAY	EDINBURGH	ROBERT DIBBLE	SCOTLAND	LOST	3	8	N/A
115	08/04/1912	HN	AWAY	PARIS	NORMAN WODEHOUSE	FRANCE	WON	18	8	N/A
116	04/01/1913	TEST	HOME	LONDON	NORMAN WODEHOUSE	SOUTH AFRICA	LOST	3	9	N/A
117	18/01/1913	5N	AWAY	CARDIFF	NORMAN WODEHOUSE	WALES	WON	12	0	N/A
118	25/01/1913	5N	HOME	LONDON	NORMAN WODEHOUSE	FRANCE	WON	20	0	N/A
119	08/02/1913	5N	AWAY	DUBLIN	NORMAN WODEHOUSE	IRELAND	WON	15	4	N/A
120	15/03/1913	5N	HOME	LONDON	NORMAN WODEHOUSE	SCOTLAND	WON	3	0	N/A
121	17/01/1914	5N	HOME	LONDON	RONALD POULTON	WALES	WON	10	9	N/A
122	14/02/1914	5N	HOME	LONDON	RONALD POULTON	IRELAND	WON	17	12	N/A
123	21/03/1914	5N	AWAY	EDINBURGH	RONALD POULTON	SCOTLAND	WON	16	15	N/A
124	13/04/1914	5N	AWAY	PARIS	RONALD POULTON	FRANCE	WON	39	13	N/A
125	17/01/1920	5N	AWAY	SWANSEA	JOHN GREENWOOD	WALES	LOST	5	19	N/A
126	31/01/1920	5N	HOME	LONDON	JOHN GREENWOOD	FRANCE	WON	8	3	N/A

GAME	DATE	TYPE	H/A	CITY	CAPTAIN	OPPONENTS	RESULT	SCORE (FOR)	SCORE (OPP)	COACH
127	14/02/1920	5N	AWAY	DUBLIN	JOHN GREENWOOD	IRELAND	WON	14	11	N/A
128	20/03/1920	5N	HOME	LONDON	JOHN GREENWOOD	SCOTLAND	WON	13	4	N/A
129	15/01/1921	5N	HOME	LONDON	DAVE DAVIES	WALES	WON	18	3	N/A
130	12/02/1921	5N	HOME	LONDON	DAVE DAVIES	IRELAND	WON	15	0	N/A
131	19/03/1921	5N	AWAY	EDINBURGH	DAVE DAVIES	SCOTLAND	WON	18	0	N/A
132	28/03/1921	5N	AWAY	PARIS	DAVE DAVIES	FRANCE	WON	10	6	N/A
133	21/01/1922	5N	AWAY	CARDIFF	LEONARD BROWN	WALES	LOST	6	28	N/A
134	11/02/1922	5N	AWAY	DUBLIN	DAVE DAVIES	IRELAND	WON	12	3	N/A
135	25/02/1922	5N	HOME	LONDON	DAVE DAVIES	FRANCE	DRAW	11	11	N/A
136	18/03/1922	5N	HOME	LONDON	DAVE DAVIES	SCOTLAND	WON	11	5	N/A
137	20/01/1923	5N	HOME	LONDON	DAVE DAVIES	WALES	WON	7	3	N/A
138	10/02/1923	5N	HOME	LEICESTER	DAVE DAVIES	IRELAND	WON	23	5	N/A
139	17/03/1923	5N	AWAY	EDINBURGH	DAVE DAVIES	SCOTLAND	WON	8	6	N/A
140	02/04/1923	5N	AWAY	PARIS	DAVE DAVIES	FRANCE	WON	12	3	N/A
141	19/01/1924	5N	AWAY	SWANSEA	WAVELL WAKEFIELD	WALES	WON	17	9	N/A
142	09/02/1924	5N	AWAY	BELFAST	WAVELL WAKEFIELD	IRELAND	WON	14	3	N/A
143	23/02/1924	5N	HOME	LONDON	WAVELL WAKEFIELD	FRANCE	WON	19	7	N/A
144	15/03/1924	5N	HOME	LONDON	WAVELL WAKEFIELD	SCOTLAND	WON	19	0	N/A
145	03/01/1925	TEST	HOME	LONDON	WAVELL WAKEFIELD	NEW ZEALAND	LOST	11	17	N/A
146	17/01/1925	5N	HOME	LONDON	WAVELL WAKEFIELD	WALES	WON	12	6	N/A
147	14/02/1925	5N	HOME	LONDON	WAVELL WAKEFIELD	IRELAND	DRAW	6	6	N/A
148	21/03/1925	5N	AWAY	EDINBURGH	WAVELL WAKEFIELD	SCOTLAND	LOST	11	14	N/A
149	13/04/1925	5N	AWAY	PARIS	WAVELL WAKEFIELD	FRANCE	WON	13	11	N/A
150	16/01/1926	5N	AWAY	CARDIFF	WAVELL WAKEFIELD	WALES	DRAW	3	3	N/A
151	13/02/1926	5N	AWAY	DUBLIN	WAVELL WAKEFIELD	IRELAND	LOST	15	19	N/A
152	27/02/1926	5N	HOME	LONDON	WAVELL WAKEFIELD	FRANCE	WON	11	0	N/A
153	20/03/1926	5N	HOME	LONDON	WAVELL WAKEFIELD	SCOTLAND	LOST	9	17	N/A
154	15/01/1927	5N	HOME	LONDON	LEONARD CORBETT	WALES	WON	11	9	N/A
155	12/02/1927	5N	HOME	LONDON	LEONARD CORBETT	IRELAND	WON	8	6	N/A
156	19/03/1927	5N	AWAY	EDINBURGH	LEONARD CORBETT	SCOTLAND	LOST	13	21	N/A
157	02/04/1927	5N	AWAY	PARIS	LEONARD CORBETT	FRANCE	LOST	0	3	N/A
158	07/01/1928	TEST	HOME	LONDON	RONALD COVE-SMITH	N/S WALES	WON	18	11	N/A
159	21/01/1928	5N	AWAY	SWANSEA	RONALD COVE-SMITH	WALES	WON	10	8	N/A
160	11/02/1928	5N	AWAY	DUBLIN	RONALD COVE-SMITH	IRELAND	WON	7	6	N/A
161	25/02/1928	5N	HOME	LONDON	RONALD COVE-SMITH	FRANCE	WON	18	8	N/A
162	17/03/1928	5N	HOME	LONDON	RONALD COVE-SMITH	SCOTLAND	WON	6	0	N/A
163	19/01/1929	5N	HOME	LONDON	RONALD COVE-SMITH	WALES	WON	8	3	N/A
164	09/02/1929	5N	HOME	LONDON	HAROLD PERITON	IRELAND	LOST	5	6	N/A
165	16/03/1929	5N	AWAY	EDINBURGH	HAROLD PERITON	SCOTLAND	LOST	6	12	N/A
166	01/04/1929	5N	AWAY	PARIS	HAROLD PERITON	FRANCE	WON	16	6	N/A
167	18/01/1930	5N	AWAY	CARDIFF	HAROLD PERITON	WALES	WON	11	3	N/A
168	08/02/1930	5N	AWAY	DUBLIN	HAROLD PERITON	IRELAND	LOST	3	4	N/A
169	22/02/1930	5N	HOME	LONDON	SAM TUCKER	FRANCE	WON	11	5	N/A

GAME	DATE	TYPE	H/A	CITY	CAPTAIN	OPPONENTS	RESULT	SCORE (FOR)	SCORE (OPP)	COACH
170	15/03/1930	5N	HOME	LONDON	SAM TUCKER	SCOTLAND	DRAW	0	0	N/A
171	17/01/1931	5N	HOME	LONDON	SAM TUCKER	WALES	DRAW	11	11	N/A
172	14/02/1931	5N	HOME	LONDON	PETER HOWARD	IRELAND	LOST	5	6	N/A
173	21/03/1931	5N	AWAY	EDINBURGH	CARL AARVOLD	SCOTLAND	LOST	19	28	N/A
174	06/04/1931	5N	AWAY	PARIS	CARL AARVOLD	FRANCE	LOST	13	14	N/A
175	02/01/1932	TEST	HOME	LONDON	CARL AARVOLD	SOUTH AFRICA	LOST	0	7	N/A
176	16/01/1932	5N	AWAY	SWANSEA	CARL AARVOLD	WALES	LOST	5	12	N/A
177	13/02/1932	HN	AWAY	DUBLIN	CARL AARVOLD	IRELAND	WON	11	8	N/A
178	19/03/1932	HN	HOME	LONDON	CARL AARVOLD	SCOTLAND	WON	16	3	N/A
179	21/01/1933	HN	HOME	LONDON	CARL AARVOLD	WALES	LOST	3	7	N/A
180	11/02/1933	HN	HOME	LONDON	ANTHONY NOVIS	IRELAND	WON	17	6	N/A
181	18/03/1933	HN	AWAY	EDINBURGH	ANTHONY NOVIS	SCOTLAND	LOST	0	3	N/A
182	20/01/1934	HN	AWAY	CARDIFF	BERNARD GADNEY	WALES	WON	9	0	N/A
183	10/02/1934	HN	AWAY	DUBLIN	BERNARD GADNEY	IRELAND	WON	13	3	N/A
184	17/03/1934	HN	HOME	LONDON	BERNARD GADNEY	SCOTLAND	WON	6	3	N/A
185	19/01/1935	HN	HOME	LONDON	DOUGLAS KENDREW	WALES	DRAW	3	3	N/A
186	09/02/1935	HN	HOME	LONDON	DOUGLAS KENDREW	IRELAND	WON	14	3	N/A
187	16/03/1935	HN	AWAY	EDINBURGH	BERNARD GADNEY	SCOTLAND	LOST	7	10	N/A
188	04/01/1936	TEST	HOME	LONDON	BERNARD GADNEY	NEW ZEALAND	WON	13	0	N/A
189	18/01/1936	HN	AWAY	SWANSEA	BERNARD GADNEY	WALES	DRAW	0	0	N/A
190	08/02/1936	HN	HOME	LONDON	BERNARD GADNEY	IRELAND	LOST	3	6	N/A
191	21/03/1936	HN	HOME	LONDON	BERNARD GADNEY	SCOTLAND	WON	9	8	N/A
192	16/01/1937	HN	HOME	LONDON	TUPPY OWEN-SMITH	WALES	WON	4	3	N/A
193	13/02/1937	HN	HOME	LONDON	TUPPY OWEN-SMITH	IRELAND	WON	9	8	N/A
194	20/03/1937	HN	AWAY	EDINBURGH	TUPPY OWEN-SMITH	SCOTLAND	WON	6	3	N/A
195	15/01/1938	HN	AWAY	CARDIFF	PETER CRANMER	WALES	LOST	8	14	N/A
196	12/02/1938	HN	AWAY	DUBLIN	PETER CRANMER	IRELAND	WON	36	14	N/A
197	19/03/1938	HN	HOME	LONDON	HERBERT TOFT	SCOTLAND	LOST	16	21	N/A
198	21/01/1939	HN	HOME	LONDON	HERBERT TOFT	WALES	WON	3	0	N/A
199	11/02/1939	HN	HOME	LONDON	HERBERT TOFT	IRELAND	LOST	0	5	N/A
200	18/03/1939	HN	AWAY	EDINBURGH	HERBERT TOFT	SCOTLAND	WON	9	6	N/A
201	18/01/1947	5N	AWAY	CARDIFF	JOSEPH MYCOCK	WALES	WON	9	6	N/A
202	08/02/1947	5N	AWAY	DUBLIN	JOSEPH MYCOCK	IRELAND	LOST	0	22	N/A
203	15/03/1947	5N	HOME	LONDON	JACK HEATON	SCOTLAND	WON	24	5	N/A
204	19/04/1947	5N	HOME	LONDON	JACK HEATON	FRANCE	WON	6	3	N/A
205	03/01/1948	TEST	HOME	LONDON	EDWARD SCOTT	AUSTRALIA	LOST	0	11	N/A
206	17/01/1948	5N	HOME	LONDON	THOMAS KEMP	WALES	DRAW	3	3	N/A
207	14/02/1948	5N	HOME	LONDON	EDWARD SCOTT	IRELAND	LOST	10	11	N/A
208	20/03/1948	5N	AWAY	EDINBURGH	EDWARD SCOTT	SCOTLAND	LOST	3	6	N/A
209	29/03/1948	5N	AWAY	PARIS	ROBERT WEIGHILL	FRANCE	LOST	0	15	N/A
210	15/01/1949	5N	AWAY	CARDIFF	NORMAN HALL	WALES	LOST	3	9	N/A
211	12/02/1949	5N	AWAY	DUBLIN	NORMAN HALL	IRELAND	LOST	5	14	N/A
212	26/02/1949	5N	HOME	LONDON	IVOR PREECE	FRANCE	WON	8	3	N/A

GAME	DATE	TYPE	H/A	CITY	CAPTAIN	OPPONENTS	RESULT	SCORE (FOR)	SCORE (OPP)	COACH
213	19/03/1949	5N	HOME	LONDON	IVOR PREECE	SCOTLAND	WON	19	3	N/A
214	21/01/1950	5N	HOME	LONDON	IVOR PREECE	WALES	LOST	5	11	N/A
215	11/02/1950	5N	HOME	LONDON	IVOR PREECE	IRELAND	WON	3	0	N/A
216	25/02/1950	5N	AWAY	PARIS	IVOR PREECE	FRANCE	LOST	3	6	N/A
217	18/03/1950	5N	AWAY	EDINBURGH	IVOR PREECE	SCOTLAND	LOST	11	13	N/A
218	20/01/1951	5N	AWAY	SWANSEA	VICTOR ROBERTS	WALES	LOST	5	23	N/A
219	10/02/1951	5N	AWAY	DUBLIN	JOHN KENDALL-CARPENTER	IRELAND	LOST	0	3	N/A
220	24/02/1951	5N	HOME	LONDON	JOHN KENDALL-CARPENTER	FRANCE	LOST	3	11	N/A
221	17/03/1951	5N	HOME	LONDON	JOHN KENDALL-CARPENTER	SCOTLAND	WON	5	3	N/A
222	05/01/1952	TEST	HOME	LONDON	NORMAN HALL	SOUTH AFRICA	LOST	3	8	N/A
223	19/01/1952	5N	HOME	LONDON	NORMAN HALL	WALES	LOST	6	8	N/A
224	15/03/1952	5N	AWAY	EDINBURGH	NORMAN HALL	SCOTLAND	WON	19	3	N/A
225	29/03/1952	5N	HOME	LONDON	NORMAN HALL	IRELAND	WON	3	0	N/A
226	05/04/1952	5N	AWAY	PARIS	NORMAN HALL	FRANCE	WON	6	3	N/A
227	17/01/1953	5N	AWAY	CARDIFF	NORMAN HALL	WALES	WON	8	3	N/A
228	14/02/1953	5N	AWAY	DUBLIN	NORMAN HALL	IRELAND	DRAW	9	9	N/A
229	28/02/1953	5N	HOME	LONDON	NORMAN HALL	FRANCE	WON	11	0	N/A
230	21/03/1953	5N	HOME	LONDON	NORMAN HALL	SCOTLAND	WON	26	8	N/A
231	16/01/1954	5N	HOME	LONDON	ROBERT STIRLING	WALES	WON	9	6	N/A
232	30/01/1954	TEST	HOME	LONDON	ROBERT STIRLING	NEW ZEALAND	LOST	0	5	N/A
233	13/02/1954	5N	HOME	LONDON	ROBERT STIRLING	IRELAND	WON	14	3	N/A
234	20/03/1954	5N	AWAY	EDINBURGH	ROBERT STIRLING	SCOTLAND	WON	13	3	N/A
235	10/04/1954	5N	AWAY	PARIS	ROBERT STIRLING	FRANCE	LOST	3	11	N/A
236	22/01/1955	5N	AWAY	CARDIFF	NORMAN HALL	WALES	LOST	0	3	N/A
237	12/02/1955	5N	AWAY	DUBLIN	NORMAN HALL	IRELAND	DRAW	6	6	N/A
238	26/02/1955	5N	HOME	LONDON	PETER YOUNG	FRANCE	LOST	9	16	N/A
239	19/03/1955	5N	HOME	LONDON	PETER YOUNG	SCOTLAND	WON	9	6	N/A
240	21/01/1956	5N	HOME	LONDON	ERIC EVANS	WALES	LOST	3	8	N/A
241	11/02/1956	5N	HOME	LONDON	ERIC EVANS	IRELAND	WON	20	0	N/A
242	17/03/1956	5N	AWAY	EDINBURGH	ERIC EVANS	SCOTLAND	WON	11	6	N/A
243	14/04/1956	5N	AWAY	PARIS	ERIC EVANS	FRANCE	LOST	9	14	N/A
244	19/01/1957	5N	AWAY	CARDIFF	ERIC EVANS	WALES	WON	3	0	N/A
245	09/02/1957	5N	AWAY	DUBLIN	ERIC EVANS	IRELAND	WON	6	0	N/A
246	23/02/1957	5N	HOME	LONDON	ERIC EVANS	FRANCE	WON	9	5	N/A
247	16/03/1957	5N	HOME	LONDON	ERIC EVANS	SCOTLAND	WON	16	3	N/A
248	18/01/1958	5N	HOME	LONDON	ERIC EVANS	WALES	DRAW	3	3	N/A
249	01/02/1958	TEST	HOME	LONDON	ERIC EVANS	AUSTRALIA	WON	9	6	N/A
250	08/02/1958	5N	HOME	LONDON	ERIC EVANS	IRELAND	WON	6	0	N/A
251	01/03/1958	5N	AWAY	PARIS	ERIC EVANS	FRANCE	WON	14	0	N/A
252	15/03/1958	5N	AWAY	EDINBURGH	ERIC EVANS	SCOTLAND	DRAW	3	3	N/A
253	17/01/1959	5N	AWAY	CARDIFF	JEFF BUTTERFIELD	WALES	LOST	0	5	N/A
254	14/02/1959	5N	AWAY	DUBLIN	JEFF BUTTERFIELD	IRELAND	WON	3	0	N/A
255	28/02/1959	5N	HOME	LONDON	JEFF BUTTERFIELD	FRANCE	DRAW	3	3	N/A

GAME	DATE	TYPE	H/A	CITY	CAPTAIN	OPPONENTS	RESULT	SCORE (FOR)	SCORE (OPP)	COACH
256	21/03/1959	5N	HOME	LONDON	JEFF BUTTERFIELD	SCOTLAND	DRAW	3	3	N/A
257	16/01/1960	5N	HOME	LONDON	RICHARD JEEPS	WALES	WON	14	6	N/A
258	13/02/1960	5N	HOME	LONDON	RICHARD JEEPS	IRELAND	WON	8	5	N/A
259	27/02/1960	5N	AWAY	PARIS	RICHARD JEEPS	FRANCE	DRAW	3	3	N/A
260	19/03/1960	5N	AWAY	EDINBURGH	RICHARD JEEPS	SCOTLAND	WON	21	12	N/A
261	07/01/1961	TEST	HOME	LONDON	RICHARD JEEPS	SOUTH AFRICA	LOST	0	5	N/A
262	21/01/1961	5N	AWAY	CARDIFF	RICHARD JEEPS	WALES	LOST	3	6	N/A
263	11/02/1961	5N	AWAY	DUBLIN	RICHARD JEEPS	IRELAND	LOST	8	11	N/A
264	25/02/1961	5N	HOME	LONDON	RICHARD JEEPS	FRANCE	DRAW	5	5	N/A
265	18/03/1961	5N	HOME	LONDON	RICHARD JEEPS	SCOTLAND	WON	6	0	N/A
266	20/01/1962	5N	HOME	LONDON	RICHARD JEEPS	WALES	DRAW	0	0	N/A
267	10/02/1962	5N	HOME	LONDON	RICHARD JEEPS	IRELAND	WON	16	0	N/A
268	24/02/1962	5N	AWAY	PARIS	RICHARD JEEPS	FRANCE	LOST	0	13	N/A
269	17/03/1962	5N	AWAY	EDINBURGH	RICHARD JEEPS	SCOTLAND	DRAW	3	3	N/A
270	19/01/1963	5N	AWAY	CARDIFF	RICHARD SHARP	WALES	WON	13	6	N/A
271	09/02/1963	5N	AWAY	DUBLIN	RICHARD SHARP	IRELAND	DRAW	0	0	N/A
272	23/02/1963	5N	HOME	LONDON	RICHARD SHARP	FRANCE	WON	6	5	N/A
273	16/03/1963	5N	HOME	LONDON	RICHARD SHARP	SCOTLAND	WON	10	8	N/A
274	25/05/1963	TEST (1)	AWAY	AUCKLAND	MICHAEL WESTON	NEW ZEALAND	LOST	11	21	N/A
275	01/06/1963	TEST (2)	AWAY	CHRISTCHURCH	MICHAEL WESTON	NEW ZEALAND	LOST	6	9	N/A
276	04/06/1963	TEST	AWAY	SYDNEY	MICHAEL WESTON	AUSTRALIA	LOST	9	18	N/A
277	04/01/1964	TEST	HOME	LONDON	JOHN WILCOX	NEW ZEALAND	LOST	0	14	N/A
278	18/01/1964	5N	HOME	LONDON	JOHN WILCOX	WALES	DRAW	6	6	N/A
279	08/02/1964	5N	HOME	LONDON	JOHN WILCOX	IRELAND	LOST	5	18	N/A
280	22/02/1964	5N	AWAY	PARIS	RON JACOBS	FRANCE	WON	6	3	N/A
281	21/03/1964	5N	AWAY	EDINBURGH	RON JACOBS	SCOTLAND	LOST	6	15	N/A
282	16/01/1965	5N	AWAY	CARDIFF	DAVID PERRY	WALES	LOST	3	14	N/A
283	13/02/1965	5N	AWAY	DUBLIN	DAVID PERRY	IRELAND	LOST	0	5	N/A
284	27/02/1965	5N	HOME	LONDON	DAVID PERRY	FRANCE	WON	9	6	N/A
285	20/03/1965	5N	HOME	LONDON	DAVID PERRY	SCOTLAND	DRAW	3	3	N/A
286	15/01/1966	5N	HOME	LONDON	BUDGE ROGERS	WALES	LOST	6	11	N/A
287	12/02/1966	5N	HOME	LONDON	BUDGE ROGERS	IRELAND	DRAW	6	6	N/A
288	26/02/1966	5N	AWAY	PARIS	BUDGE ROGERS	FRANCE	LOST	0	13	N/A
289	19/03/1966	5N	AWAY	EDINBURGH	BUDGE ROGERS	SCOTLAND	LOST	3	6	N/A
290	07/01/1967	TEST	HOME	LONDON	RICHARD SHARP	AUSTRALIA	LOST	11	23	N/A
291	11/02/1967	5N	AWAY	DUBLIN	PHIL JUDD	IRELAND	WON	8	3	N/A
292	25/02/1967	5N	HOME	LONDON	PHIL JUDD	FRANCE	LOST	12	16	N/A
293	18/03/1967	5N	HOME	LONDON	PHIL JUDD	SCOTLAND	WON	27	14	N/A
294	15/04/1967	5N	AWAY	CARDIFF	PHIL JUDD	WALES	LOST	21	34	N/A
295	04/11/1967	TEST	HOME	LONDON	PHIL JUDD	NEW ZEALAND	LOST	11	23	N/A
296	20/01/1968	5N	HOME	LONDON	COLIN MCFADYEAN	WALES	DRAW	11	11	N/A
297	10/02/1968	5N	HOME	LONDON	COLIN MCFADYEAN	IRELAND	DRAW	9	9	N/A
298	24/02/1968	5N	AWAY	PARIS	MICHAEL WESTON	FRANCE	LOST	9	14	N/A
299	16/03/1968	5N	AWAY	EDINBURGH	MICHAEL WESTON	SCOTLAND	WON	8	6	N/A

GAME	DATE	TYPE	H/A	CITY	CAPTAIN	OPPONENTS	RESULT	SCORE (FOR)	SCORE (OPP)	COACH
300	08/02/1969	5N	AWAY	DUBLIN	DICK GREENWOOD	IRELAND	LOST	15	17	N/A
301	22/02/1969	5N	HOME	LONDON	BUDGE ROGERS	FRANCE	WON	22	8	N/A
302	15/03/1969	5N	HOME	LONDON	BUDGE ROGERS	SCOTLAND	WON	8	3	N/A
303	12/04/1969	5N	AWAY	CARDIFF	BUDGE ROGERS	WALES	LOST	9	30	N/A
304	20/12/1969	TEST	HOME	LONDON	BOB HILLER	SOUTH AFRICA	WON	11	8	DON WHITE
305	14/02/1970	5N	HOME	LONDON	BOB HILLER	IRELAND	WON	9	3	DON WHITE
306	28/02/1970	5N	HOME	LONDON	BOB HILLER	WALES	LOST	13	17	DON WHITE
307	21/03/1970	5N	AWAY	EDINBURGH	BOB HILLER	SCOTLAND	LOST	5	14	DON WHITE
308	18/04/1970	5N	AWAY	PARIS	ROBERT TAYLOR	FRANCE	LOST	13	35	DON WHITE
309	16/01/1971	5N	AWAY	CARDIFF	ANTHONY BUCKNALL	WALES	LOST	6	22	DON WHITE
310	13/02/1971	5N	AWAY	DUBLIN	JOHN SPENCER	IRELAND	WON	9	6	DON WHITE
311	27/02/1971	5N	HOME	LONDON	BOB HILLER	FRANCE	DRAW	14	14	DON WHITE
312	20/03/1971	5N	HOME	LONDON	JOHN SPENCER	SCOTLAND	LOST	15	16	DON WHITE
313	27/03/1971	TEST	AWAY	EDINBURGH	JOHN SPENCER	SCOTLAND	LOST	6	26	DON WHITE
314	17/04/1971	TEST	HOME	LONDON	JOHN SPENCER	RFU PRES XV	LOST	11	28	DON WHITE
315	15/01/1972	5N	HOME	LONDON	BOB HILLER	WALES	LOST	3	12	JOHN ELDERS
316	12/02/1972	5N	HOME	LONDON	BOB HILLER	IRELAND	LOST	12	16	JOHN ELDERS
317	26/02/1972	5N	AWAY	PARIS	PETER DIXON	FRANCE	LOST	12	37	JOHN ELDERS
318	18/03/1972	5N	AWAY	EDINBURGH	PETER DIXON	SCOTLAND	LOST	9	23	JOHN ELDERS
319	03/06/1972	TEST	AWAY	JOHANNESBURG	JOHN PULLIN	SOUTH AFRICA	WON	18	9	JOHN ELDERS
320	06/01/1973	TEST	HOME	LONDON	JOHN PULLIN	NEW ZEALAND	LOST	0	9	JOHN ELDERS
321	20/01/1973	5N	AWAY	CARDIFF	JOHN PULLIN	WALES	LOST	9	25	JOHN ELDERS
322	10/02/1973	5N	AWAY	DUBLIN	JOHN PULLIN	IRELAND	LOST	9	18	JOHN ELDERS
323	24/02/1973	5N	HOME	LONDON	JOHN PULLIN	FRANCE	WON	14	6	JOHN ELDERS
324	17/03/1973	5N	HOME	LONDON	JOHN PULLIN	SCOTLAND	WON	20	13	JOHN ELDERS
325	15/09/1973	TEST	AWAY	AUCKLAND	JOHN PULLIN	NEW ZEALAND	WON	16	10	JOHN ELDERS
326	17/11/1973	TEST	HOME	LONDON	JOHN PULLIN	AUSTRALIA	WON	20	3	JOHN ELDERS
327	02/02/1974	5N	AWAY	EDINBURGH	JOHN PULLIN	SCOTLAND	LOST	14	16	JOHN ELDERS
328	16/02/1974	5N	HOME	LONDON	JOHN PULLIN	IRELAND	LOST	21	26	JOHN ELDERS
329	02/03/1974	5N	AWAY	PARIS	JOHN PULLIN	FRANCE	DRAW	12	12	JOHN ELDERS
330	16/03/1974	5N	HOME	LONDON	JOHN PULLIN	WALES	WON	16	12	JOHN ELDERS
331	18/01/1975	5N	AWAY	DUBLIN	FRAN COTTON	IRELAND	LOST	9	12	JOHN BURGESS
332	01/02/1975	5N	HOME	LONDON	FRAN COTTON	FRANCE	LOST	20	27	JOHN BURGESS
333	15/02/1975	5N	AWAY	CARDIFF	FRAN COTTON	WALES	LOST	4	20	JOHN BURGESS
334	15/03/1975	5N	HOME	LONDON	TONY NEARY	SCOTLAND	WON	7	6	JOHN BURGESS
335	24/05/1975	TEST (1)	AWAY	SYDNEY	TONY NEARY	AUSTRALIA	LOST	9	16	JOHN BURGESS
336	31/05/1975	TEST (2)	AWAY	BRISBANE	JOHN PULLIN	AUSTRALIA	LOST	21	30	JOHN BURGESS
337	03/01/1976	TEST	HOME	LONDON	TONY NEARY	AUSTRALIA	WON	23	6	PETER COLSTON
338	17/01/1976	5N	HOME	LONDON	TONY NEARY	WALES	LOST	9	21	PETER COLSTON
339	21/02/1976	5N	AWAY	EDINBURGH	TONY NEARY	SCOTLAND	LOST	12	22	PETER COLSTON
340	06/03/1976	5N	HOME	LONDON	TONY NEARY	IRELAND	LOST	12	13	PETER COLSTON
341	20/03/1976	5N	AWAY	PARIS	TONY NEARY	FRANCE	LOST	9	30	PETER COLSTON
342	15/01/1977	5N	HOME	LONDON	ROGER UTTLEY	SCOTLAND	WON	26	6	PETER COLSTON
343	05/02/1977	5N	AWAY	DUBLIN	ROGER UTTLEY	IRELAND	WON	4	0	PETER COLSTON

GAME	DATE	TYPE	H/A	CITY	CAPTAIN	OPPONENTS	RESULT	SCORE (FOR)	SCORE (OPP)	COACH
344	19/02/1977	5N	HOME	LONDON	ROGER UTTLEY	FRANCE	LOST	3	4	PETER COLSTON
345	05/03/1977	5N	AWAY	CARDIFF	ROGER UTTLEY	WALES	LOST	9	14	PETER COLSTON
346	21/01/1978	5N	AWAY	PARIS	BILL BEAUMONT	FRANCE	LOST	6	15	PETER COLSTON
347	04/02/1978	5N	HOME	LONDON	BILL BEAUMONT	WALES	LOST	6	9	PETER COLSTON
348	04/03/1978	5N	AWAY	EDINBURGH	BILL BEAUMONT	SCOTLAND	WON	15	0	PETER COLSTON
349	18/03/1978	5N	HOME	LONDON	BILL BEAUMONT	IRELAND	WON	15	9	PETER COLSTON
350	25/11/1978	TEST	HOME	LONDON	BILL BEAUMONT	NEW ZEALAND	LOST	6	16	PETER COLSTON
351	03/02/1979	5N	HOME	LONDON	ROGER UTTLEY	SCOTLAND	DRAW	7	7	PETER COLSTON
352	17/02/1979	5N	AWAY	DUBLIN	BILL BEAUMONT	IRELAND	LOST	7	12	PETER COLSTON
353	03/03/1979	5N	HOME	LONDON	BILL BEAUMONT	FRANCE	WON	7	6	PETER COLSTON
354	17/03/1979	5N	AWAY	CARDIFF	BILL BEAUMONT	WALES	LOST	3	27	PETER COLSTON
355	24/11/1979	TEST	HOME	LONDON	BILL BEAUMONT	NEW ZEALAND	LOST	9	10	MIKE DAVIS
356	19/01/1980	5N	HOME	LONDON	BILL BEAUMONT	IRELAND	WON	24	9	MIKE DAVIS
357	02/02/1980	5N	AWAY	PARIS	BILL BEAUMONT	FRANCE	WON	17	13	MIKE DAVIS
358	16/02/1980	5N	HOME	LONDON	BILL BEAUMONT	WALES	WON	9	8	MIKE DAVIS
359	15/03/1980	5N	AWAY	EDINBURGH	BILL BEAUMONT	SCOTLAND	WON	30	18	MIKE DAVIS
360	17/01/1981	5N	AWAY	CARDIFF	BILL BEAUMONT	WALES	LOST	19	21	MIKE DAVIS
361	21/02/1981	5N	HOME	LONDON	BILL BEAUMONT	SCOTLAND	WON	23	17	MIKE DAVIS
362	07/03/1981	5N	AWAY	DUBLIN	BILL BEAUMONT	IRELAND	WON	10	6	MIKE DAVIS
363	21/03/1981	5N	HOME	LONDON	BILL BEAUMONT	FRANCE	LOST	12	16	MIKE DAVIS
364	30/05/1981	TEST (1)	AWAY	BUENOS AIRES	BILL BEAUMONT	ARGENTINA	DRAW	19	19	MIKE DAVIS
365	06/06/1981	TEST (2)	AWAY	BUENOS AIRES	BILL BEAUMONT	ARGENTINA	WON	12	6	MIKE DAVIS
366	02/01/1982	TEST	HOME	LONDON	BILL BEAUMONT	AUSTRALIA	WON	15	11	MIKE DAVIS
367	16/01/1982	5N	AWAY	EDINBURGH	BILL BEAUMONT	SCOTLAND	DRAW	9	9	MIKE DAVIS
368	06/02/1982	5N	HOME	LONDON	STEVE SMITH	IRELAND	LOST	15	16	MIKE DAVIS
369	20/02/1982	5N	AWAY	PARIS	STEVE SMITH	FRANCE	WON	27	15	MIKE DAVIS
370	06/03/1982	5N	HOME	LONDON	STEVE SMITH	WALES	WON	17	7	MIKE DAVIS
371	15/01/1983	5N	HOME	LONDON	STEVE SMITH	FRANCE	LOST	15	19	DICK GREENWOOD
372	05/02/1983	5N	AWAY	CARDIFF	STEVE SMITH	WALES	DRAW	13	13	DICK GREENWOOD
373	05/03/1983	5N	HOME	LONDON	JOHN SCOTT	SCOTLAND	LOST	12	22	DICK GREENWOOD
374	19/03/1983	5N	AWAY	DUBLIN	JOHN SCOTT	IRELAND	LOST	15	25	DICK GREENWOOD
375	19/11/1983	TEST	HOME	LONDON	PETER WHEELER	NEW ZEALAND	WON	15	9	DICK GREENWOOD
376	04/02/1984	5N	AWAY	EDINBURGH	PETER WHEELER	SCOTLAND	LOST	6	18	DICK GREENWOOD
377	18/02/1984	5N	HOME	LONDON	PETER WHEELER	IRELAND	WON	12	9	DICK GREENWOOD
378	03/03/1984	5N	AWAY	PARIS	PETER WHEELER	FRANCE	LOST	18	32	DICK GREENWOOD
379	17/03/1984	5N	HOME	LONDON	PETER WHEELER	WALES	LOST	15	24	DICK GREENWOOD
380	02/06/1984	TEST (1)	AWAY	PORT ELIZABETH	JOHN SCOTT	SOUTH AFRICA	LOST	15	33	DICK GREENWOOD
381	09/06/1984	TEST (2)	AWAY	JOHANNESBURG	JOHN SCOTT	SOUTH AFRICA	LOST	9	35	DICK GREENWOOD
382	03/11/1984	TEST	HOME	LONDON	NIGEL MELVILLE	AUSTRALIA	LOST	3	19	DICK GREENWOOD
383	05/01/1985	TEST	HOME	LONDON	PAUL DODGE	ROMANIA	WON	22	15	DICK GREENWOOD
384	02/02/1985	5N	HOME	LONDON	PAUL DODGE	FRANCE	DRAW	9	9	DICK GREENWOOD
385	16/03/1985	5N	HOME	LONDON	PAUL DODGE	SCOTLAND	WON	10	7	DICK GREENWOOD
386	30/03/1985	5N	AWAY	DUBLIN	PAUL DODGE	IRELAND	LOST	10	13	DICK GREENWOOD
387	20/04/1985	5N	AWAY	CARDIFF	PAUL DODGE	WALES	LOST	15	24	DICK GREENWOOD

GAME	DATE	TYPE	H/A	CITY	CAPTAIN	OPPONENTS	RESULT	SCORE (FOR)	SCORE (OPP)	COACH
388	01/06/1985	TEST (1)	AWAY	CHRISTCHURCH	PAUL DODGE	NEW ZEALAND	LOST	13	18	MARTIN GREEN
389	08/06/1985	TEST (2)	AWAY	WELLINGTON	PAUL DODGE	NEW ZEALAND	LOST	15	42	MARTIN GREEN
390	18/01/1986	5N	HOME	LONDON	NIGEL MELVILLE	WALES	WON	21	18	MARTIN GREEN
391	15/02/1986	5N	AWAY	EDINBURGH	NIGEL MELVILLE	SCOTLAND	LOST	6	33	MARTIN GREEN
392	01/03/1986	5N	HOME	LONDON	NIGEL MELVILLE	IRELAND	WON	25	20	MARTIN GREEN
393	15/03/1986	5N	AWAY	PARIS	NIGEL MELVILLE	FRANCE	LOST	10	29	MARTIN GREEN
394	07/02/1987	5N	AWAY	DUBLIN	RICHARD HILL	IRELAND	LOST	0	17	MARTIN GREEN
395	21/02/1987	5N	HOME	LONDON	RICHARD HILL	FRANCE	LOST	15	19	MARTIN GREEN
396	07/03/1987	5N	AWAY	CARDIFF	RICHARD HILL	WALES	LOST	12	19	MARTIN GREEN
397	04/04/1987	5N	HOME	LONDON	MIKE HARRISON	SCOTLAND	WON	21	12	MARTIN GREEN
398	23/05/1987	WC (G)	AWAY	SYDNEY	MIKE HARRISON	AUSTRALIA	LOST	6	19	MARTIN GREEN
399	30/05/1987	WC (G)	NEUTRAL	SYDNEY	MIKE HARRISON	JAPAN	WON	60	7	MARTIN GREEN
400	03/06/1987	WC (G)	NEUTRAL	SYDNEY	MIKE HARRISON	USA	WON	34	6	MARTIN GREEN
401	08/06/1987	WC (QF)	NEUTRAL	BRISBANE	MIKE HARRISON	WALES	LOST	3	16	MARTIN GREEN
402	16/01/1988	5N	AWAY	PARIS	MIKE HARRISON	FRANCE	LOST	9	10	GEOFF COOKE
403	06/02/1988	5N	HOME	LONDON	MIKE HARRISON	WALES	LOST	3	11	GEOFF COOKE
404	05/03/1988	5N	AWAY	EDINBURGH	NIGEL MELVILLE	SCOTLAND	WON	9	6	GEOFF COOKE
405	19/03/1988	5N	HOME	LONDON	NIGEL MELVILLE	IRELAND	WON	35	3	GEOFF COOKE
406	23/04/1988	TEST	AWAY	DUBLIN	JOHN ORWIN	IRELAND	WON	21	10	GEOFF COOKE
407	29/05/1988	TEST (1)	AWAY	BRISBANE	JOHN ORWIN	AUSTRALIA	LOST	16	22	GEOFF COOKE
408	12/06/1988	TEST (2)	AWAY	SYDNEY	JOHN ORWIN	AUSTRALIA	LOST	8	28	GEOFF COOKE
409	16/06/1988	TEST	AWAY	SUVA	RICHARD HARDING	FIJI	WON	25	12	GEOFF COOKE
410	05/11/1988	TEST	HOME	LONDON	WILL CARLING	AUSTRALIA	WON	28	19	GEOFF COOKE
411	04/02/1989	5N	HOME	LONDON	WILL CARLING	SCOTLAND	DRAW	12	12	GEOFF COOKE
412	18/02/1989	5N	AWAY	DUBLIN	WILL CARLING	IRELAND	WON	16	3	GEOFF COOKE
413	04/03/1989	5N	HOME	LONDON	WILL CARLING	FRANCE	WON	11	0	GEOFF COOKE
414	18/03/1989	5N	AWAY	CARDIFF	WILL CARLING	WALES	LOST	9	12	GEOFF COOKE
415	13/05/1989	TEST	AWAY	BUCHAREST	ROB ANDREW	ROMANIA	WON	58	3	GEOFF COOKE
416	04/11/1989	TEST	HOME	LONDON	WILL CARLING	FIJI	WON	58	23	GEOFF COOKE
417	20/01/1990	5N	HOME	LONDON	WILL CARLING	IRELAND	WON	23	0	GEOFF COOKE
418	03/02/1990	5N	AWAY	PARIS	WILL CARLING	FRANCE	WON	26	7	GEOFF COOKE
419	17/02/1990	5N	HOME	LONDON	WILL CARLING	WALES	WON	34	6	GEOFF COOKE
420	17/03/1990	5N	AWAY	EDINBURGH	WILL CARLING	SCOTLAND	LOST	7	13	GEOFF COOKE
421	28/07/1990	TEST (1)	AWAY	BUENOS AIRES	WILL CARLING	ARGENTINA	WON	25	12	GEOFF COOKE
422	04/08/1990	TEST (2)	AWAY	BUENOS AIRES	WILL CARLING	ARGENTINA	LOST	13	15	GEOFF COOKE
423	03/11/1990	TEST	HOME	LONDON	WILL CARLING	ARGENTINA	WON	51	0	GEOFF COOKE
424	19/01/1991	5N	AWAY	CARDIFF	WILL CARLING	WALES	WON	25	6	GEOFF COOKE
425	16/02/1991	5N	HOME	LONDON	WILL CARLING	SCOTLAND	WON	21	12	GEOFF COOKE
426	02/03/1991	5N	AWAY	DUBLIN	WILL CARLING	IRELAND	WON	16	7	GEOFF COOKE
427	16/03/1991	5N	HOME	LONDON	WILL CARLING	FRANCE	WON	21	19	GEOFF COOKE
428	20/07/1991	TEST	AWAY	SUVA	WILL CARLING	FIJI	WON	28	12	GEOFF COOKE
429	27/07/1991	TEST	AWAY	SYDNEY	WILL CARLING	AUSTRALIA	LOST	15	40	GEOFF COOKE
430	03/10/1991	WC (G)	HOME	LONDON	WILL CARLING	NEW ZEALAND	LOST	12	18	GEOFF COOKE
431	08/10/1991	WC (G)	HOME	LONDON	WILL CARLING	ITALY	WON	36	6	GEOFF COOKE

GAME	DATE	TYPE	H/A	CITY	CAPTAIN	OPPONENTS	RESULT	SCORE (FOR)	SCORE (OPP)	COACH
432	11/10/1991	WC (G)	HOME	LONDON	WILL CARLING	USA	WON	37	9	GEOFF COOKE
433	19/10/1991	WC (QF)	AWAY	PARIS	WILL CARLING	FRANCE	WON	19	10	GEOFF COOKE
434	26/10/1991	WC (SF)	AWAY	EDINBURGH	WILL CARLING	SCOTLAND	WON	9	6	GEOFF COOKE
435	02/11/1991	WC (F)	HOME	LONDON	WILL CARLING	AUSTRALIA	LOST	6	12	GEOFF COOKE
436	18/01/1992	5N	AWAY	EDINBURGH	WILL CARLING	SCOTLAND	WON	25	7	GEOFF COOKE
437	01/02/1992	5N	HOME	LONDON	WILL CARLING	IRELAND	WON	38	9	GEOFF COOKE
438	15/02/1992	5N	AWAY	PARIS	WILL CARLING	FRANCE	WON	31	13	GEOFF COOKE
439	07/03/1992	5N	HOME	LONDON	WILL CARLING	WALES	WON	24	0	GEOFF COOKE
440	17/10/1992	TEST	HOME	LONDON	WILL CARLING	CANADA	WON	26	13	GEOFF COOKE
441	14/11/1992	TEST	HOME	LONDON	WILL CARLING	SOUTH AFRICA	WON	33	16	GEOFF COOKE
442	16/01/1993	5N	HOME	LONDON	WILL CARLING	FRANCE	WON	16	15	GEOFF COOKE
443	06/02/1993	5N	AWAY	CARDIFF	WILL CARLING	WALES	LOST	9	10	GEOFF COOKE
444	06/03/1993	5N	HOME	LONDON	WILL CARLING	SCOTLAND	WON	26	12	GEOFF COOKE
445	20/03/1993	5N	AWAY	DUBLIN	WILL CARLING	IRELAND	LOST	3	17	GEOFF COOKE
446	27/11/1993	TEST	HOME	LONDON	WILL CARLING	NEW ZEALAND	WON	15	9	GEOFF COOKE
447	05/02/1994	5N	AWAY	EDINBURGH	WILL CARLING	SCOTLAND	WON	15	14	GEOFF COOKE
448	19/02/1994	5N	HOME	LONDON	WILL CARLING	IRELAND	LOST	12	13	GEOFF COOKE
449	05/03/1994	5N	AWAY	PARIS	WILL CARLING	FRANCE	WON	18	14	GEOFF COOKE
450	19/03/1994	5N	HOME	LONDON	WILL CARLING	WALES	WON	15	8	GEOFF COOKE
451	04/06/1994	TEST (1)	AWAY	PRETORIA	WILL CARLING	SOUTH AFRICA	WON	32	15	GEOFF COOKE
452	11/06/1994	TEST (2)	AWAY	CAPE TOWN	WILL CARLING	SOUTH AFRICA	LOST	9	27	JACK ROWELL
453	12/11/1994	TEST	HOME	LONDON	WILL CARLING	ROMANIA	WON	54	3	JACK ROWELL
454	10/12/1994	TEST	HOME	LONDON	WILL CARLING	CANADA	WON	60	19	JACK ROWELL
455	21/01/1995	5N	AWAY	DUBLIN	WILL CARLING	IRELAND	WON	20	8	JACK ROWELL
456	04/02/1995	5N	HOME	LONDON	WILL CARLING	FRANCE	WON	31	10	JACK ROWELL
457	18/02/1995	5N	AWAY	CARDIFF	WILL CARLING	WALES	WON	23	9	JACK ROWELL
458	18/03/1995	5N	HOME	LONDON	WILL CARLING	SCOTLAND	WON	24	12	JACK ROWELL
459	27/05/1995	WC (G)	NEUTRAL	DURBAN	WILL CARLING	ARGENTINA	WON	24	18	JACK ROWELL
460	31/05/1995	WC (G)	NEUTRAL	DURBAN	ROB ANDREW	ITALY	WON	27	20	JACK ROWELL
461	04/06/1995	WC (G)	NEUTRAL	DURBAN	WILL CARLING	WESTERN SAMOA	WON	44	22	JACK ROWELL
462	11/06/1995	WC (QF)	NEUTRAL	CAPE TOWN	WILL CARLING	AUSTRALIA	WON	25	22	JACK ROWELL
463	18/06/1995	WC (SF)	NEUTRAL	CAPE TOWN	WILL CARLING	NEW ZEALAND	LOST	29	45	JACK ROWELL
464	22/06/1995	WC (3/4)	NEUTRAL	PRETORIA	WILL CARLING	FRANCE	LOST	9	19	JACK ROWELL
465	18/11/1995	TEST	HOME	LONDON	WILL CARLING	SOUTH AFRICA	LOST	14	24	JACK ROWELL
466	16/12/1995	TEST	HOME	LONDON	WILL CARLING	WESTERN SAMOA	WON	27	9	JACK ROWELL
467	20/01/1996	5N	AWAY	PARIS	WILL CARLING	FRANCE	LOST	12	15	JACK ROWELL
468	03/02/1996	5N	HOME	LONDON	WILL CARLING	WALES	WON	21	15	JACK ROWELL
469	02/03/1996	5N	AWAY	EDINBURGH	WILL CARLING	SCOTLAND	WON	18	9	JACK ROWELL
470	16/03/1996	5N	HOME	LONDON	WILL CARLING	IRELAND	WON	28	15	JACK ROWELL
471	23/11/1996	TEST	HOME	LONDON	PHIL DE GLANVILLE	ITALY	WON	54	21	JACK ROWELL
472	14/12/1996	TEST	HOME	LONDON	JASON LEONARD	ARGENTINA	WON	20	18	JACK ROWELL
473	01/02/1997	5N	HOME	LONDON	PHIL DE GLANVILLE	SCOTLAND	WON	41	13	JACK ROWELL
474	15/02/1997	5N	AWAY	DUBLIN	PHIL DE GLANVILLE	IRELAND	WON	46	6	JACK ROWELL
475	01/03/1997	5N	HOME	LONDON	PHIL DE GLANVILLE	FRANCE	LOST	20	23	JACK ROWELL

GAME	DATE	TYPE	H/A	CITY	CAPTAIN	OPPONENTS	RESULT	SCORE (FOR)	SCORE (OPP)	COACH
476	15/03/1997	5N	AWAY	CARDIFF	PHIL DE GLANVILLE	WALES	WON	34	13	JACK ROWELL
477	31/05/1997	TEST (1)	AWAY	BUENOS AIRES	PHIL DE GLANVILLE	ARGENTINA	WON	46	20	JACK ROWELL
478	07/06/1997	TEST (2)	AWAY	BUENOS AIRES	PHIL DE GLANVILLE	ARGENTINA	LOST	13	33	JACK ROWELL
479	12/07/1997	TEST	AWAY	SYDNEY	PHIL DE GLANVILLE	AUSTRALIA	LOST	6	25	JACK ROWELL
480	15/11/1997	TEST	HOME	LONDON	LAWRENCE DALLAGLIO	AUSTRALIA	DRAW	15	15	CLIVE WOODWARD
481	22/11/1997	TEST (1)	HOME	MANCHESTER	LAWRENCE DALLAGLIO	NEW ZEALAND	LOST	8	25	CLIVE WOODWARD
482	29/11/1997	TEST	HOME	LONDON	LAWRENCE DALLAGLIO	SOUTH AFRICA	LOST	11	29	CLIVE WOODWARD
483	06/12/1997	TEST (2)	HOME	LONDON	LAWRENCE DALLAGLIO	NEW ZEALAND	DRAW	26	26	CLIVE WOODWARD
484	07/02/1998	5N	AWAY	PARIS	LAWRENCE DALLAGLIO	FRANCE	LOST	17	24	CLIVE WOODWARD
485	21/02/1998	5N	HOME	LONDON	LAWRENCE DALLAGLIO	WALES	WON	60	26	CLIVE WOODWARD
486	22/03/1998	5N	AWAY	EDINBURGH	LAWRENCE DALLAGLIO	SCOTLAND	WON	34	20	CLIVE WOODWARD
487	04/04/1998	5N	HOME	LONDON	LAWRENCE DALLAGLIO	IRELAND	WON	35	17	CLIVE WOODWARD
488	06/06/1998	TEST (1)	AWAY	BRISBANE	TONY DIPROSE	AUSTRALIA	LOST	0	76	CLIVE WOODWARD
489	20/06/1998	TEST (1)	AWAY	DUNEDIN	MATT DAWSON	NEW ZEALAND	LOST	22	64	CLIVE WOODWARD
490	27/06/1998	TEST (2)	AWAY	AUCKLAND	MATT DAWSON	NEW ZEALAND	LOST	10	40	CLIVE WOODWARD
491	04/07/1998	TEST	AWAY	CAPE TOWN	MATT DAWSON	SOUTH AFRICA	LOST	0	18	CLIVE WOODWARD
492	14/11/1998	WC (Q)	HOME	HUDDERSFIELD	MARTIN JOHNSON	NETHERLANDS	WON	110	0	CLIVE WOODWARD
493	22/11/1998	WC (Q)	HOME	HUDDERSFIELD	MARTIN JOHNSON	ITALY	WON	23	15	CLIVE WOODWARD
494	28/11/1998	TEST (2)	HOME	LONDON	LAWRENCE DALLAGLIO	AUSTRALIA	LOST	11	12	CLIVE WOODWARD
495	05/12/1998	TEST	HOME	LONDON	LAWRENCE DALLAGLIO	SOUTH AFRICA	WON	13	7	CLIVE WOODWARD
496	20/02/1999	5N	HOME	LONDON	MARTIN JOHNSON	SCOTLAND	WON	24	21	CLIVE WOODWARD
497	06/03/1999	5N	AWAY	DUBLIN	LAWRENCE DALLAGLIO	IRELAND	WON	27	15	CLIVE WOODWARD
498	20/03/1999	5N	HOME	LONDON	LAWRENCE DALLAGLIO	FRANCE	WON	21	20	CLIVE WOODWARD
499	11/04/1999	5N	AWAY	LONDON	LAWRENCE DALLAGLIO	WALES	LOST	31	32	CLIVE WOODWARD
500	26/06/1999	TEST	AWAY	SYDNEY	MARTIN JOHNSON	AUSTRALIA	LOST	15	22	CLIVE WOODWARD
501	21/08/1999	WCW	HOME	LONDON	MARTIN JOHNSON	USA	WON	106	8	CLIVE WOODWARD
502	28/08/1999	WCW	HOME	LONDON	MARTIN JOHNSON	CANADA	WON	36	11	CLIVE WOODWARD
503	02/10/1999	WC (G)	HOME	LONDON	MARTIN JOHNSON	ITALY	WON	67	7	CLIVE WOODWARD
504	09/10/1999	WC (G)	HOME	LONDON	MARTIN JOHNSON	NEW ZEALAND	LOST	16	30	CLIVE WOODWARD
505	15/10/1999	WC (G)	HOME	LONDON	MARTIN JOHNSON	TONGA	WON	101	10	CLIVE WOODWARD
506	20/10/1999	WC (QPPO)	HOME	LONDON	MARTIN JOHNSON	FIJI	WON	45	24	CLIVE WOODWARD
507	24/10/1999	WC (QF)	NEUTRAL	PARIS	MARTIN JOHNSON	SOUTH AFRICA	LOST	21	44	CLIVE WOODWARD
508	05/02/2000	6N	HOME	LONDON	MATT DAWSON	IRELAND	WON	50	18	CLIVE WOODWARD
509	19/02/2000	6N	AWAY	PARIS	MATT DAWSON	FRANCE	WON	15	9	CLIVE WOODWARD
510	04/03/2000	6N	HOME	LONDON	MATT DAWSON	WALES	WON	46	12	CLIVE WOODWARD
511	18/03/2000	6N	AWAY	ROME	MATT DAWSON	ITALY	WON	59	12	CLIVE WOODWARD
512	02/04/2000	6N	AWAY	EDINBURGH	MATT DAWSON	SCOTLAND	LOST	13	19	CLIVE WOODWARD
513	17/06/2000	TEST (1)	AWAY	PRETORIA	MARTIN JOHNSON	SOUTH AFRICA	LOST	13	18	CLIVE WOODWARD
514	24/06/2000	TEST (2)	AWAY	BLOEMFONTEIN	MARTIN JOHNSON	SOUTH AFRICA	WON	27	22	CLIVE WOODWARD
515	18/11/2000	TEST	HOME	LONDON	MARTIN JOHNSON	AUSTRALIA	WON	22	19	CLIVE WOODWARD
516	25/11/2000	TEST	HOME	LONDON	MARTIN JOHNSON	ARGENTINA	WON	19	0	CLIVE WOODWARD
517	02/12/2000	TEST	HOME	LONDON	MARTIN JOHNSON	SOUTH AFRICA	WON	25	17	CLIVE WOODWARD
518	03/02/2001	6N	AWAY	CARDIFF	MARTIN JOHNSON	WALES	WON	44	15	CLIVE WOODWARD
519	17/02/2001	6N	HOME	LONDON	MARTIN JOHNSON	ITALY	WON	80	23	CLIVE WOODWARD

GAME	DATE	TYPE	H/A	CITY	CAPTAIN	OPPONENTS	RESULT	SCORE (FOR)	SCORE (OPP)	COACH
520	03/03/2001	6N	HOME	LONDON	MARTIN JOHNSON	SCOTLAND	WON	43	3	CLIVE WOODWARD
521	07/04/2001	6N	HOME	LONDON	MARTIN JOHNSON	FRANCE	WON	48	19	CLIVE WOODWARD
522	02/06/2001	TEST (1)	AWAY	MARKHAM	KYRAN BRACKEN	CANADA	WON	22	10	CLIVE WOODWARD
523	09/06/2001	TEST (2)	AWAY	BURNABY LAKE	KYRAN BRACKEN	CANADA	WON	59	20	CLIVE WOODWARD
524	16/06/2001	TEST	AWAY	SAN FRANCISCO	KYRAN BRACKEN	USA	WON	48	19	CLIVE WOODWARD
525	20/10/2001	6N	AWAY	DUBLIN	MATT DAWSON	IRELAND	LOST	14	20	CLIVE WOODWARD
526	10/11/2001	TEST	HOME	LONDON	NEIL BACK	AUSTRALIA	WON	21	15	CLIVE WOODWARD
527	17/11/2001	TEST	HOME	LONDON	NEIL BACK	ROMANIA	WON	134	0	CLIVE WOODWARD
528	24/11/2001	TEST	HOME	LONDON	MARTIN JOHNSON	SOUTH AFRICA	WON	29	9	CLIVE WOODWARD
529	02/02/2002	6N	AWAY	EDINBURGH	MARTIN JOHNSON	SCOTLAND	WON	29	3	CLIVE WOODWARD
530	16/02/2002	6N	HOME	LONDON	MARTIN JOHNSON	IRELAND	WON	45	11	CLIVE WOODWARD
531	02/03/2002	6N	AWAY	PARIS	MARTIN JOHNSON	FRANCE	LOST	15	20	CLIVE WOODWARD
532	23/03/2002	6N	HOME	LONDON	NEIL BACK	WALES	WON	50	10	CLIVE WOODWARD
533	07/04/2002	6N	AWAY	ROME	NEIL BACK	ITALY	WON	45	9	CLIVE WOODWARD
534	22/06/2002	TEST	AWAY	BUENOS AIRES	PHIL VICKERY	ARGENTINA	WON	26	18	CLIVE WOODWARD
535	09/11/2002	TEST	HOME	LONDON	MARTIN JOHNSON	NEW ZEALAND	WON	31	28	CLIVE WOODWARD
536	16/11/2002	TEST	HOME	LONDON	MARTIN JOHNSON	AUSTRALIA	WON	32	31	CLIVE WOODWARD
537	23/11/2002	TEST	HOME	LONDON	MARTIN JOHNSON	SOUTH AFRICA	WON	53	3	CLIVE WOODWARD
538	15/02/2003	6N	HOME	LONDON	MARTIN JOHNSON	FRANCE	WON	25	17	CLIVE WOODWARD
539	22/02/2003	6N	AWAY	CARDIFF	MARTIN JOHNSON	WALES	WON	26	9	CLIVE WOODWARD
540	09/03/2003	6N	HOME	LONDON	JONNY WILKINSON	ITALY	WON	40	5	CLIVE WOODWARD
541	22/03/2003	6N	HOME	LONDON	MARTIN JOHNSON	SCOTLAND	WON	40	9	CLIVE WOODWARD
542	30/03/2003	6N	AWAY	DUBLIN	MARTIN JOHNSON	IRELAND	WON	42	6	CLIVE WOODWARD
543	14/06/2003	TEST	AWAY	WELLINGTON	MARTIN JOHNSON	NEW ZEALAND	WON	15	13	CLIVE WOODWARD
544	21/06/2003	TEST	AWAY	MELBOURNE	MARTIN JOHNSON	AUSTRALIA	WON	25	14	CLIVE WOODWARD
545	23/08/2003	WCW	AWAY	CARDIFF	JASON LEONARD	WALES	WON	43	9	CLIVE WOODWARD
546	30/08/2003	WCW	AWAY	MARSEILLE	DORIAN WEST	FRANCE	LOST	16	17	CLIVE WOODWARD
547	06/09/2003	WCW	HOME	LONDON	MARTIN JOHNSON	FRANCE	WON	45	14	CLIVE WOODWARD
548	12/10/2003	WC (G)	NEUTRAL	PERTH	MARTIN JOHNSON	GEORGIA	WON	84	6	CLIVE WOODWARD
549	18/10/2003	WC (G)	NEUTRAL	PERTH	MARTIN JOHNSON	SOUTH AFRICA	WON	25	6	CLIVE WOODWARD
550	26/10/2003	WC (G)	NEUTRAL	MELBOURNE	MARTIN JOHNSON	SAMOA	WON	35	22	CLIVE WOODWARD
551	02/11/2003	WC (G)	NEUTRAL	BRISBANE	PHIL VICKERY	URUGUAY	WON	111	13	CLIVE WOODWARD
552	09/11/2003	WC (QF)	NEUTRAL	BRISBANE	MARTIN JOHNSON	WALES	WON	28	17	CLIVE WOODWARD
553	16/11/2003	WC (SF)	NEUTRAL	SYDNEY	MARTIN JOHNSON	FRANCE	WON	24	7	CLIVE WOODWARD
554	22/11/2003	WC (F)	AWAY	SYDNEY	MARTIN JOHNSON	AUSTRALIA	WON (AET)	20	17	CLIVE WOODWARD
555	15/02/2004	6N	AWAY	ROME	LAWRENCE DALLAGLIO	ITALY	WON	50	9	CLIVE WOODWARD
556	21/02/2004	6N	AWAY	EDINBURGH	LAWRENCE DALLAGLIO	SCOTLAND	WON	35	13	CLIVE WOODWARD
557	06/03/2004	6N	HOME	LONDON	LAWRENCE DALLAGLIO	IRELAND	LOST	13	19	CLIVE WOODWARD
558	20/03/2004	6N	HOME	LONDON	LAWRENCE DALLAGLIO	WALES	WON	31	21	CLIVE WOODWARD
559	27/03/2004	6N	AWAY	PARIS	LAWRENCE DALLAGLIO	FRANCE	LOST	21	24	CLIVE WOODWARD
560	12/06/2004	TEST (1)	AWAY	DUNEDIN	LAWRENCE DALLAGLIO	NEW ZEALAND	LOST	3	36	CLIVE WOODWARD
561	19/06/2004	TEST (2)	AWAY	AUCKLAND	LAWRENCE DALLAGLIO	NEW ZEALAND	LOST	12	36	CLIVE WOODWARD
562	26/06/2004	TEST	AWAY	BRISBANE	LAWRENCE DALLAGLIO	AUSTRALIA	LOST	15	51	CLIVE WOODWARD
563	13/11/2004	TEST	HOME	LONDON	JASON ROBINSON	CANADA	WON	70	0	ANDY ROBINSON

GAME	DATE	TYPE	H/A	CITY	CAPTAIN	OPPONENTS	RESULT	SCORE (FOR)	SCORE (OPP)	COACH
564	20/11/2004	TEST	HOME	LONDON	JASON ROBINSON	SOUTH AFRICA	WON	32	16	ANDY ROBINSON
565	27/11/2004	TEST	HOME	LONDON	JASON ROBINSON	AUSTRALIA	LOST	19	21	ANDY ROBINSON
566	05/02/2005	6N	AWAY	CARDIFF	JASON ROBINSON	WALES	LOST	9	11	ANDY ROBINSON
567	13/02/2005	6N	HOME	LONDON	JASON ROBINSON	FRANCE	LOST	17	18	ANDY ROBINSON
568	27/02/2005	6N	AWAY	DUBLIN	JASON ROBINSON	IRELAND	LOST	13	19	ANDY ROBINSON
569	12/03/2005	6N	HOME	LONDON	MARTIN CORRY	ITALY	WON	39	7	ANDY ROBINSON
570	19/03/2005	6N	HOME	LONDON	MARTIN CORRY	SCOTLAND	WON	43	22	ANDY ROBINSON
571	12/11/2005	TEST	HOME	LONDON	MARTIN CORRY	AUSTRALIA	WON	26	16	ANDY ROBINSON
572	19/11/2005	TEST	HOME	LONDON	MARTIN CORRY	NEW ZEALAND	LOST	19	23	ANDY ROBINSON
573	26/11/2005	TEST	HOME	LONDON	MARTIN CORRY	SAMOA	WON	40	3	ANDY ROBINSON
574	04/02/2006	6N	HOME	LONDON	MARTIN CORRY	WALES	WON	47	13	ANDY ROBINSON
575	11/02/2006	6N	AWAY	ROME	MARTIN CORRY	ITALY	WON	31	16	ANDY ROBINSON
576	25/02/2006	6N	AWAY	EDINBURGH	MARTIN CORRY	SCOTLAND	LOST	12	18	ANDY ROBINSON
577	12/03/2006	6N	AWAY	PARIS	MARTIN CORRY	FRANCE	LOST	6	31	ANDY ROBINSON
578	18/03/2006	6N	HOME	LONDON	MARTIN CORRY	IRELAND	LOST	24	28	ANDY ROBINSON
579	11/06/2006	TEST (1)	AWAY	SYDNEY	PAT SANDERSON	AUSTRALIA	LOST	3	34	ANDY ROBINSON
580	17/06/2006	TEST (2)	AWAY	MELBOURNE	PAT SANDERSON	AUSTRALIA	LOST	18	43	ANDY ROBINSON
581	05/11/2006	TEST	HOME	LONDON	MARTIN CORRY	NEW ZEALAND	LOST	20	41	ANDY ROBINSON
582	11/11/2006	TEST	HOME	LONDON	MARTIN CORRY	ARGENTINA	LOST	18	25	ANDY ROBINSON
583	18/11/2006	TEST (1)	HOME	LONDON	MARTIN CORRY	SOUTH AFRICA	WON	23	21	ANDY ROBINSON
584	25/11/2006	TEST (2)	HOME	LONDON	MARTIN CORRY	SOUTH AFRICA	LOST	14	25	ANDY ROBINSON
585	03/02/2007	6N	HOME	LONDON	PHIL VICKERY	SCOTLAND	WON	42	20	BRIAN ASHTON
586	10/02/2007	6N	HOME	LONDON	PHIL VICKERY	ITALY	WON	20	7	BRIAN ASHTON
587	24/02/2007	6N	AWAY	DUBLIN	PHIL VICKERY	IRELAND	LOST	13	43	BRIAN ASHTON
588	11/03/2007	6N	HOME	LONDON	MIKE CATT	FRANCE	WON	26	18	BRIAN ASHTON
589	17/03/2007	6N	AWAY	CARDIFF	MIKE CATT	WALES	LOST	18	27	BRIAN ASHTON
590	26/05/2007	TEST (1)	AWAY	BLOEMFONTEIN	JASON ROBINSON	SOUTH AFRICA	LOST	10	58	BRIAN ASHTON
591	02/06/2007	TEST (2)	AWAY	PRETORIA	JONNY WILKINSON	SOUTH AFRICA	LOST	22	55	BRIAN ASHTON
592	04/08/2007	WCW	HOME	LONDON	PHIL VICKERY	WALES	WON	62	5	BRIAN ASHTON
593	11/08/2007	WCW	HOME	LONDON	MIKE CATT	FRANCE	LOST	15	21	BRIAN ASHTON
594	18/08/2007	WCW	AWAY	MARSEILLE	PHIL VICKERY	FRANCE	LOST	9	22	BRIAN ASHTON
595	08/09/2007	WC (G)	NEUTRAL	LENS	PHIL VICKERY	USA	WON	28	10	BRIAN ASHTON
596	14/09/2007	WC (G)	NEUTRAL	PARIS	MARTIN CORRY	SOUTH AFRICA	LOST	0	36	BRIAN ASHTON
597	22/09/2007	WC (G)	NEUTRAL	NANTES	MARTIN CORRY	SAMOA	WON	44	22	BRIAN ASHTON
598	28/09/2007	WC (G)	NEUTRAL	PARIS	MARTIN CORRY	TONGA	WON	36	20	BRIAN ASHTON
599	06/10/2007	WC (QF)	NEUTRAL	MARSEILLE	PHIL VICKERY	AUSTRALIA	WON	12	10	BRIAN ASHTON
600	13/10/2007	WC (SF)	AWAY	PARIS	PHIL VICKERY	FRANCE	WON	14	9	BRIAN ASHTON
601	20/10/2007	WC (F)	NEUTRAL	PARIS	PHIL VICKERY	SOUTH AFRICA	LOST	6	15	BRIAN ASHTON
602	02/02/2008	6N	HOME	LONDON	PHIL VICKERY	WALES	LOST	19	26	BRIAN ASHTON
603	10/02/2008	6N	AWAY	ROME	STEVE BORTHWICK	ITALY	WON	23	19	BRIAN ASHTON
604	23/02/2008	6N	AWAY	PARIS	PHIL VICKERY	FRANCE	WON	24	13	BRIAN ASHTON
605	08/03/2008	6N	AWAY	EDINBURGH	PHIL VICKERY	SCOTLAND	LOST	9	15	BRIAN ASHTON
606	15/03/2008	6N	HOME	LONDON	PHIL VICKERY	IRELAND	WON	33	10	BRIAN ASHTON
607	14/06/2008	TEST (1)	AWAY	AUCKLAND	STEVE BORTHWICK	NEW ZEALAND	LOST	20	37	ROB ANDREW*

GAME	DATE	TYPE	H/A	CITY	CAPTAIN	OPPONENTS	RESULT	SCORE (FOR)	SCORE (OPP)	COACH
608	21/06/2008	TEST (2)	AWAY	CHRISTCHURCH	STEVE BORTHWICK	NEW ZEALAND	LOST	12	44	ROB ANDREW*
609	08/11/2008	TEST	HOME	LONDON	STEVE BORTHWICK	PACIFIC ISLANDERS	WON	39	13	MARTIN JOHNSON
610	15/11/2008	TEST	HOME	LONDON	STEVE BORTHWICK	AUSTRALIA	LOST	14	28	MARTIN JOHNSON
611	22/11/2008	TEST	HOME	LONDON	STEVE BORTHWICK	SOUTH AFRICA	LOST	6	42	MARTIN JOHNSON
612	29/11/2008	TEST	HOME	LONDON	STEVE BORTHWICK	NEW ZEALAND	LOST	6	32	MARTIN JOHNSON
613	07/02/2009	6N	HOME	LONDON	STEVE BORTHWICK	ITALY	WON	36	11	MARTIN JOHNSON
614	14/02/2009	6N	AWAY	CARDIFF	STEVE BORTHWICK	WALES	LOST	15	23	MARTIN JOHNSON
615	28/02/2009	6N	AWAY	DUBLIN	STEVE BORTHWICK	IRELAND	LOST	13	14	MARTIN JOHNSON
616	15/03/2009	6N	HOME	LONDON	STEVE BORTHWICK	FRANCE	WON	34	10	MARTIN JOHNSON
617	21/03/2009	6N	HOME	LONDON	STEVE BORTHWICK	SCOTLAND	WON	26	12	MARTIN JOHNSON
618	06/06/2009	TEST (1)	HOME	MANCHESTER	STEVE BORTHWICK	ARGENTINA	WON	37	15	MARTIN JOHNSON
619	13/06/2009	TEST (2)	AWAY	SALTA	STEVE BORTHWICK	ARGENTINA	LOST	22	24	MARTIN JOHNSON
620	07/11/2009	TEST	HOME	LONDON	STEVE BORTHWICK	AUSTRALIA	LOST	9	18	MARTIN JOHNSON
621	14/11/2009	TEST	HOME	LONDON	STEVE BORTHWICK	ARGENTINA	WON	16	9	MARTIN JOHNSON
622	21/11/2009	TEST	HOME	LONDON	STEVE BORTHWICK	NEW ZEALAND	LOST	6	19	MARTIN JOHNSON
623	06/02/2010	6N	HOME	LONDON	STEVE BORTHWICK	WALES	WON	30	17	MARTIN JOHNSON
624	14/02/2010	6N	AWAY	ROME	STEVE BORTHWICK	ITALY	WON	17	12	MARTIN JOHNSON
625	27/02/2010	6N	HOME	LONDON	STEVE BORTHWICK	IRELAND	LOST	16	20	MARTIN JOHNSON
626	13/03/2010	6N	AWAY	EDINBURGH	STEVE BORTHWICK	SCOTLAND	DRAW	15	15	MARTIN JOHNSON
627	20/03/2010	6N	AWAY	PARIS	LEWIS MOODY	FRANCE	LOST	10	12	MARTIN JOHNSON
628	12/06/2010	TEST (1)	AWAY	PERTH	LEWIS MOODY	AUSTRALIA	LOST	17	27	MARTIN JOHNSON
629	19/06/2010	TEST (2)	AWAY	SYDNEY	LEWIS MOODY	AUSTRALIA	WON	21	20	MARTIN JOHNSON
630	06/11/2010	TEST	HOME	LONDON	LEWIS MOODY	NEW ZEALAND	LOST	16	26	MARTIN JOHNSON
631	13/11/2010	TEST	HOME	LONDON	LEWIS MOODY	AUSTRALIA	WON	35	18	MARTIN JOHNSON
632	20/11/2010	TEST	HOME	LONDON	NICK EASTER	SAMOA	WON	26	13	MARTIN JOHNSON
633	27/11/2010	TEST	HOME	LONDON	LEWIS MOODY	SOUTH AFRICA	LOST	11	21	MARTIN JOHNSON
634	04/02/2011	6N	AWAY	CARDIFF	MIKE TINDALL	WALES	WON	26	19	MARTIN JOHNSON
635	12/02/2011	6N	HOME	LONDON	MIKE TINDALL	ITALY	WON	59	13	MARTIN JOHNSON
636	26/02/2011	6N	HOME	LONDON	MIKE TINDALL	FRANCE	WON	17	9	MARTIN JOHNSON
637	13/03/2011	6N	HOME	LONDON	MIKE TINDALL	SCOTLAND	WON	22	16	MARTIN JOHNSON
638	19/03/2011	6N	AWAY	DUBLIN	NICK EASTER	IRELAND	LOST	8	24	MARTIN JOHNSON
639	06/08/2011	WCW	HOME	LONDON	LEWIS MOODY	WALES	WON	23	19	MARTIN JOHNSON
640	13/08/2011	WCW	AWAY	CARDIFF	MIKE TINDALL	WALES	LOST	9	19	MARTIN JOHNSON
641	27/08/2011	WCW	AWAY	DUBLIN	MIKE TINDALL	IRELAND	WON	20	9	MARTIN JOHNSON
642	10/09/2011	WC (G)	NEUTRAL	DUNEDIN	MIKE TINDALL	ARGENTINA	WON	13	9	MARTIN JOHNSON
643	18/09/2011	WC (G)	NEUTRAL	DUNEDIN	LEWIS MOODY	GEORGIA	WON	41	10	MARTIN JOHNSON
644	24/09/2011	WC (G)	NEUTRAL	DUNEDIN	LEWIS MOODY	ROMANIA	WON	67	3	MARTIN JOHNSON
645	01/10/2011	WC (G)	NEUTRAL	AUCKLAND	LEWIS MOODY	SCOTLAND	WON	16	12	MARTIN JOHNSON
646	08/10/2011	WC (QF)	NEUTRAL	AUCKLAND	LEWIS MOODY	FRANCE	LOST	12	19	MARTIN JOHNSON
647	04/02/2012	6N	AWAY	EDINBURGH	CHRIS ROBSHAW	SCOTLAND	WON	13	6	STUART LANCASTER
648	11/02/2012	6N	AWAY	ROME	CHRIS ROBSHAW	ITALY	WON	19	15	STUART LANCASTER
649	25/02/2012	6N	HOME	LONDON	CHRIS ROBSHAW	WALES	LOST	12	19	STUART LANCASTER
650	11/03/2012	6N	AWAY	PARIS	CHRIS ROBSHAW	FRANCE	WON	24	22	STUART LANCASTER
651	17/03/2012	6N	HOME	LONDON	CHRIS ROBSHAW	IRELAND	WON	30	9	STUART LANCASTER

GAME	DATE	TYPE	H/A	CITY	CAPTAIN	OPPONENTS	RESULT	SCORE (FOR)	SCORE (OPP)	COACH
652	09/06/2012	TEST (1)	AWAY	DURBAN	CHRIS ROBSHAW	SOUTH AFRICA	LOST	17	22	STUART LANCASTER
653	16/06/2012	TEST (2)	AWAY	JOHANNESBURG	CHRIS ROBSHAW	SOUTH AFRICA	LOST	27	36	STUART LANCASTER
654	23/06/2012	TEST (3)	AWAY	PORT ELIZABETH	DYLAN HARTLEY	SOUTH AFRICA	DRAW	14	14	STUART LANCASTER
655	10/11/2012	TEST	HOME	LONDON	CHRIS ROBSHAW	FIJI	WON	54	12	STUART LANCASTER
656	17/11/2012	TEST	HOME	LONDON	CHRIS ROBSHAW	AUSTRALIA	LOST	14	20	STUART LANCASTER
657	24/11/2012	TEST	HOME	LONDON	CHRIS ROBSHAW	SOUTH AFRICA	LOST	15	16	STUART LANCASTER
658	01/12/2012	TEST	HOME	LONDON	CHRIS ROBSHAW	NEW ZEALAND	WON	38	21	STUART LANCASTER
659	02/02/2013	6N	HOME	LONDON	CHRIS ROBSHAW	SCOTLAND	WON	38	18	STUART LANCASTER
660	10/02/2013	6N	AWAY	DUBLIN	CHRIS ROBSHAW	IRELAND	WON	12	6	STUART LANCASTER
661	23/02/2013	6N	HOME	LONDON	CHRIS ROBSHAW	FRANCE	WON	23	13	STUART LANCASTER
662	10/03/2013	6N	HOME	LONDON	CHRIS ROBSHAW	ITALY	WON	18	11	STUART LANCASTER
663	16/03/2013	6N	AWAY	CARDIFF	CHRIS ROBSHAW	WALES	LOST	3	30	STUART LANCASTER
664	08/06/2013	TEST (1)	AWAY	SALTA	TOM WOOD	ARGENTINA	WON	32	3	STUART LANCASTER
665	15/06/2013	TEST (2)	AWAY	BUENOS AIRES	TOM WOOD	ARGENTINA	WON	51	26	STUART LANCASTER
666	02/11/2013	TEST	HOME	LONDON	CHRIS ROBSHAW	AUSTRALIA	WON	20	13	STUART LANCASTER
667	09/11/2013	TEST	HOME	LONDON	CHRIS ROBSHAW	ARGENTINA	WON	31	12	STUART LANCASTER
668	16/11/2013	TEST	HOME	LONDON	CHRIS ROBSHAW	NEW ZEALAND	LOST	22	30	STUART LANCASTER
669	01/02/2014	6N	AWAY	PARIS	CHRIS ROBSHAW	FRANCE	LOST	24	26	STUART LANCASTER
670	08/02/2014	6N	AWAY	EDINBURGH	CHRIS ROBSHAW	SCOTLAND	WON	20	0	STUART LANCASTER
671	22/02/2014	6N	HOME	LONDON	CHRIS ROBSHAW	IRELAND	WON	13	10	STUART LANCASTER
672	09/03/2014	6N	HOME	LONDON	CHRIS ROBSHAW	WALES	WON	29	18	STUART LANCASTER
673	15/03/2014	6N	AWAY	ROME	CHRIS ROBSHAW	ITALY	WON	52	11	STUART LANCASTER
674	07/06/2014	TEST (1)	AWAY	AUCKLAND	CHRIS ROBSHAW	NEW ZEALAND	LOST	15	20	STUART LANCASTER
675	14/06/2014	TEST (2)	AWAY	DUNEDIN	CHRIS ROBSHAW	NEW ZEALAND	LOST	27	28	STUART LANCASTER
676	21/06/2014	TEST (3)	AWAY	HAMILTON	CHRIS ROBSHAW	NEW ZEALAND	LOST	13	36	STUART LANCASTER
677	08/11/2014	TEST	HOME	LONDON	CHRIS ROBSHAW	NEW ZEALAND	LOST	21	24	STUART LANCASTER
678	15/11/2014	TEST	HOME	LONDON	CHRIS ROBSHAW	SOUTH AFRICA	LOST	28	31	STUART LANCASTER
679	22/11/2014	TEST	HOME	LONDON	CHRIS ROBSHAW	SAMOA	WON	28	9	STUART LANCASTER
680	29/11/2014	TEST	HOME	LONDON	CHRIS ROBSHAW	AUSTRALIA	WON	26	17	STUART LANCASTER
681	06/02/2015	6N	AWAY	CARDIFF	CHRIS ROBSHAW	WALES	WON	21	16	STUART LANCASTER
682	14/02/2015	6N	HOME	LONDON	CHRIS ROBSHAW	ITALY	WON	47	17	STUART LANCASTER
683	01/03/2015	6N	AWAY	DUBLIN	CHRIS ROBSHAW	IRELAND	LOST	9	19	STUART LANCASTER
684	14/03/2015	6N	HOME	LONDON	CHRIS ROBSHAW	SCOTLAND	WON	25	13	STUART LANCASTER
685	21/03/2015	6N	HOME	LONDON	CHRIS ROBSHAW	FRANCE	WON	55	35	STUART LANCASTER
686	15/08/2015	WCW	HOME	LONDON	TOM WOOD	FRANCE	WON	19	14	STUART LANCASTER
687	22/08/2015	WCW	AWAY	PARIS	CHRIS ROBSHAW	FRANCE	LOST	20	25	STUART LANCASTER
688	05/09/2015	WCW	HOME	LONDON	CHRIS ROBSHAW	IRELAND	WON	21	13	STUART LANCASTER
689	18/09/2015	WC (G)	HOME	LONDON	CHRIS ROBSHAW	FIJI	WON	35	11	STUART LANCASTER
690	26/09/2015	WC (G)	HOME	LONDON	CHRIS ROBSHAW	WALES	LOST	25	28	STUART LANCASTER
691	03/10/2015	WC (G)	HOME	LONDON	CHRIS ROBSHAW	AUSTRALIA	LOST	13	33	STUART LANCASTER
692	10/10/2015	WC (G)	HOME	MANCHESTER	CHRIS ROBSHAW	URUGUAY	WON	60	3	STUART LANCASTER
693	06/02/2016	6N	AWAY	EDINBURGH	DYLAN HARTLEY	SCOTLAND	WON	15	9	EDDIE JONES
694	14/02/2016	6N	AWAY	ROME	DYLAN HARTLEY	ITALY	WON	40	9	EDDIE JONES
695	27/02/2016	6N	HOME	LONDON	DYLAN HARTLEY	IRELAND	WON	21	10	EDDIE JONES

GAME	DATE	TYPE	H/A	CITY	CAPTAIN	OPPONENTS	RESULT	SCORE (FOR)	SCORE (OPP)	COACH
696	12/03/2016	6N	HOME	LONDON	DYLAN HARTLEY	WALES	WON	25	21	EDDIE JONES
697	19/03/2016	6N	AWAY	PARIS	DYLAN HARTLEY	FRANCE	WON	31	21	EDDIE JONES
698	29/05/2016	TEST	HOME	LONDON	DYLAN HARTLEY	WALES	WON	27	13	EDDIE JONES
699	11/06/2016	TEST (1)	AWAY	BRISBANE	DYLAN HARTLEY	AUSTRALIA	WON	39	28	EDDIE JONES
700	18/06/2016	TEST (2)	AWAY	MELBOURNE	DYLAN HARTLEY	AUSTRALIA	WON	23	7	EDDIE JONES
701	25/06/2016	TEST (3)	AWAY	SYDNEY	DYLAN HARTLEY	AUSTRALIA	WON	44	40	EDDIE JONES
702	12/11/2016	TEST	HOME	LONDON	DYLAN HARTLEY	SOUTH AFRICA	WON	37	21	EDDIE JONES
703	19/11/2016	TEST	HOME	LONDON	DYLAN HARTLEY	FIJI	WON	58	15	EDDIE JONES
704	26/11/2016	TEST	HOME	LONDON	DYLAN HARTLEY	ARGENTINA	WON	27	14	EDDIE JONES
705	03/12/2016	TEST	HOME	LONDON	DYLAN HARTLEY	AUSTRALIA	WON	37	21	EDDIE JONES
706	04/02/2017	6N	HOME	LONDON	DYLAN HARTLEY	FRANCE	WON	19	16	EDDIE JONES
707	11/02/2017	6N	AWAY	CARDIFF	DYLAN HARTLEY	WALES	WON	21	16	EDDIE JONES
708	26/02/2017	6N	HOME	LONDON	DYLAN HARTLEY	ITALY	WON	36	15	EDDIE JONES
709	11/03/2017	6N	HOME	LONDON	DYLAN HARTLEY	SCOTLAND	WON	61	21	EDDIE JONES
710	18/03/2017	6N	AWAY	DUBLIN	DYLAN HARTLEY	IRELAND	LOST	9	13	EDDIE JONES
711	10/06/2017	TEST (1)	AWAY	SAN JUAN	DYLAN HARTLEY	ARGENTINA	WON	38	34	EDDIE JONES
712	17/06/2017	TEST (2)	AWAY	SANTA FE	DYLAN HARTLEY	ARGENTINA	WON	35	25	EDDIE JONES
713	11/11/2017	TEST	HOME	LONDON	DYLAN HARTLEY	ARGENTINA	WON	21	8	EDDIE JONES
714	18/11/2017	TEST	HOME	LONDON	DYLAN HARTLEY	AUSTRALIA	WON	30	6	EDDIE JONES
715	25/11/2017	TEST	HOME	LONDON	CHRIS ROBSHAW	SAMOA	WON	48	14	EDDIE JONES
716	04/02/2018	6N	AWAY	ROME	DYLAN HARTLEY	ITALY	WON	46	15	EDDIE JONES
717	10/02/2018	6N	HOME	LONDON	DYLAN HARTLEY	WALES	WON	12	6	EDDIE JONES
718	24/02/2018	6N	AWAY	EDINBURGH	DYLAN HARTLEY	SCOTLAND	LOST	13	25	EDDIE JONES
719	10/03/2018	6N	AWAY	PARIS	OWEN FARRELL	FRANCE	LOST	16	22	EDDIE JONES
720	17/03/2018	6N	HOME	LONDON	DYLAN HARTLEY	IRELAND	LOST	15	24	EDDIE JONES
721	09/06/2018	TEST (1)	AWAY	JOHANNESBURG	OWEN FARRELL	SOUTH AFRICA	LOST	39	42	EDDIE JONES
722	16/06/2018	TEST (2)	AWAY	BLOEMFONTEIN	OWEN FARRELL	SOUTH AFRICA	LOST	12	23	EDDIE JONES
723	23/06/2018	TEST (3)	AWAY	CAPE TOWN	OWEN FARRELL	SOUTH AFRICA	WON	25	10	EDDIE JONES
724	03/11/2018	TEST	HOME	LONDON	OWEN FARRELL/DYLAN HARTLEY	SOUTH AFRICA	WON	12	11	EDDIE JONES
725	10/11/2018	TEST	HOME	LONDON	OWEN FARRELL/DYLAN HARTLEY	NEW ZEALAND	LOST	15	16	EDDIE JONES
726	17/11/2018	TEST	HOME	LONDON	GEORGE FORD	JAPAN	WON	35	15	EDDIE JONES
727	24/11/2018	TEST	HOME	LONDON	OWEN FARRELL/DYLAN HARTLEY	AUSTRALIA	WON	37	18	EDDIE JONES
728	02/02/2019	6N	AWAY	DUBLIN	OWEN FARRELL	IRELAND	WON	32	20	EDDIE JONES
729	10/02/2019	6N	HOME	LONDON	OWEN FARRELL	FRANCE	WON	44	8	EDDIE JONES
730	23/02/2019	6N	AWAY	CARDIFF	OWEN FARRELL	WALES	LOST	13	21	EDDIE JONES
731	09/03/2019	6N	HOME	LONDON	OWEN FARRELL	ITALY	WON	57	14	EDDIE JONES
732	16/03/2019	6N	HOME	LONDON	OWEN FARRELL	SCOTLAND	DRAW	38	38	EDDIE JONES
733	11/08/2019	WCW	HOME	LONDON	GEORGE FORD	WALES	WON	33	19	EDDIE JONES
734	17/08/2019	WCW	AWAY	CARDIFF	GEORGE FORD	WALES	LOST	6	13	EDDIE JONES
735	24/08/2019	WCW	HOME	LONDON	OWEN FARRELL	IRELAND	WON	57	15	EDDIE JONES
736	06/09/2019	WCW	HOME	NEWCASTLE	OWEN FARRELL	ITALY	WON	37	0	EDDIE JONES
737	22/09/2019	WC (G)	NEUTRAL	SAPPORO	OWEN FARRELL	TONGA	WON	35	3	EDDIE JONES
738	26/09/2019	WC (G)	NEUTRAL	KOBE CITY	GEORGE FORD	USA	WON	45	7	EDDIE JONES
739	05/10/2019	WC (G)	NEUTRAL	TOKYO	OWEN FARRELL	ARGENTINA	WON	39	10	EDDIE JONES

GAME	DATE	TYPE	H/A	CITY	CAPTAIN	OPPONENTS	RESULT	SCORE (FOR)	SCORE (OPP)	COACH
740	19/10/2019	WC (QF)	NEUTRAL	OITA PREFECTURE	OWEN FARRELL	AUSTRALIA	WON	40	16	EDDIE JONES
741	26/10/2019	WC (SF)	NEUTRAL	YOKOHAMA CITY	OWEN FARRELL	NEW ZEALAND	WON	19	7	EDDIE JONES
742	02/11/2019	WC (F)	NEUTRAL	YOKOHAMA CITY	OWEN FARRELL	SOUTH AFRICA	LOST	12	32	EDDIE JONES
743	02/02/2020	6N	AWAY	PARIS	OWEN FARRELL	FRANCE	LOST	17	24	EDDIE JONES
744	08/02/2020	6N	AWAY	EDINBURGH	OWEN FARRELL	SCOTLAND	WON	13	6	EDDIE JONES
745	23/02/2020	6N	HOME	LONDON	OWEN FARRELL	IRELAND	WON	24	12	EDDIE JONES
746	07/03/2020	6N	HOME	LONDON	OWEN FARRELL	WALES	WON	33	30	EDDIE JONES
747	31/10/2020	6N	AWAY	ROME	OWEN FARRELL	ITALY	WON	34	5	EDDIE JONES
748	14/11/2020	AUTC	HOME	LONDON	OWEN FARRELL	GEORGIA	WON	40	0	EDDIE JONES
749	21/11/2020	AUTC	HOME	LONDON	OWEN FARRELL	IRELAND	WON	18	7	EDDIE JONES
750	28/11/2020	AUTC	AWAY	LLANELLI	OWEN FARRELL	WALES	WON	24	13	EDDIE JONES
751	06/12/2020	AUTC	HOME	LONDON	OWEN FARRELL	FRANCE	WON (AET)	22	19	EDDIE JONES
752	06/02/2021	6N	HOME	LONDON	OWEN FARRELL	SCOTLAND	LOST	6	11	EDDIE JONES
753	13/02/2021	6N	HOME	LONDON	OWEN FARRELL	ITALY	WON	41	18	EDDIE JONES
754	27/02/2021	6N	AWAY	CARDIFF	OWEN FARRELL	WALES	LOST	24	40	EDDIE JONES
755	13/03/2021	6N	HOME	LONDON	OWEN FARRELL	FRANCE	WON	23	20	EDDIE JONES
756	20/03/2021	6N	AWAY	DUBLIN	OWEN FARRELL	IRELAND	LOST	18	32	EDDIE JONES
757	04/07/2021	TEST	HOME	LONDON	LEWIS LUDLOW	USA	WON	43	29	EDDIE JONES
758	10/07/2021	TEST	HOME	LONDON	LEWIS LUDLOW	CANADA	WON	70	14	EDDIE JONES
759	06/11/2021	TEST	HOME	LONDON	COURTNEY LAWES	TONGA	WON	69	3	EDDIE JONES
760	13/11/2021	TEST	HOME	LONDON	OWEN FARRELL	AUSTRALIA	WON	32	15	EDDIE JONES
761	20/11/2021	TEST	HOME	LONDON	COURTNEY LAWES	SOUTH AFRICA	WON	27	26	EDDIE JONES
762	05/02/2022	6N	AWAY	EDINBURGH	TOM CURRY	SCOTLAND	LOST	17	20	EDDIE JONES
763	13/02/2022	6N	AWAY	ROME	TOM CURRY	ITALY	WON	33	0	EDDIE JONES
764	26/02/2022	6N	HOME	LONDON	COURTNEY LAWES	WALES	WON	23	19	EDDIE JONES
765	12/03/2022	6N	HOME	LONDON	COURTNEY LAWES	IRELAND	LOST	15	32	EDDIE JONES
766	19/03/2022	6N	AWAY	PARIS	COURTNEY LAWES	FRANCE	LOST	13	25	EDDIE JONES
767	02/07/2022	TEST (1)	AWAY	PERTH	COURTNEY LAWES	AUSTRALIA	LOST	28	30	EDDIE JONES
768	09/07/2022	TEST (2)	AWAY	BRISBANE	COURTNEY LAWES	AUSTRALIA	WON	25	17	EDDIE JONES
769	16/07/2022	TEST (3)	AWAY	SYDNEY	COURTNEY LAWES	AUSTRALIA	WON	21	17	EDDIE JONES
770	06/11/2022	TEST	HOME	LONDON	OWEN FARRELL	ARGENTINA	LOST	29	30	EDDIE JONES
771	12/11/2022	TEST	HOME	LONDON	OWEN FARRELL	JAPAN	WON	52	13	EDDIE JONES
772	19/11/2022	TEST	HOME	LONDON	OWEN FARRELL	NEW ZEALAND	DRAW	25	25	EDDIE JONES
773	26/11/2022	TEST	HOME	LONDON	OWEN FARRELL	SOUTH AFRICA	LOST	13	27	EDDIE JONES

SELECT BIBLIOGRAPHY

An extensive array of books, autobiographies, audiobooks, match programmes, video cassettes, DVDs, online videos, newspapers, television programmes and blogs have been referenced for this book. Below is a select bibliography for those who may wish to read more on the history of English rugby.

BOOKS

History of Welsh International Rugby (1999) – John Billot (Roman Way Books)

England Rugby: A History of the National Side 1871–1976 (1976) – Barry Bowker (Cassell)

Behind the Rose: Playing Rugby for England (2014) – Nick Cain and Stephen Jones (Polaris Publishing)

Men in Black (1978) – Rod H. Chester and Neville McMillan (Pelham Books)

The Wales Rugby Miscellany (2008) – Rob Cole and Stuart Farmer (Vision Sports Publishing)

Cardiff Rugby Club – History and Statistics 1876–1975 (1975) – D.E. Davies (Cardiff Athletic Club)

Welsh International Matches 1881–2011 (2011) – Howard Evans (Y Lolfa)

The Official England Rugby Miscellany (2006) – Stuart Farmer (Vision Sports Publishing)

The International Rugby Championship 1883–1983 (1984) – Terry Godwin (Willow Books)

The Book of English International Rugby 1871–1982 (1982) – John Griffiths (Willow Books)

English Rugby 101 (2019) – John Griffiths (Polaris Publishing)

The Phoenix Book of International Rugby (1987) – John Griffiths (Phoenix House)

Behind the Dragon (2019) – Ross Harries (Polaris Publishing)

1905 Originals (2005) – Bob Howitt and Dianne Haworth (Harper Sports)

The Essential History of Rugby Union (2003) – Ian Malin and John Griffiths (Headline Book Publishing)

Football: The Rugby Union Game (1894 edition) – Edited by Rev. F. Marshall (Cassell and Company Ltd)

England Rugby: 150 Years (2021) – Phil McGowan and Richard Steele (Vision Sports Publishing)

One of Us: England's Greatest Players (2015) – Phil McGowan (Amberley Publishing)

The History of the Rugby Football Union (1955) – O.L. Owen (Playfair Books)

Prince Gwyn: Gwyn Nicholls and the First Golden Era of Welsh Rugby (1999) – David Parry–Jones (Seren)

A Game for Hooligans: The History of Rugby Union (2006) – Huw Richards (Mainstream Publishing)

The Red & White: The Story of England v Wales Rugby (2009) – Huw Richards (Aurum Press)

The Original Rules of Rugby (2016) – Intro by Jed Smith/RFU publication (Bodleian Library)

The Who, When & Where of English International Rugby Since 1947 (1997) – Dan Stansfield (Stansfield Publishing)

Fields of Praise (1980) – David Smith and Gareth Williams (University of Wales Press)

The Illustrated History of Welsh Rugby (1980) – J.B.G Thomas (Pelham)

1905 and All That (1991) – Gareth Williams (Gomer Press)

England: The Official R.F.U. History (1999) – Jason Woolgar (Virgin Books)

ANNUALS

Rothmans Rugby Union Yearbook (Multiple editions referenced) (Queen Anne Press)

Welsh Brewers Rugby Annual for Wales/Worthington Rugby Annual for Wales/Buy as You View Rugby Annual for Wales (Multiple editions referenced from 1969 to 2003)

WEBSITES

BBC, British Library, Cardiff Rugby Museum, *The Daily Telegraph*, ESPN Scrum.com, Gloucester Rugby Heritage, *The Guardian*, National Library of Australia, National Library of Wales, RFU official site, *The Times*, Swansea RFC, Twitter, Wales Online, Wikipedia, WRU official website, YouTube (various).

ACKNOWLEDGEMENTS

I am once more humbled by the kindness and support so many people have shown me over the past two years in the writing of this second book in the *Illustrated History of Rugby* series.

Once again I must extend my gratitude to Peter Burns and all at Polaris Publishing for backing this book and series. I was immensely proud to work with them on selling out the first edition of our Welsh title and very much hope we will have the same success with this volume. Raluca Moldovan, the main artist, has again delivered dozens of charming illustrations. I know how hard, long and late she has worked on these and it means so much to me. Raluca, 'mulțumesc frumos!'

Carys Feehan, my extraordinarily talented niece has outdone herself with her cover art. I am so proud to work with her. Carys, 'diolch yn fawr!' As always, thanks to Josel Nicolas and Ched De Gala for their work and creativity. Josel and Ched, 'salamat!' It was a joy again to work with the excellent Anne Cakebread on the complex task of recreating historical rugby jerseys. Anne, 'diolch yn fawr!'

I was overwhelmed by support from across the rugby and literary communities for the Wales book and this time I had even more help. For support with everything from stats to trivia; proofing and photos; social media requests and promotional advice (plus much more besides), I want to thank Aled Betts, David Brayley, Steve Coombs, Katie Field, John Griffiths, Hugh Godwin, Carolyn Hodges, Fredric Humbert, Phil McGowan, Albert Pico Sánchez, Ian Greensill, Paul Wade, Chris Miller and Paul Williams. I must also highlight the help I've had from Huw Richards. Huw has always been ready to rapidly scan and search his archives (and his own highly informed brain) whenever I've asked for help clarifying some obscure fact or historical detail. I cannot recommend his works on the history of the game enough. Special thanks again to my cousin Marc Stafford for maintaining my website *The East Terrace*, helping me spread the word about my books.

My long–suffering wife has again tolerated me working away into the early hours of the morning almost every night of the week for two years. She has the patience of a saint. Helena, 'děkuji!' Also I send love and thanks to my children: Michael and Helena. You may have no idea what I'm typing away at every day and why, but you both still inspire me to keep going.

Finally, I want to express my love and eternal gratitude to my father, Michael Stafford. My father gave me a life blessed with sport and rugby and for that, among a million other precious things he provided, I will always be grateful. He started this book with me and helped me painstakingly compile the statistics and match records. My dad did so, quite literally, yards from what was ultimately his deathbed. His love and support, despite his cruel illness and suffering, never wavered. To think he worked so hard on this for me right up until the end of his magnificent and loving life, will never cease to astound me. Dad, you were the most amazing man and father and I wish beyond words you were here to see the finished copy of this book. I will love you always. Thank you for a life of kindness and love.

James Stafford

ABOUT THE AUTHOR AND ILLUSTRATORS

James Stafford

James is founder of cult rugby website *The East Terrace* and has written on sport for a wide range of newspapers, websites and magazines. In 2017 his collection of short webcomics, *The Sorrowful Putto of Prague*, was published to critical acclaim in the Czech Republic. In 2021 he released *An Illustrated History of Welsh Rugby* with Polaris Publishing and a children's book, *How Wales Beat the Mighty All Blacks*, with Y Lolfa. Both titles quickly sold out and were reprinted, with the former title also being expanded and updated.

James broke various limbs and ruined multiple muscles, ligaments and nerves playing rugby for Barry Plastics, Old Belvedere, London Japanese and Nyrsko. Born in Cardiff and raised in Barry, he now lives in Prague.

Twitter/Instagram: *@jpstafford*
Website: *www.theeastterrace.com*

Raluca Moldovan

Raluca is a book, comics and commercial illustrator based in Constanța, Romania. Her previous published work includes *The Sorrowful Putto of Prague* and *An Illustrated History of Welsh Rugby*. She will release her third book with James Stafford in late 2023 with *An Illustrated History of Rugby Rebels, Role Models and Giant Killers*.

Instagram: *@_raloux*

Carys Feehan

Carys Feehan, who provided the book's cover art, is a Welsh animation student currently studying in California. Born and raised in Hong Kong, her Welsh heritage has consistently inspired her art work in painting, illustration and filmmaking. She also drew the cover art for *An Illustrated History of Welsh Rugby* and was the illustrator for the best-selling children's book *How Wales Beat the Mighty All Blacks*.

Instagram: *@burnthelampposts*
Website: *www.carysfeehan.weebly.com*

Josel Nicolas

Josel, who provided the player profile illustrations in each chapter, is a Filipino comics editor, artist and writer. He has been making comics since 2006 and previously collaborated with James Stafford on *The Sorrowful Putto of Prague* comics and the previous instalment in this series.

Instagram: *@joselnicolasart*
Contact: *josel.nicolas@gmail.com*

Ched De Gala

Ched, who worked on the player profile illustrations in each chapter, is a freelance Filipino comics artist who enjoys sports.

Instagram: *@ang.sa.tin*
Latest work available at Penlab.Ink

Anne Cakebread

Anne Cakebread is a freelance illustrator with over 20 years' experience in publishing and TV, including cover art and illustrations for numerous books and magazines. She also illustrated sets and props for Boomerang on S4C's award-winning ABC. Anne grew up and went to school in Radyr, Cardiff and now lives with her partner, two whippets and lurcher in St Dogmaels. She runs an art gallery in Cardigan.

Website: *www.cakebreadillustrations.com*

AN ILLUSTRATED HISTORY OF RUGBY REBELS, ROLE MODELS AND GIANT KILLERS

By James Stafford
Illustrated by Raluca Moldovan

Learn all about the players, characters and teams that shaped rugby and inspired millions. From 19th century innovators to 21st century superstars, the latest book in the *Illustrated History of Rugby* series examines players who overcame the odds to beat everything from injury and illness to racism and sexism to excel and thrill followers of our great game. It also tells the stories of giant killing teams who shocked the world and took the scalps of heavily favoured opponents. From the Tonga team that beat Australia in the 1973 to the 'Miracle in Brighton' which saw Japan topple the mighty Springboks, James Stafford and Raluca bring to life some of the most thrilling moments in rugby history.

AN ILLUSTRATED HISTORY OF WELSH RUGBY: FUN, FACTS AND STORIES FROM 140 YEARS OF INTERNATIONAL RUGBY

By James Stafford
Illustrated by Raluca Moldovan

REVISED AND UPDATED

For almost 140 years the Welsh rugby team has battled proudly on the international stage. Full of tales of fighting clergymen, poisoned arrows and deathbed confessionals, James Stafford's *An Illustrated History of Welsh Rugby* takes a unique look at the games, the players, the legends and the myths behind Wales's national game.

Blending fun and facts with trivia and social history, this is Welsh rugby like you've never experienced it before. Brimming with delightful illustrations from Raluca Moldovan and irreverent humour, this book will fascinate young readers and rugby-mad adults alike.

'A great achievement that frames the game for young readers and curious grown-ups alike' – Carolyn Hitt, *The Western Mail*

'A light-hearted, but also weighty, well researched, passionate and fun and serious look at our national game' – Gary Raymond, *The Review Show, BBC Radio Wales*

'I love it . . . If you love rugby and history, I highly recommend it' – Mike Bubbins, *BBC Wales* and *The Socially Distant Sports Bar*